FAITH
SEEKING
UNDERSTANDING

The Functional Specialty, "Systematics,"
in Bernard Lonergan's *Method in Theology*

by

Matthew C. Ogilvie

MARQUETTE
UNIVERSITY

PRESS

MARQUETTE STUDIES IN THEOLOGY
No. 26

ANDREW TALLON, SERIES EDITOR

Library of Congress Cataloging-in-Publication Data

Ogilvie, Matthew Charles, 1966-
   Faith seeking understanding : the functional specialty, systematics, in
Bernard Lonergan's Method in theology / by Matthew Charles Ogilvie.
   p. cm. — (Marquette studies in theology ; no. 26)
Includes bibliographical references and index.
   ISBN 0-87462-625-0 (pbk. : alk. paper)
   1. Theology—Methodology. 2. Lonergan, Bernard J. F.
I. Title. II. Marquette studies in theology ; #26.
BR118 .O45 2001
230'.2'01—dc21   00-012241

Cover design by
Andrew J. Tallon

MARQUETTE UNIVERSITY PRESS
MILWAUKEE

The Association of Jesuit University Presses

Contents

Faith Seeking Understanding

The Functional Specialty, "Systematics,"
in Bernard Lonergan's *Method in Theology*

Matthew C. Ogilvie PhD

Abstract

How can doctrines be made intelligible within the context of our modern world? This book intends to investigate, and to throw new light upon, Lonergan's response to this challenge in his presentation of the functional specialty, systematics, within his *Method in Theology*.

This book primarily aims to present a thorough understanding of systematics' function. We intend to investigate systematics' specific function as a promotion of understanding, of the mysteries of faith. We shall also examine the need for, and grounds of, this functional specialty and we shall place systematics in relation to the other functional specialties within Lonergan's *Method in Theology*. Of special concern to this work will be an investigation of what Lonergan could have meant by explaining systematics' function by reference to the statement of the First Vatican Council, that human reason can attain an understanding of the mysteries both by analogy with what human reason naturally knows and by the interconnection of the mysteries with each other and with humanity's last end.

We shall bolster our understanding of systematics by placing it within the context of Lonergan's theological method. To make systematics' function more intelligible, we shall investigate the conditions prevailing in Catholic theology that prompted Lonergan to develop his theological method, we shall assess the value and place of systematics, and we shall also evaluate Lonergan's presentation of systematics in relation to the goals he set himself in developing a theological method.

This book contributes to scholarship: by presenting new research on Lonergan, by explicating an instrument by which one can make doctrines intelligible and by showing how a significant philosopher-theologian has effectively responded to the challenges of the modern world.

Acknowledgments

For help in bringing this work to fruition, I first wish to thank Professor Eric J. Sharpe, of the School of Studies in Religion, University of Sydney, who supervised the doctoral thesis upon which this book is based. Without Professor Sharpe's expert guidance, this work would have never been completed.

I would also like to thank Rev. Professor Thomas V. Daly, S.J., of the Melbourne College of Divinity, the Associate Supervisor of my doctoral work. Father Daly's expert guidance and penetrating insight into the work of Lonergan were invaluable to this publication.

I would further like to thank Associate Professor James G. Tulip, Head of the School of Studies in Religion at the University of Sydney. I am grateful to him for his kind and valuable help. From the University of Sydney, I thank also Professor Garry W. Trompf, for his charitable and unselfish support.

I owe special gratitude to Rev. Peter J. Beer, S.J., of the Lonergan Centre, Canisius College, Pymble. Father Beer has been most gracious in sharing his expert knowledge of Lonergan. I am also grateful to Father Beer, the staff and residents of Canisius College, for the use of the Lonergan Centre Library.

I am also grateful to the staff at the Lonergan Research Institute, Toronto, Canada. Like many, I have benefited greatly from their diligent work, and I appreciate their indefatigable commitment.

With sadness I also belatedly acknowledge the kind assistance given me by the late Doctor William J. Jobling, Reader in the School of Studies in Religion, University of Sydney. I also am grateful to the late Rev. Timothy P. Fallon, S.J., of the Lonergan Center, Santa Clara, California, for his kind help with computer-based resources on Lonergan.

I owe thanks to many family members and friends, whom, through defect of memory rather than lack of affection, I have neglected to acknowledge.

I finally wish to express my heartfelt thanks to my wife, Elizabeth. Despite most trying circumstances, including the unexpected loss of close family members, Elizabeth has been a constant source of support to me. She has also most kindly proofread this book.

Preface

"For now problems are so numerous that many do not know what to believe. They are not unwilling to believe. They know what church doctrines are. But they want to know what Church doctrines could possibly mean. Their question is the question to be met by systematic theology." Lonergan's statement (1994, 345) is most pertinent to the modern context in which Christianity finds itself. Developments in the modern world have raised new questions concerning the intelligibility of doctrines. In the face of new notions of person, one may ask how the Hypostatic Union could be. Alternatively, with new developments in philosophy, we can ask if transubstantiation still adequately explains the mystery of the Eucharist. The experience of the modern church bears out Lonergan's point that doctrines may be faithfully affirmed, but that people also need to understand how those doctrines could be in the face of new developments in their modern culture.

Within his *Method in Theology*, Lonergan presents the functional specialty, systematics, which sets about answering questions concerning the intelligibility of doctrines, such as those we have just mentioned. In this book, we shall argue that systematics does provide a framework for answering such questions, thus adding a valuable resource to theology. However, our primary aim in this work will be to present an original and new understanding of systematics' specific function. In particular, we shall examine what Lonergan may have meant when he affirmed that systematics intends to understand the mysteries from the analogy of what human reason naturally knows and from the mysteries' interconnections with each other and with humanity's end. This latter concern will be especially challenging. While Lonergan affirms such understandings, he does not specifically explain what he may mean by understanding attained from analogy or interconnection. We thus need to ask what Lonergan may have meant in his own teaching, on the function of systematics. In pursuing this aim, our principal reference sources will be *Method in Theology* and other writings of Lonergan that throw light on systematics.

We also find that systematics is unintelligible without understanding both Lonergan's theological method and his analysis of human intentionality. Accordingly, we shall investigate these with the intention of helping us attain a better understanding of systematics. Moreover, systematics is even better understood if we refer to the motivations and influences upon Lonergan, if we understand the value and place of systematics and if we evaluate Lonergan's presentation of this functional specialty. Therefore, in addition to fulfilling our primary aim, we shall endeavour to attain these goals.

An outline of this book will help show how it meets the goals we have set for it: Our first chapter will provide introductory details on systematics and Bernard Lonergan, and it will outline our work's key issues and its structure. Chapter two will begin our investigation proper, by investigating the adverse conditions afflicting Catholic theology, under which Lonergan had to teach and which prompted him to develop his *Method in Theology*. Chapter three examines the development from Aristotelian to modern science, and the corresponding changes in philosophy, history and other disciplines. These developments had great impact on theology, and were key concerns of Lonergan's. Chapter four rounds off our foundational investigations by examining Lonergan's analysis of theology's needs. This chapter will explain Lonergan's vision for renewing Catholic theology upon a methodological theology that was up to modern standards.

Chapter five will investigate Lonergan's intentionality analysis and his transcendental method. Understanding these will be crucial, for *Method in Theology* was founded upon his intentionality analysis. Chapter six will outline Lonergan's *Method in Theology*, and explain the reasons for, and grounds of, this theological method. This chapter will place systematics within a method that fosters specialised functional operations in the process from data to results.

Chapter seven begins our direct examination of the function of systematics. In it we shall investigate: the function of systematics and its contrast to other theological activities, the object of systematics as seeking intelligibility into divine mysteries, and the reasons behind the need for systematics.

In chapters eight and nine, we shall investigate the meaning of systematics' understanding being attained from analogy with what human reason naturally knows and from the mysteries' interconnections with each other and humanity's end.

Chapter ten begins the evaluative phase of our work, drawing thematic conclusions on systematics' contribution and place regarding teaching, apologetics, ongoing cultures, communications, pluralism and non-Catholic religions. Chapter eleven reviews systematics within the context of Lonergan's general theological method. Chapter twelve ends the book, by situating systematics within the context of Lonergan's new beginning for theology, summarising the exact function of systematics, summarising the usefulness of this functional specialty, and concluding with a brief reflection.

This book will be valuable to students in several quarters. First, students of Lonergan will find a renewed presentation of systematics, which will deepen their knowledge of Lonergan and his work. This work in particular, will expand upon Lonergan's statements about systematics in *Method in Theology*, which may have left previously unanswered questions. Secondly, Catholic and other Christian theologians, scholars and pastors can find in systematics a valuable instrument with which they can more effectively make intelligible the doctrines of their church. Thirdly, in this book, students of studies in religion can find an explanation of one person's response to the challenges that the modern world has presented to religion and theology.

Abbreviations

DS   "Denziger-Schönmetzer"—H. Denziger—A. Schönmetzer, *Enchiridion Symbolorum Definitionum et Declarationum de rebus fidei et morum*, Freiburg im Breisgau, 1965.

ET   English Translation

TCF "The Christian Faith"—J. Neuner and J. Dupuis, (editors), *The Christian Faith: In the Doctrinal Documents of the Catholic Church*, (Revised edition.) London: Collins, 1983.

Chapter 1
Introduction

I. WHAT IS "SYSTEMATICS"?

According to tradition, the young boys resident in a Benedictine monastery were allowed to ask the abbot a question. Most students asked the conventional question, "Does God exist?" However, young Thomas Aquinas posed the more penetrating question, "What is God?" While this story is well known, it helps to note that Thomas' question differed in form, as well as content, from the routine manner of questions. The question concerning God's existence requires only an affirmation or negation. No matter how lengthy or complex one's deliberations and proofs may be, one's answer will ultimately be a simple "yes," or "no." However, one poses a much different and more difficult question by asking "What is God?" Such a question cannot be answered by simple affirmation or negation. Moreover, by inquiring into what God is, one also presumes that God's existence has been affirmed. In concise terms, Thomas' question illustrates the difference between inquiring into God's existence and asking about God's essence.

Aquinas' penetrating inquiry would fit well into the functional specialty, "systematics," within Bernard Lonergan's *Method in Theology*. This functional specialty "is concerned with promoting an understanding of the realities affirmed in the previous functional specialty, doctrines." Like young Thomas' specific inquiry, systematics relies upon differences between essence and existence and between the operations by which we know existence and essence. Such differentiation distinguishes Lonergan's cognitional theory from those theories that do not substantially distinguish understanding and judgement. For Lonergan and Aquinas, understanding and judgement are sharply distinguished, the first seeking what an object is, the second determining whether one's understanding of that object is correct (Lonergan 1994, 335).

To explain systematics' function, Lonergan (1994, 336) refers to the First Vatican Council's retrieval of "the notion of understanding." The Council (DS 3016/TCF 132) taught that human reason, illumined by faith, could inquire diligently, piously, soberly and with God's help, to attain a fruitful understanding of the mysteries of faith, both from the analogy of what human reason naturally knows and from the interconnections of the mysteries with each other and with humanity's ultimate end. Because it seeks understanding, systematics is not an effort to add more proof of the mysteries' existence. Systematics instead aims to take on the realities affirmed by doctrines and to discover how these realities may be made intelligible.

While we have concisely stated that systematics is essentially the effort to find intelligibility in the mysteries of faith, we have already set several significant challenges for this book: (1) to understand better the relationship between doctrines and systematics, (2) to account for the cognitional theory that distinguishes understanding and judgement, (3) to show why such a theological understanding should be needed, (4) to explain what Lonergan means in describing the function of systematics, and specifically (5) to account for what Lonergan may mean by an understanding both from analogy with what human reason naturally knows and from the mysteries' interconnections. Before dealing with these, and related, issues we should first introduce Lonergan and the more influential occurrences in his life.

2. Bernard Lonergan

While a biography of Lonergan has yet to appear, the basic events of Lonergan's life are readily available from a number of sources (Crowe 1992; Crowe 1989, 3-12; Lonergan 1974, 209-30, 263-78; Meynell 1989, 205-16). Born in Buckingham, Quebec, in 1904, he attended parish school run by the Brothers of Christian Instruction. His memories of parish school disclose an ongoing commitment to high standards. He praised the Brothers for their high standards, but later complained that the Jesuits "taught him to loaf" (Crowe 1992, 4-5). That complaint was carried into later life, when Lonergan (1984, 14) complained that minimum standards lead to minimum results. At thirteen he began boarding school at Loyola College, Montreal, where, despite a life-threatening mastoid condition and operation, he had a most successful school career (Crowe 1992, 4; Meynell 1989, 205). However, he later criticised his education for being "organized pretty much along the same lines as Jesuit schools had been since the beginning of the Renaissance, with a few slight modifications." This educational culture emphasised the classicist notion of one normative culture to which all others should aspire. It assumed that intelligent communication would occur within that culture and that one would communicate with the "uncultured" by making slight adjustments, without however, expecting the uncultured to understand. This "Renaissance" style education also emphasised the *uomo universale*, the man who could master anything. Lonergan later explained (1974, 209-10) that classicist notions, of normative culture and universal masters of learning, have been overcome by modern, specialised techniques, and by anthropological, empirical notions of culture. In this book, we shall show how he worked to bring Catholic theology to account for such developments.

In 1922, Lonergan entered the Society of Jesus, spending two years in novitiate in Guelph, Ontario. From 1926-1929, he studied philosophy at Heythrop College, Oxfordshire, while simultaneously taking an external "General Degree" from the University of London. Despite praising the Heythrop professors, who were "competent and extremely honest," he criticised the inferior Suarezian philosophy taught there (Lonergan 1974, 263; Crowe 1992, 6-17; Meynell 1989, 205). Even in these early days, we find him interested in cognitional theory. His criticism of the principal place given to universal concepts led him to assume that he was a nominalist. However, this nominalism gave way after reading J. A. Stewart's *Plato's Doctrine of Ideas*, from which Lonergan discovered that his nominalism had not been an opposition to intelligence or understanding, but a rejection of universal concepts. Stewart also taught Lonergan that Plato was a methodologist and that the scientific or philosophic process towards discovery proceeds by way of question and answer. This interest in methodology and heuristic investigation was complemented by an interest in modern science that developed at Heythrop. These interests show the foundation of Lonergan's search for a theological method that could both account for developments in modern science, and confront the objections of modern philosophy (Lonergan 1974, 263-64; Crowe 1992, 14; Meynell, 1989, 206).

In these early days, during which many of Lonergan's later ideas had their genesis, we find a key development in several unpublished papers from 1928 and 1929. In a study of Euclid's proofs, he rejected the view that one could appropriate the proof by concerning one's thought with the concept of a geometrical figure. He argued that instead of dealing with concepts, Euclid inquired into the image of the geometric figure, from which he gained his proof. We find here the emerging rejection of what we later find to be Lonergan's chief adversary—conceptualism. We also find emerging the cognitional element that he later articulated as insight into phantasm (Crowe 1992, 14-15).

The ferment of Lonergan's thought continued with his reading of Newman and H.B.W. Joseph's *Introduction to Logic*. Newman's work encouraged Lonergan to confront difficulties sincerely, and provided, in the "illative sense" the model for Lonergan's later reflective act of understanding. He further developed his cognitional theory, reading more of Plato and the early dialogues of Augustine, noting in particular how Augustine was "unmindful of universal concepts." Another key influence came with Christopher Dawson's *The Age of the Gods,* which overturned Lonergan's previous classicist notion of culture (Lonergan 1974, 263-65).

If we take account of Lonergan's life before he took any serious interest in Aquinas, we can overcome the unfortunate misconception that Lonergan began as a Thomist, and only later became interested in modern philosophy and science. During his Heythrop days Lonergan showed both an interest in modern mathematics and science and a disillusionment with Catholic philosophy at the time. We find Lonergan's notion of insight being developed through his study of Euclid, and his notion of judgement being found in Newman's illative sense. As Meynell (1989, 206) observes, "It can be seen from Lonergan's early papers that his basic ideas were solidly in place by 1929, before he had read a line of Aquinas."

After his regency, Lonergan began theological studies. He spent a brief period at Montreal's Collège de l'Immaculée-Conception, before being sent to Rome in November, 1933. Despite his delight at many aspects of student life in Rome, he was dismayed at the standards of education. Despite its allegedly soporific routine, he found decisive influences in Rome. Most importantly, Maréchal was mediated to him through a fellow student. From Maréchal he learned that human knowledge was discursive, not intuitive, and that its decisive component was judgement. This position correlated with Augustine's notion of *veritas*, and also with Aquinas' notion of *esse*. This discovery was complemented by Leeming's course on the Incarnate Word, which convinced Lonergan that the Hypostatic Union was impossible without a real distinction between essence and existence (Lonergan 1974, 265; Crowe 1992, 20-21). Another important influence was Peter Hoenen's article (1933) in *Gregorianum*, in which he argued that "intellect abstracted from phantasm not only terms but also the nexus between them" (Lonergan 1974, 266-67). These influences helped Lonergan to articulate both that intelligence operates first by insight into phantasm (a position we find germinating in his article on Euclid) and also that there is a distinct act of judgement, which corresponded to Newman's illative sense.

After completing his doctorate under Charles Boyer, Lonergan (1973, 15; 1974, 212) describes his experience as teaching "theology for twenty-five years under impossible conditions," within a system that was "hopelessly antiquated," which demanded too much of the now outdated *uomo universale* and operated with an inadequate philosophy and a classicist notion of culture. It was a time during which he continued his sharp criticisms, which extended beyond Jesuit education to include Catholic education in general, at all levels. We find illuminating Lonergan's belief that "Colonial" Universities were seen as inferior to English Universities, which in turn were seen as inferior to Continental institutions.

> In England they smile very tolerantly at colonial universities; in France and Germany they smile at English Universities. But what is galling about this smiling is that it is completely and fully justified. . . . I know that I cannot produce the stuff that a European scholar would produce with half the labor I put in (Crowe 1992, 30n10).

Despite such obstacles, he found time to produce some most constructive work. After rewriting his doctorate for publication in *Theological Studies* 1941-1942, he began researching Aquinas' views on understanding and the inner word. The resulting *Verbum* articles, originally published in *Theological Studies* between 1946 and 1949, were decisive in emphasising that essential to Aquinas' cognitional theory were neither inner words nor concepts, but understanding (Lonergan 1974, 267). While working on *Verbum*, he took a Montreal Adult education group through a course on *Thought and Reality*. The group's response convinced Lonergan (1974, 268) that his cognitional theory was "a marketable product." So, after completing his *Verbum* work, he spent from 1949 to 1953 writing *Insight: A Study of Human Understanding*. The work had several important aims, not the least of which was to help the reader personally appropriate the crucial role of understanding. This element of personal appropriation was important, because *Insight* was meant, not as a set of prescriptions, but as an aid to help people experience understanding for themselves, to advert to that experience, name it and identify that experience in subsequent occurrences (Lonergan 1974, 213, 268-69). The key results of *Insight* are covered in this book's fifth chapter, on *Lonergan's Intentionality Analysis*.

Lonergan originally intended *Insight* as the first part of a work that dealt first with methods generally, then theological method specifically. His transfer to the Gregorian University in Rome meant that he had to round off his work in the form of *Insight*, and delay his work on theological method (Lonergan 1974, 269; Meynell 1989, 205-6). Despite its part in his years of teaching under impossible conditions, Lonergan's Roman period provided fertile ground for his theological method. His Roman lectures show interest in the development of doctrine, as the ongoing, ever-deeper understanding of revealed mysteries. During this period, he also grappled with the challenges of new hermeneutics and critical history and the need to integrate modern achievements in these fields with the teachings of Catholicism. This effort can be seen in his writings of this period and in the different doctoral courses on theological method that he taught. His teaching career was interrupted by cancer in and the subsequent removal of a lung in 1965. After this illness, he took on a lighter teaching load. From 1965 to 1975, he served as Professor of Theology, Regis College, Toronto, apart from 1971-1972, when he was Stillman Professor at Harvard Divinity School. Despite his ill-health, Lonergan still worked on his theological method, and in 1972, his *Method in Theology* was published. During 1975-1983 Lonergan was Visiting Professor at Boston College, where he delivered graduate seminars on economics. He died on November 26, 1984 (Lonergan 1974, 277; Crowe 1992, 106-7; Meynell 1989, 205-6).

3. ISSUES TO BE ADDRESSED

Our introduction to systematics, and our brief coverage of key elements in Lonergan's life, give us a preliminary understanding of systematics and the man whose work we are investigating. These reflections also reveal some key issues that we must address in this book. First, we should take up the "impossible" and inadequate conditions contributing to the "antiquated" system under which Lonergan taught. We shall explain how the classicist notion of normative culture, the lack of specialisation and the failure to account for modern developments afflicted Catholic theology. This raises the need to examine the development from classicist, Aristotelian science and philosophy to modern science and the associated developments in modern philosophy and scholarship, and how these affected Catholic theology. Against this background, we shall be better able to understand Lonergan's determination of theology's needs, and his vision to renew theology with a new, methodological foundation.

We shall then have to investigate Lonergan's cognitional theory, which was a key part of his life-work, and which formed the foundation for his *Method in Theology*. In particular, we need to contrast his intellectualist model of human knowing with its focus upon understanding, against the conceptualist legacy, which focuses on concepts. Understanding Lonergan's cognitional theory is crucial, for without doing so, we can understand neither Lonergan's theological method, nor any part of the method, such as systematics. Most importantly, we need to grasp what Lonergan means by understanding, as this is systematics' main pursuit. We shall next inquire into Lonergan's *Method in Theology*, to outline the structure of this method, the division of functional specialties, the needs for and grounds of this division. More importantly, this investigation will place systematics within the wider context of Lonergan's method.

We shall next need to examine the functional specialty, systematics, in itself. We shall cover issues pertaining to the specific needs for, and foundations of, systematics. We shall have to make intelligible systematics' distinction from, and relation to, belief, doctrines and faith. Importantly, we shall have to distinguish systematics as an operation yielding understanding, from doctrines as a function yielding religious certitude. We shall also have to ask what Lonergan could have meant by taking up understanding from analogy and interconnections.

In the final part of this book, we shall explicate the value, place and attainments of systematics, before making some evaluations and conclusions on Lonergan's presentation of this functional specialty.

4. The Method of this Book

This book will be guided by its primary aim, which is to understand the function of systematics, as a functional specialty within Lonergan's *Method in Theology*. As a secondary aim, from our attainment of this understanding, we shall be able to comment upon the value and place of systematics.

Readers of Lonergan, or Aquinas, would be familiar with the two orders in which one may pursue an investigation. In the *ordo inventionis* (order of discovery) one follows an unplanned path. Issues are resolved as they arise in the course of one's path of discovery, secondary issues are likely to be concluded first, and teachers are likely to settle issues as they arise in argument (Lonergan 1994, 345-46; 1988, 121). Such an approach is useful for a chronologically ordered investigation, such as tracing development of a person's thought. However, as Aquinas (*Summa Theologiae*, Prologue) warns and John Finnis (1980, v) argues, this approach can result in repetition of subject matter and can detract from the desired outcome of one's investigation, if one's intention is to teach effectively or communicate an understanding of one's subject matter.

The *ordo doctrinae* (order of teaching), which this book primarily follows, intends a systematic presentation of one's subject matter, in which one defers deliberation over issues that assume the results of other issues and in which one begins with questions whose resolution presupposes no other solutions. In this order, one eliminates irrelevant material, avoids repetitions and provides an account ordered to the subject matter of a book (Lonergan 1994, 345-346; 1988, 121; *Summa Theologiae*, Prologue). This book will pursue the *ordo doctrinae*, with the aim of communicating an understanding of systematics, as our subject matter. However, we do not mean that because this book is not a chronological investigation, it will not be historically-minded. Our work shall be historical to the extent that it explains the key questions that were in Lonergan's mind, in addition to his answers that we explicate in this investigation. We acknowledge, however, that while our approach is suitable for achieving this book's aim, we leave open the possibility of more work on the development of Lonergan's thought. Such work would be helpful in complementing the discoveries contained in this book.

This book will refer most frequently to primary sources from Lonergan. Secondary sources, where used, will aid us in interpreting a point, which normally will be corroborated with Lonergan's own work. In using Lonergan's work, our task is made slightly less complicated by the systematic presentation of much of his work, so the work of interpretation is easier than for less systematic documents, such as the Scriptures. Our work is also made more straightforward by Lonergan's own comment that, despite his work having gone through significant development, he did not believe any of his earlier work to have been wrong (Danaher 1993, 195n63). Thomas Daly (1996) recalls that, upon confronting Lonergan with the possibility that he had disowned some parts of his earlier thought, he "smilingly defended himself from self slander with the words 'I've never said he [the early Lonergan] was wrong.'" We are saved, then, from having to uncover earlier positions that Lonergan rejected later in life.

Having introduced this book, we begin with the first element in the history behind Lonergan's work—the impossible conditions, which he endured as a professor of theology, and which prompted him to write his *Method in Theology*.

Chapter 2
Teaching Theology—"Under Impossible Conditions"

Lonergan stated (1973, 15) that he had "taught theology for twenty-five years under impossible conditions." Lest we dismiss these harsh words as an offhand remark, we should consider his earlier statement (1974, 212), that "the situation I was in was hopelessly antiquated, but had not yet been demolished." Against the challenges of such difficult conditions, Lonergan sought long to discover a theological method that could account for the progress of modern science and meet the challenges posed by modern philosophy (Meynell 1989, 206). To help us better understand the method Lonergan discovered, we find it worthwhile to examine the reasons for this discouragement over the state of Catholic theology. Doran notes (1990, 3) that these reasons were both internal to theology, and due to the "ecclesial, academic, and sociocultural dimensions of the stituation that a contemporary theology must address." Understanding those reasons, we can more accurately understand his aims and ambitions, and we can be better informed about the place of Lonergan's method in theology, specifically his functional specialty, systematics, within a renewal of Catholic theology.

I. LACK OF SPECIALISATION

The theological system, which Lonergan found "hopelessly antiquated," failed to sufficiently encourage specialisation by its teachers. Of his teaching days at the Gregorian University, he wrote (1974, 212) that

> to be a professor in dogmatic theology was to be a specialist in the Old Testament—not just in the Pentateuch or something like that—the Old Testament, the New, the Apostolic Fathers, the Greek Fathers, the ante-Nicene, Greek and Latin, the post-Nicene, the medieval Scholastics, the Renaissance period, the Reformation, contemporary philosophy and so on. There's no one who is a specialist in all that; but that was the sort of thing you had to handle. And you did what you could—(as Damon Runyon's characters put it: 'How are you doing?' 'I'm doing what I can.').

Lonergan found (1973, 32) that modern scholarship's specialisation renders obsolete the notion of such a multi-disciplinary master. Modern scholars need to be specialised because they encounter increasing amounts of information. Furthermore, new techniques in history, new methods of interpretation and new standards in language studies demand increasing specialisation. Even if an encyclopedic genius could assimilate all the information pertinent to one's field, one would nonetheless be unlikely to have mastered the manifold and specialised techniques used in the process between a scholar and one's sources. Lonergan (1974, 232) argues that such factors render it impossible for any one person to master all possible knowledge, even within a given subject area. We find support for this argument in Macquarrie's (1977, 21) and Doran's (1995 1:405) observations that the days have passed when an encyclopedic genius, such as Aristotle or Leonardo da Vinci, could master all the knowledge available in one's time.

A direct study of one's sources may be proposed to overcome problems associated with increased specialisation, with such study being evident in Melchior Cano's *De locis theologicus*. But work like Cano's belongs to a period when one could master all the available techniques for investigating the Scriptures, Patristic writings, Councils, theologians and the faith of Christians. Cano could write a manual, which proved his doctrines by appealing to his sources. Modern scholarship, however, demands rigorous and accurate interpretation of those sources and modern techniques for investigating different sources are very different. One does not, for example, understand the Council of Chalcedon by being an expert on Hebrew, nor does one interpret Genesis by being expert in investigating counter-Reformation theology. The modern techniques used to investigate any one field take many years to learn, so no one scholar is capable of mastering the techniques proper to all fields. The demands of modern investigative techniques mean that a project, such as Cano's, could be undertaken today only by a team of specialists working together. Lonergan regretted that the Catholic Church resisted a specialised approach to theology. When the Church finally realised the need for its teachers to specialise, it did so belatedly and with insufficient commitment, which left Catholic dogmatic theologians trailing the standards set by specialists in other disciplines. While most of the modern world embraced specialised scholarship, and witnessed a rise in successful science, scholarship, and philosophy, Catholic theologians worked within a system that was seriously antiquated in its expectation that they would have to master all fields and methods relevant to their discipline. Specialisation thus presented Catholic theology with a challenge that, in Lonergan's opinion (1994, 281; 1974, 210; 1973, 32), it failed to meet.

Lonergan was not alone in his concern over responses to specialisation. For example, Karl Rahner (1990, 19) wrote that "Forty years ago the ratio between what I knew, and the problems, available information, and methods, was maybe 1:4; today it's more like 1:400." If we account for Rahner's (1978, xii) related reflections, we realise that for both Lonergan and Rahner, the question facing modern theology involved the specialisation demanded by the new methods, and not just the information relevant to theology.

2. THEOLOGY'S CLASSICIST ASSUMPTIONS

Lonergan also devoted much effort in criticising "classicist assumptions" behind Catholic theology. These were assumptions that Doran finds (1990, 4) minimised the achievements of Catholic theology, stifled its creativity and ruled the thinking of those in ecclesiastical power. So repelled was Lonergan by classicism's effects on Catholic theology, he labelled it the "shabby shell of Catholicism" and he described classicism's faults at the very beginning of *Method in Theology* (1994, xi, 327).

According to Lonergan (1994, xi, 326-27; 1974, 232), classicism assumed that its culture was normative, that there was but one culture for all times and all places, and that to this universal and uniform culture all should aspire. In religion's expression of classicism, one would feel required to evangelise with one's culture firmly bound to one's Gospel, so that "A classicist could feel that he conferred a double benefit on those to whom he preached if he not only taught them the Gospel but also let them partake in the riches of the one and only culture" (Lonergan 1974, 233).

Classicism was not a specifically religious point of view. After all, as Lonergan (1974, 5) observes, classicism has "no foundation in the revealed word of God." However, if as Lonergan (1994, xi) proposes, theology "mediates between a cultural matrix and the significance and role of a religion in that matrix," a classicist notion of culture would seriously influence theology. Under a classicist notion of culture, one's theology would share that classicist world-view by considering itself a permanent achievement, universally applicable, bound to one philosophy. Such a theological system would be conceived as static.

By conceiving culture empirically, critical history has ended classicist assumptions. An empirical conception of culture holds that cultures can be manifold, develop and decline, grasp new meanings and accept new values, give to and receive from other existing cultures. Cultures are thus many and changing (Lonergan 1974, 232-33). Under an empirical conception of culture, theology changes and develops by being conceived as an ongoing process, not as a static system (Lonergan 1994, xi). After reading Christopher Dawson's *The Age of the Gods,* Lonergan (1974, 264) personally abandoned classicism. He became increasingly distressed that Catholic theology clung to classicist notions and thus failed to appropriate an empirical notion of culture, and remained more relevant to the sixteenth century than to the twentieth century (Lonergan 1973, 15).

We note that a classicist-minded theology would have little time for developments in either specialisation or specialised techniques within theology. Catholic theology's classicism thus doubled the afflictions to which we referred in our last section and brought about other effects, which we should now investigate.

3. Isolation from Modern Thought

Classicism effectively isolated Catholic theology from modern thought. Lonergan (1988, 228) mourned the fact that, before Pope John XXIII's programme of *aggiornamento*, Catholicism was unable to properly embrace and use the developments in modern thought. While being able to acknowledge certain products of modern thought, the classicist worldview could not accept the means of modern thinking. Lonergan's essential point is that a classicist theology could selectively accept some conclusions of modern thought. Beyond such conclusions though, classicist theology could neither use the tools of modern thought, nor could it appropriate a way of thinking that was empirical, developing, open to revision, open to a plurality of cultures, and thus requiring both more work than before and a commitment to specialisation. Beyond its failure to use modern methods, classicist theology was also unable to effectively or constructively criticise modern thought, when it was used within the Church. In this regard, Lonergan (1974, 112) cites the failure of classicist "churchmen" to account properly for the work of Teilhard de Chardin. So remote from the project of modern thought were the classicists, they could not understand any reason to interact with modern culture by enhancing that culture with a religious understanding. Classicists could only greet the palaeontologist-theologian's work with mistrust, because they could not appreciate the modern notion of science with which he worked. Teilhard de Chardin was not alone in being misunderstood by classicist thinkers. We note Lonergan's point (1974, 94), that:

> If their opposition to wickedness made churchmen unsympathetic to modern ways, their classicism blocked their vision. They were unaware

that modern science involved quite a different notion of science from that entertained by Aristotle. When they praised science ... what they meant to praise and support was true and certain knowledge of things through their causes.

In our next chapter, we shall be taking up the difference between modern science and the older notions that it replaced.

Another symptom of classicist theology's isolation from modern thought is manifested in Pope Leo XIII's scholastic revival, which, despite its initial success, failed to produce the long-lasting renewal for which he had hoped. Lonergan (1974, 184) blames classicist theology for the failure of the Thomistic revival. Regrettably, *Aeterni Patris* (1879) did nothing to counter classicist thinking. The scholastic revival "collapsed" because it could neither keep up with critical histories of Aquinas' period, nor could classicist theology provide the more advanced philosophy, which new human studies of theology demanded.

David Tracy (1975, 25) follows in Lonergan's line of thought, and helps to clarify Lonergan's statements on classicist theology's isolation from modern thought. Tracy observes that one of the more significant weaknesses of the older "orthodox" model of theology, was its "inability to come to terms with the cognitive, ethical, and existential counter-claims of modernity." We find a further problem with *Aeterni Patris* in Leo's failure to encourage a fully critical recovery of Thomas' thought. While he proposed that students take Thomas's doctrines from "his own fountains," he also proposed in the same sentence the "established agreement" of Thomistic commentators as a guard against new and dangerous ideas creeping into the new scholasticism. The result of such an uncritical approach is that the supposedly Thomist neo-scholasticism, which became popular after *Aeterni Patris*, often deviated from the thought of Aquinas (Lonergan 1973, 31; McCool, 1977, 233).

Classicism's isolation from modern thought manifested itself in two other ways. First, Catholic theology remained bound to the Aristotelian system of thought. Lonergan (1974, 136-37) observes that Aristotelianism was effective in Christianising the Greek and Arabic influences flooding into Europe and in bringing coherence to Christian thought. However, Aristotelianism was simply unable to account for the nature or the content of modern science. Moreover, Aristotelianism was incapable of understanding modern human and natural sciences and philosophy, and their relationship to theology. While Catholic theology adhered to this outmoded and impotent Aristotelianism, Catholic theologians had attempted to supplement their theology with the results of modern philosophic thought. However, where they lacked an effective, modern methodology, Lonergan laments that Catholic theologians had adopted modern thinking in a way that was often eclectic and superficial.

With its attachment to Aristotelianism, classicism also isolated itself from modern thought's account of the human subject. Aristotelianism maintained that there were necessarily true first principles. Moreover, classicism held to the view of normative culture. Together these factors sustained the classicist belief that, while subjective factors existed, the differences resulting from human subjectivity were inconsequential. This classicist view is far removed from modern thought's insistence that we must not ignore human subjectivity (Lonergan 1973, 12-13).

Lonergan's anxiety over Catholic theology's isolation from modern thought was more than academic. He (1973, 56) displayed pastoral concern and a broad vision of theology by declaring that "The concern of the theologian is not just a set of propositions but a concrete religion as it has been lived, as it is being lived, and as it is to be lived." At the same time, he deplored the static, or classicist, viewpoint that invariably isolates Catholic theology and theologians from concrete religion and from the concrete world in which a religion is lived out. In 1968, he observed (1974, 94) that such isolation meant that Catholic theology had only "belatedly" acknowledged the classicist system's end, as an effective worldview. In catching up with the modern world, Catholic theology, and Catholics in general, suffered gravely from their isolation from modernity:

> ... from the present situation Catholics are suffering more keenly than others, not indeed because their plight is worse, but because up to Vatican II they were sheltered against the modern world and since Vatican II they have been exposed more and more to the chill winds of modernity (Lonergan 1974, 93).

Its long isolation from modern thought made Catholicism experience modernity as "chill winds," rather than a refreshing breeze. Lonergan (1974, 93) argued that, without an adequate methodology that allowed them to constructively interact with modernity, Catholics were left in a state of confusion, with many voices, "many of them shrill, and most of them contradictory," vying for support.

4. Lack of an Adequate "Scientific" Methodology

In 1972, Lonergan saw the unfolding of a crisis in the Catholic Church, a crisis which was aggravated by Catholic theology's insufficient philosophy and scholarship and its outdated notion of science. He (1973, 63) concurred with Andrew Greeley that the foundational problem facing the Church was a problem of theory. Catholicism, especially in its theology, lacked the theoretical, methodological foundations, with which to account for modern science, philosophy and scholarship.

Lonergan's statement of 1972 echoes his criticism of Catholic theology in 1954. He observed (1988, 129) that in settling a type of question relevant to theology, scholars did not approach the question with a scientific method but they tended to settle the questions with now this and then that prevailing and transient philosophy. While at this time, Lonergan had not formulated his theological method, it is important that we appreciate his early struggle against a theological system, which lacked a sufficient methodology.

Method in Theology shows much concern over Catholic theology's inadequate methodology. Lonergan wrote (1994, 3-4) that, when judged by the standards of modern scientific method, theology had often to be content with being regarded as a nonscientific discipline. In the minds of many, theology had descended into mediocrity, being somewhat less successful and influential than the natural and human sciences. Lonergan expressed his belief that an effective method must be found, if a less successful subject like theology was not to remain a mediocrity, or to sink into "decadence and desuetude." The search for such a method was his lifework and *Method in Theology* resulted from that search (Meynell 1989, 206).

5. CONCLUSIONS

Lonergan had many complaints against Catholic theology's "impossible conditions." He found it wanting in its lack of specialisation, its attachment to classicism and its isolation from modern thought. These factors, he argued (1985a, 10), left Catholic theology unable to solve important issues, such as the theology of grace, which occupied his doctoral thesis. Catholic theology's deterioration had led to the three centuries long Dominican-versus-Jesuit controversies on grace (Crowe 1980, 16). Lonergan's investigation of this issue, and his subsequent writings, reveal that Catholic theology lacked an adequate methodology with which to resolve today's substantial problems.

This concern went beyond the purely academic pursuit of theology. Lonergan (1973, 57) was troubled by the effects of theology's problems upon the concrete living out of the Catholic religion. He was distressed that Catholic theology's problems, specifically its lack of an adequate methodology, meant that with the rejection of the scholastic foundation of theology, people simultaneously rejected the more authentic tenets of the Catholic faith. Moreover, with Catholic theology's lack of a firm methodological foundation, Lonergan (1988, 245) foresaw the formation of one party in Catholicism who held onto the classicist framework against the reality of the modern world, while another party would form in an attempt to embrace modernity, but which lacked adequate methodological foundations on which to do so.

> Classical culture cannot be jettisoned without being replaced; and what replaces it cannot but run counter to classical expectations. There is bound to be formed a solid right that is determined to live in a world that no longer exists. There is bound to be formed a scattered left, captivated by now this, now that new development, exploring now this and now that new possibility. But what will count is perhaps a not too numerous center, big enough to be at home in both the old and the new, painstaking enough to work out one by one the transitions to be made, strong enough to refuse half measures and insist on complete solutions even though it has to wait.

In our book's fourth chapter, we shall investigate Lonergan's hopes, as a "painstaking centrist," for Catholic theology. However, we should also investigate the general background behind Lonergan's concerns. With the intention of showing how they influenced Lonergan's work, our next chapter will now examine some key developments in modern thought and the responses made to these challenges.

Chapter 3
Classicism and Modernity

"Along with changes in the notion of science and the notion of philosophy, it [specialisation] has been my motive in devoting years to working out a *Method in Theology*" (Lonergan 1973, 32). The shift from the older, "classicist" worldview, to the more modern, empirical notion of culture and the changes present in modern science and modern philosophy have presented a serious challenge to Catholic theology. Lonergan (1994, xi, 3-4) lamented Catholic theology's failure to adequately account for the change from a classicist worldview to a more modern outlook. He believed that, to regain its dignity and usefulness, theology had to conceive its tasks "in the context of modern science, modern scholarship, modern philosophy, of historicity, collective practicality and coresponsibility."

While we have noted Lonergan's concern over classicist theology and its inability to account for modern thought, we have not so clearly examined the natures of, and the distinction between, the older and newer ways of thinking. To better understand Lonergan, and the motivating factors behind his theological method, we should investigate the meanings of "classicism," "Aristotelianism," "modern scholarship" and "modern philosophy." Accordingly, this chapter will investigate the Aristotelian-classicist notion of science and key developments in modern science, modern mathematics and physics, modern philosophy and modern history. We acknowledge that we shall not deal comprehensively with the following issues. With such an endeavour being beyond the scope of this book, we shall pursue the modest but more relevant task of extracting from classicist and modern thought those factors most relevant to Lonergan's motivations for developing his *Method in Theology*.

I. THE ARISTOTELIAN NOTION OF SCIENCE

The evolution of modern science was a major development in Western society. Heralded by Bacon, this development counts among its heroes Galileo, Newton and Kepler. We should emphasise that, beyond the content of science, the very notion of science also changed with modern developments. That change and development, according to H. Butterfield (1958, vii), reduces the Renaissance and the Reformation to historical trivialities. This important development, however, is only intelligible when modern science is compared with the older, Aristotelian, model of science. We now investigate the Aristotelian model of science, but we do so with the knowledge that the shift from Aristotelian to modern science was not primarily concerned with conclusions or observations. The shift regarded the very method of science (Butterfield 1958, 1). We also proceed with the clarification that we use deliberately the term "Aristotelian," rather than "Aristotle's." While the medievals took their justification for their scientific method from Aristotle, especially his *Posterior Analytics*; Aristotle did not envisage a strict application of his *Posterior Analytics* beyond the realm of mathematics. Furthermore, neither Aristotle nor Aquinas were concerned, as were some of their followers, to determine first principles for their science. It was their fourteenth century followers who pursued this quest for "necessary" truth (Lonergan 1973, 6; 1985b, 45).

Aristotelians were most importantly characterised by their belief that their method could yield *certain knowledge*. They believed that science was "certain knowledge of things through their causes" (Lonergan 1959, 27). Lonergan (1985b, 41) was well aware of the Aristotelian emphasis on certainty, writing that, within the Aristotelian system, "scientific knowledge is about things: it is knowledge of the cause, knowledge that it is the cause, knowledge that the effect cannot be other than it is." Such emphasis on certainty would have taken support from Aristotle's statement (*Posterior Analytics*, I, 2, 71b 9-16):

> We think we understand a thing *simpliciter* (and not in the sophistic fashion accidentally) whenever we think we are aware both that the explanation because of which the object is is its explanation, and that it is not possible for this to be otherwise. It is clear, then, that to understand is something of this sort; for both those who do not understand and those who do understand-the former think they are themselves in such a state, and those who do understand actually are. Hence that of which there is understanding *simpliciter* cannot be otherwise.

Next, the Aristotelians believed that they could attain certitude with a methodology relying upon *deduction* from supposedly "self-evident axioms" (Meynell 1991, 234). Aristotelian method conceived science as beginning from first principles, then deducing objective necessity from these principles (Lonergan 1973, 6). However, this approach was insufficiently attentive to experience and the facts of the world, as they could be observed. Bacon (1973, 1:n5/p26) particularly disparaged such an approach.

He upbraided "the schoolmen" [Aristotelian scientist-philosophers] who, though having excellent intellectual skills, remained isolated from the world of experience, preferring to deduce their science from books. This methodology of science, as deduction from self-evident first principles, is most unlike the approach of modern science, which pursues "theories invented, corrected and corroborated over an indefinite period through appeal to experience" (Meynell, 1991, 234).

Under a methodology that saw itself as certain and deductive, *necessity* followed as another key element of Aristotelian science, which concentrated on learning causes and their necessary effects (Lonergan 1988, 238). With things supposed to be necessary effects of their causes, the Aristotelian worldview allowed no scientific place for probability. This position did have some basis in Aristotle's writings, as Lonergan notes (1992, 151-52), because Aristotle excluded any theory of probability. This science, which regarded itself as necessary and not in any way probable, thus excluded any science of the contingent, an exclusion that created a problem with concrete observations of our apparently contingent world. The Aristotelians, however, maintained that while all terrestrial events were contingent, they remained necessary effects of their cause, unless another cause intervened. Such intervention was regarded as a mere coincidence, which could be explained by a regressive series of further coincidences. In our contingent world, an Aristotelian could thus not escape the category of the coincidental. In a system of thought with no place for a theory of probability, there could be no science of the contingent or the accidental. As Aristotle wrote (*Metaphysics* VI, 2 1027a 19), "that there is no science of the accidental is obvious; for all science is either of that which is always or of that which is for the most part." This worldview, which excluded any science of the accidental (Lonergan 1959, 29-30; 1974, 3), meant that no science of history could exist within Aristotelianism.

With Aristotelian science conceiving its proper methodology as a matter of deducing necessary effects from known causes, it is predictable that Aristotelianism considered itself a *"permanent* acquisition of truth." Aristotelians considered their science to be "an expression of truth and, what once is true, always is true" (Lonergan 1973, 6, 32). Unlike modern science, which allows for development and ongoing succession of systems, the Aristotelian system supposedly remained fixed, immobile, seemingly immutable (Lonergan 1994, 310-11). A factor that reinforced this supposed permanence was the Aristotelian system's assumption of "a somewhat instantaneous methodology." As Meynell writes (1991, 233), this assumption came from Aristotle's view that "reality could be known rather immediately as a result of inquiry into experience, rather than only at the end of an indefinitely reiterated process." Interestingly, Meynell (1991, 245) also explains that Plato comes closer to, what we shall later find is, the modern notion of science as an ongoing, indefinite process of inquiry. In *Timaeus* (29c-d), he wrote: "Enough if we adduce probabilities as likely as any others, for we must remember that I who am the speaker and you who are the judges are only mortal men."

Under the Aristotelian system, the sciences were not autonomous, as they are today. Rather, they were *dependent upon metaphysics*, forming a single block with philosophy, with strict philosophy and the sciences being distinguished only by their different objects. Underlying the sciences' dependence on philosophy was the assumption that the object of metaphysics, being as being, was the most fundamental object. Aristotelianism thus assumed that metaphysical principles held for all objects. Under that assumption, metaphysics provided the basic terms for all other sciences (Lonergan 1985b, 41). Rather than as autonomous disciplines the sciences were conceived as "prolongations of philosophy and as further determinations of the basic concepts philosophy provides" (Lonergan 1994, 95, 274). This assumed dependence of the sciences upon metaphysics was present even as late as Isaac Newton's time. Despite Newton's freedom from metaphysical dependence, he still felt compelled to give his scientific work the rather Aristotelian title, *Philosophiae Naturalis Principia Mathematica* (Lonergan 1985b, 41). To clarify Lonergan's point, we note that Newton made a definitive break from the dependence of science upon metaphysics. The title of Newton's *Principia*, however, does reflect the mood of his time, which still conceived science along metaphysical foundations. We also note that classicists found it easy to assume that the sciences were not independent, but subordinated to Church authority. They would have taken comfort from *Pius IX's Syllabus of Condemned Errors* (1864) and *Qui Pluribus* (1846) (DS 2776, 2903, 2904, 2910, 2911; TCF 107, 112/3, 4, 10, 11), when he indicated that Catholic faith could neither benefit from, nor be criticised by, modern thinking because all other disciplines were supposed to come under the authority of God and the Church.

The Aristotelian model of science had serious implications for the Catholic theology that adopted it. By conforming to the model of Aristotelian science, Catholic theology became a deductive pursuit of certainty, necessity and permanence, with an undue reliance on metaphysics. This is because of the link between theology and culture. We should first note Lonergan's point (1994, 124), that with the Aristotelian's concept of all knowledge being dependent upon a necessary, certainly deduced, and permanent philosophy, it is unsurprising that they should view culture similarly. They conceived culture as a permanent and singular achievement, and thus considered their culture universal and normative for all peoples of all times. Classicism was thus the cultural expression of Aristotelianism, which took the "view of conceiving culture normatively and of concluding that there is just one human culture."

Theology was invariably affected by such a viewpoint of culture, the reason for which is straightforward. If theologians conceive their science in very abstract terms, they may believe that they can escape the influence of culture. However, Lonergan (1994, xi) presents a more accurate and concrete picture of theology, as mediating "between a cultural matrix and the significance and role of a religion in that matrix." Of most concern to us is his statement that when classicism dominates theological thinking, theology is conceived as a permanent achievement within a static system. In Lonergan's assessment, Catholic theology was afflicted by the viewpoint in which theologians saw their science as belonging to the one authentic culture, with no room for development. We find a good example of such theology in the work of Joseph Kelutgen, a theologian responsible for the First Vatican Council's *Dei Filius*. Kleutgen rejected the "new theology," presented by Tübingen and Günther, and insisted upon an "old" theology that rejected the modern notion of development. In Kleutgen's view, the historical approach to doctrinal development was limited to determining the logical bonds that existed between the tradition's revealed truths. This theology was typical of classicist thinking, through its emphasis on deduction, necessity and certitude. To be fair, Kleutgen was a talented metaphysician, but his classicist horizon meant that he lacked the ability to deal with history, and Christianity, as it existed in the concrete, historical world (McCool 1977, 10, 167-216, 220ff).

Lonergan was distressed that such a viewpoint was untenable in the modern world. Our following sections will now be concerned with the developments in modern science and how classicism is untenable in the light of such developments. However, before studying modern science, we should qualify a point concerning Aristotle; that is, whether he should bear the blame for classicism. Lonergan acknowledges that classicist thinking took some of its confirmation from Aristotle's writings. However, he argues (1985b, 45) that, outside mathematics, Aristotle did not conceive a strict application of his *Posterior Analytics*, a key proof text for classicist thinking (Ross 1949, 14). Lonergan further argues (1973, 6, 32) that

Aristotle did not share the classicist concern to find necessary first principles. He observes that Aquinas, as an interpreter of Aristotle, did not strive towards finding first principles, and he backs up this defence of Aristotle by noting that Aquinas was sufficiently familiar with the whole Aristotelian corpus to avoid being over-concerned with the logic that so infatuated classicism. Rather than Aristotle, Lonergan holds that it was the fourteenth century scholars, such as Scotus and Ockham, whose basic concerns turned to demonstrative logic and certitude.

We can be sympathetic towards Lonergan's concern to defend Aristotle from the full blame for classicism. To be realistic, however, one is justified in identifying classicism with Aristotelianism. Even if it failed to take the philosopher's statements in their right context, medieval classicism did base itself on some of Aristotle's writings. Moreover, as Meynell observes (1991, 235-36), Aristotle did fall, at least partly, into the same error as classicism, by taking geometry as his model for science, along with its axioms, which, at the time, were regarded as necessary truths, not mere postulates.

Having dealt with classicism and Aristotelian science, we now turn to the development of modern science.

2. Modern Science and the Advent of Critical Empirical Method

As the prognosticator of modern science, Francis Bacon (1973, 1:n5/ p26) ruthlessly castigated Aristotelian science for its preoccupation with deduction. Bacon believed science's basic cause of corruption to be "the Schoolmen['s] ... wits being shut up in the cells of a few authors (chiefly Aristotle their dictator) as their persons were shut up in the cells of monasteries and colleges." Bacon meant that, instead of sufficiently attending to experience and the observable facts of nature, the "schoolmen" had been overwhelmed by the pursuit of metaphysical axioms by abstraction (Crowe 1980, 11). Accordingly, the most important part of Bacon's work was to reject the method of syllogistic deduction from first principles and to embrace an inductive method that effectively analysed experience (Collins 1956, 58; Crowe 1980, 11-12). He exemplified that change under tragic circumstances. Eager to find out if snow would retard putrefaction, rather than deducing his conclusions, Bacon stopped his carriage, killed a chicken and stuffed it with some snow that lay about. The experiment, while somewhat successful, led to Bacon's catching a chill and fatal bronchitis.

Galileo's free-fall experiments illustrated the turn to inductive or empirical method in an experiment with less lethal consequence. Galileo's method brought to fruition the movement Bacon had heralded. While the material results of Galileo's experiments are widely known, we find vitally important Galileo's method, in which he systematically analysed experience. He abandoned the methodology of taking first principles and from these, deducing scientific laws, choosing instead to perform concrete experiments, discover what happened in reality, mathematically express what he discovered and support his formulation by a "systematic appeal to experience" (Drake 1978, 44). Galileo's experiments were pivotal for modern science. Before his time, scientists did not feel compelled to appeal to experience. However, after Galileo, scientific method became based on experiment (Danaher 1988, 25). For Galileo and those who followed him, what mattered to science were not abstract conclusions from first principles, but the intelligibility detectable within the data available to experience.

Modern science's turn to an empirical basis meant that notions of permanence and certainty were replaced by the pursuit of an ever-ongoing process of seeking truth. With a potentially unlimited field of data for empirical study, one could no longer presume to know all relevant principles and to infallibly deduce one's conclusions from such principles. Bacon's notion of the scientific ideal, for example, was to seek first principles, but he avoided "rushing" into deducing general concepts from particular instances. He was content to go on cautiously, inductively, to come steadily safer, more reliable, first principles (Collins 1956, 58; Crowe 1980, 11-12).

In a manner similar to the overthrow of permanence and certainty, the Aristotelian model of necessity was replaced by modern science's pursuit of empirically verified possibility. Galileo's experiments illustrate a concern for the observed state of free-fall. Issues of necessary natures, or what should be so, did not concern modern scientists like Galileo. In contrast to such concerns with necessity, Galileo sought after intelligibility present within empirically verified patterns of free-fall (Riley 1980, 98). We note that by relying upon observation, experiment and the empirical verification of possibilities, modern science became intrinsically open to ever-new discoveries that "in turn generate new definitions and formulations to make science not *an unchanging system but an ever ongoing process*" (Lonergan 1974, 235; 1985b 43; 1973, 7, 32).

The pursuit of intelligibility is a critical point of interest. Whilst Aristotelian science resolutely adhered to certitudes, modern science was more content to find intelligibility within observed data. Lonergan (1992, 57; 1990, 60) also observes Galileo's departure from concern with causes. Galileo's distinct interest was with discovering intelligibility in how objects fall (Tracy 1970, 84-91).

In Darwinian thought, which was manifestly concerned with probability, we find a clear rejection of notions of certainty and necessity. Rather than proposing any cause of biological evolution, Darwinian thought simply proposed an explanation of the conditions, under which the emergence and survival of species were more probable or less likely (Lonergan 1992, 154-55; 1985b, 139; Darwin 1962, 138ff). We find, moreover, that Darwinian theory avoids deductivism by in no way pretending to deduce certainly the evolutionary process of the future. It only proposes to provide more accurate explanations of the intelligible probabilities present in natural selection.

We finally note that modern science has freed itself from dependence upon philosophy, especially from metaphysics. Lonergan (1985b 135-36) argues that Newton's work illustrates the definitive assertion of science's autonomy from metaphysical philosophy. While the title, *Philosophiae Naturalis Principia Mathematica,* was a concession to centuries of Aristotelian science, the contents of the *Principia* show Newton breaking free from a metaphysical framework. Newton established an independent conceptual framework, which was proper to science, and effectively manifested the "vindication of mechanics as an autonomous science."

3. Modern Mathematics and Twentieth Century Physics

Lonergan (1994, 280, 315; 1990, 85) explains that, in a manner similar to modern science, modern mathematics has discarded the notion of necessity. Such a position may be surprising, because mathematicians seem to use deductions with logical rigour to attain conclusions from initial primitive propositions. However, mathematicians have no way of showing that such primitive propositions are necessary. The basic premises of modern mathematics, as Lonergan observes, are not necessary truths, but "freely chosen postulates." He notes that non-Euclidean geometry was a key factor in establishing that mathematical postulates and axioms could no longer be considered necessary.

Despite Aristotelian science's wounding by modern science, there lingered in human minds the assumption, or at least the desire, that science could be concerned with a certain knowledge of causal necessity. That lingering notion was shattered by the quantum hypothesis of Planck and the subsequent discoveries of Einstein and Heisenberg. Such advances in physics demanded corrections to the theories of Euclid, Newton and Maxwell. Such scientific revision made it undeniably clear that physics could no longer concern itself with deductions from necessary truths. It had irreversibly become the pursuit of hypothetical theories, subjected to verifying conclusions (Lonergan 1985b, 149).

Modern physics now rejects notions of determinism or systematic compulsion, which rely upon a presumption of necessity. On the contrary, even the non-systematic has become a positive object of scientific inquiry, as is displayed by the work of scientists such as Fermi. The quantum physicist's horizon is no longer limited to necessary cause and effect. It embraces a world where the apparently non-systematic and non-necessary can, and do, occur. Instead of striving against the non-systematic and attempting an explanation through necessity, the role of the modern physicist is to determine which of these non-systematic or non-necessary events are actually significant (Heelan 1965, 39-41; Riley 1980, 100).

Physics has become a science of empirical verification. In that light, Heelan writes (1965, 29) that Heisenberg's quantum physics contributed the great methodological insight that physics "should concern itself only with *observable quantities.*" Being concerned only with the observable, physics became interested only in what is, rather than what necessarily "should be," even when this went against what was supposed to be logically so. A good example is Planck's apparent unease, after discovering that energy could only be emitted or absorbed only in discrete energy quanta, because this discovery contradicted previously established theories. However, despite his "logical" misgivings, Planck had to incorporate the observed measurements of heat radiation by Curlbaum and Rubens (Heisenberg 1962, 31-32). Furthermore, despite at least the desire to have a determinable universe, Heisenberg's principle of indeterminacy, which again is based on empirical, observable data, exemplified modern science's relegation of necessity to being a "marginal notion" (Lonergan 1985b, 42-43; Heelan 1965, 36-43).

The mood of modern physicists is captured well by Patrick Heelan (1965, 29). Their cry, "Out with metaphysics and all unobservable quantities!" is an evangelical motto that decries the older notions of necessity, certainty, deduction and permanence. "Out," is the attitude that we can know what is certainly and permanently true and what cannot be other than what it is. For modern physicists, "in" is an ongoing and advancing study of what happens to be there to be observed, whether it seems necessary, logical, or not. Modern physics has accordingly curtailed a focus on deduced certainties. In its place is the pursuit of understanding verifiable possibilities (Lonergan 1985b, 42-43).

4. MODERN PHILOSOPHY

The Aristotelian model of philosophy, just as the science relying upon it for methodological principles, was supposed to be a matter of deducing necessary truths from self-evident principles (Lonergan 1985b, 156; 1994, 316-17; 1974, 72). Because it concentrated on necessary truths and self-evident principles, Lonergan (1974, 70-72) argues that Aristotelian philosophy seriously neglected the thinking human subject, meaning that this model of philosophy, which prevailed among Catholic theologians from the days of Suarez, de Lugo, and Banez, practically presumed that philosophical truth was "so objective as to get along without minds." Lonergan (1974, 72) finds that such a concentration on necessity and self-evidence, which he argues is present in Aristotle's *Posterior Analytics* but more proximately in the rationalist concept of pure reason, also led to a presumption of human authenticity. That is, where conclusions are supposed to follow necessarily from self-evident premises, no matter who the thinker may be, it is supposed that one cannot fail to grasp what is self-evident, or to conclude what is necessary.

In sharp contrast to its Aristotelian predecessor, modern philosophy took on a more empirical approach, which took account of the human subject that did philosophy. Lonergan (1994, 96; 1985b, 236) argues that Kant's turn to the subject "marks a dividing line" in modern philosophy. When empiricist philosophy awoke Kant from his "dogmatic slumbers," he wakened to a study of the operations of the human mind and their relations to one another, in addition to philosophy's conclusions. Kant's awakening overturned the assumptions of the older philosophy. He proposed that pure reason could operate in mathematics because the mathematician could have an *a priori* intuition of the concepts of space and time used in mathematics. However, Kant (1990, A713/B741-A738/B769) argued that because a philosopher could not have a similar *a priori* intuition of being, which is his object of inquiry, he could not rely on pure reason. The philosopher must be content with the more modest and critical work of developing a transcendental method based on analysing human consciousness (Tracy 1970, 92-93).

With the advantage of historical hindsight, one notes that Kant was handicapped, for example, by relying upon a pre-Riemannian view that believed mathematics to be concerned with necessary principles (Tracy 1970, 93). Despite such limitation on his work, Kant (1990, Bxvi-Bxvii) still demanded and effected a paradigm change in philosophy similar to the change brought about by Copernicus:

> We should then be proceeding precisely on the lines of Copernicus' primary hypothesis. Failing of a satisfactory progress in explaining the movements of heavenly bodies on the supposition that they all revolved around the spectator, he tried whether he might not have better success if he made the spectator to revolve and the stars to remain at rest. A similar experiment can be tried in metaphysics, as regards the *intuition* of objects.

This philosophical "Copernican Revolution" shifted from the object of philosophy to the philosophising subject. In Kant's model of philosophy, to do metaphysics, one would first have to critically defend the "conditions of possibility" of such metaphysical knowledge. Such a challenge effectively placed all precritical philosophy, especially scholasticism, into question (Tracy 1970, 93). Not surprisingly, and as an indication of the prevailing Catholic theological mood, such a challenge resulted in Kant's *Critique of Pure Reason* being placed on the *Index Liborum Prohibitorum* in 1827.

Lonergan (1974, 70; Tracy 1970, 93) and Doran (1990, 157) both note that Kant's "Copernican Revolution" has remained incomplete, with this incomplete turn to the subject resulting in such things as relativism. Despite this revolution's incompleteness, Lonergan notes (1974, 70) that Kant's challenge to philosophy brought the subject into a technically prominent position in philosophy, with modern philosophy taking serious account of the thinking human subject. After the changes effected by absolute idealism, Lonergan (1985b, 242) finds the subject accounted for: in Kierkegaard's stand on faith, Newman's position on conscience, Nietzsche's will to power, Dilthey's *Lebensphilosophie*, Blondel's philosophy of action and Scheler's emphasis on feeling. We would also find such emphasis in Schleiermacher's writings on the human person's "sense" or "feeling" (Sykes 1983, 2-3). While these authors differ in emphasis, they are united in the belief that "pure reason" does not exist in the philosophising subject and that account has to be taken of the human mind, as it is actually found to operate. This means, as Lonergan explains (1985b, 156-57), that authenticity cannot always be taken for granted in a thinking subject, because human activity is never "pure" but a struggle between authenticity and inauthenticity.

We clarify that, regarding "authenticity" Lonergan (1994, 104, 110-11) holds that human "authenticity" is achieved through self-transcendence. One reaches cognitional self-transcendence, and therefore authenticity, when one is attentive, inquiring and understanding, reflective and judging. One reaches moral and religious self-transcendence by deciding for the truly good and loving the truly lovable. To the extent that one achieves cognitional, moral and religious self-transcendence, one is acting in human authenticity. One can be unauthentic, however, to the extent that one rejects one's human processes by not being open to data, by scoffing understanding, by refusing to reflect and judge, by committing oneself to ingenuine goods or evils, or by rejecting the love of the truly lovable.

Returning to modern philosophy's more concrete outlook, we find the drive to honestly face the complexity that arises when we are investigating human subjects. The data may be a mixture of authenticity and inauthenticity, and the investigation of the data may be affected by the level of authenticity of the investigator. Modern philosophy thus presumes neither a speculative intellect, nor a pure reason, which draws necessary truths from self-evident principles. Even when philosophy does now acknowledge analytic propositions, these are submitted to the process of critical verification, which is largely concerned with the knowing subject (Lonergan 1994, 316).

5. Modern History

The spirit of critical inquiry, which spawned modern science, generated critical history in the nineteenth century. The critical faculty, aroused into investigating the natural world, remained wanting until it had also investigated human nature and how human populations and their institutions had come to be. It was, as Alan Richardson writes (1964, 32-33), the same movement that "first culminated in the seventeenth-century scientific achievement and later in the emergence of the fully developed historical critical method of the nineteenth century" (Lonergan 1984, 2; Riley 1980, 96).

Two key factors distinguish modern history from its predecessor. First, modern history rejects the notion that history is adequately interpreted by a believer who collects, and weighs up, testimonies (Lonergan 1985b, 80; Boly 1991, 166). R. G. Collingwood (1989, 234, 258) thus criticised Greco-Roman and medieval approaches to history, which were often used to prove "a thesis, in particular some philosophical or political or theological thesis." Such precritical history was based on a "scissors and paste approach," by which one gathered testimony, assembled what one believed, and published it. Secondly, modern history eschews history as being a tradition formed for its hearers' edification. Despite the value such an approach has for building up cultures, it is pre-critical, not critical, history (Lonergan 1994, 185). John Henry Newman (1974, 91) made such a criticism of precritical history, noting how modern history had assailed the notion that history could be a matter of "an appeal ... to the supposed works of the Areopagite, or to the primitive Decretals, or to St Dionysius' answers to Paul." In a similar spirit, Geiselmann (1966, 109) notes that "It was only with the discovery of history during the transition from the eighteenth to the nineteenth century that tradition completely lost its power. History now liberated itself from tradition and made itself independent."

Collingwood (1989, 236, 240) argued that a reformation, like Kant's "Copernican Revolution," has taken place in history, which resulted in its modern critical method. A more significant element of this revolution is modern history's turn to the subject, in a manner paralleling philosophy's turn. Collingwood emphasised this change, writing that, no longer relying on an authority other than himself, the historian "is his own authority and his thought autonomous, self-authorizing, possessed of a criterion to which his so-called authorities must conform and by reference to which they are criticised."

Critical history's functions are also important to us. First, Collingwood (1989, 237) states that the critical function demonstrates the autonomy of the historian, puts one's authorities "in the witness-box," and "extorts from them information which in their original statements they have withheld." He draws a significant parallel between putting historical witnesses to the test, and Bacon's putting "Nature to the question." This parallel supports Richardson's claim that modern science and modern history are the same movement. The critical function, though, is critical of historians, as well as historical sources. We note Becker's point (1958, 25-26), which is echoed by Lonergan (1994, 222-23), that historians are neither unobstructed by the ideas of their age, nor, despite the Enlightenment's best intentions, do they operate without presuppositions. Modern critical history thus acknowledges that because historians do not operate with "pure reason," they should be subject to critical evaluation.

Modern history also has a constructive function, which further reinforces the historian's autonomy, because the historian relies on one's own powers to interpolate the phases in the historical process, which are accessible from the authorities. Collingwood (1989, 237, 238, 240) notes that this leads the historian to independence from his authorities, to the point of rediscovering what has been forgotten, or even of discovering what no one had previously known. Lonergan (1994, 195) expresses the same point by noting that modern history's constructive aspect discovers "what hitherto hd been experienced but not properly known." This constructive function represents freedom from pure deduction in history, in which one can also be creative, within critical parameters.

6. Conclusions

While this chapter has not dealt exhaustively with the developments of modern science, history and philosophy, it has examined key developments that illustrate Lonergan's concern with the shift from "classicist" thinking to more modern scholarship. Understanding such developments is most important to our notion of theology. When one's notion of theology remains limited to a static, classicist worldview, one thinks of theology as a permanent achievement and one will most likely find no need to reform theology. However, when one acknowledges theology's concrete function, which is to mediate between a religion and a culture, and when one conceives culture empirically, one recognises theology as an ongoing process and one's concern will be with theology's method. If one holds that theology must both operate in the concrete world within which theologians operate and pursue its tasks in the context of today's science, philosophy, history and scholarship, one will recognise the need for theology to account for developments in the very methodologies, in addition to conclusions, of these disciplines (Lonergan 1994, xi).

A prime motivation behind writing *Method* was Lonergan's belief that theology had to be freed from a classicist methodology, that saw itself as: certain, based on deduction, attaining necessity, a permanent achievement, reliant upon metaphysics, and which was also narrowly focussed on the contents of one's investigations. To replace this classicist methodology, theology could maintain respectability in the face of modern thought only if it adopted an empirically established foundation, employed its autonomous methods to find intelligibility within the context of an ongoing process that yielded probable and cumulative results, accounted for the subject who does such theology and accounted for a critical establishment of its own proper methods.

We have noted Lonergan's (1994, 4) concern that a theology failing to account for developments in modern thinking would "remain a mediocrity or slip into decadence and desuetude." From his other comments (1973, 15), most notably that he had to teach theology under impossible conditions, it is evident that, by the late 1960s, Lonergan found Catholic theology still not meeting the challenges of modern thought. That failure was a key motivation in the formulation of his theological method. We now turn our attention to Lonergan's views on Catholic theology's needs, and how those needs could be met. We intend to show how Lonergan sought a theological method that was up to the standards of modern thought. From this position, we can better understand his theological method, generally and his notion of systematics, specifically.

Chapter 4
Theology's Needs and Lonergan's Vision for New Methodological Foundations

Our previous chapters have examined the shift from classicist to modern thinking and the "impossible conditions" under which Lonergan (1973, 15) had to teach theology for twenty-five years. Many, including John Henry Newman (1973, 56-57), recognised that Catholic theology needed to come to terms with modern thought and to effect its own *novum organon*, a new beginning, if it were to retain any standing in modern society. We shall now investigate: Lonergan's assessment of the needs that a renewed Catholic theology should fulfil, how these needs required this new beginning and the new foundations that Lonergan proposed for the renewed theological method that he was developing.

i. The Needs of Theology

While Lonergan repeatedly expressed his dissatisfaction with the state of Catholic theology, his concern for theology prompted a search for a renewed theological method that in turn led him to formulate certain requirements for a revitalised and effective theology. He emphasised in his doctoral thesis (1985a, 11-12) that Catholic theology would benefit from meeting the standards of modern quantitative science. Again, in his article, "Theology and Understanding" (1988, 129), he evaluated theological method in the light of modern scientific method. Underlying those statements is a conviction that a Catholic theology, which was up to the standards of modernity, would both be methodical and take account of modern scientific methods. Lonergan thus stands in contrast to those like Karl Barth (1975, 6, 8-9), who rejected the need for theology to be concerned with either the results or the methods of "secular" sciences, or those neo-conservatives whom Doran finds (1995 2:130-31) afraid that a turn to the subject would corrupt Catholic faith. Underlying those contrasts is the question of whether theology should take account of the worldview or horizon of humankind, a question Lonergan answered clearly in the affirmative.

Despite Lonergan's intentions, we note that the renewal of Catholic theology, and the embracing of modern methods towards which he had worked, had not arrived during most of his theological career. Even though methodological developments had been advocated by Newman, the official Church was more notable for its coolness towards modern thought. For the greater part, Catholic theology remained within the classicist horizon. Only with the movements resulting from Pius XII's *Divino Afflante Spiritu* and John XXIII's vision of *aggiornamento* did Catholic theology truly begin to come to terms with modernity. As we have found previously, Lonergan lamented this state of theology. Instead of being a genuinely critical discipline, he (1994, 330-31) found Catholic theology to be oriented towards *"Denzigertheologie,"* a term he borrowed from Karl Rahner, which described the theologian's task as repeating, explaining and defending what was taught in church documents. Such a theologian "had no contribution of his own to make and so there could be no question of his possessing any autonomy in making it."

We should note that Lonergan had not yet articulated a clear concept of method in his earlier writings. It is only later, in *Method in Theology* (1994, 4), that we find such a conception of method, as "a normative pattern of recurrent and related operations yielding cumulative and progressive results."However, Lonergan's early writings reveal a notion of theological method, which would both bring theology to account for modern scientific method and solve the problems that we have explored earlier in this thesis. Within his notion of a "scientific" theological method, Lonergan (1985a, 16) noted that such a method would need to be both genuinely theological and sufficiently removed from the contingencies of current debates. An effective theological method thus needed a foundation that was more constant and universal than the contingencies of the theological dialectic of any one time:

> What is required is a point of vantage outside the temporal dialectic, a matrix or system of thought that at once is as pertinent and as indifferent to historical events as is the science of mathematics to quantitative phenomena.

Lonergan meant that Catholic theology needed a method that was: removed from debates and "issues" in theology, founded on a base that would account for the very processes immanent in theology and able to pass judgement on their particular authenticity, or otherwise.

By seeking a theological method removed from the "current dialectic," Lonergan effectively sought a transcultural theology that would be intelligible in contemporary terms. In *Method in Theology* (1994, 282), he later expressed this need in theology with more precision, writing that

... Christianity is a religion that has been developing for over two millennia. Moreover, it has its antecedents in the Old Testament, and it has the mission of preaching to all nations. Plainly, a theology that is to reflect on such a religion and that is to direct its efforts at universal communication must have a transcultural base.

Lonergan (1994, 276) thus upheld Catholic theology's need for a theological method that could address the plurality of theologies resulting from different brands of common sense existing over different languages, times, places, social and cultural situations. We find Lonergan's concern reflected in Macquarrie's point (1977, vii, 13) that to be intelligible, a theology must use the language of a culture within which theology finds itself. Such an approach has its attendant risks, and many consider it impossible for theologians to meet the standards of modern thought without betraying their faith. Barth (1975, 72), for example, held that "A proclamation that accepts responsibilities along these ... lines spells treachery to the Church and to Christ Himself." However, Lonergan's method meets this problem head-on. Especially in his functional specialty, doctrines, he presents an account of doctrines that is historical and critical, while simultaneously upholding the authentic dogmas of his tradition. Later in this book, we shall take up this balance of transcultural intelligibility and continuity of tradition.

Lonergan (1994, 315; 1974, 112) also maintained that a renewed Catholic theology needed a method that fostered a coherent self-image of the Christian in the modern world. He thus esteemed Pierre Teilhard de Chardin's efforts, but lamented the classicist inability to appreciate Teilhard's efforts because his theology challenged the classicist notions of permanence, immutability and universality. In his own work, Lonergan (1974, 3) believed that a coherent worldview of the Christian would come from an understanding of humanity, which did not mean an abstract, or an *a priori* understanding of supposed human nature. Rather, one would find a coherent theological worldview in beginning "from people as they are." As we shall find later, Lonergan responded to this challenge by accounting for people, especially theologians, by beginning from a cognitional theory that accounted for the way that the minds of theologians operated.

2. A NEW BEGINNING

Lonergan could not meet the abovementioned needs of theology by simply answering the questions of his day with the then-current theological techniques. Only a radical new beginning in theology's method could fulfill his vision. He observed (1974, 67) this century's movement towards "a total transformation of dogmatic theology" and he explained that to bring about that "total transformation" would require a new type of foundation. Essentially, Catholic theology's poor state meant that complete restructuring was necessary for its renewal. Crowe (1980, 14-15) argues that this project for theological renewal paralleled Bacon's new order for science. However, we note that this restructuring of theology parallelled Bacon's new order of science because it pursued not only new theological conclusions but a complete reconstruction of theological methodology. Lonergan (1974, 67) argued that theology had to be re-built, just as Bacon had called for a radical and complete reconstruction of the sciences, arts and all knowledge, based upon renewed foundations (Crowe 1980, 11).

Lonergan's project of restructuring theology is not an entirely new enterprise. He admired (1974, 49) the example of Thomas Aquinas and stated his aim "to do for our age what he [Aquinas] did for his." Lonergan (1974, 62) hoped to emulate Thomas' achievement in taking the Arabic and Greek thought dominant in Thomas' culture and fitting these "pagan sciences" into a Christian context. This enabled Thomas to master the Greek and Arabic philosophies and use these philosophies to present Christian doctrine. The *Summa Contra Gentiles* presents a prime example of Thomas' achievement. Lonergan argues (1974, 45) that in his *Summa* Thomas effectively made a presentation of Christian doctrine against its adversaries, which was coherent, up-to-date, persuasive and demonstrative, when necessary. Thomas' writings, we observe, were coherent, modern and persuasive, because his work met the standards of the dominant science of his time and also employed the science's more valid insights for his purposes. Lonergan (1974, 45) observes that, in using this approach,

> St. Thomas wrote against the Gentiles, but he used their own weapons, and used them so skilfully that he provided his age with a concrete instance in which essential features of Catholic truth and of Greek and Arabic culture were fused into a single organic whole.

Lonergan's observation manifests his desire to construct a theological method that both met the standards of the modern world and was able to take the more useful insights from modern thought and apply these to theology. Moreover, the observation that Thomas used his adversaries' own "weapons," calls to mind the work of Newman (1974, 91-92), who argued that the "the assailants of dogmatic truth" had available the tools of modern thought, thus having a clear advantage over those whose job it was to defend Christian dogma. For Christianity to retain any credibility or capability of argument, Newman maintained that it would have to adopt the tools of modern history. In his words, "An argument is needed, unless Christianity is to abandon the province of argument." While his intent was obviously apologetic, Newman responded to modern thought, not by suppressing it, but by insisting that modern history, not some precritical tradition, be used to verify the legitimacy of Christian doctrine. Newman thus aspired to defeat the assailants of Christianity, neither by repression, nor by an archaic response, but by using the same modern tools as Christianity's assailants.

We should note that there have been less-successful attempts at bringing Catholic theology up to modern standards. For example, the German theologians Günther (d. 1863) and Möhler (d. 1838), argued for a Christian faith that met the demands of contemporary cultures, and dealt with both Church and Christians as historical realities (McCool 1977, 107-8; Geiselmann, 1966, 65). Also noteworthy were the efforts of the modernists. These scholars, however, fell from favour with the Catholic hierarchy and, in the theological climate that existed until recently, their public influence rapidly waned in Catholic theology. On one level, such theologians failed because of the heresies that typified their work. On a deeper level, modernism and rationalism failed because they could neither sufficiently account for faith and reason, nor distinguish them. The manifold heresies, for which modernism became notorious, were perhaps only symptomatic of its failure to positively bridge the gap between the traditional teaching of their church and their new teachings, with the guidance of reason by faith (Lonergan 1992, 551, 664, 743-44, 756; 1974, 94, 112). Modernism failed, according to Lonergan (1992, 743-44), because of its stripping away of the meaning of "higher collaboration" between humans and God, with a corresponding failure to complement reason with "an intelligently formulated and reasonably accepted faith."

If we are to understand the import of theological modernism, it is important for us to distinguish it from modernity, as the development of modern science, scholarship and philosophy. "Modernism," was a seemingly convenient title for a theological movement, which chronologically followed on from other modern movements that brought a certain amount of misery to the world. Lonergan (1974, 94) explains that the Catholic Church's failure to come to terms with the modern world can, in part, be explained by the "wickedness" that often accompanied modern developments. Irreligious modern philosophies developed and the natural sciences were often seen as irreligious:

The new industry spawned slums, the new politics revolutions, the new discoveries unbelief. One may lament it but one can hardly be surprised that at the beginning of this century, when churchmen were greeted with a heresy that logically entailed all possible heresies, they named the new monster modernism.

We propose that Lonergan's work was more successful than the modernists, because, like Newman and Aquinas, he worked towards theological foundations that accounted for both faith and reason. He aimed to preserve his faith, while doing this with intellectual honestly and with a method up to the standards, and methods, of modern thought. As Doran observes (1995 2:301, *italics mine*), Lonergan succeeded because his writings reflect a balance by which they "can be filtered through the hermeneutic grid of his respectful attention to, learning from, and critical reorientation of *both* tradition *and* modernity."

3. Towards a New Methodological Foundation

We have already outlined Lonergan's notion of an effective theological method's requirements. Before outlining specific goals for such a method, we should make some observations on scientific method's value to theology. As early as his 1954 article, "Theology and Understanding," Lonergan (1988, 128-29) noted that an understanding of a scientific method and its presuppositions would go straight to the heart of a matter under consideration and supply the principles by which a scientific investigation can be systematically critiqued and evaluated. He argued that concern about one's performance as a theologian would be one thing, but "to discover the methodological principles on which that duty can be performed in a fully satisfactory fashion," would be a different matter. This implies that, when it lacked an adequate scientific methodology, theology would be capable only of dealing with superficial and peripheral issues. This conviction is clearly present in Lonergan's doctoral thesis, in which he argued (1985a, 10) that without a systematic method, "an inquiry would presuppose that the unimportant issues can be settled scientifically while the important ones are merely matters of personal opinion." With the advantage of hindsight, Lonergan wrote, in the first chapter of *Method in Theology* (1994, 4), that the lack of method would leave theology as a mediocrity and allow it to slip into decadence and desuetude.

Lonergan's point echoes the sentiments of Newman, who warned (1974, 69, 72) that Christianity would be seriously harmed if it did not adopt a modern, historical methodology. He argued that if Christianity ignored its own historical reality, and if it failed to engage modern critical history, Christianity would stumble into one of two errors. On the one hand, Christianity could fall into a naive biblicism, which would be guilty of "dispensing with historical Christianity altogether, and of forming a Christianity from the Bible alone." Alternatively an ahistorical Christianity could deteriorate into an immoderate relativism, whereby a Christianity outside of the province of history would be "to each man what each man thinks it to be, and nothing else." We would find the first of these alternatives within the many fundamentalist movements, which are characterised by their hostility to critical history and other critical sciences. The second alternative surfaced, to a degree, within the modernist movement, which sometimes over-emphasised the individual believer's experience, such as in Loisy's statement (1950, 5) that "No authority has the right to impose conclusions upon the critic in anything that falls within the field of his experience."

By stressing a methodological renewal of theology, Lonergan's work reflects Kant's intended "Copernican Revolution" in philosophy. Kant argued that anyone claiming to do metaphysics would first have to critically defend the conditions of possibility for such knowledge (Tracy 1970, 93). Similarly, Lonergan sought to establish the conditions under which theology was possible and authentic. In seeking these conditions, as we shall later find, he determined that the most reliable base for considering such conditions lay in the very intentional operations of the theologising subject.

We have found that Lonergan sought a theological method that: was transcultural, was scientifically methodical, provided a coherent self-image of the Christian, provided a vantage point outside current debates, was concretely based on human beings as they are and followed Aquinas' example in using the tools of contemporary thought to present authentic Christian teaching. These goals for theological method help us better understand Lonergan's search for a methodological basis in an understanding of the intentionality of human consciousness. With Riley (1980, 14), we note that Lonergan sought normative foundations for a historically-minded understanding of humanity. However, Lonergan did not find those foundations in hermenuetics, as did Gadamer or Ricouer, nor did he find these foundations in a universal history as did Pannenberg. Rather, Lonergan discovered his foundations within the concrete, but universal structures operative in human beings.

In his doctoral thesis, Lonergan suggests an intentionality analysis as the basis of a theological method. He observes (1985a, 11) that historians have intelligence and perform intelligent acts of understanding and that the way in which these intelligent acts of the historians' minds are performed predetermines their conclusions. Even at the beginning of his theological career, Lonergan had established that the method for which he was searching would be found, not in the objects, conclusions, data or dialectic of theology, but in the conscious, intentional processes that the theologian performed in generating one's conclusions.

Lonergan's search for a method based on an intentionality analysis is reflected in his contrast of two methodological procedures. One can take a method from the consideration of certain historical facts. However, one can take up the method employed by the quantitative sciences, which, as Lonergan argues (1985a, 12), have an objectivity resting upon "a consideration of the nature of human speculation on a given subject." Crowe observes (1980, 18) that this approach shows young Lonergan's search for "a 'matrix or system of thought' that would stand outside of, and be a guide for, actual theology." Already, as Crowe continues, Lonergan is trying to formulate that matrix in terms of the invariant operations of the human mind. By trying to base his theological method within the human mind's observed operations, we find Lonergan (1974, 3) attempting to turn theology from a classicist viewpoint of theology and human nature to a concrete viewpoint, gained from an empirically based analysis of people as they actually exist.

Lonergan's thought significantly developed between writing his doctoral thesis and *Method in Theology*. What both remained constant and gained clearer expression was his conviction that an effective theological method would be based upon an intentionality analysis. In a 1958 article, he (1988, 145) commented on the methodological value of understanding human intentionality, noting that if we were to understand understanding itself, we could bring order, light and unity to a totality of different disciplines. He put the point succinctly (1973, 18, 33), after writing *Method in Theology*, stating that his basic intention was to start from the human subject and his operations. Lonergan thus believed that an effective theological method's foundation would be an intentionality analysis that analysed effectively the data of human consciousness and provided an effective cognitional theory. This is what he means when, in the first chapter of *Method in Theology* (1994, 4), he maintains that the most foundational aspect of his method will be the procedures of the human mind.

We propose that Lonergan's approach to theology was more concrete, more empirical and more successful than the approach of the First Vatican Council. Despite the positive value of the Council's declarations in *Dei Filius*, it prescinded from the concrete condition of natural human reason, preferring to explain human reason's abilities by reference to a state of pure nature. By preferring such an abstract exposition of human reason, the Council made it difficult to account for the historical order in which concrete human beings encountered a personal God within God's concrete creation and revelation. Interestingly, on the specific issue of natural knowledge of God, Lonergan (1994, 338-39; 1974, 117-18) notes that, while Kleutgen's schema for *Dei Filius* contained a reference to fallen humanity, the final version of *Dei Filius* (DS 3004-28, 3015-20 / TCF 113-17, 131-36) made no reference to the concrete condition in which human beings find themselves.

By basing his theological method upon an analysis of the human mind's concrete operations, Lonergan opens the door to a method that is concrete, deals with people, theologians specifically, as they are. This leads to a method that is rooted in the historical and cultural realities of human life, and far more able to deal with human theology and theological issues as they arise in the concrete world.

The foundation of theological method, within a transcendental method based upon an intentionality analysis, fostered a theology that could be both transcultural and specialised. In the first place, a methodology based on the operations of the human mind would be transcultural. Lonergan acknowledges (1994, 282, 302) that such a method would not be transcultural in its explicit formulations. That, we note, would be a perpetuation of classicism. Rather, this method would be transcultural in the realities with which it dealt, namely the invariant operations of the human mind. Such an approach would allow one to take a normative stance while being historically conscious and avoiding the pitfalls of "classicism, dogmatism or authoritarianism" (Doran 1990, 461).

Secondly, a theological method based upon the operations of human intellect would advance the specialisation of theology. Lonergan (1973, 32; 1974, 211) was aware of this challenge, knowing that theology needed a method that could afford specialists a place in an ongoing process of distinct but interdependent and interacting functions, ranging from the unearthing of data to communicating results. Such distinction and specialisation would be impossible, though, without a method that explained what each specialist was doing at each part of the specialised process. In this light, the method towards which Lonergan worked could allow for specialisation because, being based on the operations of the human mind, it could distinguish the specialties and specialists in theology, not only by their objects, but by the specific intentional operations of the theologising subjects.

4. CONCLUSIONS

Lonergan (1994, 282, 302, 326; 1985a, 12) anticipated the objection that basing a theological method on universal operations of the human mind would perpetuate classicism by establishing another supposedly permanent and immutable scheme. But such a method is not based on classicist assumptions about culture. Moreover, Lonergan's position on human intentionality was not based on any abstract reasoning about what human intentionality ought to be, it was concretely, empirically based on an investigation into human knowing as it actually occurred. Lonergan could lay claim to invariance in a general methodological scheme based upon an intentionality analysis, because, as he argues, "the human mind is always the human mind."

The most important finding of this chapter is that, in an attempt to do for our time what Aquinas and the greater scholastics did for theirs, Lonergan (1994, 328) intended to emulate these scholars in transposing Catholic faith and belief into a contemporary philosophy that was based upon analysing human consciousness. In a manner similar to Rahner's (1978, xi) aim of situating Christianity within the intellectual horizon of today's people, Lonergan's project would give modern theologians a renewed standpoint from which to explore Christian faith with a method that was both up to the modern world's standards, and intelligible to it. Moreover, this methodological foundation would account for both faith and reason, establish the conditions of possibility for effective theology, and provide theologians with a coherent self-image. Such a foundation would go beyond modern secularism by calling one to conversion, but it would also call the advocates of classical culture to refine their achievements so as to overcome a "cultural lag" and bring their discipline into the contemporary world (Doran 1990, 151).

While Lonergan acknowledges the scholastics as inspiration for his work, we also find an echo of Newman's (1974, 69) work in the strong desire to remain within the traditions of his church, while at the same time making genuine use of the available tools of modern scholarship. Most revealing are Newman's statements, in his *Essay on The Development of Christian Doctrine*: First, that "CHRISTIANITY has been long enough in the world to *justify us in dealing with it as a fact of the world's history.*" Secondly,

"Christianity is no dream of the study or the cloister. ... Its home is in the world; and to know what it is, we must seek it in the world, and hear the world's witness of it." For Newman, because Christianity cannot escape being part of the history of the world, it cannot be understood properly without using the available tools of history. Similarly, Lonergan held that theologians cannot escape using their minds. A theological method, then, could not be properly discovered and used, without an adequate understanding of the human mind's operations.

We acknowledge that theologians may, under different specific circumstances, use their minds well or badly. However, this does not detract from Lonergan's point that theologians have minds and use them. In fact, by highlighting and analysing the operations of the human mind, Lonergan's method has the advantage of giving us a clearer idea of when a mind has operated authentically or not.

We find Lonergan's and Newman's work more successful than, for example, Leo XIII's scholastic revival. To his credit, Leo acknowledged the need for Catholic theology to meet the challenges of modern thought, and he promulgated *Aeterni Patris* both as a practical application of the principles set forward by the First Vatican Council and as a modern renewal of Catholic theology based on a recovery of scholastic philosophy. However, while Leo wrote favourably of those scholars who augmented the old philosophy with the new, he was, as Crowe notes (1989, 379), "not really pushing the *nova*—the context rather is a condemnation of innovators who abandon the old and run after the new, instead, Leo says, of saving the old and adding the new." Leo believed ([1879] 1981, n24, 27) modern thought to be confused, subjective, and lacking proper foundations. Against modernity, he proposed a restorationist model of scholasticism, which was supposed to be objective, abstract and certain. Leo was firmly entrenched within the "classicist" framework, so his restoration did not renew Catholic theology in the face of modernity. Rather, it isolated Catholic theology from the modern world. In a concrete sense, this left the Roman congregations and theologians unable to appreciate the problems and challenges of modern exegesis, philosophy and historical method. Catholic theology thus could not constructively deal with these challenges, when they arose under the form of modernism (McCool 1977, 240; Lonergan 1974, 94).

We would acknowledge the possible objection that theology would become profane, were its method based upon an understanding of the human mind's operations. We find an effective answer in Newman's work. Against the argument that one demeans Christianity by applying, to a supernatural community of faith, such natural and secular methods, Newman argued (1974, 149-50) that to investigate Christianity as an "earthly," historical reality was "no irreverence." After all, Christianity teaches that Christ himself bore such an earthly form. We are justified in studying Christianity with "earthly" sciences, because Christianity is not above its founder by being exempted from the realities of being earthly and historical. If we take up Lonergan's approach, we find that Christianity, specifically Christian theology, is likewise not immune from the human cognitional operations of its theologians.

We have explained the importance of intentionality analysis, as a basis for Lonergan's theological method. Our most pressing task now is to explore this intentionality analysis. Without doing so, our explanation of his method in general, and systematics in particular, would be as intelligible, as Lonergan puts it (1994, 7) as giving a printed book on colour to the blind.

Chapter 5
Lonergan's Intentionality Analysis

Our previous chapters have shown how Lonergan found classicist-based theology unable to meet the questions, challenges and standards of modern thought. To overcome such shortcomings and to develop a theology that was up to modern standards, he sought a new foundation of theology and found it in an analysis of the operations of human consciousness. Rather than basing his method on notions of a supposedly unchanging culture, Lonergan found that his theological method needed to be based on the genuinely invariant operations of the human mind.

If we are to understand *Method in Theology*, either in whole or in a part such as "systematics," we must understand Lonergan's intentionality analysis. The importance of such an understanding is manifested in two statements. The first, in *Method* (1994, 24), is that "theologians always have had minds and always have used them." Secondly, in his doctoral thesis (1985a, 11), Lonergan remarks that "even historians have intelligence and perform acts of understanding." Because the human mind's conscious operations are the foundation of an authentic theological methodology, he argues that having a clear and precise understanding of the operations of the human mind "add[s] considerable light and precision to the performance of theological tasks."

Lonergan's approach conflicts, however, with the negative attitude towards philosophy, typified by Karl Barth (1975, 6), who argues that,

> Directly, in all the three areas of theological enquiry philosophy, history, psychology, etc. have always succeeded in practice only in increasing the self-alienation of the Church and the distortion and confusion of its talk about God. ... There never has actually been a philosophia christiana, for if it was philosophia it was not christiana, and if it was christiana it was not philosophia.

Barth (1975, 6, 8) reinforces his rejection of the use of "other sciences" within theology by writing that it must "sacrifice all concern for what is called science elsewhere." Barth's hostility to judgements, of the Church's utterances about God, are aimed at the introduction of "alien principles." Barth may be defended then, if his rejection of philosophy is limited to its possible role as arbiter or judge over Christian doctrine. Reading on, however, we find Barth rejecting even the methodological use of other sciences: "As regards method, it [theology] has nothing to learn from them."

How can we justify Lonergan's use of a philosophy to lend methodological support to theology? A clue comes from Barth himself (1975, 11-13). Dogmatics, according to Barth, is an enquiry, and the Church's talk about God needs to serve "as the object of human enquiry." We gather that Barth acknowledges, at least implicitly, a human action as well as a divine principle within theology. It is this human action, not the divine principle, that Lonergan intends to understand and evaluate in an intentionality analysis. More importantly, it is not so much the content, or conclusions of "philosophy" that interest Lonergan. Rather, as Doran notes (1995 1:54), self-appropriation or self-knowledge is the key to his philosophy, and in this light Lonergan argues (1984, 3) that "philosophy is the basic and total science." If we consider the reasons behind it, we find that this is not an audacious declaration disposed towards classicism. Philosophy is basic because it is a cognitional theory, which accounts for the operations of all people, including specialists in particular sciences (Lonergan 1990, 3; Daly 1991, 45). Lonergan would thus reject Barth's position as a denial of the human subject's action in theology and he would insist that because theology involves human questions about God, one's theological method must account for the nature of those human inquiries. The positive resource that philosophy brings to theology, in Lonergan's view, is a clear understanding of what the human subject is doing when one is doing theology. Such an enterprise accords with the Second Vatican Council's decree, in *Optatum Totius* ([1965]1984b n14-15), that students of theology should be well trained in philosophy, which should bring clarity to the mysteries of faith and help students in a knowledge of "man, the world and God." Lonergan's aim is such an understanding of human theologians, precisely in their contact with God and "the world." We also emphasise that this focus on the theologians' cognitional operations represents a turn to the subject, which reflects the shift found in modern philosophy, which we discussed above.

Having noted the importance of an understanding of human intellectual operations for Lonergan, we turn to a study of his cognitional theory. This investigation will be necessary, for without the understanding gained from this inquiry, we shall be left unable to understand Lonergan's theological method (Lonergan 1994, 7). We acknowledge, though, that this chapter can present only a modest overview of Lonergan's intentionality analysis. For a more detailed analysis, we direct the reader to Lonergan's (1992) extensive treatment of the operations of human intentionality in *Insight: A Study of Human Understanding*. Lonergan presents his thought in a more compact form in "Cognitional Structure," (1988, 205-21) and *Method in Theology* (1994, 6-20).

i. Preliminary Clarifications

We begin our study of Lonergan's intentionality analysis by clarifying that, as a self-appropriation of rational consciousness, it involves an observation of human rationality in act. Lonergan (1992, 11) neither first proposes suppositions on whether human beings know, nor does he propose ideas on what knowing should be. Rather, by analysing human consciousness in act, he addresses the question of what knowledge is. That is, he concerns himself with what happens when we know (Sala 1994, 10). The exercises proposed at the beginning of *Insight* (1992, 11ff) bear out this point, because through them we are invited to discover within ourselves the same processes of human rational consciousness that he has discovered for himself. Moreover, the very term "self-appropriation" is important, for it stands in contrast to the post-modern literature that explicates not self-appropriation, but loss of self (Doran 1990, 462).

Lonergan and Newman take a substantially similar approach to investigating human knowing. Both authors take knowing as a basic fact of human existence. They do not question the existence of human knowing, they question its nature and activity. As Dessain observes (1970, 4), they approach knowing as "something to be described, not proved." Lonergan, like Newman, thus takes an approach of observing the matters of fact of human knowing. Newman (1985, 109) is outspoken on this point, criticising Locke, for taking "a view of the human mind, in relation to inference and assent, which to me seems theoretical and unreal. ... I think, because he consults his own ideal of how the mind ought to act, instead of interrogating human nature, as an existing thing, as it is found in the world."

Doran notes (1995 2: 133) that Lonergan also differs from many Catholic thinkers who began with the Kantian question "What are the conditions for valid knowing?" Lonergan, rather, begins with the more radical, and more foundational question "What am I doing when I am knowing?" This reflects the approach, common to Lonergan (1992, 16-17) and Newman (Dessain 1970, 6), which is a psychological, not logical, investigation of human knowing. Only after an investigation of what one is doing when one knows, does Lonergan proceed to the consequent question of what is known when one does that knowing. This orientation of Lonergan's intentionality analysis means that, as Doran points out (1990, 43), Lonergan's is not a theory simply to be placed alongside other theories. Rather, he moves the theory to a higher context where it assists the human subject in concretely knowing and constituting oneself.

Before our exposition of Lonergan, we note his important clarifications regarding his terminology and his description of cognitional operations. First, Lonergan (1988, 206; 1994, 6) identifies some examples of human intending's different operations: seeing, hearing, smelling, touching, tasting, inquiring, imagining, understanding, conceiving, formulating, reflecting, marshalling and weighing the evidence, judging, deliberating, evaluating, deciding. He assumes our familiarity with these operations, or our familiarity with at least some of them. Regarding his terminology, Lonergan (1994, 7-8) first explains that these operations have objects, and it is by these operations that one becomes aware of an object. That coming to awareness is what is meant by the verb, *intend*; the adjective, *intentional*; the noun, *intentionality*. Secondly, the operations described are operations of an operator, who is termed a subject. The operator is a subject in the grammatical sense that he is the subject of verbs referring, in the active, to the operations. More importantly, the operator is called the subject in the psychological sense that he operates consciously. Lonergan would agree that he has not presented an exhaustive list of conscious operations, such as those presented by Tallon (1997, 33). Apart from intentional operations, there are nonintentional states such as fatigue and irritation and teleological trends such as thirst and hunger. Rather than exluding or ignoring other conscious operations, Lonergan has focussed his philosophy on intentional operations as these are more pertinent to the intentional exercise of theology.

Lonergan (1994, 17; 1988, 210-11) defends the reality of the operations he describes by drawing our attention to the fact that one who wishes to dismiss such operations in oneself would be "merely disqualifying himself as a non-responsible, non-reasonable, non-intelligent somnambulist." Later in this chapter, we shall take up Lonergan's defence of this position.

2. The Triple Cord of Human Knowing

To correctly understand Lonergan's intentionality analysis, we must appreciate both his (1988, 207-8; 1992, 299-300) distinction of the different operations indicated above and his indefatigable argument that human knowing is a pattern of distinct cognitional acts, with these acts being distinguished and related in a functional and dynamic structure. Most importantly, Lonergan maintains (1988, 206) that no one alone of the above-mentioned cognitional acts is human knowing, properly speaking. Only a formal pattern, of related but distinct acts, constitutes human knowing. He illustrates this point with the example of ocular vision. By itself, vision may be perfectly enacted, but it provides not human knowing, only mere gaping. Similarly, with other sense activities, he argues that none of these alone constitutes full human knowing.

Just as sense experience alone does not constitute human knowing, Lonergan (1988, 206-7) stresses that neither understanding alone nor judging alone account for human knowing. If understanding lacked the presentations of sensible data, it would have nothing to understand. If understanding lacked judgement, there would be no distinction between fact and fiction. Judgement to the exclusion of understanding is not knowing, but arrogance. Furthermore, judgement isolated from experience simply sets aside fact. For Lonergan, human knowing is neither experience alone, understanding alone, nor judging alone, but a dynamic structure of all three, together constituting human knowing.

To explain the notion of a dynamic structure, Lonergan refers (1988, 205-6, 208) to human knowing as a whole. A whole, he argues, can be made up of similar or identical parts that are related arithmetically, such as the four quarts of a gallon of milk. Alternatively, a whole may be constituted by dissimilar, but related parts, the absence of any of which would disintegrate the whole. A motor car is such a whole, incorporating dissimilar, but functionally related parts such as the engine, tyres and muffler. The motor car, as a dynamic structure, is made up of different parts, no one of which alone is the car, but without any one of them, the car would cease to be a car.

This explanation shows what Lonergan calls (1994, 213-14, 238-39) the "cognitional myth," that human knowing is either a single activity or a compound of similar acts, such as the arithmetically related parts of a gallon of milk. He finds a key example of this cognitional myth in Kant and repeatedly distances himself from Kant's account of human knowing. We grasp some of the ground for Lonergan's disagreement with Kant in Heidegger's (1951) criticism that, "To understand the *KRV* [Critique of Pure Reason] one must, as it were, hammer into one's mind the principle: Knowledge is primarily intuition" (Trans. in Sala 1994, 9). To clarify this point, Sala explains that Kant tends to reduce human knowing to a single act of intuition. As Kant writes in the opening of his "Transcendental Aesthetic," (1990, A19/B33) "IN whatever manner and by whatever means a mode of knowledge may relate to objects, *intuition* is that through which it is in immediate relation to them, and to which all thought as a means is directed." Kant further writes (1990, A19/B33) that the object of human intuition is only yielded by *sensibility* and it alone yields intuitions. Thus, "all thought must, ... relate ultimately to intuitions, and therefore, with us, to sensibility, because in no other way can an object be given to us." The essence of Kant's position is that knowing is looking and that the known is simply what is looked at (Sala 1994, 10). Lonergan, however, argues that human knowing is formally dynamic, made of dissimilar, but related parts, just as the motor-car. The different parts of human knowing, as indicated above, are experience, understanding and judgement. To understand Lonergan, and his distance from writers like Kant, we turn to a more detailed analysis of these cognitional operations and their dynamic relationship.

3. Experience

Lonergan (1994, 9) locates the first level of human intentionality in being attentive. On this level, we experience by sensing, perceiving, feeling and by generally being alert to our world. In experience, the intellect gains its raw material, namely, the data upon which understanding and other cognitional operations will subsequently operate. It is important to note, with Lonergan (1992, 298), that experience alone does not constitute human knowing. While experience provides to intelligence the data within which intelligence can discover intelligibility, the data itself, prior to understanding, remains non-understood and, in itself, quite ineffable.

We also note that insofar as we regard knowledge's beginning in experience, and the intrinsic ineffability of sense-data, Kant and Lonergan would be in agreement. Kant writes (1990, A1-2) that "Experience is, beyond all doubt, the first product to which our understanding gives rise." He further notes that, experience "gives us no true universality; and reason, which is so insistent upon this kind of knowledge, is therefore more stimulated by it than satisfied."

We find helpful three clarifications regarding Lonergan's understanding of experience. First, the "free images and utterances" provided in the data of experience, are not always obtained in a haphazard and random fashion. A subject's attentiveness is often under the influence of one's intelligence or rationality seeking further or specific data (Lonergan 1992, 299). Secondly, the subsequent cognitional act of intelligent understanding cannot occur without the presentations of experience. Aquinas (*In De Anima,* lect 11 n758) effectively makes this point, in writing that the mind's first cognitional act is the apprehension of sensible objects. Lonergan also explains (1988, 206) that, "Without the prior presentations of sense [data], there is nothing for a man to understand; and when there is nothing to be understood, there is no occurrence of understanding."

Thirdly, it may be proposed that Lonergan is advancing an intentional consciousness that is merely animal. Indeed, he acknowledges (1994, 9-10) that our empirical consciousness, where experience occurs, does not seem to differ from the consciousness of other higher animals. However, human empirical consciousness is differentiated from animal consciousness, because our empirical intentionality is only a foundation for the operations of the further intentional acts we are about to explore.

Before commencing our next section, we may observe that the necessity of human experience, for cognitional operation, rules out the possibility of innate ideas. As Aristotle argues (*De Anima* III, 4, 430a 1), our human intellects begin like a clean writing table on which nothing has yet been written. Aquinas (*DeVeritate,* q16,a1c) follows Aristotle in denying innate ideas, precisely because the human intellect begins only in potentiality to understanding. This human potency only begins to be actuated by the reception of sense-data through intentional experience.

4. The Pure Desire to Know

Human intentionality is dissatisfied with merely absorbing the data of experience. Lonergan (1997, 100) emphasises this point by citing Aristotle's (*Metaphysics*, I, 1, 980a 21) statement, that "All men by nature desire to know," and by referring to Aquinas' account of the human desire to know:

> Aristotle opened his *Metaphysics* with the remark that naturally all men desire to know. But Aquinas measured that desire to find in the undying restlessness and absolute exigence of the human mind that intellect as intellect is infinite, that *ipsum esse* is *ipsum intelligere* and uncreated, unlimited Light, that though our intellects because potential cannot attain naturally to the vision of God, still our intellects as intellects have a dynamic orientation, a natural desire, that nothing short of that unknown vision can satisfy utterly. For Augustine our hearts are restless until they rest in God; for Aquinas, not our hearts, but first and foremost our minds are restless until they rest in seeing Him.

In accord with Aristotle and Aquinas, Lonergan maintains (1992, 28) that within all people there exists a drive to know, to understand, to explain and to discover reasons and causes. Importantly, this emphasis on the desire to know reflects a turn to the subject. The human drive to know is not because of any impulse from data, nor is it a passive operation of reception, it is rather the active desire with which a human subject

greets intelligible objects. Tallon observes (1997, 20) that our active desire, means that the mind is not "empty like a wastebasket," but it is more
like a stomach, hungering for knowledge, with the fulfillment of this
hunger bringing joy and peace.

Lonergan illustrates this drive to know with the joy accompanying its
fulfilment, as in Archimedes' hydrostatic discovery. What better symbol,
Lonergan asks us (1992, 28-29), could be found for the drive to know,
than the man who had fulfilled his drive to know, running naked though
the streets of Syracuse, crying excitedly, "I've got it"? To this example we
may add two instances cited by Eliot Dole Hutchinson, an author to
whose work Lonergan refers (1992, 28n1) for a "profusion of instances
of insight."[1] "The moment of insight," wrote Bertrand Russell, "is excit-
ing, like quick motoring." Similarly, Tchaikovsky wrote of this moment
of fulfillment, "I forget everything and behave like a madman. Everything within me starts pulsing and quivering; hardly have I begun the
sketch, than one thought follows another with great rapidity ..."
(Hutchinson 1949a, 433). While we have not yet explored the meaning
of human "insight," we emphasise the force of the drive to know, which
is reflected in the joy and engrossment accompanying its fulfillment.

From this desire to know, cognitional activity gains its intentional, objective character. That is, human intelligence greets the objects of experience with the desire to know them and intends knowledge of such objects (Lonergan 1988, 211). Lonergan explains though (1992, 33-34),
that this desire to know is an unrestricted intention, for there is nothing
that we cannot at least desire to know. He calls this drive to know the
intellectual *eros* of our human spirit, the pure question. We seek answers
to questions of data, intelligibility and fact. He clarifies however, that
such questions are not necessarily thematised questions. While such questioning intends answers to inquiries, the "pure question" can more accurately be related to a wanting of knowledge. This wanting, or the "pure
question," corresponds to Aristotle's above-mentioned universal, essential desire of all people to know. Lonergan (1997, 193) also notes that,
efficiently, human intellect is "the light of intelligence within us, the drive
to wonder, to reflection, to criticism." This drive, he observes, with
Aristotle (*Metaphysics* I, 1, 982b 10-20), is the source of all science and
philosophy. We may thus contrast purely sensitive consciousness with
active, intellectual consciousness. Merely sensitive consciousness is like a
"pure reverie," with image after image coming before the senses, but with
no human care for why or wherefore. Active human intelligence inter-
venes by asking why and wherefore, thus transforming the object into

something-to-be-understood (Lonergan 1997, 185; *Summa Theologiae*, I,q85a1ad3).

We should remember that the pure desire to know cannot, and does not, operate without an object. As Lonergan writes (1992, 34), "no one just wonders. We wonder about something." That "something" is found in the data of experience, as indicated above. Human knowing thus begins with the experience of an object, with that object being greeted by human intelligence with the intentional desire to gain knowledge of that object. The aspect of "knowledge" first intended, is an understanding of the object, so to this act we now turn.

5. Understanding I—Insight

It is vital to this investigation that we come to terms with Lonergan's account of understanding. He emphasises, in *Method in Theology*, that to comprehend his notion of systematics, we must have a clear comprehension of what he means by understanding. Without this firm appropriation of understanding's meaning, our appropriation of systematics will be remote and incomplete. As a most critical part of our work, we must understand Lonergan's account of understanding, and we begin with his account of the act of insight. Insight, as Hutchinson writes (1949c, 386), is "one of the most experiential facts of creative life," yet it is also "less commonly understood in process, than almost any other aspect of the productive mind." Lonergan's analysis is thus more significant because he deals with this largely overlooked aspect of human knowing.

5.1 Examples of Insight

To help us to intelligently appropriate what insight is, Lonergan proposes two examples. The first is a dramatic instance—the hydrostatic discovery of Archimedes. The second is a personal exercise involving our discovering the intelligibility present in a circle's roundness.

In the dramatic instance, Lonergan recalls (1992, 27-28) the story of Archimedes. Having been set the task of determining whether King Hiero's crown was made of pure gold, Archimedes had grasped the solution, to weigh the crown in water. While in a bath, he had grasped that, when weighed or floated in water, the crown would displace its own weight equivalent in water (Sears 1982, 249; Pitt 1975, 26). The joy of having reached this discovery lead to Archimedes' famous dash through the streets of Syracuse.

In the personal exercise, Lonergan proposes (1992, 31-32) that we imagine a cartwheel, with its hub, spokes and rim, and ask ourselves,

"Why is it round?" We may consider the suggestion that the wheel is round because of its spokes are all of equal length. Yet, our intelligent inquiry reveals this as insufficient. We grasp that the spokes could be unequally sunk into the hub, or the rim could be flat between spokes. Lonergan suggests, however, that we do have a clue. If we let the hub decrease to a point and the rim and spokes thin out to lines, and if we allow an infinity of exactly equal spokes, we grasp that the rim must be perfectly round. Conversely, were any of these conditions not met, the rim would have bumps or dents in it. In grasping this necessary relation, we understand that the cartwheel is round inasmuch as the distance from the hub's centre to the outside of the rim is invariably equal.

For further references, Lonergan refers us (1992, 28n1) to the "profusion of instances of insight," offered by Hutchinson in his series of articles on insight, originally published in *Psychiatry*. One key example is from Bertrand Russell, as cited by Hutchinson (1949c, 388):

> In all the creative work that I have done, what has come first is a *problem*, a *puzzle involving discomfort*. Then comes concentrated voluntary application entailing great effort. After this a *period without conscious thought*, and finally a solution bringing with it the *complete plan of a book*. This last stage *is usually sudden*, and seems to be the important moment for subsequent achievement.

We can propose another illustration of insight. A schoolboy, talented in physics, was perturbed by a man's claim that something was wrong with the local water of the mountain town in which they lived. The mountain water, it was claimed, boiled at a lower temperature than the city water, which boiled at the normal one hundred degrees Celsius, and contamination of the mountain water, possibly by radioactive waste, caused this lower boiling point. The boy verified the lower boiling point of the mountain water, but he wondered if there may be a more plausible explanation for the phenomenon. The problem puzzled him for weeks. Perhaps his thermometer was inaccurate? But he found that the same thermometer, used at his school, which was in the city at sea level and on a different water supply, registered a boiling point of one hundred degrees. He then thought that conditions unrelated to the water itself could affect its boiling point. He verified this insight by boiling city water at his home in the mountains, and boiling mountain water at his school. He found that it was the location, not the source of water, that affected the boiling point. For weeks he wondered how it could be that water boiled at a lower temperature in the mountains, than the temperature at which it boiled in the city. Although deeply disturbed at this discrepancy, he almost despaired of finding a solution. But he awoke one night with an inspiration, an event he later described as a time of energy, when ideas seemed to come from nowhere and what had seemed confused and puzzling became clear and plausible. Upon recalling his observations that the steam from boiling water seemed to force itself under pressure, up and out into the external surrounds, he realised that it could possibly be that the external air pressure, which varied with altitude, affected the water's boiling point. In an almost feverish state he experimented by heating water in a vacuum flask and found that he could make very hot water boil by reducing the air pressure inside the flask. Next day, in a thrilled state, he announced his discovery to his physics teacher, who informed the poor boy that he had discovered what scientists had already known for many years, namely, that the temperature of phase transition, such as boiling, is affected by external pressure (Sears 1982, 305).

For the less scientifically inclined, the solution of an old problem serves to help us to personally experience the moment of insight. A king died, leaving two sons, both of whom are excellent horsemen. The sons each own one horse. These horses are reputed to be the fastest two animals in the kingdom. The king has willed that the son owning the slower horse should be compensated by becoming the new king, and that a race should be held to determine which of the two is the slower horse. A problem develops on the day of the race. Each son naturally mistrusts the other, believing that the other will make his mount underperform so as to lose the race and win the crown. An atmosphere of intellectual and emotional tension ensues, until a wise old man makes a two-word suggestion that could solve the problem—"Swap Horses!"

5.2 The Act of Insight

The cognitional contents of the above examples may occupy us for many pages. However, for Lonergan's explanation of understanding, the important discoveries are in neither hydrostatics nor the definition of a circle, but in the intellectual act they illustrate. The key experience, in which we are interested, is what is variously called the hunch, illumination, revelation or, as Lonergan calls it, the insight. Platt and Baker (1931, 1975), in an article that inspired Hutchinson's work on insight, give a good preliminary description of an insight, under the name "scientific hunch."

> A scientific hunch is a unifying or clarifying idea which springs into
> consciousness suddenly as a solution to a problem in which we are
> intensely interested. In typical cases, it follows a long study but comes
> into consciousness at a time when we are not consciously working on the
> problem. A hunch springs from a wide knowledge of facts but is
> essentially a leap of the imagination, in that it goes beyond a mere
> necessary conclusion which any reasonable man must draw from the
> data at hand. It is a process of creative thought.

Such activity is what Lonergan understands to be insight. To elaborate
upon Platt and Baker's description, we can reflect on our above-cited
examples of insight. If we prescind from the actual contents of the discoveries and focus on the act of insight, we find important aspects of the
act of insight that we need take up. Insight, we shall find: (1) is a release
of the tension caused by intellectual inquiry, (2) grasps the "must" or
necessary relations in a case under question, (3) grasps intelligible unity,
(4) discovers intelligible possibility, (5) relies on inner intellectual conditions, (6) requires a sensible image, (7) is not imaginable, (8) comes suddenly and unpredictably, (9) pivots between the concrete and abstract,
(10) passes into the mind's habitual texture, (11) is creative and (12) is
fertile. We now turn to investigate these aspects of insight.

5.3 Aspects of Insight

(1) Insight is first characterised by its coming as the *release of the tension
formed by intellectual inquiry*. It is the primary fulfilment of the pure desire to know. That intellectual tension, Lonergan notes (1992, 28), develops as we experience our earnest desire to know, understand, grasp reasons why, determine causality, and to explain; that is, to discover intelligibility in the object of our desire to know. We find this desire, and its
corresponding intellectual tension, in our own desires to know why the
circle is round, how it is that water could boil at different temperatures or
how to solve the problem facing the king's sons. We have also seen this
tension described above, in Russell's periods of intellectual bafflement.

Hutchinson notes (1943, 347-49; 1949b, 406-13) that the creative
thinker, when facing unresolved problems, often suffers from "a state of
problem-generated 'neurosis,' or its lesser equivalent *tension*." When the
desire is more intense, there can arise repression, regression, neurotic com-
pensation and emotional excess. In a religious sense, one can suffer the
"dark night of the soul," with its attendant experience of introvertiveness,
brooding and psycho-pathology. Such experience, when one's desire to
understand is unfulfilled, reflects the pre-insight despair at perhaps never

finding a solution to one's problem. Some symptoms, of the desire to understand, can be seen in the years-long struggles and wanderings of the Buddha, and Mohammed, before their intellectual tensions were released, as it were, in a flash (Hutchinson 1943, 355; Carrithers 1986, 50).

On the other hand, we experience the release of this tension within ourselves when we grasp the conditions under which a wheel is round, or how it could possibly be that water can boil at varying temperatures. We also find this release remotely, but more dramatically, in Archimedes' naked run through Syracuse and in Tchaikovsky's "pulsing and quivering." Lonergan explains (1992, 28-29) that, even if our joy is typically less ecstatic than Archimedes', we nonetheless have the same drive to know. He explains, moreover that this desire to understand is shown in its fulfillment, by the scientist's naked dash to announce the fulfillment of his desire to know, with a cry of "Eureka!"

We can find several other illuminating cases of the dramatic release of intellectual inquiry's tension. Hutchinson (1943, 351; 1949a, 434, 442, 445) refers to the *raptus* that Beethoven experienced and to the aesthetic pleasure and apprehension of beauty that Einstein experienced when he solved a problem. Hutchinson writes that in insight there comes a thrilling "surge," that leaves one in peace, often in ecstasy. Interestingly, he remarks (1943, 348) that what is "sometimes called 'ecstasy' or 'union' with all their theological implications, are more accurately described as simple insight." While Hutchinson's remark may "demythologise" ecstatic states, it does serve to highlight the force of insight and its relief of inquiry's tension. We also observe the positive release of inquiry's tension in children. Jessica Rees (1983, 20-23), a deaf author, recounts her childhood experience of feeling "elated" as she grasped how words were related to concrete objects. Thomas Daly (1991, 49) has observed joy in children when they focussed on their intellectual processes in solving puzzles. The question, "How do you feel?" put to these children, drew the positive response, "I am something that enjoys insights."

(2) We have explained that insight is a release of inquiry's tension. But what releases this tension? One way in which Lonergan (1990, 40-41) expresses the pure desire's fulfilment in the act of insight itself, is that insight is intelligence grasping *the must* in a particular case. In the circle exercise, insight grasps that the circle *must* be perfectly round, if the radii are equal in length and sharing a common point of origin. Another way of expressing this point is that insight grasps the necessary relations in a case. It grasps, for the circle, the necessity of roundness where the radii are equal and the impossibility of roundness where the radii are unequal.

Archimedes' insight, we note, grasped that the crown must displace its own weight equivalent of water. We find that, by insight, Lonergan means the grasp, by intelligence, of intelligible relations within an object of inquiry.

We note that Lonergan openly owes to Peter Hoenen the notion that the act of understanding grasps the relations in an intelligible object. In *Verbum,* and later writings, Lonergan (1974, 266-67; 1997, 39n126) notes that Hoenen (1933; 1938; 1939) first made him explicitly aware that "intellect abstracted from phantasm not only terms but also the nexus between them." That is, intellect, in the intelligent act of insight, grasps the intelligible relations within objects that are sensibly perceived.

We may also clarify insight's grasp of relations in a case like Russell's solution of his "bafflement." In such a case we may propose that one has much data, perhaps a puzzle like Russell's in which seemingly disparate and unrelated ideas are present to one's intellect. The act of insight grasps how these data are related, and how intellect can apprehend them in a single viewpoint. This unifying, we propose, is how Russell could have a solution that brought with it "the *complete plan of a book*" (Hutchinson 1949c, 388).

(3) To reduce the above considerations to a more concise statement, we find that insight, as Lonergan writes (1997, 187, *italics mine*), "adds to our knowledge a grasp of *intelligible unity in sensible multiplicity*." In our cartwheel example, within the manifold sense data of points/hubs, lines/spokes and rims, we grasp the intelligible unity of the relationship between roundness and equality of radii. Similarly, from the multiple data before him, Archimedes' insight was a grasp of the intelligible unity between the weight of the crown and the amount of water that it displaced. Furthermore, Russell's reported insight experience was a grasp of the unity of the ideas to be contained in his book. Lastly, the schoolboy's insight was into the relationship between air pressure and boiling point.

Another aspect of insight's grasp of intelligible unity, Hutchinson notes (1949c, 387), is that insight can be interpreted as "a reorganisation of the perceptual field." From a seemingly unrelated and perhaps confusing field of data, insight realigns the data, to grasp how it is that elements in that "perceptual field" are related to one another. On this point, we can clarify that insight is not a content taken from one's apprehended data. Insight, in fact, adds a new content to the data of experience, that content being intelligence's grasp of the relations between data. Such relations, we emphasise, are not in the data themselves.

To help us understand the content which insight adds to the data of experience, we can take up Lonergan's account (1992, 112) of "enriching abstraction." The first moment of enriching abstraction is when intelligence anticipates something that insight can know. That is, intellect seeks something beyond mere sensible presentations. The second moment, is "the erection of heuristic structures and the attainment of insight." One then discovers, in the data, the answer to one's question. This answer contains, in Lonergan's words, "what is variously named as the significant, the relevant, the important, the essential, the idea, the form." He then notes the further process of enriching abstraction, but this is more concerned with conception, to which we shall turn our attention later.

Of greater concern to us now is that insight adds to the images presented to sense. Lonergan holds (1992, 336) that insight adds "intelligible unities and correlations and frequencies." He acknowledges that these do have reference to images and data, but insight's additional content goes beyond what sense presents to intellect.

(4) Insight is also characterised by its *grasp of intelligible possibility*. That is, by insight, one discovers a possible explanation for the object of one's inquiry. Galileo's insight into gravity and the boy's insight into boiling water both revealed, in the first place, possible explanations of how the respective phenomena may be intelligible. The positive content of insight, by way of intelligible possibility, is in its explanation of how a thing may be so. In this way, insight of itself is only hypothetical. As we find later in this chapter, the hypothetical nature of insight means that one's understanding must be complemented by the verification attained in judgement.

(5) On the conditions under which insight occurs, Lonergan notes (1992, 29-30) that "insight is a function, not of outer circumstances, but of inner conditions." He illustrates this point with the case of Archimedes's insight. Many others patronised the Syracuse baths, and underwent the same sense experiences, but only Archimedes came to any hydrostatic insights. Insight is thus resolutely distinguished from the essence and occurrence of sense experience. As Lonergan explains, unless one's senses are lacking, one cannot avoid seeing or hearing. The occurrence of sensible acts simply corresponds with outer events. Insight's occurrence, however, is primarily dependent on inner personal conditions. Lonergan explains that insight depends, first, upon a certain native endowment found frequently in the intelligent, but less often in the backward. Insight secondly depends on the presence of the desire to know, and the persistent question, "why?" Thirdly, and very importantly, insight depends on the

accurate presentation of a particular problem. Had Archimedes not diligently thought upon the king's problem, "the baths of Syracuse would
have been no more famous than any others."

Our key sources, especially Hutchinson, offer an abundance of cases
that support Lonergan's position. His point (1992, 66), that insight relies
primarily on a "native endowment" that we find frequently in the intelligent, is supported by the experience of any teacher, who finds that students manifest different levels of ability to catch on and understand. From
another perspective, Hutchinson points out (1948c, 392-93) that insight
is exacting, in terms of "psychic energy." The intelligent are more capable
of utilising such mental energy, while the slow are less adept in this enterprise.

On Lonergan's second point, we affirm that insight depends on human
inquiry. Despite being surrounded by a plethora of sense data, people do
not come to insights unless they make intelligent inquiries into the data.
For example, Platt and Baker (1931, 1974) point out that Darwin may
have spent years accumulating information on the varieties of life on earth,
but he would never have had the slightest notion of evolution, had he not
asked "why?" The answer to that question only came after a long period
of intellectual tension (Darwin 1993, 119-20). In Hutchinson's numerous examples of insight (1949b, 404-06; 1949c, 387, 390, 392, 394-95,
397), a common factor is the inquiry that different scientists and thinkers put into their objects. While the degree of intellectual tension varies,
ranging from short-lived mild bafflement to many years of tension and
the experience of phobias and nightmares, what remains constant is that
these people did not just passively experience their objects, they actively
inquired into the objects.

We also emphasise that inquiry into objects is a spontaneous and often
compulsive human activity. Aristotle (Metaphysics I, 1, 980a23) affirms
that "All men by nature desire to know." Hutchinson's work (1949b, 406)
also indicates that human intellect has a creative desire to understand,
but when this desire is unfulfilled, there results emotional conflict. We
propose that insight can be considered as a positive reaction to emotional
conflict that people experience when they find an object unintelligible.
In that light, we can appreciate the joy and peace that one experiences
upon reaching an insight.

We finally affirm Lonergan's point, that insight depends upon the presentation of a problem. In the many cases reported by Platt and Baker
(1931, 1977ff), a consistent factor in the scientific "hunch" was the hunch's
being a response to a particular problem. Hutchinson's reports of insights

(1949b, 404, 406; 1949c, 390-91, 395, 397) also manifest the truth that these insights develop in response to particular problems. To state the point concisely, we do not have insights into nothing, we have insights into problems of intelligibility in specific objects.

(6) Lonergan also observes (1992, 33) that human *intellect requires a sensible image* upon which to operate and in which to grasp an insight. In the cartwheel exercise, we find that insight grasps the intelligibility present between the imagined equal radii and the imagined curve that must be perfectly circular. Without the sensible image of the circle, we simply could not have the insight. Without thinking upon the image of steam rising from boiling water, the schoolboy would not have had his insight. We further note Lonergan's point (1997, 28), that "The act of understanding leaps forth when the sensible data are in a suitable constellation." Such an understanding of insight's relation to, and reliance on, sense data reminds us of Hutchinson's point (1949b 405; 1949c, 387), that insight involves "a reorganisation of the perceptual field."

We find support for Lonergan's position in Aquinas and Aristotle. Aristotle maintained that intelligible objects exist only in concrete extension, with sensible forms. Consequently, one lacking sense perception could neither learn nor understand anything (Lonergan 1997, 41).

> Since it seems that there is nothing outside and separate in existence from sensible spatial magnitudes, the objects of thought are in the sensible forms, viz. both the abstract objects and all the states and affections of sensible things. Hence, no one can learn or understand anything in the absence of sense, and when the mind is actively aware of anything it is necessarily aware of it along with an image; for images are like sensuous contents except in that they contain no matter (*De Anima* III, 8, 432a 3-10).

Aquinas (*De Veritate*, q2a6c) appropriated and elaborated on Aristotle's position, relating phantasm to intellect as sensible objects are related to sense and as colours are related to sight. For Aquinas (*De Veritate*, q10,a2,ad7m), the sensible image is to the intellect, as object is to potency. Accordingly, phantasm—the sensible image, is necessary as the object of intellect.

> No power can know anything without turning to its object, as sight knows nothing unless it turns to color. Now, since phantasms are related to the possible intellect in the way that sensible things are related to sense, as the Philosopher points out, no matter to what extent an intelligible species is present to the understanding, understanding does

not actually consider anything according to that species without referring to phantasm.

Later, Aquinas (*De Veritate* q18,a8ad4) made a stronger statement on
the necessity of phantasm, for understanding:

> According to the Philosopher [*De Anima* III, 7, 431a 14], the intellec-
> tive soul is related to phantasms as to its objects. Consequently, our
> understanding needs conversion to phantasms not only in acquiring
> knowledge but also in using knowledge once it is acquired.

Aquinas' point will be vital to bear in mind when we explore the implications of systematics as an understanding and using of already acquired
knowledge of the truths of faith.

In accord with Thomas and Aristotle, Lonergan states (1997, 41) that,
"since phantasm is the object of intellect, a phantasm is always necessary
for intellectual activity, no matter how perfect the *species intelligibilis*."
One cannot understand without understanding something, and that
"something" is found in the phantasm—the sensible image. In Lonergan's
cartwheel exercise, to intellectually grasp the necessary circularity is to
grasp the relation between the imagined equal radii and the imagined
equal uniform curvature. The terms to be intelligently related are sensibly experienced and their necessary relation is intelligently grasped by
insight into this sensitive presentation (1997, 42).

We find further support for this position in Finnis' work. He writes
(1980, 399-400) that "we need images, figures, symbols, to help us understand even the most abstract terms and relations." We also find a concrete instance of understanding's reliance on a sense image in Rees' description (1983, 22) of how she grasped the relation between the abstract
concept "five" and concrete collections of five objects. The insight came
to her, "Suddenly something clicked," in her words, when she saw the
word "five" spelled next to several collections of five objects. Lonergan's
point is reinforced by Thomas Daly's observation (1982, 28) that we
learn foreign languages more easily when the words are applied to concrete images taken from "real life" than when words are translated into
other words. We suggest that the application of sensible images is actually the way that we learned our first language. After all, do not parents,
when teaching their children, point to a sensible object, and then say
"mama," "cat" or whatever else the object may be?

To operate, the intellect depends on sense to provide its object. Lonergan
(1997, 45) acknowledges that his position, for which he finds the above-

mentioned support in Aristotle and Aquinas, contradicts any theory of innate ideas, and the Kantian notion of *a priori* forms. Lonergan likewise (1997, 39n126) both opposes his position to that of Scotus, who flatly denied the reality of insight into phantasm, and maintains that it was this denial of insight into the sensible image that led Scotus to reduce understanding to being a "seeing" a nexus between concepts. For Scotus, conceptualisation preceded understanding. Two key points that Lonergan makes (1997, 39n126), are important to bear in mind. The first, that Scotus' position gave Kant the analytical judgements which he criticised, and led him to form the idea of synthetic apriori judgements. The second, that Scotus' position was in sharp contrast to the Aristotelian-Thomist tradition, which found understanding to precede conceptualisation. This is despite the all too common misconception that Scotus was in substantial agreement with Aquinas on human knowing.

(7) If we further consider the examples and exercises above, we find with Lonergan (1992, 32) that the content of the insight, the "must," necessary relations, or intelligible possibility, which insight grasps, *is definitely not imaginable*. We are able to form sensible images of dots or fine threads. These images can be formed because these have magnitude. The actual points and lines that we consider, though, lie beyond the imagination, as they have no observable magnitude. Similarly, we are able to see the image of boiling water, but we cannot see the insight into why water boils at different temperatures. We find, with Lonergan (1990, 25), that we cannot see an insight, nor can one imagine the intelligibility in an insight. One does not see, or otherwise sensibly experience this intelligibility—one understands it. There is present a difference between experience and understanding. One can see or imagine a circle, but one cannot see that it must be a circle, one needs to understand this intelligibility. Again, one can see all aspects of boiling water, but nowhere in the sense data is there the cognitional content, "this water boils at temperatures that vary with external air pressures." The non-imaginable reality of insight illustrates the sharp and substantial difference between the act of experience and the act of understanding. We recall Lonergan's constant reminder (1994, 238; 1988, 206)—knowing is not looking!

(8) Lonergan also notes (1992, 29) that Archimedes' moment of insight demonstrates how *insight's advent is not predictable* but a sudden and unexpected event. Archimedes' insight came, not in a speculative moment or posture, but in a more trivial moment of bath-time recreation. Lonergan explains that insight comes, not by rote-learning rules, nor by following precepts, nor by studying method. These techniques cannot

produce insight, which is a discovery, a new beginning. As a discovery, insight is a new beginning, the outcome of creative genius. Were such genius the subject of rules, discoveries would only be conclusions, and the genius only a mere "hack."

William Danaher (1988, 49-50) finds a more contemporary example of insight's unexpected advent in Kekule, who had spent much time on the structure of carbon compounds. The insight, which became a major contribution to structural organic chemistry, came to Kekule, neither when he was in the laboratory nor even in learned company, but while he was in a reverie on a bus! We find further support for Lonergan's observations in the research of Hutchinson, and Platt and Baker. Platt and Baker repeatedly refer (1931, 1973, 1974, 1977-1980) to the "scientific hunch," which comes suddenly and unexpectedly. They cite Helmholtz's report that "happy ideas come unexpectedly without effort like an inspiration." They also refer to many scientists, who write of the occasion of their insight, or "hunch" as: sudden and emphatic, "suddenly as a flash of lightning," a flash through the mind, a springing into mind, or a sudden dawning. Hutchinson similarly notes (1949a, 445; 1949c, 387, 392, 402) that insights come in unpredictable ways and times. He emphasises that insight is spontaneous. "In the case of insight the process must wait upon purely chance factors, since there is no prediction as to just what element or what kind of experience will release the repressed system." Hutchinson observes that insight's spontaneous occasion may lead one to suppose oneself to be the "mouthpiece" of higher forces. Such is the unpredictability of insight, that thinkers may mistake their own unpredicted flashes of insight to be extra-personal moments of "inspiration" from outside. Hutchinson would suggest that we give human intellect more of its due credit, and acknowledge that even though it is occasional, and unpredictable, human insight is a natural product of the mind.

Lonergan's point, that the moment of insight is unpredictable, means that he would reject the notion that insight comes only as the result of a deductive process. If insight is a sudden and often unexpected event and if we cannot prescribe rules for its occurrence, then understanding can hardly be knowledge deduced with certainty from self-evident axioms, as was assumed under the classicist scientific model. A reflection from Adrienne Clarke (O'Neill 1989, 3-4) illuminates this point:

> At one time we were working on a problem that we had come to call 'The Chinese Puzzle'. We had all these fragments of information stuck on a

chart, but they made no overall sense. We would keep designing new
experiments to find out what it meant.
The day it all became clear, it was like the electric light bulb switching
on in the bubble over your head in a cartoon.

Clarke's research team-members had all the necessary data before them,
but the understanding of what those data meant was not forthcoming by
any process of deduction. The clarity only came "one day" when a creative, though unpredictable, insight occurred.

The foregoing reflections on insight hold true not just for an original
discovery, but also for a teacher's success in communicating his or her
discoveries. As Lonergan explains (1992, 29, 31), no teacher can make a
student understand. One can only dispose data in a meaningful manner.
Ultimately, students will understand a teacher according to the students'
own abilities. He reminds us of what any teacher knows, that students
vary widely in their ability to catch on and understand.

(9) Lonergan observes (1992, 100) that *insight pivots between the concrete and the abstract*. This point means that, while an insight arises from
inquiry into concrete issues, it can be applied, in an abstract way, to the
world beyond the original concrete issue.

By way of example, Lonergan explains (1992, 30) that Archimedes had
a concrete problem, to which he found the concrete answer, to weigh
King Hiero's crown in water. However, Archimedes' insight into the concrete problem had universal and abstract applications, for the hydrostatic
principles that he discovered could be applied to any objects.

So what does it mean for insight to pivot between the concrete and the
abstract? Lonergan clarifies (1992, 30) that insight arises in response to
concrete situations. Geometers use concrete diagrams, doctors see individual patients, mathematicians use pen and paper to resolve particular
questions. After inquirers have had their insights, it is in the abstract
formulation of those insights that the insight takes on universal significance. In the example of Archimedes, the concrete question concerned
the crown's composition. The insight was to weigh it in water. The abstract application was gained once scientists abstracted from the crown,
the bath and the king. What remained were abstract and universally applicable principles of displacement and specific gravity. Importantly
though, between the concrete situation and the abstract formulation and
application of the discovered principles, there is the pivotal insight, without which the concrete problem would remain unsolved, and the abstract principles would remain unknown.

By emphasising the pivotal role of insight, Lonergan manifests a break with classicist science, which emphasised deduction of certainties from abstract principles. For Lonergan, what comes first is insight into the concrete, not deduction from abstract "first principles."

(10) Lonergan also observes (1992, 30) that *insight passes into the mind's habitual texture*. He notes that, before his insight, Archimedes required an inspirational moment in which to solve his problem, but he did not require a similar moment when he presented his solution to the king. As Lonergan writes, "Once one has understood, one has crossed a divide." Once one has gained that grasp of intelligibility in insight, what had been an overwhelming problem before the moment of insight becomes quite obvious. This is a most common experience. When we understand a point, we tend to wonder how it was that we never previously understood. The solution that is grasped in insight also tends to remain quite simple, and personal repetitions of the insight occur almost at will. This point essentially means that the act of insight produces a personal appropriation of that solution. In the act of insight, one gains the content of that insight for oneself. Moreover, to the extent that one's memory does not fail, the content of that insight continually stays with a person.

Tallon (1997, 135n2) helps clarify in general reference to intentionality what Lonergan makes specific in reference to insight. Intentionality has three moments, the pre-intentional disposition (which we would apply to the desire to know), the actual act of intending (which we would apply to the inquiry and insight), and the subsequent moment of post-intentionality, which refers generally to the reside left upon the subject, and specifically to the insight as part of the mind's habitual texture, that becomes part of one's predisposition and one's pre-intentionality for future intending.

(11) Earlier, we noted Lonergan's brief point (1992, 29) that "Genius is creative." This point is worth elaborating, especially as Hutchinson writes (1949c, 386) that "We may even go so far as to call the phenomenon *creative insight* since it is usually in connection with constructive work that its most brilliant illustrations are to be found." Because of this constructive, creative nature of insight, Hutchinson notes (1949c, 393) that when insight is present, "science approaches art in its methodology."

Platt and Baker (1931, 1970-72) illuminate insight's creative nature, noting that the "flash of genius," which constitutes the scientific "hunch," involves a "*leap of the imagination*" that fills in gaps in the evidence before the scientist. Platt and Baker illustrate such leaps of imagination by reference: to Wilder Bancroft, who noted that judgements from the facts at hand are often not sufficient, one needs to make a guess; to Bancroft's description of Faraday, who noted the work of guessing by hypothesis; to Pasteur, whom Bancroft described as a "brilliant guesser;" and to Newton, whom Platt and Baker report stating that "no great discovery was ever made without a bold guess."

Hutchinson notes (1949c 398) that even though it involves a "reorganisation of the perceptual field," insight is more than this. We understand, from Hutchinson, that insight brings a new content of understanding, a new grasp of how that perceptual field can be unified, or how a problem can be solved. Platt and Baker (1931, 1977-79) offer many instances of insight being creative, and adding a new cognitional content that brings intelligible unity. These examples include: Measuring hydrolysis of ammonium salts by the new method of slow rotation, the invention of Sun Fast colours in blinds by beating in colour with water, and photographing free-rising bubbles in water by a new technique, namely taking pictures of downward-flowing water. In these cases, the "new" discoveries were not found in the sense-data available to the scientists. The discoveries came from their creative process of intelligent insight.

Insight is *creative*. We thus re-emphasise our earlier point that insight does not strictly come from a deductive process. Lonergan's vision of insight would exclude the classicist notion that human knowledge is attained with certainty by deducing truths from self-evident axioms. The creative element of insight, we further note, goes to explain why some people "catch on" and have insights, and others do not, and why individuals vary in their ability to make discoveries and understand. *Creative* insight is unpredictable, for there are no set rules for creativity. Creativity is a human reality that, though able to be used, is not able to be caused or brought into being. It remains mysterious, and enigmatic, but nonetheless a very real part of human life.

(12) Insight is also *fertile*. We have indicated something of insight's fertility or power when we examined the exaltation, joy and sometimes ecstasy, associated with insight's release of intellectual tension. John Finnis (1980, 399) refers to this power when he follows Aquinas in observing that "The power of human understanding far exceeds ... what we would expect to be the intrinsic capacity of the brain material."

On more familiar territory, Hutchinson remarks (1949b, 405; 1949c, 398) that insight is often "accompanied by a flood of ideas." This flood of ideas, or the surpassing power of understanding, indicates that insight is both a powerful and productive part of human knowing. Some key examples found in Hutchinson (1949c, 388, 393-95) are illuminating. Bertrand Russell, Gibbon and Lilian Whiting, all report that a moment's insight gave each of them the plan of an entire book. Rousseau's "sudden vision" of Summer 1794, was an insight that conveyed a "multitude of 'truths'." Descartes "illumination" advising him to combine mathematics and philosophy took him the greater part of a season to elaborate in a fruitful fashion. Finally, the culture-changing power of the Buddha's revelation of the Fourfold Noble Truths would be very familiar to us (Hutchinson 1943, 355).

A final example is also illuminating. Hutchinson (1949a, 433) cites Tchaikovsky as writing that in his moment of inspiration, when all within him is "pulsing and quivering," "one thought follows another with great rapidity." Such a reflection reminds us of Lonergan's point (1964c, 16) that a fertile act of understanding does not only resolve one question, but a whole series of subsequent questions.

We need bear in mind two observations then. First, that insight is not an incidental part of human knowing. It is powerful and sometimes overpowering, often to the point of being extravagant and needing the later critical temperance (Hutchinson 1949c, 393). Secondly, the power of insight is such that it ranges beyond the tension of the primary question that it answers. An act of insight can, and often does, answer not just one question, but an entire series of questions. By way of example, the schoolboy, to whom we referred above, found later in life that his insight into the variation of boiling point with external pressure helped make more intelligible such diverse matters as pyrotechnics, explosives detonation, and the treatment of decompression illness associated with SCUBA diving.

6. Understanding II—Conception
6.1 The Notion of Concept

Hutchinson notes (1949a, 435-37) that at the moment of insight, the psychic energy that has been "dammed up" demands a delivery into some motor channel. More often than not, this channel is speech. Though verbal forms are not the only ways of expressing insights. Insight brings with itself the psychic need to express the content of this new insight. However, as Hutchinson notes (1949b, 405), full expression of an insight is not always attainable immediately. There is, after insight itself, a period of elaboration in which one attempts to express one's insight.

Lonergan (1990, 42) expresses this "period of elaboration" by proposing that the next stage in cognitional process is the formation of concepts, which express in a general manner what is essential to having an insight. In the cartwheel exercise, we find that our insight, into the circle's roundness depending on the equality of its radii that originate from a common point, is conceptually expressed by the definition of a circle—as a locus of coplanar points equidistant from a centre. Conception, as expressing the essential conditions for having an insight, is thus a matter of abstraction. In this case, from particular radii and roundness, one abstracts what is essential to having that insight again.

The process of abstraction is necessary for forming a concept, because in any case of insight into sensible multiplicity there is the intelligible unity that is necessary for the insight, and there is the residue that is merely given (Lonergan 1997, 187; 1992, 112). Accordingly, in what Lonergan (1990, 42; 1992, 112) calls "enriching abstraction," we select what is essential to having that insight and eliminate what is incidental to having the insight again. That is, in the "third moment" of enriching abstraction, we abstract from "the insignificant, the irrelevant, the negligible, the incidental, the merely empirical residue." In the circle case, and our boiling water example, the empirical residue, or inessential qualities would include colour or size. If however, an object fulfils the essential conditions of being a circle, being a coplanar locus of points equidistant from a centre, then it is still a circle (Lonergan 1990, 42). Again, if an object fulfils the basic conditions of being water boiled under air, we can conceive the water's boiling point as being proportionate to the surrounding air pressure.

Lonergan (1990, 39) offers a historical example to illustrate concepts. Socrates wandered around Athens asking the citizens, "What is it to be a brave man? What is it to be a temperate man? What is it to be a wise man? What is it to be a just man?" The Athenians correctly believed that they had a good idea of whether any particular person was brave, temperate, just or wise. However, while they had effective insights into particular cases, they could not answer Socrates' questions and he "would make monkeys of them every time."

While the Athenians had correct insights into particular cases, their capabilities stopped there. Socrates' interrogations, however, went further by asking about the general formulae that accounted for all cases of bravery, temperance, wisdom or justice. The Athenians had simply not considered such general formulae. They were incapable of abstracting from the empirical data of particular cases, what was necessary for them to intellectually grasp such virtues again.

We find another illustration in Rahner's contrast (1961, 63-64) of "propositional knowledge and primordial consciousness." In matters such as love, Rahner writes, one may know much about this state of love, but one may know much more than one can state, or express in propositions. Lonergan would agree substantially with Rahner, proposing that one in love may have an insight into this love, but may not yet be able to adequately express this love in a concept.

6.2. Concept and Image

With reference to his circle exercise, Lonergan reminds us (1992, 32) that concepts are not necessarily imaginable. The intellect's act of conception can thus create objects that lie beyond the imaginable. Conception can create objects simply by supposing. In the cartwheel exercise, the points and lines that we conceived are concepts. Moreover, the imagined dot, the hub, has magnitude but a geometer supposes it, as a point, to have only position. The imagined line has breadth, yet the geometer supposes it to have only length.

Despite the rather random appearance of such supposing Lonergan (1992, 32) clarifies its purpose. The imagined hub was reduced to a conceived point, without magnitude, for if it had magnitude, the spokes could rest in it unevenly. The imagined spokes were reduced to conceived lines, for if they had breadth, the wheel could be flat, bumped or dented. Accordingly, by Lonergan's suggestion, we supposed, conceived a point without magnitude and lines without breadth, in order to conceive a perfectly round circle.

6.3. Properties of Concepts

Lonergan (1992, 32-33) observes two important properties of concepts. First, they are constituted by the act of supposing, defining, considering, thinking, formulating. They may be more than that, but even if they are only supposed, considered or thought about, they are still constituted as concepts. Secondly, concepts do not occur randomly, they originate from thinking, supposing, considering, defining and formulating. That manifold activity, Lonergan emphasises, occurs only in conjunction with an act of insight. He thus (1990, 31) aligns his position to that of Aristotle and Aquinas, but distinguishes it from that of Kant, writing that "In Kant there is no talk of the insight, but only of the concept, the image, and the concept governing the image." He also explains that, "In Aristotle and St Thomas, on the other hand, the insight and the concept are distinguished, and the phantasm, the image, causes the insight." Lonergan thus maintains that the insight is prior to concept and that the concept only arises in conjunction with the insight, and as insight's expression.

Regarding his crucial distinction between insight, which relies on a sensible image, and concept, which does not, Lonergan outlines a concrete example from the work of Athanasius. In *The Way to Nicea*, Lonergan (1976, 99) finds that Athanasius, in referring to the consubstantiality of the Son with the Father, specifically excludes the spatio-temporal, that is, the imaginable, from this concept of consubstantiality. By using such unimagined concepts, Athanasius could insist in *De Decretis* (1978a) that "the Son is begotten of the Father in a manner altogether different from that of human generation."

Lonergan explains (1976, 99-100) the working of Athanasius' mind by observing that, beginning with images, mostly taken from Scripture, he grasped in these a certain intelligibility that was expressed in the concept of consubstantiality. It was this concept that was then taken to describe the Son's divine generation. Significantly, the concept itself is not expressed in terms of, nor does it rely on, sensible images. As Athanasius writes in *De Synodis* (1978b):

> When we speak of him as offspring, we do not understand this in a human way, and when we acknowledge God as Father, we do not attribute bodily characteristics to him: these words and images we apply to God in a fitting manner, for God is not like man. In the same way, when we hear him described as consubstantial, we must transcend the senses utterly and, following the Proverb (23, 1), understand spiritually what is laid before us (Lonergan 1976, 100).

Athanasius' statement tells us that a concept, such as consubstantiality, transcends every image, and even in a way, transcends every intelligibility grasped in a sensible image. Lonergan (1976, 103) finds a scientific parallel in Maxwell's electromagnetic equations. While these first emerged from images, in themselves, they have no corresponding images. We clarify that, while Maxwell's formulations do employ images in the symbols belonging to the electromagnetic equations, these symbols are not received directly from the magnetism itself. Likewise, Athanasius' rule refers to concepts and judgements rather than to images. The rule of Athanasius prescinds from all images, there being nothing imaginable that can serve as intelligence's object to formulate this rule.

6.4 Concept's Dependence on Insight

Lonergan's (1990, 41-42) next observation on concepts is that they are dependent on insight. In the cartwheel exercise, we found that insight grasps a necessary relation in an intelligible object. Insight grasps the relation between equal radii and circular curve. It is when, and only when, one has had that insight, that one is able to proceed to the definition of a circle. This is, as Lonergan insists, because "Insight is prior to concepts." The conceptual definition of a circle attends to the general case, but this act is not a reflex action. For example, we may define a circle as "a locus of points equidistant from a center," but we find that this definition could fit a map of Africa on a globe. The correct definition and concept of a circle is, "a locus of *coplanar* points equidistant from a center." That conceptual definition expresses the essential conditions for having the insight. Conception then, Lonergan re-emphasises, expresses in a general manner what is essential to having the insight.

If we grasp Lonergan's point, that a concept expresses an insight, we can understand his conviction, for which he takes support from Aristotle and Aquinas, that insight is prior to concept. Lonergan insists (1997, 192-95) that in the genuine exercise of intelligence, a conceptual definition remains an expression of the insight, and not the other way around. Thomas Daly (1982, 27) likewise emphasises that while a definition may assist communication, ultimate clarity lies with the prior insight, without which the definition is meaningless. Lonergan further states (1997, 194) that intellectual habits are not concepts, judgements or inferences, but habits of understanding. It is from these that intelligence in act results, and it is intelligence in act that is the intellect. The implication that we find for conceptual definition is that to define intelligently, intelligence must be acting, for definition is the expression of intelligence in act.

We can illustrate Lonergan's point by noting that one who endeavoured to operate with concepts as being prior to insights, those whom Lonergan calls conceptualists, can easily rattle off the conceptual definition, "two plus two is four." However to make this definition with genuine intelligence, one must have intelligence in act, and have insight's grasp that two objects added to two other objects results in four objects. Essentially, one must first intelligently grasp, in an act of insight, the relation between a two, the other two, and the four. To properly define this relation is to express intelligence in act. We also find that the very "proof" of the proposition "two plus two equals four," as a concept, cannot be self-evident. One could present the "proof" but if the hearer had no intelligent grasp of what two, four, addition and equality were, one could do no more than dumbly repeat the definition. To appreciate the sufficiency of the proof, the hearer must use one's own intellect to grasp these necessary relations.

If insight is prior to concepts, we may ask why the common view holds that concepts are prior to understanding. Daly (1982, 27-28) provides reasons for both the existence of this conceptualist view and the need to reject it. He observes that we normally encounter understanding expressed in words and sentences. This is normally taken as the basic form of understanding. Conceptualists thus conclude that "since words represent concepts, and sentences represent propositions, it seems that we get the concepts first through the words and then understand them." Daly (1982, 28) refutes this conceptualist assumption, negatively, by noting that the understanding of words is not basic because we do not understand the words of foreign languages. Positively, he notes that with puzzles and machines, we understand these, and then only after we understand them do we formulate our understanding by concepts, which express this understanding.

6.5 Insight and Discovery

We should also observe that the intellectualist position, which gives priority to insight over concept, has the advantage of being able to account for the human reality of discovery. We simultaneously observe that a conceptualist view-point cannot account adequately for discovery. Concepts are categorical, and can only refer to already understood intelligibilities. Because it is a new discovery, insight is actively open to grasping new, as yet ungrasped intelligibilities.

We recall the role of insight in scientific discovery. Specifically, we note Platt and Baker's (1931, 1976ff) and Hutchinson's (1949c, 386ff) discovery of the role of "the scientific revelation or hunch in the solution of an important problem." We also recall one physicist's testimony:

> Nearly all important ideas come quick as a flash, faster than they can be expressed in words; but always after long gathering and analysis of data and usually after considerable unsuccessful thought (Hutchinson, 1949c, 392).

This statement corresponds to Lonergan's idea of human understanding. That is, understanding begins with inquiry into an object, one then gains an unformulated insight into that image, then that insight is expressed in a concept. Lonergan's example of Archimedes further illustrates this point, for no apprehension of concepts lead to Archimedes' hydrostatic insight. We also note that no concepts brought about Kekule's understanding of carbon bonding. In both cases, the scientists had insights that were only later formulated and expressed, and not the other way around. In particular, we note Kekule's recollection that his grasp of carbon bonding came in what we would call an unformulated, non-conceptualised fashion. Only later did he spend the evening trying to formulate and express this insight (Danaher 1988, 49-50). Likewise, Daly also notes (1982, 28-29) that a similar personal act of understanding must occur in appropriating others' discoveries, and such understanding must lie at the foundation of any genuine assent to a proposition.

6.6 Historical Influences

As noted before, Lonergan's insistence in giving priority to insight over concept firmly places him in the Aristotelian-Thomist tradition. However, we should recall Augustine's substantial influence on Lonergan's concern for intelligent insight. In the nineteen-thirties, Lonergan (1974, 264-65) read Augustine's early dialogues, finding that while Augustine was concerned with understanding, he was nonetheless quite unmindful of universal concepts. Despite Lonergan's later misgivings, about Augustine's Platonist leanings, we find that, at this early stage, Augustine's account of understanding motivated Lonergan into spending much time trying to write an intelligible account of his convictions. Lonergan however (1997, 39n126), sharply distinguishes himself from the cognitional positions of Scotus and Kant. Scotus, Lonergan observes, put concepts first and held understanding to be the apprehending of the nexus between concepts. He further argues that this viewpoint directly resulted from Scotus' denial of insight into phantasm. It was this position of Scotus that lead Kant to the idea of a purely discursive intellect and assert synthetic *a priori* judgements.

7. Understanding III—Intellectualism and Conceptualism

After exploring Lonergan's account of understanding, insight and concept, we can appreciate his sharp and vigorous distinction of the two theories of knowing, which he calls intellectualism and conceptualism. This distinction corresponds to the position of Aquinas (*Summa Contra Gentiles* II, 98§19, 20), who argues that,

> ... for Aristotle, who asserts that understanding occurs as the result of *the thing actually understood being one with the intellect actually understanding;* ...
>
> On the other hand, according to Plato's position, understanding is effected through the contact of the intellect with the intelligible thing.

Lonergan explains (1997, 192-93) that the Platonist holds knowing to primarily be a confrontational act, with a definite duality existing between knower and known. This duality is highlighted by Plato's deduction that because we can know ideas, ideas subsist. Furthermore, for Plato, knowing consists in a consequent, added movement, which is illustrated by the dilemma of the subsistent idea of Being needing to be in motion, or without knowing.

> If knowing is to be acting on something, it follows that what is known must be acted upon by it, and so, on this showing, reality when it is being known by the act of knowledge must, in so far as it is known, be changed owing to being so acted upon—and that, we say cannot happen to the changeless (*Sophistes,* 248 d-e).

In tracing the successors to this position, Lonergan notes (1997, 192) that, by holding that knowing abides in seeing and consulting the eternal reasons, Augustine reflected Plato's view. Medieval followers of Augustine perpetuated the doctrine of confrontational knowing by holding to an intuitive cognition of material and singular existents. In modern times, Lonergan also observes that many "escape the critical problem by asserting a confrontation of intellect with concrete reality." We find that in asserting understanding to consist in an object being apprehended and immediately understood, these Platonist and neo-Platonist positions maintain a confrontation of a knower who confronts the object in a knowing analogous to ocular looking.

Conversely, Lonergan finds (1997, 192-93) that Aristotelians hold that confrontation is secondary to knowing as perfection, act and identity. For the Aristotelian, "Sense in act is the sensible in act. Intellect in act is the intelligible in act." In our material world, we find the knower and the known in act, and these are identical. Lonergan explains that there are also the knower and known in potency, and these are distinct. He thus observes that because potency is non-essential to knowing, distinction is non-essential to knowing. Accordingly, in immaterial substances, when one decreases potency, one also decreases distinction. Aristotle effectively supports this position:

"As, then, thought and the object of thought are not different in the case of things that have not matter, they will be the same, i.e. the thinking will be one with the object of its thought." (*Metaphysics* XII, 9, 1075a 3-4);
"For in the case of objects which involve no matter, what thinks and what is thought are identical; for speculative knowledge and its object are identical." (*De Anima* III, 4, 430a 3-5) and
"Actual knowledge is identical with its object." (De Anima III, 5, 430a 20)

Lonergan notes (1997, 193) that Aristotle's view of knowing overcomes the Platonists' problem, when conceiving subsistent being, in that they required the introduction of movement for knowledge. However, because he could conceive knowing as identity in act, Aristotle could affirm the intelligence in act of his unmoved mover.

In appropriating the above points, Chesterton's *The Secret of Father Brown* is a most helpful illustration of understanding as being an intellectual identity. In Father Brown's explanation of how he solves crimes we find a clear explanation of understanding from an intellectualist perspective.

We first note how Father Brown rejects, with "animated annoyance," the idea that science is an outside study of an object. The model of science that Brown rejects as providing only dry light, and no success in detection, is a "getting *outside*" of the object and studying that object from "a long way off." Conversely, Brown explains that the secret of his detective work is that "I don't try to get outside the man. I try to get inside the murderer" (Chesterton n.d. 12-13). Father Brown thus presents a concrete example of understanding as identity with the object to be understood. In the light of Lonergan's cognitional theory, we can say that Father Brown does not solve his crimes by an act of confronting the clues, rather he gains his insights by identifying his intellect with the reality of the murder.

As Father Brown explains (Chesterton n.d. 9), he could solve murders because, "it was I who killed all those people. ... You see, I had murdered them all myself. ... So of course, I knew how it was done." Of course, Father Brown only killed those people in his mind, but for our investigation, we note particularly that he rejects the notion that he only killed those people "as a figure of speech." Rather, he attempts to explain how he killed those people in a spiritual, though not a material sense, in the manner of "a sort of religious exercise, until "I am really a murderer" (Chesterton n.d. 10-11, 13).

As Brown later recounts, someone else played the part of the murderer and played out the "material experience." The way in which he solved the crime was by imagining the mind of the criminal, placing his own mind in the place of the criminal, then clearing his mind of those things that would not have been in the mind of the criminal. Having eliminated such irrelevant data, he would then endeavour to align his mind with the intellect that perpetrated the crime. Then, Father Brown notes, when your intellect has grasped the same things as the criminal, when in fact you are thinking in the same way as the criminal then "'you contract your mind like the camera focus ... the thing shapes and then sharpens ... and then, suddenly, it comes!'" So powerful is this experience of insight, that "He spoke like a man who had once captured a divine vision" (Chesterton n.d. 299-300, 304-5).

Chesterton's account of Father Brown illustrates several points. The more manifest point is the meaning of understanding as being identity. When Aristotle and Lonergan write of understanding as identity, they mean the same thing as Father Brown. One experiences intelligent insight when one's intellect has grasped the intelligibility that is in the object, when the same intelligibility as there is in the object is in the mind. Father Brown also illustrates other aspects of insight. In the first place, his account of detective work shows that insight does not result from only deductive process proceeding from facts to certainly deduced truths. Rather, insight comes suddenly and unexpectedly, and only from a creative thought process, in which one has filled in the gaps in one's data. Chesterton illustrated well the joy that accompanies insight, when he wrote how Father Brown spoke of his crime solutions with the disposition of one who had beheld a divine vision.

To conclude this section, we note that understanding begins with the image formed by the act of experience. The pure desire to know intends questions regarding intelligibility in the presented data, and the act of insight intelligently grasps the intelligibilities, or necessary relations, present in the experienced data. Then intelligence abstracts what is essential to having the insight again from the sensible residue, and the abstracted concept expresses in a general form what is necessary to having that insight again. We note that this notion of understanding closely corresponds to Aquinas' notion (*De Veritate* q14,a1c) of the first operation of "the understanding" in determining an object's "quiddity." The question remains though, as to whether such understanding is invulnerable. Human experience witnesses to understanding's fallibility and, as Lonergan notes (1994, 13), "insights are a dime a dozen." Tallon observes likewise

(1997, 229) that humans are finite spirits, with the finitude of our understanding meaning it must be complemented by discursive judgement. That is, there is required an act by which understanding can be tested for authenticity, and to this act of judgement we now turn.

8. JUDGEMENT

Lonergan (1992, 296-97) invites us to find the notion of judgement for ourselves by considering two types of questions. First, there are questions for reflection that may be answered by a simple "yes" or "no." Such a question would be, "Is there a logarithm of the square root of minus one?" Secondly, there are questions for intelligence, which cannot be met by a "yes" or "no" answer. Such a question would be "What is the logarithm of the square root of minus one?" We would find it absurd to answer this question with a simple affirmation or denial. Such questions show how one can take two attitudes to propositions. One can consider the proposition, making it the object of thought, the content of an act of conceiving, defining, supposing. Alternatively one can make the proposition the content of an act of judging, whereby it becomes the content of an act of affirmation or denial, agreement or disagreement, assent or dissent.

Lonergan also brings our attention to these two parts of human knowing and cites a number of texts from Aquinas in support of his position in *Verbum* (1997, 20-21). He notes that the first act of intellect is knowledge of the *quod quid est*. That is, intellect's first act is the understanding of quiddity. He emphasises though, that understanding quiddity does not involve knowledge of truth or falsity. The question of truth only arises in intellect's second act, which attains truth or falsity.

In proceeding to affirmation or denial, we advance to the cognitional level of being reasonable, in which we exercise our rational consciousness. On this level of consciousness, we regard the understanding gained by intelligence as a mere possibility until the evidence for its reality has been settled. We thus discover the rational level of human consciousness, in which we reflect upon an object, marshal evidence and pass judgement on its truth or falsity (Lonergan 1994, 9).

In considering judgement, we discover that in addition to presupposing a level of experience, the level of understanding is also presupposed and complemented by a third level of knowing. While understanding can yield valuable concepts, definitions, objects of thought and suppositions, the authentically acting person requires more, by way of asking "But is it true?" or "Is it so?" In this asking "Is it so?" there emerges the search for truth and falsity, certitude and probability. In judgement, the knowing person takes an object of thought and transforms the object from a mere idea to an object of affirmation (Lonergan 1990, 110; 1992, 298). Lonergan (1997, 57) reminds us that this process is the way in which people live their everyday lives. Tell any "bumpkin" a plausible tale and we shall be greeted with the remark that, "Well now, that may be so." While our provincial friend may not be knowingly exercising the rational faculty, he nonetheless shows that by grasping intelligibility, his understanding has grasped possible being. However, to affirm reality, our "bumpkin" tells us that more than a well-conceived account is needed. There is needed a judgement regarding the correspondence between the tale and reality.

Lonergan notes (1994, 10) that when one engages in such affirmation, as one who is critically conscious, one gives oneself over to the criteria of truth and certitude and makes one's concern the determination of what is, and is not so. This notion, of concern for truth, finds support in Aquinas, who wrote that the intellect tends towards the true just as an appetite tends toward a good (*Summa Theologiae*, I,q16,a1c). In a more modern setting, Lonergan refers (1974, 271) to Herbert Fingarette (1963), who conceives neurosis as "cumulatively misinterpreted experience." Fingarette would uphold the view that persons naturally tend towards a correct understanding of experience. The incorrect, or unreal, understanding of experience cumulatively leads to neurosis.

We find further support for this position in Arthur Janov's *The Primal Scream*, a work to which Lonergan makes general references in *Method* (1994, 68n9, 285n8). Janov (1981, 22-37) holds the psychological split from reality to be neurotic. To flee from reality, and to try to live in an unreal world is not naturally human, but a psychological illness. We may also refer again to Hutchinson's writings on human insight. He notes (1949c, 398) that after the insight itself, there is "*A Period of Verification, Elaboration, or Evaluation.*" In this period, Hutchinson notes that possible exaggerations and overstatements from the *period of insight* are "checked against external realities." We find that Hutchinson points to the same reality as Lonergan, namely, that beyond understanding, there is a cognitional act that asks, "is my understanding accurate?" "Do I need to correct my understanding?" To eliminate this step of verification, would seem, from Hutchinson's analysis, to eliminate a stage in the process of creative thinking.

8.1 Judgement's Relation to Understanding

Lonergan (1994, 10) relates judgement to understanding first, by noting that without the prior effort to understand, and understanding's indefinite results, there would be no occasion for judgement. In other words, without the prior understanding of an object, the judgement is totally meaningless. He states (1988, 207) that "To pass judgement on what one does not understand is, not human knowing, but human arrogance."

For Lonergan, understanding and judgement are distinct cognitional acts and they both add distinct cognitional contents to human knowledge. Lonergan's position is thus distinct from that of Kant who, as Sala notes (1994, 5), maintains a composite make-up of knowledge, but does not acknowledge that later phases of the cognitional process add their own distinct contents to the "full and final object of knowledge."

8.2 The Character of Judgement

We have a notion of what judgement does, but we must also address the question of what judgement is. Lonergan's (1992, 304) first observation is that judgement, like the act of understanding, relies on an insight. Judgement's "insight," however, grasps the sufficiency of evidence for a prospective judgement. We also note that Lonergan's idea of judgement is that judgement is an active, not a passive, operation. As Vertin writes (1983, 3), to judge is neither to intuit nor perceive, nor see real existence in some concrete, intelligible object. Rather, judgement is to affirm of, assert of or attribute to, that concrete intelligible object a relation to intellect's ultimate objective term, a term one anticipates *a priori*, and that is what one means by "real existence." This account of judgement as an active operation recalls Newman's (1985, 223) similar point that the illative sense, which leads to certitude, "is not a passive impression made upon the mind from without, ... but ... it is an active recognition of propositions as true, such as it is the duty of each individual himself to exercise at the bidding of reason."

In this active operation, which Lonergan calls reflective understanding, one grasps the "weight" of evidence at hand. This is an act with which we are all familiar, though perhaps not in a reflective fashion. Lonergan reminds us (1990, 112) that when one does not grasp the evidence at hand, but nonetheless says, "It is," or "It is not," one is merely guessing. When one does grasp the evidence, but refuses to affirm or deny, one is just being silly. He clarifies though (1992, 305), that terms, such as "weighing the evidence," are only metaphorical. To foster precision, he intro-

duces the term, "unconditioned." That is, "To grasp evidence as sufficient for a prospective judgement is to grasp the prospective judgement
as virtually unconditioned."

Lonergan means that a "conditioned" relates to the conditions under
which a thing really exists. In this light, he (1990, 118; 1992, 305) first
names the formally unconditioned, which can have no conditions what-
soever. A virtually conditioned, though, has conditions, but these are
fulfilled. Lonergan (1992, 305) identifies the three components of a virtually unconditioned:

(1) "a conditioned,
(2) a link between the conditioned and its conditions, and
(3) the fulfilment of the conditions."

Accordingly, a prospective judgement will be virtually unconditioned if:

(1) "it is the conditioned,
(2) its conditions are known, and
(3) the conditions are fulfilled."

Lonergan explains (1992, 305) that if a question is posed for reflection,
that much is sufficient to make the prospective judgement a conditioned.
Thus, even if conditions did not exist, the mere act of questioning would
create conditions for the judgement. Reflective understanding meets such
questioning by grasping the conditions of the conditioned, and perhaps
also their fulfilment, thus transforming the prospective judgement to a
virtually unconditioned.

Lonergan (1992, 306) illustrates the general form, of the grasp of the
virtually unconditioned, with two syllogisms, one abstract, the other more
concrete:

Syllogism One:	Syllogism Two:
If A then B,	If X is material and alive, X is mortal
But A	But men are material and alive
Therefore B.	Therefore, men are mortal.

In both syllogisms, the second part of the major premise, B or the
mortality of X, are conditioned. The minor premise brings the conditions' fulfilment. Reflective insight grasps the pattern and, being rationally conscious, the subject judges the truth of the conclusion. The foregoing is the technical expression of, what Lonergan had metaphorically
called, "weighing the evidence." One has "weighed the evidence" when
one has reached a virtually unconditioned (Lonergan 1990, 10, 112-13).

8.3 Sources of the Notion

Lonergan's first acknowledged source of the notion of reflective under-standing is Newman. Lonergan states (1990, 351) that his account of reflective understanding is expressed in different terms, but is roughly equivalent to Newman's illative sense, which was a key influence in form-ing his notion of reflective understanding. Lonergan (1971c, 48, 48n29) shows his early debt to Newman in his doctoral dissertation, writing that,

> when error exists in matters of principle, it can be corrected, not indeed by deduction which supposes true principles, but by collative thought and by the acquisition of the virtues which effect a right attitude toward principles.

Lonergan (1971c, 48, 48n29) clearly associated this thought with Newman. We find that, like Newman, he found the attainment of certi-tude to be a natural part of human cognitional operation. As Newman wrote (1985, 222), "That is to be accounted a normal operation of our nature, which men in general do actually instance." Thus, the notion of judgement, or the illative sense, is a specific instance of how neither Lonergan nor Newman passed judgement on what knowing should or might be, they simply observed and reflected on what knowing was.

Lonergan's position is most clearly and precisely founded on the thought of Aquinas, for whom the act of judgement is the final increment in the process of knowledge. The human mind reaches this truth and attains its term, that is, "it judges that a thing corresponds to the form which it apprehends about that thing, [only] when first it knows and expresses truth" (*Summa Theologiae*, I,q16,a2c). This position was first made clear to Lonergan by the influence of Maréchal, whose thought he learned from his fellow student Stephanou. Maréchal, albeit indirectly, taught Lonergan that judgement is a separate act and is the decisive element in knowing. Lonergan acknowledges (1973, 62; 1974, 265; 1990, 276-77) that it was Maréchal who introduced Catholic scholarship to the notion that human knowledge is discursive, not intuitive, and that knowledge is attained on the level of affirmation. He also observes that, as well as put-ting him in accord with Maréchal and Aquinas, his position distinguishes him from Kant, for whom experience, confrontation, and sense percep-tion is the decisive element in knowing. Michael Vertin observes (Lamb 1981, 419) that the basic point of agreement between Maréchal and Lonergan, namely, their assertion that judging is discursive and not intuitive, is also their basic point of disagreement with many other philosophers.

The distinction of judgement as a separate act in cognitional process is upheld by Aquinas (*Summa Theologiae*, I,q16,a2c) when he writes that truth is the conformity of the intellect with the thing intended and that this is in no way known by sense. Sight, Aquinas maintains, can know the likeness of a visible object, but cannot know the comparison between the seen object and the sight apprehending it. Furthermore, the intellect can know its conformity with the intelligible thing, but it cannot do this by understanding quiddities. He continues:

> When, however, it judges that a thing corresponds to the form which it apprehends about that thing, then first it knows and expresses truth. ... Therefore, properly speaking, truth resides in the intellect composing and dividing; and not in the senses; nor in the intellect knowing *what a thing is* (*Summa Theologiae*, I,q,16,a2c).

Thomas likewise distinguishes the intellect's two operations in *De Veritate* (q14,a1). The first operation of the intellect, which Lonergan calls understanding, forms understandings of what things are. The second operation, which Lonergan calls judgement, joins and divides concepts by affirmation or denial, and it is in this second operation that truth and falsity are determined. Thomas writes:

> For according to the Philosopher [*De Anima* III, 6, 430a 26ff, 430b 26], our understanding has a twofold operation. There is one by which it forms the simple quiddities of things, ...The second operation of the understanding is that by which it joins and divides concepts by affirmation or denial.

We note that the loose and somewhat confusing terms "joins" and "divides" come from Aristotle's *De Anima*. However, Thomas clarifies their meaning by adding "by affirmation or denial." In Lonergan's more precise terminology, "joining" is strictly part of understanding.

Aristotle, as Thomas observes, similarly differentiates the assertion of truth or falsity from definition. He writes that:

> Assertion is the saying of something concerning something, as too is denial, and is in every case either true or false: this is not always the case with thought: the thinking of the definition in the sense of what it is for something to be is never in error nor is it the assertion of something concerning something (*De Anima*, III, 6, 430b, 26ff).

Aristotle effectively means that a statement of assertion must be either true or false. A statement of understanding though, has a simple object, and need not be true or false. Truth or falsehood comes from a comparison of one thing, or another, as when the mind asserts the union of what it combines or distinguishes (Aquinas, *Commentary on De Anima,* Book III, Lect 11,n760*).*

Finally, we again note that Lonergan's view of judgement, especially in its being a separate cognitional act, sharply differentiates Lonergan from the Platonist position, which conceives knowing as an essentially confrontational act that is analogous to ocular looking.

8.4 Understanding Established Facts

In our previous sections on understanding, we found that Lonergan concentrated on understanding as insight into the data of experience. However, we note that by the time of *Method in Theology*, he explicitly acknowledged that in addition to an understanding of data, there is also an understanding of facts. These two modes of understanding have notable differences.

First, Lonergan finds (1994, 325, 347) that when one understands data there result new theories, and the rejection of older, outmoded positions. Understanding data relies on the images that are presented to consciousness as given, and only as given.

Secondly, understanding facts, or truths, is quite different, for when we better understand a truth, it is the same truth being understood. Lonergan (1994, 325, 336, 348) uses the example of the truth that two plus two equals four. While being the same truth, this truth has been understood with varying levels of skill, by the Babylonians, the Greeks and modern mathematicians. Unlike data, facts are not just given, they have been formed by the conjunction of experience, understanding and judgement. Lonergan uses the example of scientific theories, which are established as truths. One can return from such facts through applied science and technology to transform the commonsense world of man. As we shall find in greater detail below, he finds that one can, and indeed must, understand truths, to answer the questions of just what such truths can possibly mean and how it can be that these facts are what they are. The two forms of understanding, we note, both involve a grasp of intelligibilities and relations in objects. With understanding data, this understanding operates upon unthematised experience, whereas in understanding facts, understanding operates on established objects of knowledge.

9. INFLUENCES ON LONERGAN'S POSITION

Having investigated Lonergan's cognitional theory, it is helpful to recall some influences on his position. We should emphasise that it is mistaken to assume that his cognitional theory was initially Thomist, with concern for modernity coming only later (Lonergan 1990, 428n[d]). As Meynell notes (1989, 206), Lonergan's "basic ideas were solidly in place by 1929, before he had read a line of Aquinas." Only in the nineteen-forties, with his *Verbum* articles, did Lonergan begin any serious study of Aquinas' cognitional theory. Before then, he states (1974, 38) that Aquinas had been mediated to him through conceptualist interpreters. It helps to clarify, though, that while Lonergan had studied Aquinas in his doctoral work, it was only with the *Verbum* articles that Lonergan began any specific study of Aquinas' cognitional theory.

A key influence in Lonergan's early development was Newman's work, especially *Grammar of Assent*, key sections of which Lonergan (1974, 38) read at least six times. Newman remained an influence on Lonergan's work, especially in the correspondence of Newman's illative sense to Lonergan's notion of judgement, as indicated above. In the nineteen-thirties, Lonergan was particularly interested in Augustine and Plato, and, as mentioned above, he began to take a serious interest in the cognitional philosophy of Aquinas in the nineteen-forties. This interest came through the influence of a fellow Jesuit student, Stephanos Stephanou, who mediated Maréchal's theory of knowing to Lonergan (1974, 38; 1990, 350).

There is some contradiction, even in Lonergan's own writings, as to whether his interest in Plato or in Augustine came first. In "Theories of Inquiry," Lonergan maintains (1974, 38) that "I began to delight in Plato, ... and then went on to the early dialogues of Augustine." In *Understanding and Being*, Lonergan recalled (1990, 350) that his development was "from Newman to Augustine, from Augustine to Plato." In "Insight Revisited," though, Lonergan notes specifically (1974, 264-65), how he went from reading Plato's early dialogues, to Augustine's early dialogues written at Cassiciacum. It would appear then, that this is the more correct order. We note though, that regardless of which came first, it does not alter the more important fact that Lonergan's interest in Aquinas was a later development in his thought.

With our advantage of hindsight, we can understand the decisiveness of Maréchal's influence on Lonergan, even though this influence was only second-hand. By his own affirmation (1974, 276), "I had become a Thomist through the influence of Maréchal mediated to me by Stefanos Stefanu." The most important element in Maréchal's thought was that with it,

Lonergan (1974, 265) could articulate the ideas that human knowing was discursive, and that human knowing completed its term in judgement. We should note Lonergan's debt to Maréchal in his finding that knowing is not a matter of one single cognitional act, such as looking. Maréchal emphasised, particularly in his criticism of Kant, that human cognitional acts must be distinguished and that judgement must be emphasised (Lonergan 1990, 177-79). From Maréchal, Lonergan took the notion that judgement was distinguished from understanding and that it was an essential, though distinct, component of human knowing.

Peter Hoenen also had a critical influence on Lonergan. Hoenen's articles in *Gregorianum* brought to light and formed Lonergan's idea (1997, 224) of understanding as apprehending of nexus in phantasm. Hoenen's articles also furthered an interest in Aquinas, and specifically led to Lonergan's own work on the thought of Aquinas in the *Verbum* articles. In his reading of Thomas, enkindled by Hoenen, Lonergan found the keys to formulating his cognitional theory. First, there was the fact that understanding and judgement are distinct and dissimilar though dynamically related and mutually dependent acts. As Aquinas expresses this theory (*De Veritate*, q14,a1c), "assent [judgement] and discursive thought [intelligent understanding] are not parallel, but the discursive thought leads to assent, and the assent brings thought to rest." From the theory of Aquinas, we find Lonergan taking up human knowing as being constituted by a dynamic triple cord of attentiveness, intelligence and rationality. Secondly, there was the notion of understanding as being an act of insight that grasps intelligible relations in phantasm, with the insight then being expressed by a concept, and not the other way around.

10. Consciousness and Self-Knowledge

At this point, it is helpful to clarify Lonergan's distinction between consciousness and self-knowledge, a distinction that separates him from most other scholars. Importantly, he rejects (1992, 344) the notion that consciousness is a manner of looking into oneself. He finds that, just as knowing is often confused with looking, consciousness is similarly confused with knowing, so that consciousness is often misconceived as an inward look.

Lonergan (1992, 344) furthermore holds that consciousness is an essential factor in human knowing, but that it is neither identical with, nor analogical to, knowing. As Michael Vertin helpfully clarifies (Lamb 1981, 416, 420), Lonergan holds consciousness to be a primitive, non-reflexive internal experience and awareness of self. To assist us in grasping this notion of consciousness, Lonergan directs our attention (1992, 344-45) to the difference between cognitional acts, such as seeing, hearing, imagining, and insight; and their corresponding cognitional contents, colour, sound, image, and idea. In this light, consciousness is meant as an awareness that is immanent in the cognitional acts. Thus, to affirm consciousness is not just to affirm that cognitional process involves a series of contents, but that it involves a succession of cognitional acts. Consciousness, then, is the primitive, as yet not understood self-awareness immanent in these intentional acts.

To further help us in grasping the idea of consciousness, Lonergan (1992, 345) distinguishes the conscious character of intentional acts from the unconscious nature of other human acts, such as cellular metabolism and our organs' maintenance. Both varieties of acts are quite human. Conscious acts, however, such as hearing and seeing, are not just responses to stimuli, they are intentional responses that involve becoming aware of the stimuli such as sights and sounds. It is important to note that in conscious acts, there are not just the contents of the acts, but there are the conscious intentional acts from which one appropriates those contents. This notion of consciousness is consistent with a rejection of the Platonist position, which holds to a notion of a passive intellect coming into confrontation with subsistent ideas. Lonergan's view of consciousness accords with his acceptance of Aristotle's view of the human intellect, as being active, reasoning and intentional.

For Lonergan, consciousness is a non-reflexive awareness of cognitional acts. It is an instance of experience. He clarifies though (1988, 209), that experience can be internal or external. External experience, with which we would be more familiar, is of the apprehended external object, such as a sight or sound. Internal experience is an awareness of one's own activities as an intentional operator.

In the affirmation of consciousness as an experience of intentional acts, we can now understand the clear distinction between consciousness and self-knowledge. Human knowledge is a compound of experience, understanding and judgement. Lonergan accordingly notes (1990, 227) that self-knowledge involves the affirmation of a reply to the question, "Am I a knower?" That is, "Is there an I, a unity that perceives, understands and judges?" There is a shift here, he maintains (1998, 209-10; 1992, 558), from the conscious subject as self-present, to the self-presence of oneself as an object of inquiry. In such self-objectification, one first experiences oneself as simply conscious. Intelligence then operates upon this internal experience of one's operations, gaining insight into such operating, and formulating it. Then, in rationally reflecting and affirming, one judges that one is rationally conscious and that one is a knower. Such operating, Lonergan notes (1990, 140), is thinking upon oneself, where one is both subject and object. For example, as one intelligently acting, I am a conscious subject, but as intelligently understanding my operating, I am an object. Self-knowledge then, is a process of going from oneself as conscious, subjectively self-present, to objectifying such consciousness, understanding it, and reasonably affirming such conscious knowing to be so. In short, self-knowledge is an objectification of the conscious self. That objectification and affirmation, as Doran points out (1990, 66) does not result in mere factual affirmation, rather, it affirms the task and value of the knowing subject, and affirms the value of that knower and what one's authentic self would be.

ii. Moral Decision

Lonergan (1974, 168) introduces the idea of a fourth, existential level of human intentionality. It is on the level of what Tallon (1997, 18) helpfully calls "volitional consciousness." This level lies beyond a bare knowledge of what is real, by realising that above and beyond questions of intelligent understanding and reasonable judgement on facts, there are further questions of deliberation. Such questions go beyond the affirmation "This is true" to the question, "What am I going to do about it?" (Doran 1995, 1:406-7) There are questions of value that affect not just what we know to be real, but what we deliberate over, evaluate, decide for or against, and act upon—for in volitional consciousness, knowledge leads to action (Tallon 1997, 23). Beyond the cognitive knowledge gained by experience, understanding and judgement, human intentionality becomes moral, asking if its object is truly worthwhile, truly good, or not (Lonergan 1994, 104).

Lonergan (1994, 268) identifies this level of intentionality with decision, that is, decision about for whom and what one is for, and for whom and what one is against. The level of decision arises, we note, because the knowledge of the real gained by judgement presents us with manifold objects, which are often in conflict. The level of decision then, selects from these manifold objects which are truly good and compatible with human authenticity, and which are not. On the good, it helps to note Doran's point (1995 1:72) that a distinct notion of the good was a development in Lonergan's thought that was present in *Method*, but not in *Insight*.

Lonergan argues (1994, 37) that the level of decision involves judgements of value. He emphasises that such judgements of value, while sharing the same structure as judgements of fact, have a different content. To clarify this point, Tallon's analogy (1997, 200, 208) is helpful—"insight is to truth what feeling is to value." The difference in content is evident if we consider that we can approve of the value of something that does not exist. However, one can decide in the negative and disapprove of the value of something, the existence of which one can reasonably affirm. The structure of both sorts of judgements is identical, Lonergan asserts, in the distinction of criterion and meaning. In both, the criterion is the self-transcendence of the intending subject, who goes beyond oneself in matters of fact to moral truth in judgements of value, but cognitive truth in matters of fact. In both types of judgement, the meaning is also held to be independent of the subject, that is, with judgements of fact affirming what is or is not so, and judgements of value affirming what is or is not truly good.

The structure of judgements of value is also similar to judgements of fact in that the judgement does not rely on one act, or a series of similar acts, but a compound of different, but dynamically related acts. In the first place, Lonergan notes (1994, 38) that there is the knowledge of reality. That is, there is the knowledge of the thing upon which we are deciding. Secondly, there are intentional responses to values, which come from the apprehension of value perceived by the subject in the object of decision. The apprehensions are not given in strictly cognitive terms, Lonergan explains, but in feelings, which are intentional responses to values. Thus moral decision, the operation of will is analogous to, but not identical to cognition. Thus the will's dependence upon feeling parallels, but is not identical to intellect's dependence upon phantasm (Tallon 1997, 123). Lonergan further explains that such apprehensions occur in a field of intentional responses that regard the qualitative value, "of beauty, of understanding, of truth, of noble deeds, of virtuous acts, of great achievements." It is helpful to note that Lonergan would not exclude feelings from other levels of intentional consciousness. Tallon clarifies (1997, 204-5) that feeling "is analogous to the level of consciousness on and in which it is experienced," ranging from the simple physical experiences of empirical consciousness through to the affective acts and states reached on the fourth level of consciousness.

The third element in the judgement of value arises in the thrust of the subject toward moral being, or self-transcendence, as Lonergan puts it (1994, 38), that is caused by the judgement of value itself. That is, the judgement of value drives the subject not just into grasping an authentic judgement of value, but one is driven to acting in accord with that judgement of value. It is this driving and subsequent acting that leads one to the existential discovery of oneself as a moral being. One becomes intentionally conscious, on the fourth level of human intentionality. One becomes conscious of one's choosing between different courses of action, and thereby making oneself an authentic human being or an unauthentic one. Accordingly, Lonergan calls the fourth level of human intentionality, whereby one judges upon values and acts in accord with them, the level of being responsible. Thus, just as intellectual conversion leads us to becoming self-transcending subjects of truth, moral conversion brings us to being self-transcending subjects of value (Tallon 1997, 205).

It is worthwhile to note that Lonergan explains (1994, 36) that judgements of value are not only simple, such as a certain object being either truly or only apparently good. Judgements of value can also be comparative, in saying that one is better or more important than another.

12. Being in Love

Those of us who have at one time or another done what is right, without necessarily having felt affectionate about that action, would understand Lonergan's point that there remains another level of human intentionality beyond that of responsibly deciding for what is right. He finds this level to be "being-in-love" with the intended object. The problem of conceiving and writing about this level of human intentionality, as Lonergan wrote in 1943 (1988, 23), arises from the essential concreteness of love, and the complexity of the concrete. It is also a fact that through the history of philosophy, questions about cognition have been far more prominent that efforts to explain feelings and emotions (Tallon 1997, 201). Doran notes (1990, 9, 30-31) that substantial references to being-in-love, or affective conversion appear relatively late in Lonergan's writings, and that his acknowledgement of a fifth level of consciousness occurs only after *Method* and only in "brief" and "offhand manner." Yet Doran also finds love becoming increasingly central in Lonergan's post-*Method* writings, as found in his *Third Collection* (1985b). We are further limited by Lonergan's not really discussing what love is, most certainly not to the extent that he has explained understanding. We are thus left to speculate what he may have said on the topic, though one may endorse the work of Doran (1990, 1995) and Tallon (1997), which we have found helpful in building upon Lonergan's work, and in which one may find the differentiation of affective conversion and its integration with cognition and volition.

Despite these limits, we do find some helpful clarifications regarding the character of "being-in-love," the first of which is that Lonergan does not situate love in the cognitive or rational realm. As Tallon points out (1997, 212-13) with reference to Barry Miller, love is not restricted by the limits of knowledge as such, love comes from what we are, rather than what we know. Taking inspiration from Blaise Pascal (1966, iv.22/n423), Lonergan (1994, 129) identifies love with the heart's reasons that reason does not understand. He thus identifies reason with the triple cord of experience, understanding and judgement. The "heart's reasons," however, are intentional responses to value. He explains that further to the factual knowledge gained in human cognition, there is a "knowledge" gained by a person discerning value and being in love with an object. This means, as Tallon writes (1997, 200), that affective consciousness does not intend knowledge, in the strictest sense. What is intended is not truth or fact *per se*, but value, which is parallel to, but not identical to the intention of truth. Pascal's "heart's reasons" are not understood by "reason" because the "knowledge" of love is affective and nonconceptual (Tallon 1997, 222).

Authentic being-in-love leads one to self-surrender to the loved object. This means in the first place, that in a manner paralleling understanding, love is not being affected by contrast or confrontation, but it is an identity with the beloved. It is the radical discovery of one's suitable proportion or affinity with another (Tallon 1997, 222). Thus, when "falling in love" the lover finds a new beginning in the beloved, and one's world undergoes radical transformation, in which "we evaluate and decide and act differently, we judge and understand our world differently, and we even experience our world differently (Tallon 1997, 239). Where such loving is authentic, Lonergan notes (1994, 242) that in surrendering oneself to the lovable, one finds deep peace, joy and fulfilment in the beloved. This is a point that is not lost on any of us who have fallen in, and (hopefully) remained in love.

The dynamic state of being-in-love, Lonergan explains (1974, 172), becomes a first principle in human living. As noted before, it dismantles one's old horizon and establishes a new horizon in which one's values and knowing take on a new perspective, a perspective or horizon in which one surrenders to or identifies with and makes one's own authentic values which one does not seek to distort (Tallon 1997, 211). Lonergan hastens to note though (1994, 242), that such being-in-love does not nullify the products of reason or moral decision. Rather, it includes them within a higher context and purpose. Thus, as Tallon notes (1997, 133), affection, volition and cognition can be brought into a "higher operational synthesis." To illustrate this point Lonergan cites (1994, 39) Augustine's *"Ama Deum et fac quod vis."* In the measure that one loves God, one's judgements of value and moral decisions will be made in the light of that love. Accordingly, Augustine counsels us to feel safe in our deciding, for if one loves God, one may do as one pleases. One would clarify that such an approach does not lead to an uncritical pietism. Rather, such loving is more correctly termed by Doran (1995 1:32) "precritical." It is a love that leads to, not flees from, moral decision and rationality. The operation of such love is explained by Aquinas (*Summa Theologiae* II-II, q45,a2), as noted by Tallon (1997, 201-2). A right judgement may come about by the use of reason, or one may arrive at that judgement by one's affinity or fellowship with God. He thus esteemed the man who could not only learn about divine things, but also "suffer them," for such activity resulted from the charitable love in which one is united with God.

A final, but pertinent, point on the level of being-in-love, is that Lonergan situates religious faith on this level. Faith, he holds (1994, 115), "is the knowledge born of religious love." It is a "knowledge" we hold, in the same manner as that described by Aquinas above. Lonergan explicitly identifies such knowledge born of religious love with the trans-cognitive reasons that Pascal outlined in his *Pensées.* He elsewhere (1974, 162) distinguishes such faith from religious belief, which is found in the cognitive knowledge of a religion, and by doing so, he finds that religion, and theology, can be emancipated from the rationalistic need to prove the truths of a religion from reason or history.

13. FORMAL DYNAMISM AND SUBLATION IN HUMAN INTENTIONALITY

It is important to remember that the intentional pattern described above is formally dynamic. Each part of the whole calls forth, supplies the material for, and is complemented by, the next part (Lonergan 1994, 13). Lonergan explains (1988, 206-2; 1992, 300) that each intentional act is incomplete when it is not complemented by the contents of subsequent levels. Conversely, the subsequent acts are quite meaningless without the content of the antecedent acts. We come to grasp then, the formally dynamic structure of human intentionality. It is a self-constituting, self-assembling process.

The dependence of each component upon antecedent acts is highlighted when Lonergan reminds us (1994, 13) that for the human spirit, "To know the good, it must know the real; to know the real, it must know the true; to know the true, it must know the intelligible; to know the intelligible, it must attend to data." However, the dependence also works in the reverse, upward order. For our attending is but gaping if it is not complemented by inquiry. Inquiry leads to the delight of insight, but, as Lonergan puts it, "insights are a dime a dozen." Reflective understanding is called for, to verify the truth of our insights. When we have settled the true, we are faced with alternative courses of action, and so we consider which is truly good. Thus, each intentional act remains incomplete and dependent upon the higher acts in order to gain their full significance and meaning.

Lonergan explains (1994, 241) that he does not mean us to understand that the higher levels of intentional consciousness diminish or demean the lower ones. Rather, their relationship can be conceived in the manner of sublation. He does not mean sublation as Hegel would have conceived it, as when the higher view reconciles a contradiction present in the lower level, but Lonergan aligns himself, with Rahner's position, whereby

> what sublates goes beyond what is sublated, introduces something new and distinct, puts everything on a new basis, yet so far from interfering with the sublated or destroying it, on the contrary needs it, includes it, preserves all its proper features and properties, and carries them forward to a fuller realization within a richer context.

By way of example, we note that within cognitional structure, intelligence goes beyond sensitive attentiveness, but it cannot get by without that sensitivity. Similarly, judgement transcends both attentiveness and intelligence, and completes them, but again judgement cannot operate except in accord with them (Lonergan 1974, 80). So too, moral decision sublates cognitive knowledge. Moral decision goes beyond the one value, truth, to values in general, and promotes the subject from cognitional to moral authenticity. The subject still needs truth, however, for without the true, the real, one cannot respond to its value. So too, being-in-love sublates moral decision and cognitive knowledge. These are preserved by love, but now, as Lonergan puts it (1994, 241-42), they are caught up and furthered by a cosmic context and purpose where there accrues the power of a person to love, and give oneself for the true and the good.

We thus find that each of the higher levels of intentional consciousness sublates the lower, in no way diminishing the purpose or value of the lower levels, but presupposing them, complementing them, and bringing them to fruition. We should note that Lonergan's account of sublation reflects his turn to the subject, in what is more properly called an intentionality analysis, because it accounts for more than just a cognitional analysis (Doran 1995 1:241). That there are different, related and sublating levels of human intentionality is in no way due to differences in the objects being beheld, for one intends the same object. What is different on each level is the specific act of the human subject. The relationship between intellectual, moral and religious conversion is due not to the objects, but because of the one conscious subject. The different intentional levels are, as Lonergan writes (1974, 130), "distinct phases in the unfolding of the human spirit [human subject]." They work together in the one conscious subject in what Tallon calls (1997, 212) an "operational synthesis."

The reality of the sublation of different intentional acts and the priority of moral and religious conversion over intellectual conversion reveal Lonergan's simple, yet important point (1994, 340), that "the speculative intellect or pure reason is just an abstraction." He stresses that the process of reason, experience, understanding and judgement, no matter how scientific or philosophical, do not occur in a moral or affective void. Human reason, he continues, involves the operations of a subject who has made a moral decision regarding the pursuit of understanding and truth, and who, in varying degrees of success maintains fidelity to one's commitment. The life of pure intellect, then, is a fiction. To live under the operation of reason uninfluenced by moral decision, Lonergan notes (1994, 122), would be "something less than the life of a psychopath." This point is reinforced by Tallon's observation (1997, 123-24) that the real human self is triune consciousness, and that cognition, affection and volition are as inseparable and interrelated as they are distinct. There remains, however, a prejudiced myth that higher intelligence leads to human consciousness' unbinding from the emotions (Tallon 1997, 2). This myth is overcome by Lonergan's model, further support for which we find in the observation of neuroscience that when patients have their affective abilities damaged, their rational ability suffers likewise. It seems, in Tallon's words (1997, 8) that "[r]educed affection meant defective thinking and deciding."

14. REPLIES TO DISPUTES

Does there really exist an intelligent subject, who operates on the distinct levels of intentional consciousness described above? Lonergan directly confronts those denying that human intentionality exists in the manner in which he has described it. This confrontation takes the strategy of *Insight*, but in reverse. That is, *Insight* (1992, 11) was not so much a prescription of human knowing's nature, but an invitation to discover one's own intellectual operations within onself. Lonergan challenges those who would dispute his intentionality analysis by inviting them to discover within themselves what would happen if they denied the pattern of intentional acts, which he describes. The success of such a challenge would, as Tallon notes (1997, 23) show the value of Lonergan's theory as self-verifiable.

Lonergan (1988, 210; 1994, 17) challenges positivists and behaviourists to admit that they have never had the experience of seeing, hearing, touching, smelling tasting, imagining or perceiving. Alternatively, if such people claim to appear to have such experiences, would they hold that such experience was merely apparent, because their whole lives had been spent like a sleep walker, utterly unaware of one's own experiences? He also issues to positivists the challenge to admit that they had never experienced intellectual inquiry, or coming to understanding and expressing that understanding. Could even relativists, he asks, admit that never had they experienced the act of making a rational judgement? Would a determinist, he lastly demands, deny that one had ever acted responsibly? Lonergan means that a denial of the verity of his intentionality analysis would be an effective denial of one's own humanity.

Lonergan (1994, 16-17) explicitly argues that one who denied the levels of intentional consciousness, which he proposes, would have to disqualify "himself as a non-responsible, non-reasonable, non-intelligent somnambulist." Meynell (1989, 208) puts the argument this way:

> It might be objected that the 'transcendental precepts' are simply not applicable to all areas of inquiry. But this objection does not stand up to examination. The physicist, the sociologist and the historian all, in the course of their investigations, have to decide responsibly to attend to evidence, to accept provisionally the account which best fits that evidence, and so on. No more in organic chemistry than in palaeontology does one advance towards the truth by brushing relevant data aside. (One may well create more favorable prospects for oneself; or gratify those in a position to advance one's career; but that is another matter.) In cosmology, just as much as in ancient history, one has to be at once bold and ingenious in formulating hypotheses (intelligent), and stringent in testing them against the available evidence (reasonable.)

We find within this sharp rebuttal, a reflection of the point with which we opened this chapter, namely that Lonergan's intentionality analysis has a strong empirical base. Like Newman's account of human knowing, the strength of Lonergan's theory is that people can examine their own cognitional operations and discover within themselves the activities that he describes. The alternative to this self-discovery and self-appropriation would seem to be the loss of self that Doran (1990, 461) finds within postmodernism.

Lonergan (1994, 18-19) makes four points to meet the challenge of one who would grant that his intentionality analysis is valid, but could be substantially revised. First, a revision of the analysis must appeal to data to which one had not previously adverted, thus using the empirical level of operations. Secondly, a revision would offer a better explanation of such data, thus presupposing an intelligent level of operating. Thirdly, a revision would claim that the revised model is true, or at least more probable, thus presupposing a rational level. Fourthly, a revision would promote itself as being more worthwhile than the previous model, so that there would be presupposed a fourth, responsible level. It follows then, Lonergan writes, that the normative pattern of operations does not admit of revisions, and any attempt to revise it, would, in fact, be making use of the already verified operations.

15. The Notion of Transcendental Method

It remains now to clarify what Lonergan means by *transcendental* method. He (1994, 11, 13-14) first contrasts transcendental notions to categories, and follows scholastic usage in finding the categorical, or predicamental, to be concerned with determinations. That is, categories: have a restricted denotation, vary from culture to culture, are concerned with putting determinate questions and with giving determinate answers. Transcendental notions are thus opposed to categories, because "transcendentals are comprehensive in connotation, unrestricted in denotation, invariant over cultural change." Moreover, rather than with the content of questions and answers, transcendental notions are concerned with the intending that is prior to any answers. Transcendental notions thus constitute intending of the human spirit, that is, the pure desire that moves us from ignorance to knowledge, moral decision and love. They are, Lonergan notes, *a priori*, because transcendental notions move us beyond what we do know to what we seek to know and do not yet know. Furthermore, they are comprehensive, because they intend the unknown whole of which our present answers only reveal a part.

The pattern of intentional operations, which Lonergan has described, is therefore a *transcendental* method. It is a method because it meets his

(1994, 4, 5, 125) definition of method as a recurrent pattern of related operations that yield cumulative and progressive results. It is transcendental because, as already noted, its results are not categorically confined and because they are unrestricted, the transcendental notions can intend any result. Lonergan (1994, 13-14) importantly emphasises the universality of this method, for, while other methods aim at the contingencies and needs of particular fields, transcendental method is concerned with the exigencies of the human mind itself, that investigates any, and all, fields of human inquiry.

There are three key functions of Lonergan's (1994, 20, 53) transcendental method that should be borne in mind. First, transcendental method makes specific the transcendental precepts: be attentive, be intelligent, be reasonable, be responsible. These precepts concisely state the demands that transcendental method places on the authentically acting person. These are to be: attentive by being open to the data provided by experience, intelligent by intending questions and forming understandings of our experience, reasonable by judging upon the truth or falsity of our understandings and responsible by morally deciding upon the value of the real known in judgement. Lonergan maintains that the transcendental precepts exist in the spontaneous dynamic structure of authentic human consciousness. They exist even before they are spoken of. Importantly, they may not be known or acknowledged under these names by all cultures, seeing as they exist in consciousness prior to their being formulated and expressed in words. That is, the precepts exist, but whatever names by which they may be called is a matter of cultural diversity. Another way of considering the transcendental precepts is that they give expression to the guiding desire, or *eros* in authentically acting human beings.

This function of transcendental method helps to clarify a misconception. If, as this writer has observed (Ogilvie 1997, 37-41), Lonergan's stated transcendental precepts include the precept to be attentive, it is bewildering that Karen Armstrong (1994, 441) should write that "Bernard Lonergan also emphasised the importance of transcendence and of thought as opposed to experience ... In all cultures, human beings have been driven by the same imperatives: to be intelligent, responsible, reasonable, loving and, if necessary, change." Armstrong not only misorders Lonergan's transcendental precepts, she omits the precept "be attentive." Moreover, her statement ignores Lonergan's (1988, 207) point that, "To pass judgement independently of all experience is to set fact aside." Armstrong's statement is similar to Tracy's (1970, 4) statement of "the 'transcendental' imperatives 'be intelligent, be reasonable, be responsible, be loving, develop and, if necessary, change.'" From this statement, Armstrong may have taken the impression that Lonergan advocates certain transcendental "imperatives," which exclude being attentive. Despite misgivings we may have over calling the transcendental precepts "imperatives," we note that, in the same book, Tracy does (1970, 228, 231, 237) in fact refer to Lonergan's transcendental precept, "be attentive."

Returning to its functions, transcendental method secondly ensures continuity by assuring us of basic terms and relations. But it does not impose rigidity, for it does not impose a system on a thinker, but, it simply heightens one's attention to a set of operations that already exists (Lonergan 1994, 21). Thirdly, transcendental method guides and brings to light the heuristic process in transforming an unknown into a known. Between ignorance, and knowing, Lonergan notes (1994, 22), is an intending, and transcendental method is that intending.

At this point, we note the common misconception that Lonergan uses "transcendental" in a purely Kantian sense. It is held, for example, that Lonergan's method is based on imperatives that are transcendental in the sense of being *a priori* structures within the subject. Lonergan explains (1994, 14n4), however, that this is not quite the manner in which he intends "transcendental" to be taken:

> Here, the word transcendental, is employed in a sense analogous to Scholastic usage, for it is opposed to the categorical (or predicamental). But my actual procedure is also transcendental in The Kantian sense, inasmuch as it brings to light the conditions of the possibility of knowing an object in so far as that knowledge is *a priori*.

Accordingly, he insists that he uses "transcendental" in both the Scholastic and Kantian senses. Alongside this clear statement, we also find that Lonergan spends three paragraphs over pages eleven to fourteen in *Method* explaining how he opposes "transcendental" method to the categorical, thus employing a Scholastic usage, as well as a Kantian usage. It seems inaccurate then, to write as if Lonergan meant transcendental in an exclusively Kantian sense. Also, if Lonergan uses "transcendental" method in the sense of being opposed to the "categorical," it is doubly mistaken to believe that Lonergan presents a "categorical framework" as suggested by Mary Hesse (Corcoran 1975, 60).

We note, with Lonergan (1994, 282), that transcendental method is the transcultural method for which he had been searching. He acknowledges that the explicit formulation of transcendental method is not transcultural. However, the realities that transcendental method affirms are transcultural and universal. For, whatever the activities are called, all people value being attentive, intelligent, reasonable and responsible.

Unfortunately, this is precisely the point Nicholas Lash misses (Corcoran 1975, 127, 133-36) when he accuses Lonergan's method of neglecting "cultural discontinuity." Even though he acknowledges that Lonergan manifests a serious awareness of cultural diversity and development, Lash argues (Corcoran 1975, 127, 135) that Lonergan fails to provide a categorical framework within which inter-cultural communication would be possible. Because "transcendental method *is* transcendental, and not categorical," Lash complains that Lonergan does not tell us how to "transpose propositions" from one cultural context to another. But Lash fails to acknowledge the strength of Lonergan's transcendental method, which is to identify cognitional activities undertaken by people in all cultures. By finding a pattern of intentional operations common to all people, Lonergan provides a key starting point for intercultural communication. Lonergan does not do this by specifying categories, which are limited to certain cultures. Moreover, to specify categories for communication would betray Lonergan's aims to have theologians discover intentional operations within their own consciousness, and to attain independence in their theology. Lonergan did not intend to have people attain transcultural communications by following another person's model, or by blindly following another's method. Rather, Lonergan's transcendental method allows one to cross cultural divides: first by helping one to identify one's own cognitional operations and secondly, by helping one to identify those same operations in other people, even though the categories with which those operations may vary. Contrary to Lash's statements, Lonergan takes cultural diversity very seriously, it was a key motivation behind his *Method in Theology* (1994, xi, xii, 7, 344).

Having noted how his transcendental method is not strictly Kantian, we should also note that, in a general sense, Lonergan holds (1985b 83) his method to be post-Kantian. His method does not consider only an object of inquiry, nor is it only concerned with the inquiring subject. Lonergan's transcendental method is concerned with both the subject and the object in themselves and with their dependent relationship with the other. A post-Kantian transcendental method

> embraces in their complementarity *both* man as attentive, as intelligent,
> as reasonable, as responsible *and* the human world as given and as

structured by intelligence, by reasonable judgement, by decision and action (Lonergan 1985b 82).

As we have indicated before, this method is a transcendental method. Within such a method, all of a subject's cognitional operations would be recognised, and related. A transcendental method does not only account only for the object of cognition. Furthermore, in a post-Kantian manner, the transcendental method does not refer only to the *a priori* of the subject. This method refers to both object, and subject. In the first place, there is the *a priori* of the subject's questions. Secondly, Lonergan explains (1985b, 76) that a transcendental method would apply itself "to the range of objects disclosed in answers." We note that Lonergan's turn to the subject is illustrated here by the heuristic definition of his transcendental method, with such a definition being founded upon the subject who asks questions. We further note that, while the object is still given its due attention, the object is regarded in the light of being the object disclosed by the answers given to a subject's questions.

16. CONCLUSION

Lonergan's intentionality analysis is characterised by its empirical base. It is a concrete investigation of what human intellect actually does, not what it logically could be in any abstract sense. This intentionality analysis and transcendental method is thus both modern and scientific, inasmuch as it deals with the concrete, observable, and empirically verifiable operations of human intellect. In this regard, Lonergan is more concrete in his account of intellect than either Aristotle, whose pure theory of intellect can be found in his account of separate substances, or Aquinas, whose pure theory of intellect is found in his account of angelic knowledge.

This point is missed in Patrick McGrath's criticism (Corcoran 1975, 34-35) of Lonergan's cognitional theory as being what Wittgenstein called "language gone on holiday." McGrath wonders if Lonergan has ever "examined the concept of knowing." We would reply that, instead of speculating on the concept of knowing, Lonergan has made a concrete and empirically verifiable study of what knowing is. Rather than analysing concepts, Lonergan's concern with knowing is with human knowing's concrete activities. As Meynell notes, such an enterprise is most valuable. McGrath's argument, Meynell retorts (1976, 51), is akin to encouraging the pursuit of ornithology "by examining the concept of a greenfinch."

Lonergan's intentionality analysis also meets other criteria of modern thought. By explaining the operations of human intellect, he meets Kant's challenge to account for the conditions of possibility for human knowledge. Moreover, by explaining a human subject's intentional operations, Lonergan's work helps a person to attain a self-appropriation of one's own intentional consciousness. Such self-appropriation is a cardinal step in achieving intellectual autonomy.

But what specific relevance does Lonergan's intentionality analysis have to theology? In the first place, we note that his intentionality analysis yields a transcendental method that is beyond the "temporal dialectic" of any specific issue. This transcendental method provides a method which can be applied to any, and all, of the possible objects of human inquiry. Secondly, the specific application of Lonergan's intentionality analysis and transcendental method to theology is most straightforward. On the one side, transcendental method is applicable to any field of human inquiry, and so it is applicable to theology. On the other side, as Lonergan repeatedly pointed out (1994, 23-24), theologians have minds, and use them, and transcendental method is simply the account of the unfolding work of such minds.

Lonergan would never have meant to cover the full range of the human mind. As Doran points out (1990, 42ff), one may complement intentionality analysis with an account of psychic conversion. Nonetheless, Lonergan analysed human intentionality to the extent that his transcendental method could account for the operations he discovered in one's doing theology. How he did this is the object of our next chapter.

NOTE

[1] In *Insight*, (1992, 28(n1)), Lonergan refers to several articles by Hutchinson, found in Patrick Mullahy, ed. 1949. *A Study of Interpersonal Relations: New Contributions to Psychiatry*. The articles to which Lonergan makes reference are: "Varieties of Insight in Humans," (Mullahy 386-403); "The Period of Frustration in Creative Endeavour, (Mullahy 404-420); "The Nature of Insight," (Mullahy 421-445). These articles originally appeared in the journal *Psychiatry*, 2(1939):323-32; 3(1940):351-59; 4(1941):31-43.

As mentioned in the editor's notes to *Insight*, (1992) 28n1, Lonergan does not mention either Hutchinson's "The Period of Elaboration in Creative Endeavour," *Psychiatry*, 5(1942):165-76; or "The Phemonenon of Insight in Relation to Religion," *Psychiatry*, 6(1943):347-357. We further note that the editors of the "Collected Works" edition of *Insight* do not mention Hutchinson's fifth article in the series, "The Phenomenon of Insight in Relation to Education," *Psychiatry*, 5(1942):499-507.

It is also of interest that Hutchinson's work was prompted by an earlier article, which offered many other examples of insight. cf. Washington Platt and Ross A. Baker, "The Relation of the Scientific 'Hunch' to Research," *Journal of Chemical Education* 8(1931):1969-2002.

Chapter 6
Lonergan's Method in Theology

To complete the background to systematics, we shall now pursue a general investigation of Lonergan's theological method, as expressed in *Method in Theology*. We intend to discover the notion of theology with which he worked and his vision for a renewed theological method. We also intend to outline the different functional specialties and the reason for their division. After having understood Lonergan's theological method, we shall be in a strong position from which to understand the functional specialty, systematics.

1. Lonergan's Notion of Theology

Within the classicist framework, as exemplified by Ott (1974, 1), theology is conceived in terms of its formal and material objects, namely, God and all things in relation to God. Lonergan (1994, xi), however, takes a different, functional, perspective towards theology, conceiving it according to its purpose, to mediate "between a cultural matrix and the significance and role of a religion in that matrix."

In the first place, this notion of theology means that a theology is not identified with its religion. Rather, Lonergan (1994, xi) conceives theology functionally, as having the task of communicating to a culture to which a religion addresses itself an understanding and appreciation of a religion and its role. Secondly, Lonergan's notion of theology means that a theology should be both required and able to be developed into a form that is relevant to the culture to which it is addressed. This point is reflected by Rahner's (1978, 7) observation that "Every theology, of course, is always a theology which arises out of the secular anthropologies and self-interpretations of man. ... Hence this situation too necessarily produces an immense pluralism of theologies." Thirdly, this notion of theology differs again from the classicist conception of theology, which conceives both culture and theology statically and thus concerns itself with the nature of theology. A classicist would consider theology to follow science and culture in being a permanent and certain attainment. In such a system, one can only reflect upon an object's nature. Lonergan points out (1994, xi), though, that those who share his empirical notion of culture would be more disposed towards concern with theology's method. From an empirical viewpoint, theology would, like science and culture, be thought of as ongoing and cumulative. Moreover, within a modern, empirical horizon, theologians would have to establish the conditions of possibility for their science and for their method, they would have to provide for an ongoing enterprise, which used an empirically established set of operations.

2. LONERGAN'S INTENTIONS FOR A THEOLOGICAL METHOD

At this stage, it would help our understanding of Lonergan's theological method if we were to review his aspirations for a method in theology. As we found earlier, Lonergan had expressed the need for a renewed and adequate theological method when he wrote his doctoral thesis (1985a, 10-12). Later, in his article "Theology and Understanding" (1988, 129), he explicitly focussed his search for a theological method upon the intellectual operations of a theological subject, believing that a method would simply be human reason's own specific account of the principles governing its own operations. Lonergan's *Insight*, accordingly, was written not just as a work on human understanding, even though it stands as a respectable work in its own right. He (1974, 268) began writing *Insight* with the intention of exploring methods so as to prepare for a study of theological methods. Lonergan's goal (1974, 52) was to find a method in theology that was based on the consistent intellectual operations of those who did theology. He sought for a method that made explicit the conscious, intentional operations of theologians.

We note that, by basing his theological method on the operations of human intellect, Lonergan accounted for a genuine source of continuity in theology. However, he did not view continuity in a classicist fashion, by seeking uniform concepts and words. Rather, Lonergan would mean that the drive for people to be attentive, intelligent, reasonable, responsible and in love brings a certain continuity to theology. The drive towards "authenticity" leads to the excision of counter-positions, the search for truth rather than error, and the desire to increase human understanding. The normative, or universal, nature of human intentionality leads to a union or continuity in theology. This means that theology does not need rigid controls on the expressions or concepts it uses. Such "police work" cannot maintain genuine continuity, it keeps only a facade of homogeneity. Genuine continuity is achieved by systematics when it realises that people of different times and places operate under the same normative structure of intentional consciousness. One thus seeks for continuity, not in concepts, but in the cognitional operations of different peoples and times. This work is more difficult, but in the long term, it is more productive and more genuine. Moreover, we find that intentional consciousness seeks to build upon past achievement. While this also implies development, it means that contemporary work is linked to, and continuous with, the past (Lonergan 1994, 326-27, 351-52).

Lonergan brought his methodological ambitions to fulfilment in *Method in Theology*. Most importantly, we observe that *Method in Theology* is an explication of the human mind's working in doing theology. In this work, Lonergan (1994, xii, 24) returned to an old theme by noting that "theologians always have had minds and always have used them." He intended his theological method to be a specific theological application of the general transcendental method, which was based upon an intentionality analysis. He accordingly wrote *Method in Theology* with the intention to lead readers in discovering their own dynamic structure of operations, which exists within their own cognitive, moral and affective beings when they do theology.

It is crucial to appreciate that Lonergan's theological method is in fact a method, and neither another resource for theology's contents, nor a solution to any particular problem. His concern in *Method in Theology* (1994, xii, 24, 254) was with neither the content, nor the objects of theology, but with theology's method. By making explicit the operations of the theologian, Lonergan intended to add clarity, intelligbility and precision to the theologian's tasks. He did this by outlining what human authenticity was, in relation to theological activity. A theological method, he argued, would take its power in showing how to appeal to human authenticity. We find implied within this statement, a notion of a theological method's authority, namely, to evaluate the degree to which a theologian is operating with human authenticity.

3. Lonergan's Notion of Method

Having written about the theological method for which Lonergan sought, it remains for us to clarify what he meant by using the term "method." In *Method in Theology* (1994, 4, 5, 125), he referred to method as "a normative pattern of recurrent and related operations yielding cumulative and progressive results." He (1994, 4) expanded upon, and clarified, the notion of method, explaining that one has a method when:
(1) There are distinct operations,
(2) each operation is related to the others,
(3) the relations form a pattern,
(4) the pattern is verified as the correct way of performing the task,
(5) the pattern's operations may be repeated indefinitely,

(6) the results of such repetition are cumulative and progressive.

In a specifically theological context, Lonergan explained (1994, 125) that putting method into theology would mean conceiving theology as "a set of related and recurrent operations cumulatively advancing towards an ideal goal."

We acknowledge Hesse's criticism of Lonergan for basing his notion of method supposedly upon the notion that science yields progressively better results. Hesse claims (Corcoran 1975, 62) that such a position "was only an unstable resting point between classical nineteenth-century confidence and late twentieth-century scepticism and relativism." However, with Meynell (1976, 52), we would argue that, regardless of the plethora of relativistic philosophies of science, scientists in the real world do, and will, continue to seek after what is in fact so. We have found no text-book of science that prefaces its contents by explaining that it in no way attempts to explain what is real.

We must emphasise that it would be mistaken to think that, with his method, Lonergan attempted to impose upon his readers a procedure that he had deduced from supposed principles of theology. On the contrary, this method is an exposition of a set of operations, which he has discovered within authentic theology. Where did Lonergan discover these operations? Although he did not draw explicit attention to his own achievements, it is clear that *Method in Theology* was based on his inquiry into his own theological and philosophical career. In that light, we understand the significance of Lonergan's point (1994, 3) that what often counts, when method is thought of as an art, is the example of the master. The source of all thought on method, he continued, must always be a reflection upon a master's example, the students' efforts to emulate the master, and the master's evaluation of the students' performances. We also note that Lonergan did not expect his readers to unintelligently follow a set of prescribed operations. Rather, his invitation was for readers to attend to their own conscious activities and to find within themselves the conscious operations that he described. Lonergan wrote that (1994, 7) "He [the reader] will have to evoke the relevant operations in his own consciousness. He will have to discover in his own experience the dynamic relationships leading from one operation to the next." Were a reader to fail in Lonergan's invitation to self-appropriation of one's conscious activities, one would find Lonergan's reflections on method "about as illuminating as a blind man finds a lecture on color."

The foregoing reflections indicate that, for Lonergan, method is not dictated purely by the objects of its investigations. Rather, method is concerned with the conscious operations of the subject who is doing that investigating. Lonergan therefore has a notion of method as being heuristic. He conceives method in transcendental terms, as being an open structure for questions and inquiries. This is opposed to a categorical method, which would be concerned primarily with determinate objects and answers. A method, for Lonergan, would thus take the general transcendental method, and apply this general method to a specific area like theology, so that one may address the question of how, in this specific discipline, one may follow the transcendental precepts, to be: attentive, intelligent, reasonable, responsible and in love.

Before moving onto his answer to that question, we must heed a strong warning from Lonergan. Method, he emphasised (1974, 201; 1994, 5-6), is not a prescribed set of operations that can, when followed to the letter, generate acceptable results. Such a notion of method would represent a reversion to classicism's vision of a deductive system based upon notions of necessity. Lonergan's vision of method, on the other hand, is concerned with obtaining cumulative and progressive results. Such progress and accumulation of results is only possible in the light of new discovery, which is only possible when new data can be found and when synthesis is attained by adding new insights to the old. Lonergan brusquely reminds us (1994, 6) that neither discovery nor synthesis can be constantly summoned forth by rules. This point reminds us of his earlier arguments (1992, 29), that insight does not follow any rules of logic, that insight's advent is unpredictable and that insight's ease of occurrence varies between individuals. He also (1994, xi) makes the abrupt point that "Method is not a set of rules to be followed meticulously by a dolt. It is a framework for collaborative creativity." The two most important aspects of Lonergan's argument against method as a "set of rules," are creativity and discovery. Neither creativity nor discovery are subject to logic, deduction, or any rules. We note that because he conceived method as being creative, inquiring, and open to ongoing and progressive results, Lonergan has firmly broken out of the classicist framework, which saw theological method within a deductive process that drew necessary conclusions from self-evident principles.

Lonergan's notion of method, as cumulative and progressive, gave him a necessary tool with which to bring theology towards the standards of modern science. This application of method to theology, he argued (1994, 6), fostered a theological method which would not be governed by the rules of deductive logic. However, we should not be misled, though, into believing that Lonergan dismissed the true value of logic. Hesse claims

(Corcoran 1975, 72) that Lonergan rejected logic when he wrote on the Athanasian conception of consubtantiality, "'Now the meaning of this declaration is luminous'—only to a *logically trained mind* does it raise a question...(277)!" First, one is appalled at Hesse's blatant misrepresentation of Lonergan, who actually wrote (1994, 277), "Now the meaning of this declaration [from Chalcedon] is luminous, but to a logically trained mind it raises a question. Is the humanity the same as the divinity?" Clearly, Lonergan shows more concern for logic than Hesse's misquotation implies. Secondly, Lonergan never rejects logic. He simply places logic within the wider context of method. Logic, we find, is included within Lonergan's account of human intentional operations (1994, 6, 66, 72, 85, 92, 305, 353).

Rather than being bound to deductive logic, he (1974, 50) proposed a new theological method, which could encompass a recurrent set of operations, which would form a cycle of theological activities using progressively more data, and yielding increasingly more results. Lonergan's notion of method then, incorporated the process of research, which uncovers new data, provides new observations, and generates new insights that may verify or challenge old hypotheses. As he writes (1994, 5):

> The wheel of method not only turns but also rolls along. The field of observed data keeps broadening. New discoveries are added to old. New hypotheses and theories express not only the new insights but also all that was valid in the old, to give method its cumulative character and to engender the conviction that, however remote may still be the goal of the complete explanation of all phenomena, at least we now are nearer to it than we were.

It would be unfair, though, to approach such cumulative results as does Gerald O'Collins (1975, 48) by asking whether a theologian can "derive 'cumulative and progressive' results from the mass of past dogmas, so that he knows more about God than Augustine or Francis of Assisi because he has more dogmas to draw on?" He further argues that, while science can enjoy cumulative and progressive results because it relies upon progressive discoveries, theology "in its essential 'given'" cannot be increased because Christian revelation "closed with the apostolic age."

O'Collins argument does not adequately account for Lonergan's presentation of a theological method that conceives theology as both answering concrete questions and mediating a religion's value and function to a culture. He would not base his notion, of cumulative and progressive results arising from theological method, on the spurious basis that we have more dogmas upon which to draw than Augustine or Francis. Lonergan would argue, however, that human cultures have grown, progressed and raised new questions to which Christian theology should address itself. By way of example, we can propose that neither Francis nor Augustine ever provided a theological reflection upon nuclear warfare. The question simply had not been raised within the saints' cultures. Modern culture, however, has presented Christian theology with the question of nuclear warfare and many responses have been given. Those responses are manifestly a progress in Christian theology. We also note, by way of pertinent example, that many responses to nuclear warfare, such as that by the National Conference of Catholic Bishops (1983, nn80-82, 144ff) have built explicitly upon Augustine's just war theory. Surely such building upon past achievement represents a cumulative and progressive result in theology.

Having attained an understanding of Lonergan's notion of method, we now turn towards an examination of his specifically theological method.

4. The Division of Functional Specialties

The most notable feature of Lonergan's theological method is his division of theology's operations into eight distinct functional specialties: research, interpretation, history, dialectic, foundations, doctrines, systematics, communications. In the first place, these functional specialties represent a response to the need for specialisation by any modern area of study, including theology. Lonergan (1994, 125) thus justified his functional specialisation of theology by arguing that contemporary theology has become specialised to the point that it can no longer be considered one set of operations, but it should be thought of as a series of independent sets of operations. It is crucial, though, that we appreciate the nature of these theological specialties as being "functional specialisations." We can better appreciate this point, by following Lonergan's outline of three distinct forms of specialisation.

First, "field specialisation" is obtained "by dividing and subdividing the field of data," so that one narrows the field of data with which one will be concerned. Such a division or selection is necessary, as Lonergan argues (1994, 125), because in modern times, with an ever-increasing volume of information available, no one can master all fields of knowledge. Even within the broad scope of "theology" no one can be an expert in Scripture, Patristics, Church History or Doctrinal Theology. Accordingly, a "division of labor" is needed, whereby scholars confine their investigations to a relatively narrow field of study.

Secondly, "subject," or "department" specialisation is obtained by arranging and dividing the results of investigations. The aim of subject specialisation corresponds to the aim of field specialisation, to provide the opportunity for deeper study of fewer details, rather than attaining superficial knowledge of many items of information. Lonergan cites (1994, 126), as examples of subject specialisation the division of Old Testament studies into: "Semitic languages, Hebrew history, the religions of the ancient Near East, and Christian theology." The key difference between the specialisations is that field specialisation divides the data to be investigated, while subject specialisation divides the results of those investigations to be taught.

The third form of specialisation, and the one in which we are more interested, is Lonergan's (1994, 126) more original contribution to specialisation, namely, functional specialisation. This specialisation divides neither data nor results, but as the term "functional specialisation" suggests, it "distinguishes and separates successive stages in the process from data to results." For example, we propose that functional specialisation would divide and organise the different tasks to be undertaken between a study of the data of the Patristic writers and the communication of what they taught about Trinitarian theology. Lonergan illustrates functional specialisation (1994, 126) with familiar examples: Textual criticism determines what is written. Interpretation, or commentary, takes over from textual criticism and determines what was meant by the text. History takes over from interpretation, and attempts to construct a unified viewpoint from the accumulated texts. We note, importantly, Lonergan's point that functional specialties are not disparate operations, they are, he argues, successive stages of a united process. Functional specialisations are operations both dynamically and intrinsically related to one another, so that earlier functional specialties remain wanting without the later. Later functional specialties also both presuppose and complement the earlier ones. "In brief," Lonergan writes (1994, 126), "functional specialties are operationally independent."

We note that Lonergan's attention to functional specialities shows his awareness that theology, just as a religion, has a function. We also find that in his notion of theology, which we earlier noted, he was equally aware that theology had a function. While classicist theologians would have been well aware of the content and nature of theology; theologians who operate within an empirical notion of culture will be very aware that their scholarship also has a function within their culture (Sharpe 1988, 14).

It would be more expedient if we left until later in this chapter, an investigation of the need for, and grounds of, functional specialisation. We turn now, to outline the eight functional specialties that Lonergan identifies within theology.

5. THE FUNCTIONAL SPECIALTIES

5.1 Research

If functional specialisation is based on dividing the process from data to results, it is fitting that Lonergan's (1994, 127) first functional specialty within theology is *research*. As a functional specialty, research is relatively easy to understand, it simply "makes available the data relevant to theological investigation." In this way, research, as a functional specialty, corresponds to the transcendental precept "be attentive to data." The aim of research is thus to gather data that can be used by subsequent theological activities.

Within the broader functional specialty, Lonergan (1994, 127) distinguishes general research from special research. He argues that general research is sweeping and, in a way, unspecified in its goals. General research is the activity that locates and retrieves previously unknown data. It fills museums and libraries with new material. It contributes to reference works such as dictionaries and encyclopedias. A possible outcome of general research, Lonergan argues, could be "a complete information-retrieval system." On the other hand, Lonergan characterises special research as an activity concerned with collecting data on a specific issue, "such as the doctrine of Mr. *X* on the question *Y*."

When *Method* was published in 1972, the notion of general research providing a complete information retrieval system may have seemed fanciful. Yet, with the growth of the "Internet" and related information storage systems, a near-complete data bank of human knowledge seems possible. However, even if the "Internet" were to contain all information known to humanity, its data would have to be interpreted, verified, and its value established. Lonergan's point, that research must be complemented by interpretation, history, dialectic and the following functional specialities, would not be lost on the "Internet" user who has wandered the electronic wastelands created by the lunatic fringe of "Internet" contributors.

We note that Lonergan does not prescribe techniques for either general or special research. In conceding to the practical and concrete, rather than theoretical, nature of research, his main advice (1994, 149) is to seek a master in the field in which one wishes to pursue research and learn from the master's example.

We also note that Lonergan's notion of the functional specialty, research, provides theological method with a properly empirical base. Furthermore, because it is heuristically defined, the range of research, under this method, is not fixed. Accordingly, Lonergan's notion allows for new data, and new discoveries, which thus contribute to the ongoing, cumulative and progressive character of his method.

5.2 Interpretation

In Lonergan's intentionality analysis and transcendental method, we found that attention to the data of experience was incomplete without the subsequent levels of intentional consciousness. Corresponding to understanding's complement of experience, Lonergan proposes (1994, 127) that the functional specialty, *interpretation*, takes over and operates upon the data of research. Interpretation is needed because the data of research provokes questions concerning matters such as: the meaning of a document within its historical context, an author's meaning in writing that text and what the author intended to say. While such an enterprise can be "replete with pitfalls," it is a necessary undertaking, which is familiar to us by its production of commentaries and monographs.

Interpretation thus seeks intelligibility within the data yielded by research. Lonergan does make the point (1994, 153-54) that the methods of interpretation, and the level of difficulty of interpretation differs from object to object. Interpretation faces the challenges of discerning what can be meant by texts that originate from other times and cultures, which to lesser or greater degrees, possess different brands of common sense, hold to different values and interests, operate within different horizons, and vary in their intellectual developments. Moreover, texts can vary in their degree of systematic presentation, so that a systematic work such as Euclid's *Elements* does not require laborious interpretation, while the less systematic Gospels arouse incalculable commentators. In brief, by seeking the meaning of the data provided by research, the functional specialty, interpretation, corresponds to understanding in general transcendental method.

5.3 History

While the interpretation of texts is a step forward in theology, such interpretation remains insufficient if we cannot pass judgement on what these texts reveal to be going forward in religious *history*. It is not enough to understand what an author meant when writing one text or another, without a resolution of the historical realities, the social and political situation of an author's time, upon which those texts may throw light.

In the light of such theological questions, Lonergan proposes (1994, 128) history as a third functional specialty. To help clarify this functional specialty, he argues that there are three forms of history. First, "basic" history is more concerned with events and activities. It aims, Lonergan writes, to tells us *who* did *what, when* and *where*. So basic history aspires to account for events, their participants, their times and locations. Secondly, he proposes "special" history, which is more interested in movements, rather than events. Such movements can be cultural, institutional, or doctrinal. As part of a functional speciality within theological method, special history would be most dedicated to activities within religion, doctrine and theology. We also note that Lonergan's notion of "special history" would come closer than "basic" history to fulfilling Collingwood's (1989, 281) idea of "scientific history," which was in turn inspired by Acton's precept, "Study problems, not periods."

Thirdly, Lonergan proposes (1994, 128) "general history," which he acknowledges to be only a possible ideal for history. General history would comprise basic history that was augmented and clarified by special history. Such a general history, if possible, would offer an evaluation of all human movements, within their concrete circumstances. Lonergan argues that history, as a functional specialty, must first be open to basic history, so that it is open to all relevant evidence. He adds, however, that history's prime interest would be in special history, in evaluating the doctrinal history of theology. Lastly, the functional specialty, history, cannot ignore the project of general history. We note that general history like science, is an ever ongoing and never completed project. Lonergan argues, though, that general history is needed, if we are to determine the relations and differences between different sects and religions, and their respective places within world history.

5.4 Dialectic

If history judges upon what was going forward within a religion and its world, we also find that history reveals a multiplicity of movements. Such movements are dynamic, concrete and often contradictory and they call for a responsible decision concerning the respective values of different movements. The contradictions between particular movements provide the materials for the fourth functional specialty, *dialectic*. Within theological method, dialectic's material concern is with the conflicts, both external and internal, of different Christian movements. Lonergan dryly adds that dialectic also takes material from the conflicts between historical accounts and theological interpretations of the different movements (Lonergan 128-29).

Further to the materials of dialectic, its function is to seek a "comprehensive viewpoint," of different conflicts. Such a viewpoint can only be attained by going beyond the mere facts of these conflicts, to a grasp of the reasons for the conflicts. Lonergan proposes (1994, 129) that such a viewpoint can be attained by understanding the character, oppositions and relations involved in these contradictory movements. Dialectic, then, is a critical comparison of conflicts, that can clarify where such differences are irreducible, where they share some complementarity and could be reconciled, or where they are simply stages in a united process of development.

Dialectic corresponds to the transcendental precept, "be responsible." So, beyond its role of comparing, dialectic has a critical function of evaluating the relative values of contradictory movements. Dialectic thus decides which movements are worthwhile and coherent and which movements should be, as Lonergan charitably writes (1994, 246), invited to a more coherent position. He later puts this point more bluntly. Dialectic, he writes, adds to history an evaluation of achievements, and discerns within them, either good or evil. Dialectic also goes beyond the products of Interpretation by different movements, by evaluating the horizons within which those movements make their own interpretations and judgements.

Dialectic thus fills, within theological method, the need for responsibility. It aims to purge viewpoints based on unsound reasons, *ad hoc* explanations, suspicions, resentments or malice. We may ask if such unsound reasons could not be overcome by presenting fresh evidence? Lonergan's answer (1994, 130, 246) is that presenting new data will not affect such unsound reasons, for the new data will be just as vulnerable to unsound interpretation and judgement. In a point not lost on those who have dealt with fundamentalism, he argues that the cause of unsound reasoning is in the horizons of thinkers. That horizon is formed by what a thinker or movement holds to be intellectually worthwhile. Lonergan proposes that dialectic can purge unsound reasons and invite a resolution of conflict, not by adding new data, but by conversion to a more sound horizon. In short, dialectic's function is to provide a comprehensive viewpoint which acknowledges substantial, as opposed to insubstantial, differences, determines their grounds and eliminates superfluous conflicts.

Dialectic, as Doran observes (1990, 67; 1995 2:95-96) is a higher viewpoint needed when data lie beyond a single conscious subject. This viewpoint "from above" examines whether these result from conscious subjects' relations with each other of their historical milieu, or the relations of consciousness with unconsciousness.

5.5 Foundations

Lonergan bases the next functional specialty, foundations, upon conversion, which he conceives (1994, 130-31) as "a transformation of the subject and his world." Conversion is a change in mind and heart of the subject, whose life takes on a new direction, with new values, new concerns and new interests. While conversion is normally an ongoing, lasting process, it is known best by its pivotal moments of judgement and decision. Doran argues (1990, 150-51) that this emphasis on conversion as being foundational is one of Lonergan's most controversial proposals, for it challenges the mainstream "decision to live an intellectual life in abstraction from the flow of existence in the Metaxy, the In-between... ." In that way, by finding conversion as the theologian's foundational reality, Lonergan recognises and affirms the concrete operating conditions of the theologian. Tallon helps (1997, 207) by referring to Lonergan's statement (1994, 32-33) that love is both a feeling and state, and that one's state becomes "the fount of all one's actions." Thus, Tallon argues, as acts become habits, feelings become moods, which are "superactual, virtual, habitual, dynamic states." Foundations then, flow from the mood of theology, or the theologian specifically, which flows from one's attunement or loving conversion, or otherwise.

But one could ask if conversion does not occur within dialectic. After all does not Lonergan propose dialectic as a functional speciality of intentional responsibility? He replies (1994, 268), however, that dialectic simply reveals the variety of possible views. Dialectic, in itself, does not take sides on one issue or another, but it is the subject who makes a personal decision to take one side or another. That is, a subject decides whom one is for, or against, based upon one's deliberation and evaluation of the diverse views made manifest by dialectic. Conversion, then, is an ongoing movement from one viewpoint to a new conscious decision about new horizons within which a subject will view, judge, evaluate and relate with his or her world. Ultimately, one's conversion will determine the teachings one finds meaningful and those teachings one will not find meaningful.

In that light, it is puzzling that Pannenberg (Corcoran 1975, 97) should think that Lonergan confines people to the "prisons" of "separate worlds" from which there is no escape, save by an irrational act. By more accurately reading Lonergan's account of foundations, we find Lonergan arguing that foundational horizons are ongoing, and that these horizons are established and revised by intellectual, moral and religious conversion. Horizons are hardly irrational and imprisioning, they are decided upon in a manner that is attentive, intelligent, reasonable, responsible and loving (Lonergan 1994, 130, 267-68). Moreover, as Tallon notes (1997, 207) affectivity is self-transcendence to objective value. We also note that Pannenberg could only be right if a conscious subject was acting affectively to the exclusion of cognitional and volitional operations. Lonergan's view, on the other hand, is a person operating knowingly, morally and lovingly, in a process of liberation from counter-positions and counter-horizons to self-transcendence to the horizon of authentic truth, goodness and value.

If conversion is a movement from one world of meaning to another, we can understand the point that conversion is an existential and personal movement. But while conversion is personal, Lonergan reminds us (1994, 130-31) that conversion may be shared, so that many share a movement towards the same horizons. When this happens, a community forms that holds in common a horizon, which affects the community's conscious and intentional operations. That conversion augments their understanding, directs their judgements, and influences their decisions.

When such conversion is spoken of explicitly and made the object of deliberation, Lonergan proposes (1994, 131) that we have the functional specialty, foundations. Foundations is a function of theology in making responsible decisions about what is valuable and meaningful, and what is not. It is a functional specialty that defines the horizons within which a religion's beliefs can be meaningfully appreciated. Lonergan illustrates this functional specialty with a Pauline image. Paul argues (I Cor 2:14-15) that an "unspiritual man" cannot grasp or find meaningful the message of God's Spirit. That is, only within the distinct "spiritual" horizon can one find the teaching of God meaningful. Lonergan likewise argues that in theology one must establish and distinguish the horizons within which religious teachings can be meaningful. This distinction is foundational and found in the functional specialty, foundations.

Lonergan importantly clarifies that (1994, 132), while horizons are manifold and different, not all horizons reflect authentic conversion. The functional specialty, foundations, is proposed as a responsible function that evaluates whether horizons reflect or do not reflect authentic conversion. Foundations, accordingly, both conveys a clarification of the manifold conflicts revealed by dialectic and gives a principle of selection with which to guide the subsequent functional specialities: doctrines, systematics and communications.

We note that Lonergan (1994, 131) distinguishes foundations from the older "fundamental theology." Fundamental theology was a matter of doctrines concerning: the true religion, the divine law, the Church, the inspiration of Scripture and so forth. However, as a functional specialty, foundations does not tell us of doctrines, but it presents the horizons within which doctrines can be apprehended.

5.6 Doctrines

Within a theological method, the next functional specialty, doctrines, makes specific the transcendental precept, be reasonable. Lonergan proposes (1994, 132, 299) that doctrines express judgements of fact and judgements of value. We note that Lonergan's notion of doctrines does not imply arbitrary truths given instantly and immutably in divine revelation. Lonergan's concept of doctrines envisages doctrines as resulting from a definite process, and a determinate method. First, the functional specialty, "dialectic" manifests the various options between the truths attained and the errors disseminated in the past. Next, foundations decides between truth and fallacy by considering the options of dialectic, in the light of the horizon within which certain propositions may be meaningful, and others meaningless. Within a methodical theology, doctrines stand within the horizon of foundations, without which they would lack meaning. In other words, doctrines are judgements within a determinate horizon from which are selected and affirmed certain of the options presented by dialectic, which are compatible with, and intelligible within, the horizon of foundations. The options of dialectic, we also note, are gained from the affirmations made in history, which were made upon the understandings formed in interpretation of the data uncovered in research.

Lonergan clarifies two points (1994, 132, 333) pertinent to the relationship between dogmatic theology, and doctrines. First, doctrines do not only encompass the judgements of fact or value more traditionally associated with dogmatic theology, they incorporate the range of specialised theological subjects, including moral, ascetical, mystical and pastoral theology. Secondly, doctrinal theology differs from the older dogmatic theology. While dogmatic theology worked under the classicist tendency to assume there to be only one correct proposition on any given issue, historically-minded doctrinal theology knows that doctrines are meaningful and determinate only within manifold specific contexts. These contexts manifest a plurality of cultural conditions, differentiations of consciousness and conversions. Lonergan thus further distinguishes a religious apprehension of doctrines, in which one apprehends doctrines from one's own context of culture, common sense, differentiation of consciousness, and conversion, from a theological apprehension of doctrines, in which one can appreciate the manifold historical and dialectical contexts in which one doctrine is expressed in a plurality of forms.

5.7 Systematics

Lonergan argues (1994, 336) that doctrines cannot be a terminal operation in theology because the facts and values affirmed by doctrines give rise to questions of meaning. In that light the functional specialty, systematics, seeks to establish what the meaning of doctrines could be, and how it could possibly be that the doctrines are so. How this is done is the main object of our investigation. For now, it suffices to recall Lonergan's notion (1994, 132) of systematics' aim to work out systems of conceptualisation of doctrines, which solve apparent inconsistencies and aim for some grasp of the mysteries affirmed in doctrines. Systematics thus corresponds to the transcendental precept, to be intelligent, because this specialty searches for the meaning present in doctrines.

5.8 Communications

Finally, as the result of the ongoing theological process, Lonergan (1994, 355) finds the last functional specialty, communications, in which the other theological functional specialties come to fruition and maturity by mediating the results of theology to the "outside" community.

Communications, in Lonergan's words (1994, 132-33, 357), "is concerned with theology in its external relations." Those relations may be with the arts, sciences, or with other religions. On the other hand, communications can be concerned with the relations that come from the transpositions that theology must make so that a religion can retain its integrity, while simultaneously appealing to the minds and hearts of many peoples. Such a communication to different people means that the theologian must find common meaning and common understanding with those to whom one is addressing oneself. It is on that basis of common understanding that one can thus transmit one's acquired knowledge to others.

On communications, we note two points. First, because communications is conceived on the basis of a common understanding, there is ruled out a crass form of dogmatising whereby one would consider the gospel to be preached where the hearers could simply repeat the concepts of the preacher. Secondly, communications makes specific the transcendental precept, "be attentive," by providing the data of theology to those who can be attentive to and hear the message of communications.

Before leaving our outline of the functional specialties, we should respond to William Shea's declaration (1976, 281n17) that "I [Shea] do not understand how Lonergan situates the question of God (and the answer to the question) in relation to the functional specialties." Shea's lack of understanding may arise from an attempt to place the question of God within one functional specialty. However, one can reply to Shea by noting Lonergan's points (1973, 48, 52): first, that method's function is to make specific the transcendental precepts "Be attentive, Be intelligent, Be reasonable, Be responsible," and secondly that "the question of God arises on a series of successive levels." From a reading of *Method*, it is clear that the question of God can, and does, occur in relation to all of the functional specialties. Research uncovers what has been said about God, interpretation asks what is meant about God, history determines how questions and answers about God were unfolding in ongoing cultures, dialectic decides between divergent positions on God, foundations thematises what is within us as regards the horizon within which we apprehend God, doctrines affirms what we acknowledge in God, systematics seeks an understanding of God and communications expresses, to other people, what we understand about God (Meynell 1978, 409). With questions about God occurring within all of the functional specialties, we may resolve Shea's problem by moving away from the positing of a "question" of God, towards the realisation that human beings raise numerous questions about God, which occur on different levels of intentional consciousness.

6. THE NEED FOR THE DIVISION

We have so far outlined the division of functional specialties within theology. We now turn to asking about the reasons that Lonergan offers in support of such a division.

In the first place, functional specialisation is prompted by the increasing level of specialisation in theology, which in turn is provoked by developments in modern thought. As Lonergan writes (1994, 141-42), with the ongoing refinement of theology's techniques and with a corresponding increase in the delicacy of theology's operations, it becomes increasingly difficult for any one specialist to competently master the whole range of theological operations. In *Philosophy of God and Theology*, he reflected upon the way in which modern hermeneutics and history have forced Catholic dogmatic theology out of its belief that any one dogmatic theologian could effectively master the range of theological fields. This increasing specialisation was a key factor in prompting Lonergan's development of a theological method. His firm belief (1973, 15; 1974, 212) was that without a method that allowed for, and encouraged, specialisation within theology, Catholic theology would be left languishing under the weight of the "impossible conditions," under which he had long worked.

We can appreciate Lonergan's argument (1974, 212; 1994, 137), that by dividing and distinguishing functional specialties, we can prevent immoderate demands being placed upon a theologian. Moreover, we would argue that functional specialisation would allow theologians to maintain their professional self-respect, while simultaneously being able to abandon the pretence of being omniscient and omnicompetent within the theological disciplines.

Lonergan further argues that (1994, 137), not only would functional specialisation curb excessive demands, it would also provide due recognition for a scholar's work within his functional area. Although all eight functional specialties are required for theology's full process from data to results, he proposes that one can still acknowledge a serious and important contribution from a scholar who substantially contributes to theology in one of the eight specialties. Such a contribution, would be "as much as can be demanded of a single piece of work."

From a more negative perspective, Lonergan argues that (1994, 137), by recognising the division of functional specialties and by giving due acknowledgment to the value of contributions in each functional specialty, we can restrain the totalitarian attitudes of those who consider their specialty to be more excellent than other parts of the theological process. Lonergan laments that such a one-sided, totalitarian outlook has afflicted theology from the middle ages until the present day. In contrast to such parochialism, he proposes a total view of theology, which affirms the value and place of the different functional specialties within the whole process of theology.

We should clarify that Lonergan does not specify that each functional specialty necessarily be performed by one specialist and that each specialist only engage in one functional specialty. Rather, he argues (1994, 136) that functional specialty is not a distinction of specialist personnel, but of specialised operations. While it is often the case that one scholar will work in one specialty, it is not Lonergan's intent to confine the work of a scholar, but simply to differentiate different tasks within the theological project, and prevent their confusion with one another.

7. The Grounds of the Division

When considering the grounds for the division of the functional specialties, it is important to bear in mind Lonergan's assertion (1994, 136) that he is not proposing an utterly novel idea. The first four specialties: research, interpretation, history and dialectic, have their parallels in the already familiar fields pertaining to: textual criticism, commentaries and interpretive monographs, church and dogmatic history, controversial and apologetic theology. The second four specialties: foundations, doctrines, systematics, and communications, have some correspondence with the older divisions of: fundamental theology, dogmatic theology, speculative theology and pastoral theology. However, the most notably different and novel element in Lonergan's conception of these distinct operations, is his division of these operations into functional specialties and their dynamic interrelationship as components of a single process from data to results.

Turning to the actual grounds for dividing the functional specialties, we first note Lonergan's argument (1994, 133, 135-36) that theological operations take place in two distinct phases. In the first phase, which he calls "mediating theology," one investigates the manifestations of one's religion and one appropriates the reality of that religion and its history. As this first, mediating, phase is essentially an assimilation of a religion's past, this phase is where one apprehends the religious situation as it presently exists. In other words, the first phase of theology involves one's working towards a personal encounter of a religion. It is a phase of theology, *in oratione obliqua*, where one discovers what various authorities have handed down to us in a religious tradition.

Lonergan submits (1994, 133-36, 144) that this first phase challenges a theologian towards a personal decision about a religion. From the first phase of harkening to a tradition, one is challenged to pass on the products of that tradition. This second phase of theology is called "mediated theology" insofar as one turns, from others mediating that tradition to oneself, to one's activities of making that tradition mediated to others. Thus, while the first, "mediating" phase of theology is concerned with assimilating past achievement, the second, "mediated" phase of theology is more concerned with working towards future achievements. This second phase, Lonergan argues, exists to the extent that one takes the responsibility of maintaining continuity or initiating change within a tradition. To state briefly the difference between the two phases, we note that in the first phase one encounters past attainments within a tradition. In the second phase, one takes past achievement and in the light of that achievement, one confronts the questions of one's own day so as to work towards the future of that tradition.

In addition to the two phases of theology, Lonergan argues (1994, 133-34) that theological method can be divided according to the operations of intentional consciousness. There exist four levels of operation that correspond to the four levels of intentional consciousness, which we investigated in chapter five, with each level having its own proper goal. While Lonergan acknowledges that, in everyday "commonsense" activity, the four levels are employed unreflectively and without care for their distinction, he argues that in scientific inquiry, one would pursue the end proper to one level of intentional operation. The textual critic's work illustrates this point. The critic uses all four levels of one's intentional consciousness, by acting responsibly to decide upon what one intelligently understands to be the best method, by which one can reasonably affirm to be written in the original text. Thus, a textual critic acts responsibly, reasonably, intelligently and attentively. However, Lonergan argues, the textual critic's task is oriented towards the proper end of intentional consciousness' first level, being attentive. The textual critic, by one's research, acts to provide the data upon which other specialists will perform their tasks. Lonergan helps us to grasp this division of specialties by also noting the interpreter's task. While the interpreter also performs responsible, reasonable, intelligent and attentive operations, his or her task is ordered to the end of understanding those data made available by research. Effectively, the textual critic researches, to provide data to which scholars may be attentive. The interpreter, however, provides exegesis by which scholars may attain understanding of those texts. The vital point is that functional specialties can be divided according to the proper ends of four different levels of intentional consciousness.

The different functional specialties thus arise because, although one operates on all four levels of intentional consciousness, one operates towards a goal proper to one specific level. It is important to bear in mind this point, as noting it prevents us from Hesse's (Corcoran 1975, 60-61, 66-67) mistaken impression that Lonergan presents a "four-fold categorical framework" in which common sense is limited to being attentive, science terminates at being intelligent, history terminates in being reasonable, theology is concerned with all four levels of consciousness, but feels most at home in being responsible. Hesse also argues that Lonergan implies a division between natural and human sciences corresponding to the second and third levels of intentional consciousness. Were Hesse correct in her summary of Lonergan, we would readily agree that Lonergan's distinctions of levels of intentional consciousness amount to nothing. However, Hesse is right to lack confidence in her own interpretation (Corcoran 1975, 60). Nowhere does Lonergan restrict different fields of study to particular levels of consciousness, accounted for in his transcendental (not categorical!) method.

Having clarified that point, we observe Lonergan's point (1994, 134) that theology occurs in two phases, "mediating" and "mediated" theology. A functional speciality is thus one's operation towards an end proper to one level of human consciousness, in one phase of theology. Accordingly then:

> It follows that the very structure of human inquiry results in four functional specializations and, since in theology there are two distinct phases, we are led to expect eight functional specializations in theology. In the first phase of theology *in oratione obliqua* there are research, interpretation, history, and dialectic. In the second phase of theology *in oratione recta* there are foundations, doctrines, systematics, and communications.

To more explicitly match each of the eight functional specialties to their corresponding levels of intentional consciousness, Lonergan (1994, 134, 135) first notes that, in "mediating" theology, in which we assimilate the past, we find: (1) Research, which is concerned with finding data, to which one is attentive, (2) Interpretation, which seeks intelligent understanding of that data, (3) History, which passes reasonable judgement upon what happened in the religion and (4) Dialectic, which responsibly decides between conflicting accounts. Secondly, in theology's "mediated" phase, in which one takes a tradition towards the future, there are: (5) Foundations, in which one responsibly decides between manifold available horizons, (6) Doctrines, which is concerned with judging upon the facts and values of a religion, (7) Systematics, in which one seeks intelligent understanding of those doctrines and (8) Communications, which is concerned with mediating that understanding to attentive hearers.

Lonergan importantly acknowledges (1994, 135-36) that there is an inverted order with the sequence: attention/research, intelligence/interpretation, judgement/history and responsibility/dialectic, in the first phase; with the sequence in the second phase being: responsibility/foundations, judgement/doctrines, intelligence/systematics and attention/communications. He argues that the inverted order exists because, in the first phase, one moves from data, towards a personal encounter with one's religion as it exists. In the second phase, one moves from this personal encounter towards providing data for others' encounters with the ongoing, renewed tradition.

8. Conclusions

To conclude our chapter, we need to address several issues. First, we need to note that Lonergan's theological method allows an articulation of the difference between a theology and a religion. Throughout *Method in Theology*, he insists that theology is a reflection upon a religion and he conceives theology as mediating the meaning and value of a religion to its culture. That theological process, as Lonergan's method indicates, is hardly a simple matter of a religion meeting a people in one simple act of encounter, so that if we were to identify a theology with a religion, in its whole or parts, we would regress to the less complex, early period of Christianity. But the complexities and questions of modern times differ greatly from early Christianity's cultural context. Despite the core of the faith remaining constant, theology must change to meet the new questions and challenges of modern times. If we were to make the mistake of identifying Christian religion with Christian theology, we would run the risk of meeting the challenges of the twentieth century with answers more appropriate to ancient Antioch, Corinth or Rome (Lonergan 1994, 140).

Secondly, Lonergan's theological method, and his division of functional specialties, can also help solve some conflicts between different approaches to theology. He argues (1994, 145) that the older Aristotelian model of theology relied upon subject specialisation, which emphasises the theological operations that he finds in the mediated (second) phase of theology. On the other hand, he argues that more modern theologies have focussed on field specialisation, which concentrates more on the operations pertinent to the mediating (first) phase. Lonergan suggests that his functional approach has the advantage of giving due attention to both phases, while simultaneously preserving their proper interdependent and dynamic unity.

Thirdly, and most importantly, Lonergan's theological method meets a standard of modern science, insofar as it constitutes theology as an ongoing process. The aim of the functional approach is to ensure a patterned unity of interdependent parts, with each adjusting to meet the changes effected in the others (Lonergan 1994, 144). We add, at this stage, that the process is ongoing, because, contrary to a widespread misconception, Lonergan's method (1994, 6) is not a step-by-step approach that terminates with communications. Apart from his renunciation of method as being such a one-way, linear process, we also note that, throughout the process, especially in communications, new questions will be raised, which stimulate new incentive for further research, with the consequent addition of new data, which in turn generate new understandings and judgements.

We lastly note that Lonergan's functional division, within a methodological theology, reflects a dynamic structure, which exists in a framework of interdependence between functional specialties. To illustrate that reciprocal dependence, we note the explanation that, not only does interpretation demand the data of research, but research also calls forth, and requires interpretation to bring the task of research to fulfilment. Moreover, not only does history depend upon research and interpretation, but the demands of historical inquiry furnish research and interpretation with the context and perspectives within which they operate (Lonergan 1994, 141). We find then, in Lonergan's words (1994, 144), an outline of "the dynamic unity of theology. It is a unity of interdependent parts, each adjusting to changes in the others, and the whole developing as a result of such changes and adjustments." Given that interdependence, one cannot sustain Pannenberg's suggestion (Corcoran 1975, 96) that Lonergan only reluctantly concedes this interdependence. Pannenberg also argues that such interdependence debilitates the distinctiveness of each functional specialty. Pannenberg's argument is understandable if we note his argument (Corcoran 1975, 92-94) against the distinction of cognitional activities. Pannenberg's key problem with appreciating Lonergan's distinction of dynamically interrelated functional specialties within a methodological theology evidently corresponds to his inability to appreciate the distinction of the dynamically related, though distinct, cognitional activities that constitute human knowing.

We now have a general overview of Lonergan's method in theology. Having grasped the meaning of his intentionality analysis, his general transcendental method, and his specific theological method, we are now in a position to more fully understand his function specialty, systematics. To our investigation of systematics, we now turn.

Chapter 7
The Functional Specialty, Systematics

> Lord, I do not attempt to comprehend Your sublimity, because my
> intellect is not at all equal to such a task. But I yearn to understand some
> measure of Your truth, which my heart believes and loves. For I do not
> seek to understand in order to believe but I believe in order to
> understand. For I believe even this: that I shall not understand unless I
> believe (Anselm *Proslogion*, 1).

Lonergan conceives the functional specialty, systematics, to be principally concerned with promoting an understanding of the mysteries of
faith. He situates (1994, 335-36) his conception of systematics within
the tradition of theological understanding represented by Augustine,
Anselm as cited above, Aquinas and the First Vatican Council. After having laid the foundations necessary for our investigation of what Lonergan
means in systematics, we turn now to the central concern of our work.

In this chapter, we shall investigate the basic elements of systematics.
We shall outline the general function of systematics, the factors that make
systematics necessary, and the way in which systematics comes to be within
a methodological theology. In the two chapters following, we shall investigate two specific manners in which Lonergan proposes systematics' understanding to come about, by analogy and by the interconnections of
the mysteries.

1. The Function of Systematics

Systematics is conceived as the functional specialty, within theology,
that is concerned with promoting an understanding of the mysteries of
faith. We must immediately note Lonergan's point (1994, 336) that these
mysteries of faith are affirmed in the functional specialty, doctrines. Importantly, systematics both follows on from, and presupposes, doctrines.
We secondly observe that Lonergan uses the First Vatican Council both
as an authoritative support and as a means of expression for his idea of
systematics. He argues that the Council (DS 3016/TCF 132) "retrieved
the notion of understanding," from the Augustinian, Anselmian, Thomist tradition, by declaring that:

> ... if [human] reason illumined by faith inquires in an earnest, pious and
> sober manner, it attains by God's grace a certain understanding of the
> mysteries, which is most fruitful, both from the analogy with the objects

of its natural knowledge and from the connection of these mysteries with one another and with man's ultimate end.

We can better understand the Council's teaching, and Lonergan's intention in citing it, if we follow his earlier observation (1974, 119) that *Dei Filius* represented the Council's concern to defend both reason and faith against the respective challenges of fideism and rationalism. Against rationalism, the Council maintained that faith was necessary to know revealed mysteries, because these mysteries lay beyond the reach of natural human reason. The Council (DS 3008, 3009/TCF 118, 119) was also concerned to declare that faith, while being a supernatural virtue, is "nevertheless in harmony with reason." On the other hand, the Council simultaneously upheld the cause of reason. Against fideism, it maintained that reason was of great value to the human understanding of faith. A significant factor behind this affirmation of reason's value is the Council's departure from the classicist focus on the object of faith and theology, a departure shown by the focus upon the abilities of the subject doing theology in the declaration above. According to the Council (DS 3016/TCF 132), the human subject was capable, if one's intellect was aided by faith, of attaining a "highly fruitful understanding" of the mysteries of faith, both from an analogy with things naturally known and from the interconnection of the mysteries with each other and humanity's ultimate end. To that capability, we add our observation that the Council's focus upon the subject doing theology allowed the Council to advocate an approach to theology that could maintain a continuity between human intellect's natural and supernatural operations. The Council was thus able to teach (DS 3004-5, 3015-16/TCF 113-14, 131-32) that the same human intellect, which could approach a certain natural knowledge of God by reasoning to God from one's knowledge of natural objects, could also attain a "supernatural" understanding of divine mysteries by reason operating under the guidance of faith. We would acknowledge, though, that if we take this declaration in its historical context, it seems unlikely that the Council meant to prescribe an exhaustive set of means by which we can understand doctrines. Moreover, we would find that the Council would in no way reject the validity of other forms of expressing doctrines, such as prayer, liturgy, music and visual art.

Lonergan's first authority, for the function of systematics, expressed continuity and integration. However, his second authority, Thomas Aquinas, helps to distinguish the understanding of mysteries from other activities of human intellect. Both in his theory and practice, Aquinas shows the difference between the establishment and affirmation of the mysteries of faith, which we find in the functional specialty, doctrines, and the understanding of those mysteries, which we find in the functional specialty, systematics. For the distinction of doctrines and systematics, Lonergan (1994, 336-37) first cites Aquinas' practice, in Book Four of his *Summa Contra Gentiles*. The first forty-nine chapters of this book encompass divisions between those series of chapters that establish the fact of existence of certain mysteries, and those series of chapters that are concerned with the manner in which these mysteries can be conceived. Lonergan also refers to Aquinas' theory, in his *Quodlibetal Questions* (IV,q9a3 [18]). When asked whether authorities or reasons were more useful for instructing students, Thomas replied that an argument could have either of two intentions. On the one hand, an argument could be aimed at removing doubts, so that one was concerned with establishing the intellectual certainty of what is so. In that case, one was better served by appealing to the authorities that the listener recognised. Lonergan (1994, 132) would identify such removal of doubt, or judgement about what is so, with the primary role of doctrines.

Thomas explained however (*Quaestiones Quodlibetales* IV,q9a3 [18]), that one could also intend to bring a student to understand the truth at hand. If one sought understanding, one would leave a student empty if one appealed only to authorities, for the student would have neither understanding, nor any grasp of the principles of the matter. Aquinas argued that one is better served by establishing the reasons that both illuminate the grounds of the truth, and also enable one to know how what is said is in fact, true. It is this second intention, of showing a student how what is said is true and guiding the student to understand the reasons and principles underlying a matter of faith, which Lonergan identifies (1994, 337) with his understanding of the functional specialty, systematics. We note that the same text from Aquinas was cited by Karl Barth (1975, 1,16) to illustrate "the distinction between dogmatic enquiry and authoritative quotation," a distinction that we find parallels Lonergan's distinction of doctrines and systematics. We further note with Doran (1995, 1:181) that by seeking through systematics "reasons and principles" Lonergan promotes an explanatory understanding, rather than a merely descriptive exercise.

We also note that, in attempting to balance doctrinal stability with theological development, the First Vatican Council (DS 3020/TCF 136) also affirmed a difference between dogmas and the understanding of those dogmas. In an important text the Council declared:

... that meaning of the sacred dogmas is perpetually to be retained which our Holy Mother Church has once declared, and there must never be a deviation from that meaning on the specious ground and title of a more profound understanding. *'Therefore, let there be growth and abundant progress in understanding, knowledge and wisdom, in each and all, in individuals and in the whole Church, at all times and in the progress of all ages, but only within the proper limits, i.e., within the same dogma, the same meaning, the same judgement.'*

As a matter of historical interest, the text that we have italicised is the Council's citation of Vincent of Lérins', *Commonitorium primum*, 23, which was a polemic against the doctrine of Augustine and Prosper of Aquitaine on predestination. Vincent was an extreme conservative, and his concessions to development were made only with manifold reservations (Walgrave 1972, 86-90).

If we take account of the Council's text, along with the other declaration cited above, we find it dealing with two distinct, though not separate, issues. While the Council was most concerned to affirm the permanence of Catholic dogma, it also gave its endorsement to a growth and development in the understanding of the mysteries affirmed by those doctrines. Clearly, the Council considered doctrines and the understanding of mysteries to be two distinct activities, with their own distinct characters and proper operations.

We have introduced a foundational idea of systematics, noted its basic distinction from doctrines and written something about the main sources for Lonergan's idea of this functional specialty. We should now investigate why systematics would be needed within a modern, methodological theology.

2. Mystery, Problem, and the Need for Systematics' Understanding

Having introduced systematics, we face the question of "... how the Christian religion ever allowed itself to be involved in systematic thinking; after all, such thinking is not mentioned in the sermon on the mount." Lonergan (1973, 22-23; 1994, xi) would answer this question, first, by recalling that theology is not a discipline that communicates immutable certitudes to a static and universal culture, but it is a mediation of a religion's significance and function to a concrete ongoing culture. If theologians take seriously the empirical reality of culture, they face the challenge of making a religion intelligible to people within the various historical, social and cultural contexts within which a religion may be found. The challenge arises because the words of a religion have meaning only within a concrete cultural context. Culture, we further note with Lonergan (1994, 344), is hardly static, but it is ongoing and manifold. There is the added historical-cultural challenge created when one culture develops into another. Moreover, two cultures may meet and interact. Each of these manifold cultures will have its own common sense, science, scholarship and philosophy.

Within an empirical notion of culture, the essential challenge to theology and theologians is to make the mysteries of faith intelligible within the concrete life and history of one's specific culture. Despite the verity of the mysteries that doctrines can reveal, no simple repetition of those doctrines can make the mysteries of faith intelligible to different people. Instead, theologians need to conceive the mysteries in terms comprehensible in concrete, specific contexts. Such is the aim of systematics, which as Lonergan points out (1973, 58), is concerned not only with "supernatural" aspects of theology, but also with the concrete effect of God's grace on humanity and our world. Systematics accordingly promotes an understanding of the mysteries in terms of its audience's acquired culture. It does this by using not only religious categories, but also categories from more human fields of study, most notably philosophy.

To further illustrate the need for the understanding of mysteries, which systematics promotes, Lonergan turns (1973, 23) to Fuller's account (1979, 243-47) of the New Testament's development. Fuller's theory was that within the New Testament, one finds several different strata, which correspond to attempts to preach the same Gospel message to several different cultures. A first stratum presents the Gospel message, as it was communicated to Jews who read the Old Testament within a Hebrew culture. A second layer shows the Gospel as it was preached to Jews who had read the Old Testament within a Greek context. A third stratum presents the Gospel, as it was communicated to Gentiles who had no cultural contact with the Old Testament. The varying strata of the New Testament illustrate the need to conceive and communicate the Gospel message in as many different ways as there were different cultures to which that message was addressed. To give the Gospel any chance to success, Christian missionaries had to conceive and present it in ways intelligible to different cultures. The neglect of cultural variations, which required different conceptualisations of the Gospel, would have meant the misunderstanding and misrepresentation of the Gospel.

Lonergan also argues (1973, 25-26; 1994, 344) that systematics' promotion of understanding is prompted by the conditions of presenting the divine mysteries to people, or cultures, on different levels of intentional consciousness. By way of example, he first notes that people in a culture could express their understanding of God in mainly symbolic terms. To transform that expression, one would only need to change the relevant symbols. Alternatively, in Clement of Alexandria's culture, which came under Xenophanes' influence, one could no longer take seriously anthropomorphic conceptions of a God who stands and sits, who has right and left hands, who increases and declines in emotion. To overcome that problem, and to make God intelligible within his cultural context, Clement conceived God (*Stromateis*, V, xii*)* by abstracting from all corporeality. Similarly, Origen conceived spiritual beings, including God, in line with middle Platonism. This enabled Origen (*De Principiis*, I,1) to defend the strict spirituality of spiritual beings, within the philosophic culture of his time. Importantly, Clement and Origen promoted, neither a denial of the doctrine of God nor a rejection of the realities affirmed by Scripture, but a new understanding of God in line with the philosophic and cultural contexts of their times. These ongoing developments show that while the faith itself remained constant, its theological activity needed to devise new conceptions of its doctrines in order to meet the exigences of different times. It is important to us that ongoing developments in culture are still occurring. Lonergan emphasises (1994, 345) that our own contemporary culture has produced a range of new problems. In today's concrete world, people may be familiar with Church doctrines. From within their concrete context, though, people still ask what these doctrines could possibly mean. Such inquiry, he holds, is the object of systematics' efforts. This means that systematics is not a project inclined towards vain speculations. Systematics is a more "homely" project because it deals with the truths of faith confessed by practising Christians, who at different times ask what those truths may mean (Lonergan 1994, 350). Systematics' focus on the truths of faith thus engenders a theology that is more concrete and more manifestly relevant to the faith into which it inquires.

Lonergan's 1975 investigation of Christological concerns illustrates contemporary culture's new challenges to theology and how systematics can meet these challenges. He recalls (1985b, 88) that in many and varied cultural contexts, Jesus has been known as the "Son of God." The contemporary challenge, however, is to resolve in our own minds how we can find Jesus' divine sonship intelligible within our own cultural context. On this issue, Lonergan (1985b, 91) writes that,

> If in earlier ages it was enough to adore the mystery, if from the medieval period some metaphysical account of person and nature were all that was sought, it remains that in our age of psychology and critical philosophy, of hermeneutics and history, something both different and more exacting is required. We have to be able to say what it means for a divine person to live a fully human life.

The essential point is that theologians must conceive the mystery of Christ's person with expressions that are intelligible to a culture influenced by modern psychology and philosophy. A new understanding of the doctrine is thus called for by new questions and new contexts. This contention concurs with Pope John XXIII's vision for the Second Vatican Council to remain faithful to the constant deposit of faith, while simultaneously promoting the mutable modes of presentation and conceptualisation, which meet the challenges of different times (Lonergan 1985b, 225).

If ongoing modes of conceptualisation are needed for an understanding of the mysteries of faith, a key concern is why anything would be needed beyond doctrines, faith or belief. To answer that question we must now turn to investigate these realities, and their relationship to theological understanding.

3. Judgement and Understanding

Lonergan (1994, 336) conceives systematics as the promotion of an understanding of the mysteries. To correctly appreciate the meaning of understanding, as the intent of systematics, Lonergan (1994, 335) emphasises the critical difference between understanding and judgement. We have studied this difference earlier in this book. However, we note that, when Lonergan begins his outline of "The Function of Systematics," his first priority is to distance himself from those thinkers who would identify judgement with understanding. He first singles out Kant, for whom "understanding (*Verstand*) was the faculty of judgement." It may be objected that Kant does regard human knowing as a composite reality, but as Sala points out (1994, 5), Kant does not really acknowledge a difference between the products of the activities of understanding and reflection upon what has been understood.

Against the Kantian position, with its sources in Platonism and Scotism, Lonergan again aligns himself with Aquinas and Aristotle, for both of whom the operations of human intellect were definitely distinct. In the

Aristotelian-Thomist position that Lonergan maintains (1994, 335), human intellect's first operation addresses questions of quiddity, or nature. The second intellectual operation answers questions of existence, or fact. On the one hand, Lonergan thus holds understanding to be the source of definitions and hypotheses. Judgement, on the other hand, provides knowledge of the existence of what is defined, and judgement verifies a hypothesis' content.

As we found in chapter five, Lonergan takes much support for his distinction of understanding and judgement from the writings of Aquinas and Aristotle. First, we find that Aquinas *(Summa Theologiae*, I,q16a2c) holds that the human intellect can know truth. But Aquinas argues that truth is known neither by sense, nor by knowing "what a things is." That is, truth is not known by understanding quiddity. "Truth," Thomas writes, "resides in the intellect composing and dividing; and not in the senses; nor in the intellect knowing *what a thing is.*" In *De Veritate* (q14a1c), he similarly distinguishes the intellect's two distinct operations: "There is one by which it forms the simple quiddities of things, as what man is or what animal is. ... The second operation of the understanding is that by which it joins and divides concepts by affirmation or denial."

Secondly, we find that, in the context of correctness in thought, Aristotle similarly differentiates the assertion of truth from definition. Assertion or denial, he writes (*De Anima* III, 6, 430b 26ff), is "the saying of something concerning something." Assertion always regards what is either true or false. On the other hand, the thinking of a definition, of what something is, is never incorrect in itself, but nor is definition like assertion in being "the assertion of something concerning something."

In the early part of his outline of systematics' function, Lonergan simply reiterates the point that judgement and understanding are distinct intellectual operations. We are thus led to expect that he will comment upon corresponding theological functional specialties that differ in their operation and content. However, prior to outlining the function of systematics, he makes some points on belief and understanding, which further help us to understand the specific function of systematics. Because Lonergan's contrast of belief and understanding is important, we should expand upon this distinction, before going any further.

4. Faith, Belief and Understanding

Lonergan argues (1994, 336) that the tradition of theological understanding, which the First Vatican Council promoted, came from the heritage of Augustine, Anselm and Aquinas. In this regard, he emphasises the

Augustinian and Anselmian distinction between belief and understanding, arguing that if we accept the distinction of understanding and belief, we can make sense of the precept *Crede ut intelligas*, "believe that you may understand." If understanding was indistinguishable from either belief or judgement, the precept would mean that one should believe so that one may judge, or demonstrate. Lonergan argues, however, that such a proposition would be superfluous. In the first place, belief is already a judgement. Secondly, he reminds us that the truths of faith cannot be humanly demonstrated. Accordingly then, *crede ut intelligas* means "believe that you may understand." This interpretation finds support in the fact that the truths of faith are intelligible to a believer, while they seem absurd to an unbeliever, a point that reminds one of Paul's statement:

> For what human being knows what is truly human except the human spirit that is within? So also no one comprehends what is truly God's except the Spirit of God. Now we have received not the spirit of the world, but the Spirit that is from God, so that we may understand the gifts bestowed upon us from God. And we speak of these things in words not taught by human wisdom but taught by the Spirit, interpreting spiritual things to those who are spiritual (I Cor 2:11-13).

Lonergan's distinction of belief and understanding presents an effective statement that systematics is not primarily concerned with promoting belief. To better understand this conception of systematics, and how he distinguishes systematics from belief, we must outline what he understands by belief and faith.

We need to take special care with Lonergan's concept of faith, because he distinguishes the terms "faith" and "belief." He makes this distinction (1994, 123) knowing fully the traditional usage of the terms, which tended to identify faith with belief. However, we must bear in mind that when Lonergan writes of faith and belief, he intends to bring more precision than the conventional usage to which we may be accustomed.

Lonergan's definition of faith (1994, 115, 321) has its foundations in the First Vatican Council's position (DS 3008/TCF 118) that faith is a "supernatural virtue" whereby one is "inspired and assisted" by God's grace to believe what God has revealed. He also situates faith, not within the realm of experience, understanding or judgement, but within a context of love and decision. "Faith," he writes, "is the knowledge born of religious love," so that the "knowledge" of faith is distinguished from the knowledge, more strictly speaking, which human intellect attains by the operations of experience, understanding and judgement. Tallon (1997,

119) similarly finds faith not within discursive reason or deliberative will, but within "affective cognition." In such light, Lonergan likens the "knowledge" of faith to Pascal's heart's reasons that reason does not understand. To be more precise, Lonergan explains that by the "heart's reasons," he means feelings that are intentional responses to values. By the "heart," he means the human subject acting on the fourth level of intentional consciousness, in which one operates on the level of moral decision, and acting "in the dynamic state of being in love." Taking inspiration from Pascal's statement, Lonergan proposes that, further to the factual knowledge attained by experience, understanding and judgement, there is another mode of knowledge attained though the discernments and judgements of value of a person in love. When that love is the love of God in one's heart, that "knowledge" is faith. Therefore, beyond one's apprehension of life values, as well as social, cultural and personal values, by being in love with God, one apprehends transcendent value, a point we find echoed in John-Paul II's notion of faith (1993, n66) as a decision, a self-commitment to God that works through love, which comes from the "heart" of a person, and in which one submits one's intellect and will to God.

In short, Lonergan holds (1964a, n10) that faith is a kind of knowledge that results from being in love with, and deciding on the value of, God. One of the effects of this being in love with God, which is a purely gratuitous love, is that a person may increase his or her intellectual horizon by opening oneself to intellectual cooperation with God. Lonergan's position accords with Tallon's observation (1997, 240) from Aquinas (*Summa Contra Gentiles* IV,21§1) that "from affection for divine things comes their manifestation," so that one converted in love is attuned to the other and feels the befittingness of possible acts toward and for the other." In the case of faith, this means that by so being in love with God, one can trustingly open oneself to the truth which God would communicate by way of revelation. In faith, one can then be open to intellectually attain more than one could naturally know by having faith, strictly speaking, in the revelation of God. We thus note that it is primarily by faith, as an intellectual virtue, by which we can accept the verity of God's revelation.

To understand Lonergan's exposition of faith, it is vital that we appreciate his point that faith is grounded upon love, not in reason's operation from experience through understanding to judgement. To illustrate this point, he draws our attention (1974, 154) to Paul's writing of "faith active in love," and to the Scholastics' teaching that faith without love is deficient. For Lonergan, faith is not so much concerned with theological facts or conclusions, as it is constitutive of a theological horizon. Just as love determines our total context or horizon in other matters, faith, as the religious "eye of love," discerns the range of God's work in the world and "his self-disclosure in revelation."

For our present investigation, we note that, in accord with the First Vatican Council, Lonergan holds faith to be a virtue, in which we love God and through which we may attain what God has revealed. We should emphasise that this attainment is not because of experience, understanding and judging, but it is grounded upon our decision regarding the value of God as revealer. More importantly, faith itself does not give us understanding. As a virtue on the level of decision, faith is distinct from any act of understanding. Thus, systematics, as the promotion of understanding, does not directly promote faith, strictly speaking. We cannot exclude the enrichment of faith by understanding, but the two activities are distinct. We may ask then, could not systematics be concerned with belief?

To answer that question, we reiterate that faith is a virtue. We may alternatively call faith a decision. However, the act of faith, which is belief, is a more cognitional act. In the intellectual collaboration with God, as a result of faith, one discovers and assents to the truths that God reveals to human intellect. The assent, which comes from faith, is what Lonergan (1992, 741-42) calls belief. This assent is not the result of human demonstration—it does not result from the natural mode of assent that comes from experience, understanding, and judging. Rather, the assent of belief comes from one's decision to accept the knowledge, goodness, and power of God. Belief, importantly, is a decision of faith that discerns the value of believing the word of God and chooses to seek this value. Faith in God introduces our intellect to a supernatural good, by taking our intellects beyond what it can naturally know, to the truth that God reveals. It is on the basis of this value and trust that we put on God, that we believe and assent to this truth (Lonergan 1962, 243, 239; 1994, 118).

The foregoing means that in the first place, there is faith, a supernatural virtue born of religious love. This love of God leads us to trust what God reveals and so assent to what God reveals as true. This assent of belief, as Lonergan (1994, 321) and the First Vatican Council (DS 3008/ TCF 118) emphasise, is not an assent based on human reason's intrinsic grasp of divine truths, but it is an assent based on our faith in the authority of God. It is vital that we appreciate how belief is an assent, not an understanding. It helps to note Tallon's point (1997, 229) that belief does not first involve conceptual judgement, because it is prior to understanding. The assent of belief is not based on a judgement upon the truth of one's understanding, it is an assent based on one's trust of one's sources. Lonergan illuminates this point (1994, 243) by explaining that the act of faith, which is belief, regards the mysteries of faith, not with the intention of understanding "what is it?", but with the intention of judging, "is it?" He means that belief is an intention of truth, not of essence. Furthermore, belief does not immediately concern understanding, because the mysteries of faith are believed, that is, assented to, on account of the authority we acknowledge in God's word, not on account of our own understanding.

Lonergan thus distinguishes faith from belief. Faith is identified with a love and decision that precedes knowledge, while belief involves the religious facts and values to which one assents. We emphasise that as faith is associated with love and decision, and belief is associated with assent, neither faith nor belief directly involve understanding of the mysteries of faith. While faith and belief fulfil a positive role in bringing the mysteries of faith to the human intellect for assent, we find that the human desire to understand remains unfulfilled by only faith and belief.

Lonergan further clarifies the distinction of belief and understanding by pointing out that assent to doctrines is the assent of faith. While religious people will hold this assent to be firm, different people have different degrees of understanding of the same truths, in which they all have faith. To support this argument, Lonergan notes (1994, 349-50) that; "Irenaeus [*Against the Heresies* I, 10, 3] for instance acknowledged that one believer could be far more articulate than another, but he denied that the former was more a believer or the latter less a believer." We also find support for the distinction of belief and understanding in Aquinas' writings. Aquinas categorically states (*De Veritate*, q14a1c) that belief does not occur in the operation of understanding. Belief occurs only in the operation of judgement, "for we believe what is true and disbelieve what is false." In support of his own position, Thomas explains that even the "Arabians," such as Averroes [*In De Anima III*, comm 21], called the intellect's first operation "imagination of understanding" and the second operation, "faith."

It is important for us to realise that the understanding, which systematics promotes, is not directly found in belief. Belief is essentially a judgement or assent based upon the faith we have in God. We may ask, however, if belief is opposed to human rationality, as is often claimed. By answering this question, we shall not only uphold the value of belief, but we shall also be able to show the relative places of belief and understanding within human intentionality.

In the first place, belief is often maligned as religious superstition. But Lonergan shows that belief is not confined to religious matters. He makes this point by reference to the widely accepted "scientific" use of belief. Before outlining Lonergan's examples, we should note the methodological question that he sets regarding belief. He asks (1992, 726),

> ... whether each man should confine his assents to what he knows in virtue of his personal experience, his personal insights, and his personal grasp of the virtually unconditioned or, on the other hand, there can and should be a collaboration in the advancement and dissemination of knowledge.

While many would answer the first part of this question in the affirmative, Lonergan cites concrete examples that place doubt upon the practicality of such a solution.

In the first case, which also illustrates the two ways of reaching truth and certitude, one seeks the logarithm of the square root of minus one. A mathematician may use the relevant definitions and postulates to deduce the answer for oneself. However, if one is a non-mathematician, one may ask a mathematician and to the extent that one has faith in the mathematician's competence and honesty, one will believe the truth of the mathematician's answer. As Lonergan points out (1992, 724-25), truth and certitude is attained in both cases. In the first case, it is immanently generated, while in the second, it is attained by the communication from one who knows to one who believes.

Lonergan (1994, 46-47) also cites the example of an engineer who uses a slide rule to perform quickly, what may have otherwise been a tedious calculation. He explains that the results are not entirely the product of the engineer's immanently generated knowledge. The slide rule's markings represent trigonometric and logarithmic tables that the engineer has not worked out for oneself. Importantly, the engineer "... does not know but believes that such tables are correct." This example still holds true toady, when the same engineer would be more inclined to use, and believe, the output of an electronic calculator or microcomputer. Accordingly, an engineer does not immanently generate all of one's knowledge, but at least a proportion of that knowledge comes from belief. Lonergan (1974, 88-89; 1992, 727; 1994, 46-47) challenges anyone to propose that all engineers should refrain from working until they have each personally derived the mathematical tables and results upon which they rely.

With Lonergan, we find it unlikely that anyone would propose such a methodology.

Lonergan (1974, 89; 1992, 727; 1994, 42-43) similarly refers to the work of a scientist. He argues that when a scientist either makes an original contribution to his subject, or when the scientist successfully repeats experiments which others have previously performed, what is attained is immanently generated knowledge, and not belief. He observes, though, that scientists do not suffer from a mania, which drives them to repeat one another's work, so that they may attain pure, immanently generated knowledge, unblemished by "non-scientific" belief. This could be the case, we note, if science was a static discipline that could be concerned with the work that one person could achieve in one's lifetime. However, if science is to be an ongoing advance, the results of previous experiments need to be assumed, so that new work can begin. Such presupposition of the others' work is another example of belief, not of immanently generated knowledge. It is also a simple illustration of the value of belief, even in science.

As an example of belief that may appeal to the non-scientific reader, Lonergan cites (1974, 88; 1994, 42) the use of maps. He draws our attention to our knowledge of the relative positions of the United States' cities. If one has read a map of the United States, one has no doubt that one's knowledge is correct. Yet is the map accurate? Lonergan reminds us that, rather than having immanently generated knowledge of the map's accuracy, we believe it. It may be counter-argued that the accuracy of maps is verified by the countless persons who use the maps to fly, sail or drive. Yet, only a small proportion of such verification is the result of one's own immanently generated knowledge. The larger part of one's knowledge, Lonergan contends, is belief based upon the many witnesses who have found the maps acceptable.

We thus have four examples of belief, in which Lonergan argues for the value of believing. We may clarify the good of believing by examining the consequences of its rejection. To reject belief, as Lonergan notes (1992, 728), is to reject human collaboration in knowledge, which means leaving humanity in a state of primitive ignorance. In the first example, the vast majority of humanity would be robbed of the benefits of complex mathematics if each of us who wished to use the results of mathematics had to derive each result for himself or herself. Similarly, engineering and scientific research would be obstructed, were each engineer required to derive one's own logarithmic and trigonometric tables, or to design, build and test one's own calculator. Science too, would be at a virtual standstill, as no scientist would be able to proceed with new experiments until she or he had personally repeated, understood and verified all the experiments that revealed the information that could have been presupposed by belief. More familiar to many would be the predicament in which we would find ourselves when travelling. Were we to reject the value of belief, and rely on our own immanently generated knowledge, an international trip would be an ordeal. One would even be unlikely to find one's way to the airport, unless one were to yield to temptation, and believe the road maps and street signs that were produced as a result of the knowledge of other people.

We find, with Lonergan (1992, 728), that the alternative to belief is "a primitive ignorance." Against such ignorance, he proposes a symbiotic combination of belief and knowledge. More directly important for this investigation is the distinction between belief and understanding. In the above examples, we have a suggestion that belief is an assent to the knowledge proposed by others and that such assent does not itself involve understanding. To explain this point, and to indicate something of the "downward" mode of human intentionality that belief illustrates, we should investigate Lonergan's explanation of the process of belief.

In exploring this process, we note that for Lonergan, belief, no less than human intentionality in general, is a compound of different though dynamically related acts, not a single act. We note, though, that Lonergan outlines five steps or stages in the process of belief in both *Method in Theology* (44-46) and in *Insight* (728ff). We note that Lonergan uses different outlines of the process of belief in *Method* and *Insight*. The key difference between the two accounts apparently lies in Lonergan's emphasis, in *Method*, upon the persons involved in belief, in contrast to the greater emphasis on the propositions involved in belief, in the account presented in *Insight*.

The first of Lonergan's (1994, 44-45) five steps of belief is taken by one who wishes to be believed. One recognises the impossibility of giving another one's own senses, one's own understanding or one's own judgement, with which the other could have one's own cognitional acts. One can only communicate what one has experienced and one can only relate to another what one has understood and passed judgement upon. Accordingly, as one cannot give another one's own mind, one can only report one's own experience, understanding and judgement, and propose what one communicates for belief by another.

Belief's second step is a general judgement of the value of believing. It judges that no one person can immanently generate all knowledge. The judgement affirms a social and historical division of labour, in acquiring knowledge. Lonergan does note (1992, 729, 737-39; 43-45), though, that such affirmation is not uncritical. Believing is fallible, and he takes up the question of rectifying mistaken beliefs in both *Method in Theology* and *Insight*. However, in accepting the value of belief, Lonergan argues that one affirms that error would multiply, rather than diminish, in a regress to primitivism. One judges that believing is valuable therefore, as advancing the collaboration in, and advancement, of human knowledge. Belief thus affirms that just as affectivity can substitute for, or complete what is lacking in, any other level (Tallon 1997, 226), one can substitute for immanently generated experience, affective trust in another's witness.

The third step in belief is a particular judgement of value. This particular judgement concerns the worth of the witness. One asks if the witness is trustworthy, competent and of sound judgement. As Lonergan explains (1994, 45):

> The point at issue ... is whether one's source was critical of his sources, whether he reached cognitional self-transcendence in his judgements of fact and moral self-transcendence in his judgements of value, whether he was truthful and accurate in his statements.

This third step, however, may not be as simple as assessing the authenticity of one witness. One may have to evaluate the credibility and coherence of many witnesses to one subject. Nonetheless, this step addresses whether one's witness or witnesses are worthy of belief (1992, 729; 1994, 45-46).

The believer's decision to believe is belief's fourth step. Lonergan explains (1992, 730; 1994, 46) that this decision follows upon the judgement of value of belief in general and the particular judgement of the value of believing a particular witness. Here, one judges that a certain statement from a witness is credible and can be believed by a reasonable and responsible subject. Through a decision, the subject decides to accept from this other, in this instance, what the other communicates as an unconditioned.

The fifth step is the act of believing. In one's own mind, one assents to the communicated judgement of another. As Lonergan emphasises (1992, 730; 1994, 46), such assent comes not because of one's own immanently generated knowledge, but because one has accepted and assented to the immanently generated knowledge of another. He explains that belief's assent resembles ordinary judgement in its affirmation or denial of a statement's truth. However, while ordinary judgement results from a personal grasp of the unconditioned, belief's assent results from the decision to collaborate with others, in a concrete instance, in the pursuit of truth.

From the process of belief, which we have described above, we find several key implications that are relevant to our investigation. In the first place, Lonergan's account of belief shows a specific difference between knowledge and belief. Knowledge, strictly speaking, results from one's own experience, understanding, and judgement. Belief, however, becomes possible when the truth, which one has not personally attained, has been attained by another who is able to communicate that truth. In a wider context, this means that coming to know is a "group exercise." One person may perform the different cognitional operations, but many others may benefit from the performance of these operations if the person communicates the results of them, and if he or she is trustworthy and the others believe him or her (Lonergan 1962, 230; 1974, 87).

Lonergan (1992, 725; 1994, 43-44) places belief within a general context of collaboration in the advancement and dissemination of knowledge. Human knowledge is thus seen as a common reserve to which all may contribute by communicating the results of their own experience, understanding and judgement, and from which all may draw by believing the results of others' work. He argues that through communication and belief, people collaborate in the advancement of human knowledge by generating common sense, common knowledge, common science, common values and a common climate of opinion.

Secondly, the human collaboration in knowledge, which is associated with belief, results in an extension of truth. Belief carries truth from the mind of one who knows to the minds of those who do not know, and who rely on the knowing process having been performed by the first one. Accordingly then, belief "... increases the number of minds in which truths can be found" (Lonergan 1962, 230-31). Belief extends truth when one decides, even though one does not know the truth by one's own experience, direct and reflective understanding, that the truth is a good thing to have and that one is willing to believe a reliable and competent person in order to attain the truth.

The decision, indicated in the above paragraph, leads to our third point, that the impetus for belief lies in the fourth level of intentional consciousness. As indicated above, belief comes about when a subject decides on the value of accepting from another, in a particular instance, what the other communicates as an unconditioned (Lonergan 1992, 730; 1994, 46). Belief then, to be accurate, depends not so much on the knowledge, but on the attitude of the believing subject towards the other who is believed (Lonergan 1992, 452). Following this line of argument, we note Lonergan's point (1974, 90, 93) that beliefs are stable in times of social stability, while in times of social and cultural upheaval, beliefs are also more open to challenge and change. In a time of confusion, when less trust or value is put on social and cultural structures, unbelief is more likely to prevail.

Fourthly, and most importantly, we note that while belief is motivated by a moral decision of value, it results in a judgement of fact that is based on the knowledge of another. Lonergan thus notes (1994, 336) that belief is a judgement. In this respect, by judgement, he (1992, 731; 1994, 46) does not mean an affirmation of the truth of one's understanding, but it means the assent to the virtually unconditioned that is communicated by another. We note that belief in itself conveys facts, not understanding. Accordingly, religious belief cannot be expected to provide one with an understanding of how the mysteries of faith are what they are. Belief can only allow a person to assent to the facts of the mysteries.

Our investigation of Lonergan's account of belief shows the grounds for his interpretation (1994, 335-36) of Anselm's and Augustine's maxim, *Crede ut intelligas*. In the first place, belief is not done so that one may judge, because, as we have seen above, belief already involves assent. In the second place, in belief one does not attain understanding of the mysteries in which one believes. Thus, the functional specialty, systematics, as a promotion of understanding, cannot be constituted by religious belief alone.

Another point, which Lonergan's account of belief illustrates (1985b, 106-7, 181, 196-97; 1984, 10), is the difference between the "upward" and "downward" modes of human development. In the first place, there is human development from below upwards. Beginning from one's experience, one proceeds to growing understanding, through to growing and better judgement and from balanced judgement to being more responsible. On other hand, there is a development from above downwards, in which one begins in an affective intentionality with respect to one's family, one's state, to humanity, or to God. Children are born into a world of immediacy, but as Lonergan notes, from a nurturing environment of love, they are socialised and educated from this world of immediacy into the wider world mediated by meaning and motivated by values. This process depends on trust and belief, so that development may begin with one's affectivity. On this affectivity may rest one's apprehension of values, upon which in turn may rest one's belief, when one has found a trustworthy and competent teacher who can pass on one's heritage. From the belief that one has in the teacher's doctrine, one can grow in understanding, and then, with an experience made mature by one's understanding, one may begin the inverse process in which one operates on one's own experience. This point reflects that made by Tallon (1997, 225, 231), drawing on Aquinas, that a person may make a moral judgement, such as chastity, which is based on one's affections. In this case, one makes a non-conceptual assent, which is not based on prior understanding. In such a case, one may not be asked to write a book on ethics, but as Aristotle reminds us, the observation of such a person's actions would be the prime task of one who wanted to write such a book. The difference here is that the person who operates morally by affection, or connaturality, operates in the downward mode of intentionality, while the book writer would operate in the upward mode.

As we have noted before, we find these "upward" and "downward" modes of human development in the mediating and mediated phases of Lonergan's theological method. By appreciating the downward process operative in belief, we can better understand how we may assent to a truth, about which we may not have had personal experience of understanding. Likewise, with the downward mode, we can appreciate how we may seek understanding of the mysteries affirmed by doctrines, even though we may never directly experience these mysteries in this life. Lonergan's account of belief thus helps us to understand both how systematics is not concerned with belief in itself, and also how doctrines and systematics can fit into a theological method, in its "downward" mode. We are now almost in a position from which to understand systematics' positive function. Before doing that, however, we must say something of doctrines, as a functional specialty, so that we can both relate it to, and distinguish it from, systematics.

5. Doctrines and Understanding

Lonergan proposes (1973, 67-68; 1994, 132, 298-99, 331) that "Doctrines express judgements of fact and judgements of value." Moreover, doctrines' normative function is to discriminate between truth and error, and to manifest the truth of a religious tradition. Doctrines achieve this goal by the addition of foundations to dialectic. That is, from the manifold positions of "evaluators, historians, interpreters and researchers," which dialectic assembles and classifies, foundations decides upon which of these are compatible with intellectual, moral and religious conversion. The judgements of doctrines thus follow, and rely upon, the previous functional specialties. As Lonergan writes (1994, 132), "Such doctrines stand within the horizon of foundations. They have their precise definition from dialectic, their positive wealth of clarification and development from history, their grounds in the interpretation of the data proper to theology." While this functional relationship exists, we should note that doctrines occurs in the "downward," "mediated" phase of theology. Importantly, doctrines' affirmations are based upon the horizon of conversion, thematised in foundations, not upon judgement regarding the correctness of our understanding. Doctrines' selection from the options presented by dialectic is thus based upon the trust, or faith, one places in religious authorities. This helps clarify Lonergan's point (1994, 298), that the outer word, which comes to us from Christ, is doctrine because it comes from an authoritative source. We would emphasise that such authorities are not arbitrary, nor are they slavishly and unintelligently followed. Rather, they are established by intellectual, moral and religious conversion, and thematised in foundations.

As a functional speciality, doctrines works by: research uncovering revelation in sources, interpretation determining what those sources mean, history judging upon what is revealed in that meaning, dialectic assembling the manifold options presented in religious history, foundations thematising the horizon within which teachings are meaningful, and doctrines determining which specific teachings are compatible with that horizon.

The key issue for us is what doctrines manifest. Essentially, doctrines present religious truths. Those truths are presented with the certitude that stems from one's faith in the truthfulness of the God, in whom one has faith, and in whom one has faith in revealing certain truths to us. More important, though, is that doctrines neither show, nor are based upon, an understanding of the realities that they affirm. Doctrines are based upon authority and they are established in the "downward" mode. Within doctrines, we should not expect to find an understanding of the realities affirmed by doctrines. While doctrines do manifest some understanding, this is only a "catechetical" understanding of the doctrine's message. Alternatively, one can have a historical understanding inasmuch as one has studied the history of the doctrine (Lonergan 1973, 68). However, this understanding is only of the doctrine, not an understanding of the reality that the doctrine affirms.

Doctrines essentially manifests the truth of divine revelation. Doctrines are certain to the extent that one has faith in one's authorities. However, because doctrines operates in the downward mode, as a judgement following upon moral decision regarding one's horizon and authorities, doctrines does not itself intend understanding of the revealed object, nor is it based upon such an understanding. Doctrines thus stand as the truths affirmed by belief, as affirmations that take their certainty from faith, but affirmations that as yet do not yield understanding. Doctrines are thus clear affirmations, but they tend to be empty if the meaning of what they affirm is not worked out and if their coherence is not also determined (Lonergan 1994, 142). Such search for meaning and coherence is the work of understanding, which we find in systematics.

6. Does Systematics Seek Certitude?

Having covered the essential manner in which belief and doctrines attain certitude, we can now appreciate why Lonergan emphasises (1994, 336) that "The aim of systematics is not to increase certitude but to promote understanding. It does not seek to establish the facts." In the first place, he argues that systematics cannot add proof to doctrines because doctrines result, in the downward mode, from human intentionality following upon foundations added to dialectic. Moreover, it would be superfluous for systematics to pursue further certitude, because that certitude is already established in doctrines. In the second place, we note Lonergan's point (1964c, 8; 1994, 336) that supernatural truths are manifested to us only by divine revelation. Theological certitude is gained from authority and faith, neither of which, we note, rely on understanding. He proposes systematics as a pursuit of theological understanding. We note then, that because it is concerned with understanding, systematics cannot add proof, because understanding deals only with what an object is, not whether it exists or not.

The distinction of doctrines as the pursuit of certitude, from systematics as the pursuit of understanding, parallels a distinction made in Aquinas' *Summa Contra Gentiles* (I,9§1-2). Thomas argues that there is a "... twofold truth of divine things," from the point of view of our knowledge. While there are divine truths that can be demonstrated, there are also those truths that can only be revealed and are only usefully approached by probable arguments that are for the "training and consolation of the faithful." Thomas brings out the two manners of approaching divine truth more explicitly in his *Quodlibetal Questions* (IV,q9,a3 [18]), as noted above, when he differentiates arguments that advance certitude, from those that advance understanding.

Our investigations of systematics, up until this point, have primarily focussed on clarifying systematics by way of explaining what systematics is not. We have shown that Lonergan does not conceive systematics as a promotion of certitude, truth, faith or belief. Having noted what systematics is not, we now turn to a more positive statement of systematics' function, as the promotion of theological understanding.

7. Systematics as "Reason Illumined by Faith"

To more accurately understand the positive function of systematics, we find it helpful to outline the operations of the subject who does systematics. The need to study the subject becomes clearer if we consider the point of *Dei Filius* (DS 3016/TCF 132), that reason can attain a highly fruitful understanding of the mysteries of faith. One can easily overlook the Council's specific reference to *human reason* and its emphasis on the subjective nature of theological understanding. After all, the Council's specified conditions for understanding—faith, diligence, piety and sobriety, are conditions of the theologising human subject, not conditions of the theological object.

If systematics is done by a human subject, we note that, while human reason is illumined by faith and assisted by God's grace, the subject will still be affected by the same drives, capabilities, and limitations of human reason, which we have discussed earlier in this work. On the limiting side, one will still be unable to attain an immediate or quidditative understanding of the divine mysteries. However, one will still be an attentive, intelligent, reasonable, and responsible subject, who has the pure desire to know. That desire to know naturally includes the desire to understand quiddities. To help situate the function of systematics, we shall now consider the desire to know in the context of theological understanding.

Lonergan holds that the pure desire to know, which is natural to all people, manifests itself in a twofold manner. Just as essence and existence coincide to the extent that neither one can be found without the other, the intellect's two fundamental questions, "What is it?" and "Is it?" are integrated to the extent that we truncate our intellectual inquiry if we attempt to answer one question without the other. Lonergan importantly states (1964c, 7-9) that questions of existence and essence arise in response to the answers to each other. Intelligence's operation leads to reason's operation, for we spontaneously want to know if what we have understood is true. He also significantly maintains that the operation of reason prompts intelligence, for we spontaneously strive to better understand what we already know to exist. Moreover, he proposes (1992, 661) that even when we have attained certainty of fact, our reason still prompts further exercise of understanding, so that we may more fully understand what we know to exist. We would both flee from understanding and truncate the human subject, were we to ignore questions of intelligibility, including questions into the realities affirmed by doctrines.

In the light of the desire to know, which includes the desire to understand, Lonergan maintains (1985b, 82) that an effective theological method must address humanity as attentive, responsible, and intelligent. Despite the value inherent in a theological method that provided only data, certitude and values, this method would truncate the fulfilment of the human drive to know by neglecting human intelligence. Alternatively, fostering an understanding of the mysteries of faith, such as the understanding promoted by systematics, helps theology penetrate and direct the whole human mind. Promoting an understanding of the mysteries, affirmed in doctrines, thus assists in fulfilling a key desire of human intellect (1964a, n10).

Notwithstanding this human desire to know God, can God actually be the object of human knowledge? Lonergan acknowledges (1974, 123) that God "cannot be an object in the etymological sense, in the Kantian sense, in the sense acceptable to a logical atomism, positivism, or empiricism." However, in the light of Lonergan's intentionality analysis, we may turn to the subject, and consider thinking subjects as asking questions about God, and sometimes gaining answers to these questions. In this way, God is the object of human intentionality, as the object of human inquiry. So, in the same way as any other object, God is the object of what is intended in questioning and becomes known ever-better as the questions are answered and the further questions become more accurate (Lonergan 1974, 123; 1994, 343), a point that echoes Rahner's statement (1971b, 61) that Christians come into contact with God by raising questions about God. For the specific concerns of systematics, God can be the heuristic object of human intelligence. To the extent that human beings ask questions about the intelligibility of God and the divine mysteries, they become objects of human understanding.

Lonergan uses Aquinas' writings to support his position. He observes that (1997, 100), while Aristotle opened his *Metaphysics* by observing that all people naturally desire to know, Thomas was more inclined to define that desire by an unrestricted desire to know God's essence. This desire, though naturally unfulfillable, still provides what Lonergan later calls a "dynamic orientation" towards understanding God, which would in turn mean the understanding of all else. Accordingly, "For Augustine, our hearts are restless until they rest in God; for Aquinas, not our hearts, but first and most our minds are restless until they rest in seeing Him." Aquinas (*Summa Theologiae*, I,q12,a1c, I-II,q3,a8c) situates the ultimate human beatitude in our intellect, which is our highest function. This beatitude, Thomas further argues, has intellectual knowledge of God, the supremely knowable object, as its highest goal. On this point, Thomas first explains that human intellect remains unfulfilled with objects remaining unknown. Secondly, as the intellect's object is quiddity, human intellect attains perfection insofar as it grasps the essence of a thing. Accordingly, a human intellect has a desire to know God that is fulfilled as much as it grasps something of the essence of God. We find then, that Aquinas would maintain, in a manner similar to Lonergan, that the desires and beatitude of the human intellect require some understanding of the mysteries of faith, and not only assent. Aquinas notes though (*Summa Contra Gentiles*, I,8§1), that while any understanding that we may attain may be imperfect, such an understanding is still useful. To even partly fulfil the desire of the human intellect to grasp the mysteries of faith would be the source of great joy.

If we place systematics within the context of the human desire to know, we can better appreciate Lonergan's statement (1973, ix) that the functional specialty, systematics, is "the effort of human understanding to gain some insight into revealed truths." While systematics operates in the downward mode of human intentionality and our previous investigations of insight have focussed on its occurrence in the "upward" mode, systematics still manifests the key aspects of insight that we have earlier discovered. So, when investigating systematics, we should bear in mind that its insight: results from and resolves intellectual restlessness, bafflement, tension or neurosis. Furthermore, insight: grasps intelligible possibility, relies on a question, is creative, explains reasons why, grasps relations and unity, requires an image, provides personal appropriation and is very powerful.

Of the above points, we note three of particular importance. In the first place, the insight that systematics promotes is in response to a human desire. We should ask if this desire is blind, at all attainable, and in sum, whether this desire actually produces anything beyond its own fulfilment. We thus ask if systematics has a purpose. To this question, for the present, we suggest that the purpose of systematics could be found in the value of insight. In the light of Lonergan's intentionality analysis, we find that one who genuinely understands is able to reformulate this insight. Such reformulation is crucial to teaching and so to communications, in which one needs to construct expressions of one's discoveries that are intelligible to one's hearers. We thus propose that systematics, as insight into revealed truths, will be useful in helping others to come to their personal intellectual appropriation of these divine truths. Later, we shall evaluate Lonergan's functional specialty, systematics, in terms of the personal understanding of the mysteries of faith that systematics can provide.

Secondly, because it promotes human insight, systematics requires a humanly attainable image with which to enunciate a doctrine. We recall the necessity of sensible image, in Lonergan's example (1992, 33) of insight into a circle's roundness. In that case, insight is the act of grasping necessary relations between imagined equal radii and a curve that must look perfectly circular. Aquinas (*De Veritate,* q2a6c), we also recall, held sensible image to be necessary for the act of human understanding. With Aristotle (*De Anima* III,7, 431a 17, 431b 2, 432a 3-10), he maintained that phantasm is related to human intellect as sensible objects are related to sense, and colour is related to sight. He further argued (*De Veritate,* q10a2ad7m) the necessity of phantasm as intellect's object:

> No power can know anything without turning to its object, as sight knows nothing unless it turns to color. Now, since phantasms are related to the possible intellect in the way that sensible things are related to sense, as the Philosopher points out, [*De Anima,* III, 7, 431a 14] no matter to what extent an intelligible species is present to the understanding, understanding does not actually consider anything according to that species without referring to phantasm.

Lonergan maintains (1997, 41) with Aquinas that a sensible image is necessary for intelligent activity no matter, he emphasises, how perfect the *"species intelligibilis."* As we shall find in more detail below, this means that the insight gained in systematics will rely on an image, which is on the level that people can naturally attain.

We need mention a final caveat. Intelligent insight is neither into existence, nor into the fact of being of an object. That is the role of judgement. As mentioned before, intelligent insight is understanding: of causes, reasons, explanations of what and why. It is a grasp of intelligible possibility. As insight into revealed truths, we should expect systematics to be concerned with seeking intelligibility, not with judging existence.

We must turn to investigating in more detail, the nature of the understanding that systematics promotes and provides. However, before dealing with these questions, we note that systematics' insight is not into raw data, but into established facts, namely, revealed truths. So we must first explore the implications of systematics aiming to understand revealed truths. The first step however, is to explore why these truths are necessarily revealed.

When explaining the function of systematics, Lonergan writes (1994, 336) that "the truths of faith do not admit human demonstration." We shall now explore the grounds for this statement and we shall bring out implications of this position for theological understanding.

Lonergan's position (1994, 320), on the mysteries being indemonstrable, corresponds to the First Vatican Council's teaching (DS 3020, 3041/TCF 136, 137), which aimed at countering a rationalist position that simultaneously denied the existence of mysteries and proposed that theological dogmas could be demonstrated. Against rationalism, the Council declared that "the doctrine of faith which God has revealed has not been proposed like a philosophical system to be perfected by human ingenuity." The Council restated its position by anathematising those who proposed "that in divine revelation no true and properly so called mysteries are contained but that all dogmas of faith can be understood and demonstrated from natural principles by reason." The Council's position, which Lonergan takes up, is that in revelation, there are given certain mysteries and that these mysteries are beyond discovery by human reason. Furthermore, the dogmas concerning these mysteries can neither be demonstrated nor understood by natural human reason. Such is the doctrine of the Council and Lonergan. We ask though, how it is that these mysterious truths of faith lie beyond human discovery or demonstration?

To explain how we cannot demonstrate or discover the truths of faith by natural human reason, we first recall the structure of human knowing. As we outlined in our sixth chapter, human knowing is neither a single act, nor a combination of similar acts, it is a dynamic structure of experience, understanding and judgement. We do acknowledge that reason's demonstration ultimately results in an establishment of fact, which is on the level of judgement. However, prior to the establishment of fact, demonstration relies on the previous activities of experience and understanding. We recall Lonergan's statement (1988, 207),

> Nor can one place human knowing in judging to the exclusion of experience and understanding. To pass judgement on what one does not understand is, not human knowing, but human arrogance. To pass judgement independently of all experience is to set fact aside.

One's judgement of fact is thus judgement on the correctness of one's understanding. That understanding, upon which judgement operates, is attained by insight into the sensible image. We recall how Lonergan (1997, 41-42), Aquinas (*De Veritata*, q10,a2,ad7m, q18a8ad4m; *Summa Theologiae*, Iq84,a7c) and Aristotle (*De Anima*, III, 7, 431a 17) insisted that natural human knowledge is impossible without a sensible image.

If we directly consider the divine mysteries, we should first note Aquinas' answer to whether created intellect can understand the essence of God. He answers (*Summa Theologiae*, Iq12,a1c) that God's essence, being pure act, is supremely knowable in itself and that the ultimate beatitude of human beings is to behold God's essence. Thus, there is both the desire, and the goal of, people to reach the delight of the blessed, in apprehending the essence of God. Thomas acknowledges, however, that some knowable objects may not be knowable by certain intellects, due to some disproportion between the object and the knowing intellect, such as a supremely visible object like the sun being inaccessible to the limited vision of a bat. In such way, Aquinas (*Summa Theologiae*, I,q12,a11c) clarifies that we cannot understand the essence of God, with natural human intellect, in this life. He observes that because natural human intellect is bound to corporeal, or sensible, objects, human intellect cannot understand God's essence in this life, unless it is supernaturally gifted with freedom from its natural dependence on sensible images.

Because the natural human intellect's act of understanding operates on the phantasm attained by the operation of the senses, Thomas argues (*Summa Contra Gentiles*, I,30§3) that the human intellect "does not transcend the mode which is found in sensible things, in which the form and the subject of the form are not identical owing to the composition of form and matter." Aquinas thus dissociates himself from Plato's teaching. Plato held that, not only are these immaterial or non-sensible substances understood by the human intellect, but that these immaterial substances are first understood by human intellect. While Aquinas holds his position to be the same as Aristotle's, he also notes that human experience corroborates his position. We find that our intellect has a natural relationship to material objects. Thomas notes (*Summa Theologiae*, I,q88,a1c) that "immaterial substances which do not fall under sense and imagination, cannot first and *per se* be known by us, according to the mode of knowledge which experience proves us to have." We note, though, that Thomas means that immaterial substances are not accessible to natural human knowing in this life. In accord with his abovementioned points, he means to exclude neither any supernatural gift of knowledge in this life, nor the direct understanding of God enjoyed by the blessed.

Our intellect relies upon the experience of sensible objects for its natural operation. Aquinas thus argues (*Summa Contra Gentiles*, III,41§2, 47§1; *Summa Theologiae*, Iq88a1c) that natural human intellect cannot possibly understand immaterial or separate substances, because these separate substances are not subject to natural human experience. With specific reference to the divine essence, Thomas argues that because we cannot experience the divine essence in the sensible realm, natural human intellect cannot grasp it. Aquinas states his position concisely in his *Summa Contra Gentiles* (IV,1§1), writing that:

> The human intellect, to which it is connatural to derive its knowledge from sensible things, is not able *through itself* to reach the vision of the divine substance in itself, which is above all sensible things and, indeed, improportionately above all other things.

According to Aquinas, the divine essence is beyond natural human experience, and it thus remains a mystery beyond human understanding or demonstration.

Lonergan continues Aquinas' line of reasoning in a more contemporary form. He notes (1974, 95) that modern science proceeds from data and to this data it adds verifiable hypotheses. God cannot be the object of such scientific endeavour, because God is not a datum of human experience. In this life, "we do not know God face to face." Moreover, because a natural, human mode of verification relies on a relationship between data, one cannot verify God by the objects of this world, for there is no sensible relationship between God and the objects of this world, which are accessible to our experience. Aquinas and Lonergan therefore hold that as God's essence lies beyond natural human experience, it is a mystery that cannot be intelligently understood by natural human intellect. Natural human intellect can neither demonstrate nor prove the nature of the divine essence, because no understanding is present to be verified.

This section has so far outlined Lonergan's position that the mysteries of faith are beyond human demonstration, we have shown how this position accords with both the First Vatican Council and Aquinas and we have found how Lonergan and Aquinas justify their position. We must emphasise that this position has key implications for the understanding of these truths of faith. We noted that the truths of faith ultimately cannot be demonstrated because we cannot have any natural human experi-

ence of the mysteries that these truths affirm. Most importantly, because
we have no experience of these mysteries, we cannot form a sensible image of them, so we cannot have any natural human understanding of
these mysteries. Because there is no phantasm of the mysteries, human
intellect can gain no immediate insight into them. From this position,
we concur that the truths of faith cannot be demonstrated, simply because there is no understanding upon which judgement can act.

If one's main concern is with proof, one can easily miss the more pertinent point that because there is no natural human experience of the mysteries, no immediate understanding is possible into these mysteries. The
significance of this position is that, as far as the mysteries of faith are
concerned, no understanding is possible when human intellect operates
in its natural, "upward" mode from experience, through understanding,
to judgement then decision. This position is reflected in *Dei Filius'* (DS
3041/TCF 137) treatment of understanding and judgement the same
way, declaring them impossible through natural means.

This section has established two points. For this book, the more important point is that the immaterial, non-sensible, nature of the divine
mysteries places them beyond the insight attainable by natural human
intellect. We have also shown Lonergan's explanation for the
indemonstrability of the truths of faith by natural human reason. The
way is not closed, though, for intellect to attain the mysteries by a "supernatural" mode, and we should turn to Lonergan's account of this supernatural attainment.

While human intellect cannot naturally attain understanding, or verification of the mysteries of faith, it still desires more than it can attain
naturally. The fulfilment of this desire comes first, not by any humanly
natural act, but by the supernatural revelation of these indemonstrable
mysteries. The indemonstrable mysteries, rather than being the result of
human discovery or deduction, are given by God in revelation as "a divine deposit" (Lonergan 1994, 322-23). It is important to keep in mind,
as Lonergan (1994, 321) and the First Vatican Council (DS 3008/TCF
118) emphasise, that the truth of the mysteries of faith is apprehended,
not by human reason's natural operation, but because their truth is based
on the authority of God, "who reveals and can neither deceive nor be
deceived."

We should make two points concerning revelation. First, it is helpful to
clarify that divine revelation gives simply the "truths of faith," not an
understanding of the mysteries (Lonergan 1994, 336, 321-23). Specifically, these are truths that "man could not reach by the development of

his understanding" (Lonergan 1992, 746). The vital point is that revelation conveys the "facts" of faith. It does not convey much understanding of how the facts may be what they are. We therefore distinguish the revelation of truths from any possible understanding of the mysteries by human intellects.

Secondly, we note that Lonergan leaves open what he may mean by "revelation." He does give a clue, about what he accepts as constituting revelation, in an earlier part of *Method in Theology* (1994, 150). He observes that the sources for Christian theology are disputed, and that what is recognised as revelation, and hence theology's sources, is a matter for the specialty, doctrines. However, within his own horizon, Lonergan (1994, 321) recognises the authoritative witnesses to revelation as, "all that has been revealed by God in scripture or tradition and, as well, has been proposed to be believed as revealed either in a solemn pronouncement by the church or in the exercise of its ordinary and universal teaching office."

Our investigations above show the implied point that revealed mysteries are not attained in an "upward" mode of human intentionality. Mysteries are revealed to us, Lonergan would say, in a "downward" mode, in which we assent to truths, not on the basis of our understanding, but on the basis of our moral decision on the value of God as revealer. We should thus investigate the implications of revealed truth and systematics' aim to understand it, being in the "downward" mode.

8. Understanding Revealed Truth and the "Downward" Mode

Systematics is concerned with promoting an understanding of *revealed truths,* so it differs from those scientific pursuits that operate upon data, rather than truths. As Lonergan explains (1964c, 20), the natural sciences begin by attempting to understand the presentations of sense. However, the functional specialty, systematics, begins with established truths, which are the revealed truths of God. Systematics is therefore found in a "downward" mode of human intentionality. In the "upward" mode we operate by virtue of our own experience, then understanding, then judgement. However, in the "downward" mode, we assent to already established truths, we assent to the propositions put forward by one whom we decide on as valuable.

We can thus make sense of the two orders of knowledge, and the difference between understanding data and understanding facts, to which

Lonergan refers. The first order of knowledge is the more familiar process, whereby one attains factual knowledge by attending to data, forming intelligent hypotheses, then verifying the correctness of one's understanding. The second order of knowledge, in which we understand facts, is more complex. In this order, our understanding is concerned not with understanding data but understanding the facts established in the first order. We noted the difference between these orders We also recall Lonergan's example of the truth that "the sum of two and two is four." In the second, "downward," order of knowledge, this same truth has been increasingly better and more fully understood by the ongoing work of mathematicians. He offers (1994, 325, 348) two further examples that illustrate the difference between the two orders of knowledge. First, in critical history, one initially determines the sources of witnesses' information, interprets the witnesses' checking procedures, then evaluates how well the witnesses used their information. The historian's second inquiry is to use this appraised information to expound upon what happened in the period under examination. In a like manner there is the scientist's first mode of investigation, in which commonsense observations are taken as data for scientific hypotheses. In the second mode, one can use these scientific theories to expound science in an applied manner, and so change the commonsense world.

Naturally, these reflections on understanding data and understanding facts become much clearer in the light of Lonergan's distinction of the "upward" and "downward" modes of human intentionality. We find the understanding of data in the upward mode, in which understanding data is part of the process of working towards the truth of facts. The understanding of facts, however, occurs in the downward mode, and produces not factual knowledge *per se*, but the "truth of the account or explanation." This difference echoes the difference between science and theology, noted in *De Deo Trino* II. Lonergan explains (1964c, 20) that science begins with data. On the other hand, theology begins with divinely revealed truths, and then attempts to understand these divine truths. In *Method in Theology* (1994, 348-49), he clarifies that, while the first order takes initial precedence, for without the facts of the first order there is nothing to understand in the second order, the two orders are actually interdependent. This interdependence arises because, when one, in the second order, explains the truth attained in the first order, one may revise one's "upward" understanding in the first order. While Lonergan only refers explicitly to revising scientific or historical understandings, we can easily grasp how our theological understanding of data could be re-evaluated in the light of one's understanding of doctrines, which occurs in systematics in the "second order." To take a negative perspective on the matter, if one's inquiries in systematics lead one to conclude the intelligible impossibility of a doctrine, one would need to re-evaluate one's "first order" interpretation of theological data. One would actually be advised to re-evaluate all of the methodological steps leading to doctrines.

We can better appreciate the difference between the understanding present in doctrines and systematics. In Lonergan's method (1994, 349), doctrines is primarily concerned with establishing the verity of religious realities. The understanding present in doctrines is an understanding that only goes so far as determining doctrines' clarity and definition. Systematics, however, is more properly concerned with understanding something of the nature of the mysteries affirmed by doctrines and something of those mysteries' interconnections. We can thus better understand Lonergan's point (1994, 336) that systematics' function is neither to establish facts, nor to reinforce them, but to take on the facts established in doctrines and to find some intelligibility within these facts.

We also find that the downward mode adds clarity to Lonergan's point, that systematics would be subordinated to doctrines. This subordination, or dependence as we prefer to call it, would reflect the natural dependence of any other act of understanding to the exigences of existence. This means that any systematic understanding must still be subjected to the critical question, "Is it so?" However, systematics would have the added control of doctrines, by virtue of having its origins in doctrines. These factors lead Lonergan (1988, 126) to state that:

> The basic relation, then, of speculative theology to the teaching authority of the church is the subordination of both understanding and science to wisdom. It is a supernatural subordination that runs parallel to the natural subordination of *quid sit* to *an sit*, of speculation to judgement.

The "downward" mode also gives us a clue as to the need for systematics. We should not expect to find an understanding of the mysteries of faith to be found in doctrines, which provide, as Lonergan reminds us (1994, 349), "a clear and distinct affirmation of religious realities." This affirmation is an assent to the mysteries of faith, which is a response to the additions of dialectic to foundations. The assent, effected in doctrines, is based on prior authorities, not on a reflective grasp of the unconditioned. The essential point is that this assent is not made regarding

168 Matthew C. Ogilvie: *Faith Seeking Understanding*

prior understanding, so that when we assent to doctrines, we are assenting to something we do not yet understand.

The difference between understanding data and understanding facts provides one possible reason for proposing a growth in understanding of doctrines, while at the same time maintaining a constancy in these doctrines. As with the progressively better understanding of a mathematical truth by successive generations of mathematicians, so too, the occurrence of systematics' understanding in the downward mode allows us to promote and attain growth in understanding of the same doctrine. This point helps clarify Lonergan's (1994, 352) contention that, in the context of systematics, the permanence of dogma contributes to continuity. He does not make a detailed defence of dogmatic permanence here, and such a debate is beyond the scope of this investigation. However, if we grant the permanence of dogma, as Lonergan understands it, we find that inasmuch as systematics is an understanding of the mysteries of faith that are established in the functional specialty, doctrines, systematics is part of a continuous, ongoing theological process. Doctrines, as we have previously found, are the result of our reflection, in the light of our conversion, on the achievements of the first, mediating phase of theology. Thus, where systematics is done in the context of doctrines, systematics maintains continuity by seeking its insights into the mysteries within the context of an ongoing, living tradition. Moreover, by its relationship with doctrines, systematics is part of a ongoing, continuous process, by its operation upon dogmas, which remain constant. On the other hand, Lonergan notes (1994, 350) that when systematic theology attempts to operate without sufficient reference to the historical dogmas of a religion, it runs the serious risk of becoming speculative, abstract, and irreligious.

9. THE PRIMACY OF LOVE

With our understanding of systematics' operation in the "downward mode" of human intentionality, we can better understand Lonergan's notion of the primacy of love, which is also more intelligible if we recall that systematics is driven neither by proof, nor by deduction, but by one's love of God. In other words, the impulse behind systematics is one's conversion and experience of transcendent orientation to God. It is critical to appreciate that systematics does occur in this "downward" mode of human intentionality. With this recognition, we can understand how love takes primacy in human intentionality generally in theology, and more particularly in systematics.

From the broad statements in our last paragraph, we can turn to some specific implications of systematics, as regards the primacy of love. First, Lonergan argues (1994, 340) that if love of God is primary, we can be excused from universal acceptance of the adage, "*Nihil amatum nisi praecognitum.*" Moreover, with reference to Paul, (Romans 5:5), he proposes that the love of God neither results from, nor is formed by, human knowledge of God. What is primary then, is not knowledge of God, but a dynamic, loving orientation to God as an as-yet unknown object. Such an orientation results from God's gratuitous love, which captures the will, intellect and sensitivity of a person (Lonergan 1964a, n10; 1994, 340-41). Aquinas makes a similar point (*Summa Theologiae*, I-II,q113,a1, ad2m), by noting that faith and charity direct the human mind towards God. Peter Beer (Danaher 1993, 189) also observes that the love of the Holy Spirit is primary, in guiding our intellects to find data relevant to Christ, to whom we are lovingly converted. Essentially, prior to our knowledge of God, we are lovingly gifted to inquire and direct our intentionality, so that we come to understand, judge, and decide upon God.

The primacy of love, which we find in systematics, is intrinsically linked to the sublation of different intentional operations of the human mind. In systematics, we find, beyond a sequential primacy of love, a distinct manifestation of the way in which one's religious conversion of love sublates one's moral conversion, which in turn sublates one's intellectual conversion (Lonergan 1994, 243). In concrete terms, one's faith in God, which is in the order of love, forms one's horizon that is thematised in foundations. Those foundations decide between the many options presented to doctrines. In turn, doctrines sublates systematics by directing it to understand the affirmed mysteries of faith, rather than, for example, engaging in vain speculation. Lastly, systematics sublates communications by guiding it into communicating an intelligible, rather than unintelligible message. Systematics is thus part of a general process of the human spirit's unfolding. In this process, experience is not blind because it seeks intelligibility, understanding is not irrational because it pursues affirmation, judgement is not irresponsible because it demands that its truth be also good, and moral decision seeks after ultimate value in that which is lovable. After careful consideration of systematics, if we understand how it is part of a "downward" sublated and sublating process, with love being primary in that process, we can better appreciate the general way in which being in love affects our moral decision and intellectual knowing. We can also appreciate how intellectual, moral and religious conversions can be placed within one integrated process of human intentionality. Lastly, we can also find one reason for the myriad of conflicting opinions, which are held by scholars who research, interpret and pass judgment upon the same data.

The primacy of love also makes intelligible the dynamic orientation of human intellect. We recall Lonergan's statement (1997, 100):

> Aristotle opened his *Metaphysics* with the remark that naturally all men desire to know. But Aquinas measured that desire to find in the undying restlessness and absolute exigence of the human mind that intellect as intellect is infinite, that *ipsum esse* is *ipsum intelligere* and uncreated, unlimited Light, that though our intellects because potential cannot attain naturally to the vision of God, still our intellects as intellects have a dynamic orientation, a natural desire, that nothing short of that unknown vision can satisfy utterly. For Augustine our hearts are restless until they rest in God; for Aquinas, not our hearts, but first and most our minds are restless until they rest in seeing Him.

Whether we take up Augustine's or Aquinas' account, Lonergan's point (1994, 340-41) remains valid. Human insight into the mysteries of God occurs in a downward mode of human intentionality, in which love of, or a dynamic orientation to, God is primary. Human beings are primarily driven to understand the mysteries of God by the dynamic state of being in love with God, not by an experience of data. The intellectual "restlessness" in Aquinas and Augustine reflects the reality that our mind's intellectual response to God is consequent to, and prompted by, the love of God in our intentional consciousness.

The primacy of love over knowledge leads us to the primacy of conversion over proof. In basic terms, one's moral and affective horizon is invariably established before one attempts to establish proofs. Lonergan observes that "Proof always presupposes premises, and it presupposes premises accurately formulated within a horizon." He most importantly emphasises (1973, 40-41) that one's horizon cannot be logically proven, it is established by conversion, though we recall our earlier point that Lonergan does not reject logic, he simply puts it into a wider, methodological context. This point has significant implications for the relationship of natural, or philosophical theology, and systematic theology. If we acknowledge that even the most logical philosophical proofs regarding God occur while sublated by the moral and religious conversions of the thinking subject, we find a common point of reference for natural and systematic theology. That common point of reference is the intentional subject who can do both natural and systematic theology. If we appreciate that proofs occur within a horizon dependent upon one's love and commitment to, or one's apathy towards, God, and if we understand that a subject performs one's "logical" reflections upon God under the same horizon as one makes one's reflections upon systematic theology, we can make a step towards positive integration of the two disciplines. With Lonergan (1973, 41; 1994, 337-39), we propose that this integration is possible not so much in the contents of natural and systematic theology, but in the intentional subject who may at one time do natural theology and at another time do systematic theology, with both forms of theology being done under the subject's same horizons.

Two further points are pertinent. First, the primacy of love, or orientation to transcendent mystery, gives a more universal meaning to God as systematic theology's object. Rather than concepts or proofs, it is this loving, transcendent orientation to divine mystery that unites people across cultural boundaries in their inquiries into God. Concepts and proofs, which may not be transculturally intelligible, cannot unite minds and hearts in investigating divine mystery. That union is made possible by the gracious love of God (Lonergan 1985b, 197; 1994, 341). This means that inter-religious or ecumenical dialogue may be more fruitful if all parties appreciate the affective relationship that the others have with God. While finding such a common love of God may help in a small way to resolve doctrinal differences, it would no doubt go a long way towards dispelling the suspicion and hostility that so often sullies inter-religious relations. Secondly, the primacy of love shows how a negative theology can be worthwhile. A theology that speaks of what God is not, or states that God cannot be fully understood, cannot take solace from indifferent logic. We hold that such a negative theology by itself would lead to despair, which can only be overcome by the faith and hope flowing from love (Tallon 1997, 214). A negative theology only makes sense if it is first nourished by God's gift of his love, which is a blessing towards the human spirit, calling it into love of the mystery (Lonergan 1994, 341).

The primacy of love and the "downward" mode also help explain how Lonergan's model of systematics overcomes the problem of systematic theology's intermittent phases of irreligiosity. By being based on conversion, at the heart of which is the love of God, systematics maintains its religious focus. This position echoes Aquinas' statement (*Summa Theologiae*, I,q1,a7c) that the subject of theology is neither this nor that proposition, but that "God is the object of this science." Lonergan similarly argues (1994, 350-51) that systematics is religious inasmuch as it maintains the love of God as the focal meaning of the name "God." This point is reflected in Rahner's statement (1978, 53) that "the meaning of all explicit knowledge of God in religion and in metaphysics is intelligible and can really be understood only when all the words we use there point to the unthematic experience of our orientation towards the ineffable mystery." Lonergan further argues that systematics is religious when it acknowledges that no theology can ever fully fathom the meaning of the mystery of God. He also acknowledges that systematic theology can become fruitless. He argues that such futility occurs when one takes on and systematises counter-positions, but that the answer to fruitlessness, is dialectic, which can excise counter-positions and invite systematics to more satisfactory solutions.

10. Conclusion

Our examination of Lonergan's functional specialty, systematics, has most importantly noted that systematics is essentially concerned with promoting an understanding of the mysteries, which are affirmed by doctrines. Rather than to ideals of interpreting classical works, systematics thus correlates more closely to Doran's vision (1990, 4) of systematic theology as constructively presenting intelligibly to modern cultures a coherent and grounded statement of Christian faith's meanings and values. We note that the notion of systematics as an operation of understanding, which is distinct from doctrinal affirmation, is also not entirely novel, as evidenced by Lonergan's citations (1994, 336) of the First Vatican Council (DS 3016/TCF 132) and Thomas Aquinas (*Quaestiones Quodlibetales*, IV,q9a3 [18]).

We also found that systematics, no less than any other functional specialty, is not an isolated operation. It both presupposes and builds upon doctrines, for without doctrines systematics would either have no object of inquiry or it would be the vain speculation that sometimes plagues theology. We should also note that systematics also presupposes the horizon, thematised in foundations. Not only are doctrines selected and affirmed within that horizon, systematics also works with that horizon, within which it finds religious objects meaningful and outside of which, objects lack meaning.

Systematics is needed to complement doctrines, and is prompted by the ever-new questions presented by ongoing cultures and varying differentiations of consciousness. Human reason, in its manifold cultural manifestations and differentiations of consciousness, brings to doctrines the question, "What could those doctrines possibly mean?" This means that systematics, as an operation of human reason, affirms the roles of both faith and reason, and such an affirmation is evident in *Dei Filius* (DS 3016/TCF 132) and Aquinas' *Quodlibetal Questions* (IV,q9a3 [18]). Systematics first relies upon faith, without which one could not possibly apprehend divine revelation. Systematics, however, also relies upon human reason, aided by faith, in inquiring into the divine mysteries, with the search for some humanly attainable understanding of those mysteries.

From the negative side, this chapter has found, first, that systematics is not the pursuit of certitude because, as Lonergan emphasises (1973, 67-68; 1994, 132, 298-99, 331), certitude is found in doctrines and seeking further certitude is needless. As we have found, doctrines provide certitude by affirming truths within one's religious horizon. Importantly, doctrines provide certitude, in the judgements of faith. Doctrines do not provide an understanding of the mysteries, only an understanding of meaning of the doctrine itself, or of the doctrine's history. Secondly, systematics is not the pursuit of faith or belief. We have found that faith is precisely described as a virtue, a loving commitment to another. Belief on the other hand, is the act of faith, being an assent to a truth on the basis of one's faith. If systematics is the pursuit of understanding, it is thus identified properly with neither belief, which is on the level of assent, nor with faith, which is on the level of love. We should note though, that faith, belief and doctrines do not in themselves provide understanding of the mysteries they apprehend. Because they operate in the downward mode of human intentionality, they do not operate upon a previously established understanding, as does judgement in the upward mode. Instead, the downward mode begins with loving trust, then proceeds to assent based on that love. Understanding is not provided at that point and it is up to the operation of understanding in the downward mode, such as systematics' understanding, to seek some intelligibility in the affirmed reality (Lonergan 1962, 239, 243; 1964a, n10; 1994, 115, 118, 123, 321, 336).

While systematics is neither the pursuit of certitude, nor the addition of extra proof to doctrines, it is a positive promotion of understanding. Essentially, systematics promotes understanding of the mysteries affirmed by doctrines. It is the effort of human intelligence, guided by the light and horizon of faith, to find intelligibility within the affirmed mysteries of faith (Lonergan 1994, 336). That search for understanding is prompted by the unrestricted human desire to know, which includes the drive to understand. The search is needed because the mysteries in themselves are indemonstrable, and they are apprehended in the downward mode, so that their affirmation does not imply a prior understanding.

A key question, though, regards the possible forms of understanding the mysteries. In this regard, we note Lonergan's citation (1994, 336) of *Dei Filius* (DS 3016/TCF 132). Systematics intends an understanding of the mysteries attained "both from the analogy of what it [human reason] naturally knows and from the interconnection of the mysteries with one another and with man's last end." If we are to adequately understand systematics, we must take up what Lonergan may mean by understanding attained from "analogy" and understanding from "interconnections." This task is necessary, but it will be the most challenging part of this work. We shall cover this issue in our next two chapters. We shall then inquire into the attainments and value of systematics, before making some evaluations of Lonergan's presentation of systematics.

Chapter 8
Understanding the Mysteries "by Analogy"

We have previously investigated Lonergan's conception of systematics as the promotion of an understanding of the mysteries of faith. In holding that when human reason inquires piously, diligently and soberly, under the illumination of faith, it can attain this understanding; we have found that this position correlates with the teaching of the First Vatican Council. We must be careful, though, not to think mistakenly that either Lonergan or the Council mean that human beings can attain a complete understanding of the mysteries of faith, even when human intellect is illumined by faith. In fact, such a position was explicitly rejected in *Dei Filius* (DS 3016/TCF 132). Instead of a complete or quidditative understanding, both Lonergan (1964c, 13; 1994, 336) and the First Vatican Council (DS 3016/TCF 132) affirm a partial understanding, which is "both from the analogy with the objects of its [human reason's] natural knowledge and from the connection of these mysteries with one another and with man's ultimate end."

The functional specialty, "systematics," is characterised by its intention to foster an understanding of the mysteries of faith both by analogy and by interconnection. However, we should note that neither Lonergan, nor the First Vatican Council, intended to restrict the understanding of mysteries to these two forms. Our investigation will, however, focus on analogy and interconnections, as the two forms of understanding explicated in these sources. We must determine what Lonergan means by "analogy" and "interconnection," for without doing so, we cannot adequately understand Lonergan's presentation of systematics. In this chapter, our concern will be with analogy, as the first of these parts of systematics. To meet this concern, we should inquire into the exact character of analogical understanding, the conditions under which human reason can understand by analogy, and the possible achievements of analogous understanding.

To determine what Lonergan meant by "analogy" is one of the more difficult parts of this investigation, because, as Crowe writes (Lonergan 1988, 283'a'), Lonergan enjoyed tracing analogous concepts through a series of analogates, but he "rarely discussed analogy itself." While Lonergan often referred to an understanding "by analogy," he has not given us a detailed account of what he means by analogy. He has not even left us with a list of analogy's possible meanings (Crowe 1983, 38). More positively, we find that Lonergan wrote briefly on analogy in several works. *Insight* (385-86) contains a paragraph distinguishing univocal concepts and notions from analogous concepts and notions. *Method in Theology* (3-4, 87, 225-27, 333) contains several short sections that: contrasted analogy with mimesis, referred to the analogy of science, outlined how theological methods are analogous, not similar, and noted that historians hold the past and present to be analogous "when they are partly similar and partly dissimilar." Such reflections on analogy are brief and they do not reveal much detail of what Lonergan meant by analogy. We shall make use of them in this chapter, however, in an effort to understand his notion of analogy. Our more productive task will be to examine examples of Lonergan's actual use of analogy. As noted above, he used analogy often. So we shall take concrete examples of his use of analogy, and learn from these what he intended to do when he was forming these analogies.

We also aim to supplement our investigation by referring to Aquinas' conceptions of analogous understanding. We have previously noted Lonergan's debt and dedication to Aquinas, especially in his stated aim to pursue the Leonine program, *vetera novis augere et perficere*. In that light, he (1997, 222) has declared his aim to "understand what Aquinas meant and to understand as Aquinas understood." In his early work, such as *Verbum*, Lonergan aimed at recovering Aquinas' thought [the *vetera*]. His subsequent work represented his augmentation and improvement of Aquinas, as stated in *Insight* (1997, 768) and *Method in Theology* (1994, 339-40). In this light, we should investigate Lonergan's thoughts on analogy in the light of his more general recovery of Thomas' thought. We note, though, that we do not mean by this to restrict Lonergan to a Thomist model of analogy. Rather, by examining Aquinas, we intend to acquire a means by which to understand how Lonergan's work either corresponds to, or differs from, the Thomist tradition. A secondary effect of investigating Aquinas should be our attainment of a basic grasp of analogical thinking.

After briefly investigating Aquinas' concept of analogical understanding, our plan for this chapter is: (1) to investigate those texts where Lonergan wrote on the nature of analogy, (2) to investigate several key examples of analogy, which give a clue as to Lonergan's conception of analogous understanding and (3) to examine Lonergan's systematic, concrete and thematic use of analogy in the "Analogous Conception of the Divine Persons," in *De Deo Trino II*. From the foundations laid in our investigation of Aquinas and Lonergan's writings on analogy and from our outline of shorter examples of analogy in Lonergan's work, we shall use *De Deo Trino* to show the way in which an analogical conception is formed, the conditions under which such an analogy is possible and the understanding that analogy can provide. This chapter will thus proceed from a general overview, gleaned from Lonergan's brief reflections on analogy, through to an interpretation of what he was doing when he was pursuing and attaining an analogous understanding.

1. Aquinas' Formulations of Analogy

Thomas Aquinas presented a teaching on an analogical understanding of God, which has remained central to Christian theological reflection on analogy until the present day (Ferré 1967, 96). Aquinas' most important exposition of analogy is in the *Summa Theologiae* I, question 13, which is entitled "The Names of God." Before investigating Thomas' actual texts, we should first note that a conceptualist reader may misinterpret Aquinas' thoughts by focusing on his reflections on the names, that is, the concepts, predicated of God. The intellectualist interpreter though, would bear in mind Aquinas' statement (*Summa Theologiae*, I,q13,Intr) that we name things only "according to our knowledge of it." This point is reinforced by Aquinas (*Summa Theologiae*, I,q13,a1c), noting that:

> "Since according to the Philosopher [*De Interpretatione* 1, 16a 1-19] words are signs of ideas, and ideas the similitude of things, it is evident that words relate to the meaning of things signified through the medium of intellectual conception. It follows therefore that we can give a name to anything in as far as we can understand it."

Accordingly, the significance of Aquinas' explanation of the names predicated of God lies in his telling us how human intellect can, and cannot, know God.

Aquinas held (*De Veritate* q2a11c; *Summa Theologiae* I,q13,a5c) that the names predicated of both God and creatures are predicated in neither a purely equivocal nor a purely univocal manner. He argued that we cannot express our knowledge of God with univocal names, because human intellect is not proportionate to the divine essence. On the other hand, to express our knowledge of God with purely equivocal names would imply that, from creatures, we could know nothing at all about God. Instead of equivocation or univocal predication, Aquinas upheld the "middle way," of predication by analogy, "that is, according to a proportion."

Thomas argued (*Summa Theologiae*, I,q13,a5c; *Summa Contra Gentiles*, I,34§1) that such analogous names could be used in two ways. Proportion could be employed in the first sense that many objects are proportionate to one other object. Proportion could secondly mean that one thing is proportionate to another. An instance of many things being proportionate to one is Aquinas' favourite example, of health. "Healthy" may be predicated of medicine and urine, in relation and proportion to the health of a body. One is the cause, the other the sign, of the body's health. Aquinas warned, though, that this sort of analogy cannot hold for God. To maintain such an analogy would mean positing something prior to God, or as Copleston notes (1985, II,353), it would mean relating God and creatures to a third object.

Aquinas proposed the alternative proportion of one thing to another, such as medicine and animal both being "healthy." Medicine is the cause of health in the healthy animal body. In this way, Thomas writes (*Summa Contra Gentiles*, I,34§3), we can analogically predicate some things of God and creatures. This manner of analogy obtains "according as the order or reference of two things is not to something else but to one of them." We can thus name God, according to our mode of knowledge from creatures, in the manner of naming God from creatures. This naming is by virtue of the creature's relation to God as principle and cause, and by virtue of God's being the one in whom all the creature's perfections pre-exist super-eminently. Thomas states (*Summa Theologiae*, I,q13,a5c) that his analogical method is a "mean between pure equivocation and simple univocation." The analogical understanding, therefore, does not present predication of one and the same thing, as in univocal predication. However, it does not present a totally diverse understanding, as in equivocal predication.

One may ask what exactly Thomas proposed that we understand in such analogical predication. We must say that in the case of "health," neither Aristotle, nor the scholastics who followed him, were entirely clear on analogy when they wrote on health. For the present time, though, we can make the point that Aristotle and Aquinas meant that if one has an understanding of "health," one can have at least a partial understanding of the signs and causes of health.

In addition to the analogy of proportion, Aquinas (*De Veritate*, q2,a11c) also affirmed an analogy by proportionality. In *De Veritate*, Thomas distinguished the two manners of analogous predication. The analogy of proportion exists where things have a relation between each other. That analogy obtains, for example, in the relation of two to unity, two being the double of unity. However, the analogy of proportionality involves the relationship between two proportions, not the relationship between two things. Aquinas cites the analogy of proportionality between the relations of six to three, and of four to two. The analogy between six and four lies in their relations with their halves.

It is helpful here to note how Thomas distinguished (*De Veritate*, q2,a11c; *Summa Theologiae*, I,q13,a6c) between a symbolic or metaphoric analogy of proportionality and a proper analogy of proportionality. If we speak of God as "the Sun" we mean that what the Sun is to our bodily eye, God is to the soul. Likewise, if we speak of God as "a lion," we mean that what a lion is to his works of strength, so God is to his creation. Such predicates must be metaphorical, because the objects predicated include matter that can only be attributed to God, or any other spiritual being, in a symbolic manner. The other side of metaphorical predication, Thomas notes, is that any name metaphorically predicated of God is applied primarily to the creature, rather than to God. This is "because when said of God they mean only similitudes to such creatures." However, an analogy of proportionality, Thomas tells us, could be properly employed if the term predicated of God and creature implied nothing, in its principal meaning, that prevented our finding a similitude between God and creature. Such predicates, Thomas notes, include attributes with no defect or material dependency, such as being, or the good.

We have found two forms of Thomist analogy. In the analogy of proportion, Thomas notes that one object can be understood by another's relation by similitude to the first object. In the analogy of proportionality, an unknown object can be analogically understood in terms of its relations with another object, which stand in a proportion to the relations between two known objects. Our outline of what Aquinas meant by analogy now gives us a tool by which we can understand something of what Lonergan means by "analogy," while simultaneously allowing us to resolve how Lonergan follows, departs from, or develops, traditional Thomist forms of analogy.

While Aquinas does give us a useful entry point into the world of analogical thinking, we have two concerns about his statements on analogy. First, even though Aquinas clearly belongs to the intellectualist tradition, his writing on analogy carries remnants of conceptualist language. In particular, we note his repeated references to "predication." Secondly, Aquinas outlines two legitimate forms of analogy, proportion and proportionality. We can ask though, if restricting analogy to these two forms does not limit the range of intellect? If human intellect is unrestricted, insofar as the range and form of its inquiry is unlimited, we may ask if analogy may not take other forms with which to answer different types of inquiries. In Lonergan's reflection upon, and use of, analogy, we shall find other forms of analogy that both build upon and augment Aquinas' work, but which also indicate that his use of analogy is not bound to the forms of analogy presented by Aquinas. We now turn our attention to Lonergan's writings on analogy.

2. Lonergan's Writings on Analogy

In this section, we aim to investigate Lonergan's statements on analogy. By doing so, we intend to gain a basic idea of analogy, which will give us a foundation from which we can more ably approach the actual examples of analogy that we find in his writings.

In most basic terms, Lonergan holds that analogous understanding of the divine mysteries is an understanding of these mysteries in their relation to creatures. This mode of understanding is prompted by the inability of human intellect, in this life, to quidditatively understand the divine essence. This inability, as we have noted previously, is because human intellect can only understand objects by grasping the intelligibility of finite species. As no finite species is proportionate to the divine essence, human intellect cannot directly understand the essence of divine mysteries. Analogical understanding thus emerges as an indirect and non-quidditative understanding of intellect's objects, which are here the divine mysteries. To understand the divine mysteries, we take our understanding of finite objects and extend this understanding to grasp something of the mysteries. How this "extension" or extrapolation occurs will be taken up later. For the purposes of our preliminary investigations, however, it is sufficient to note that Lonergan follows Aquinas, who maintained that, despite human intellect's inability to naturally understand the essence of God, we can be led to a certain understanding of God through our understanding of God's creatures. Aquinas proposes (*Summa Theologiae*, I,q12,a12) that active human intellect can transcend its starting point in human sensitivity and can gain some grasp of God by comparing him to creatures. Such "going beyond" what we can naturally know is possible because human intellect's range of questions is unrestricted by its range of knowledge. After attaining proportionate knowledge, human intellect can ask further questions about transcendent objects, including God. Included in such questions are inquiries about whether God could in any way be like the objects of proportionate human understanding.

Lonergan warns however (1964c, 11-12), that our efforts to understand the divine mysteries through finite objects can never yield quidditative understanding of the mysteries. Human intellect, he notes, is always tied to its direct, sensible objects and "what directly regards what is finite is extended to the infinite solely by way of analogy." However, this statement also means that the analogical extension of human knowledge comes from human intellect raising more questions than the number to which it can give quidditative answers.

From his statement that analogous understanding is through creatures, we are lead to Lonergan's preliminary statement (1964c, 75), that analogous determination occurs when "the mode of an unknown nature is determined on the basis of a similitude to a known nature." He also provides another short definition (1988, 82), writing that "Analogical fulfilment is by the reception in intellect of some lesser form or species that bears some resemblance to the object to be understood and so yields some understanding of it." Our basic notion of analogy is that one partially understands an object by understanding the characteristics that a lesser object shares with the main object, which we are attempting to understand.

We can augment our preliminary notion of analogy by examining Lonergan's reference (1990, 92-93) to the "commonsense" use of analogy. Common sense operates on the principle that a nucleus, or core, of what is common to two situations can be used to help understand what is unknown in one object, but known in the other. That is, an object can be understood by the characteristics it shares with another object. However, because this understanding is analogical, there is a differentiation of this nucleus, so that there are different acts of understanding corresponding to these differences. The commonsense use of analogy is thus to understand one object, through another, by virtue of their known commonalities. In commonsense analogy there are both a common core and differences in the understood object, and the object through which it is understood. There are, as Lonergan notes (1990, 47), a fixed element lying in the object's mutual relations, and variable elements. In summary, analogical understanding understands an object: (1) by extending one's inquiries and going beyond what one can normally attain, (2) by positively grasping what the intended object shares with the object through which it is understood, but (3) also understanding it by its distinction from the second object, by virtue of their differences.

To finish our preliminary investigations on analogy, we note the basic difference between proportionate and analogical understandings. Proportionate understanding is attained when one's intellect grasps a form or species that is proportionate to one's intended object. Proportionate understanding thus grasps the very essence of the object. Analogical understanding, however, does not regard the essence of its object but understands its object indirectly, mediately, by means of a lesser form, which is attainable by human intellect. In analogical understanding, Lonergan clarifies (1988, 82; 1990, 201) that we do not understand the object itself, but we understand its proportion to another object. It is important to note that he makes this distinction on the basis of knowing processes, not on concepts. In a critical text, he distances himself (1988, 178n47) from conceptualists, who tend to emphasise "the distinction between univocal and analogous concepts," and aligns himself with the intellectualist position, which "emphasizes the distinction between quidditative and analogous knowledge."

3. Brief Examples of Analogy

After having gained an initial notion of what Lonergan means by analogy by reference to his writings on analogy, we now turn our attention to some examples of his use of analogy. In this section, we shall outline briefly the analogies that Lonergan uses and determine the manner in which each case is analogous. In this way, we intend to bring out something of what he means by "analogy."

3.1 Analogies of Motion and Operation *(Gratia Operans)*

Lonergan twice makes detailed analyses of analogies in his doctoral thesis (1971c, 55-61, 84-88). While in these texts he does not comment upon analogy in general, they reveal an awareness of analogies and their positive use in theology.

First, Lonergan (1971c, 55, 60-61) shows that Aquinas (*Summa Theologiae*, I-II,q113,a6c) was better able to explain habitual grace, as operative and cooperative, by using the Aristotelian analogy of motion. The infusion of grace could be seen as motion of the mover, corresponding free acts could be conceived as the movement of the moved, and the remission of sin could be understood as the consummation of the end, or the attainment of the movement.

Secondly, Lonergan (1971c, 85-86, 90) outlines Thomas' analogy of operation. The basic analogy maintained "that God acts by his substance, while creatures act by an accidental form or act." The proximate analogy used the analogy of the swordsman's use of his sword, in which the causation of the Creator is an unconditioned procession, while the causation of the creature is itself caused.

Lonergan did not focus on the form of these analogies. However, as a preliminary step, we can affirm that these analogies from motion and operation helped to explain, by similarity to natural processes, supernatural processes in grace, causation and justification.

3.2 The Concept of Being *(Verbum)*

"The concept of being," according to Lonergan (1997, 58-59), "cannot but be analogous." He also notes that the concept of being, in common with all other concepts, "is an effect of the act of understanding." However, the concept of being is also indeterminate by human intellect because "it is conceived from any act of understanding whatever; it proceeds from intelligibility in act." How the concept of being is analogous, is because of the identity of the intellectual process which conceives being so that "being is always conceived in the same way—as the expression of intelligibility or intelligence in act." Lonergan emphasises that the content of that act of intelligibility or intelligence does not affect the concept of being. While different contents make the terms of the proportion different, "it is the identity of the process that necessitates the similarity of the proportion."

In this case, Lonergan presents an analogy in line with a Thomist analogy of proportionality, which corresponds to the analogy of proportion, in modern terms.[1] Even though the concept of being is not "determinate" by human intellect, it can be analogously conceived by the similarity of the proportion between each intelligible or intelligible content and the expression of that act of intelligibility or intelligence. The analogy therefore means that while we cannot conceive being in itself, we can conceive being by its reference to certain relations, which are attainable by human intellect.

3.3 The Analogy of Matter *(Verbum)*

In *Verbum* (1997, 154), Lonergan also takes up Aristotle's analogy of prime matter. He notes that matter itself, according to Aristotle, could be no "determinate type of reality." In Aristotle's own words (*Metaphysics*, VIII, 3 1029a 20), "By matter I mean that which in itself is neither a particular thing nor of a certain quantity nor assigned to any other of the categories by which being is determined." Aristotle later states more directly and more significantly that "matter is unknowable in itself" (*Metaphysics*, VII 9 1036a 8). Matter, as Lonergan (1997, 157) concludes from Aristotle, is defined as "what is known by intellect indirectly." Human intellect can only know prime matter by analogy. Thomas (*Commentary on Aristotle's Physics*, [Book I], lect 13, n118; lect 15, n138) outlines Aristotle's analogy of matter as follows:

> Primary matter is, ... known according to analogy, that is, according to proportion. ... This 'something', then, is related to these natural substances as bronze is related to the statue, and wood to the bed, and anything material and unformed to form. And this is called primary matter. Primary matter is knowable by way of proportion, insofar as it is related to substantial forms as sensible matters are related to accidental forms. And, prime matter "is related to all forms and privations as the subject of qualitative change is to contrary qualities"(*Commentary on the Metaphysics*, [Book VIII] lect 1, §1689).

The immediate significance of Aristotle's analogy of matter, commented on by Aquinas and taken up by Lonergan (1997, 154-55), is in its illustration of the notion of analogy by proportion [proportionality], which Lonergan used at that time. First, there is the unknown and essentially unknowable element—prime matter. While prime matter is not completely knowable, Lonergan follows Aristotle and Aquinas in holding that one can analogically know prime matter by the proportions:

The proportion of
              Natural form   is to   natural matter;
as the proportion of
              intelligible form   is to   sensible matter
which is the same as the
proportion of
              the object of insight   to   the object of sense.

Lonergan (1997, 158) calls this proportion the "specifically Aristotelian analogy." It reveals his own understanding of analogy by proportion [proportionality], in which we understand an object not in itself, but in its proportional relation with another object.

3.4. God as "Ipsum Intelligere" *(Verbum)*

In the last chapter of *Verbum*, we find an example of analogy that is significant for not fitting into the pattern of an analogy of proportion [proportionality]. Lonergan writes that in *Verbum* (1997, 198-99) he has worked through four chapters to the conclusion that, when Aquinas wrote of God as *ipsum intelligere*, he meant that God was analogously conceived as "a pure act of understanding." Lonergan expressed this analogy in the form, "that *ipsum intelligere* is analogous to understanding, that God is an infinite and substantial act of understanding, that as the Father is God, the Son is God, the Holy Spirit is God, so also each is one and the same infinite and substantial act of understanding."

The important characteristic of this analogy is that Lonergan's analogy of God does not rely on our grasping the relations between different sets of objects. Rather, the analogy relies on our understanding an object something like God, here, the image of God in our intellects' operation. This analogy relies on an understanding of the image of God, which Aquinas states (*Summa Theologiae*, I,q93,a7c), "first and chiefly, ... is to be found in the acts of the [human] soul." Lonergan is not only referring to any analogy of proportion [proportionality] that may exist between God and human nature, but he effectively maintains that there is an analogy, or proportion, of attributes between God and human nature, because human beings image the divine attributes in their mental operations. In this example, we find the mode of analogy called attribution [proportion]. Here, Lonergan proposes that we can understand one object [God] by virtue of the similarity that is present in one other object [our understanding].

3.5. The "Isomorphism of Thomist and Scientific Thought" *(Collection)*

Lonergan's article (1988, 133-34) expounds "a protracted analogy of proportion, that concentrates on a structural similarity to prescind entirely from the materials that enter into the structures." The main point of this paper is that the "relation of hypothesis to verification is similar to the relation of definition to judgement." Thus, the relation between the scientist's hypothesis and his verification of that hypothesis is similar to the relation between Thomist definition and Thomist judgement. He clarifies, most importantly, that he asserts no identity between scientific hypothesis and Thomist definition. Nor, he adds, does he assert any identity between scientific verification and Thomist judgement. However, he does assert a similarity in the relations between the elements in the two sets.

The analogy thus lies in the isomorphism of the two structures. Lonergan (1988, 133) gives the general case of isomorphism as being two sets of terms, *A, B, C,* and *P, Q, R,* which are isomorphic when:

The relation of A to *B* is *similar to the relation of P* to *Q, and the relation of A* to *C* is *similar to the relation of P* to *R,* and so forth.

This formula reflects a similar one used by Aristotle *(Metaphysics,* IX, 6, 1048b 5-10), that one can analogically understand actuality in relation to potentiality, in the same way as one can grasp that, "as *A* is in *B* or to *B*, *C* is in *D* or to *D*."

We note, with Lonergan, that no similarity is affirmed, or denied, between the terms in one set and the terms in another set. The critical element in this isomorphism / analogy of proportion is that the relations between the elements of one set are similar to the relations between the terms in another set.

3.6 Theology as Analogously a Science *(De Constitutione Christi)*

Within Lonergan's *De Constitutione Christi* (1964a, n47), specifically in the section on "The Analogy of Methods," we find a more difficult and challenging example of analogy. He argues that "Theology is analogously a science," and that their similarity lies in their functioning within our knowledge. To understand the form of this analogy we need to follow his explanation of his meaning at that time, of "science" and "theology." Science, being "the sciences of created realities," posits both the causes of knowing and the causes of being in its object. Science can proceed by the way of resolution, from causes of knowing, to conclude to causes of being. It can also take the way of composition, to employ causes of being as causes of knowing. Theology, however, can know nothing of the cause of being of God, for God has no cause of being. From the foregoing, it is manifest that theology cannot be univocally called a science.

Science and theology can be analogical, Lonergan argues, because of their similar functions. The scientist, he argues "concludes to an understanding of the attributes of reality from an understanding of that reality's essence." In a similar process, he argues that a theologian proceeds from an analogous conception of God's essence to analogously conceive God's attributes. Again, the analogy is shown by the similarity between:

> science's function as —
> *"certain knowledge* of realities *through the causes* of their being,"
> and theology's function as —
> *"certain knowledge* of God *through causes* of knowing..." *[italics added]*

The challenge of this analogy arises if we try to fit the analogy into a conventional Thomist form of analogy. At first glance, we may conclude that Lonergan is drawing out an analogy of attribution [proportion] between science and theology. One may make this conclusion from the common characteristics of science's and theology's positing of causes of knowing. If however, we were to consider the analogy in terms of the functions of science and theology, that is, in terms of their relations to human intellect, Lonergan would hold that they have a similar proportion. We could conclude then, that the analogy of scientific and theological methods is another example of isomorphism, in which the realities themselves may differ, but they have common networks of relations.

If, however, we were to take into account this analogy's use of similarities both from within the two objects and from their respective relations, it would seem that Lonergan is using an analogy that does not fit into an established Thomist paradigm of analogy. We may thus speculate that he is breaking out of the constraints of Thomist conceptions of analogy by attribution [proportion] and proportion [proportionality]. We may propose that Lonergan is moving towards a use of analogy in which what is essential is a grasp of relations between analogates, but that the form of these relations is not as rigidly specified as in Thomist conceptions of analogy.

3.7. A Pivotal Case of Analogy: The Notion of Being *(Insight)*

In chapter twelve of *Insight*, Lonergan presents "The Notion of Being." This presentation is significant, first, for outlining a profound change in the account of being and secondly, for changing the paradigm of analogy. While our primary concern is with the second of these elements, we cannot understand Lonergan's meaning of the analogy present in the notion of being, without understanding something of his notion of being.

Lonergan (1992, 372-98) intends us to understand the notion of being as that anticipation of being intrinsic to human intentionality. This notion of being is not a definition of being itself, neither is it a concept, nor is it an idea, of being. Lonergan's (1992, 374) "definition of being" is of "the second order" because it does not assign the meaning of being, but it assigns how one ascertains that meaning. To help us understand what he means, we can contrast his account with the classic conception of being, as conceived by Cajetan.

When Lonergan (1990, 201-2) later wrote on the metaphysician's analogy of being, he observed that metaphysics is concerned with "being and all being." Its key problem, though, is that it cannot account for the essences proper to each being. The metaphysician knows being by concerning oneself "with the proportion between essences and existences, with the analogy of the series x_1/y_1, x_2/y_2, etc., where existences are indicated by the y's and essences by the x's." The analogy here is an analogy of proportion [proportionality], in which the analogy lies in the similarity found, not in the terms themselves, but in the relationships between terms in their different sets. The metaphysician thus understands the proportion of being in relation to each different essence.

This is the form of analogy used by Cajetan, as representative of the Thomistic tradition, to account for being. Believing that it was the only analogy in the true and strict sense (Mascall 1966, 57), Cajetan advocated the analogy of proportion [proportionality], which indicated a "functional relation between essence and existence" (Lonergan 1990, 360). Cajetan's function held that in the same way as "double" indicated the relationship between two and one, four and two, six and three, so too did "being" indicate the proportion between essence and existence. In other words, the proportion of A's existence to A's essence is the same as the proportion of B's existence to B's essence. Useful enough as such an analogy may be, Lonergan observes (1992, 393) that it does not present a unified notion of being. Cajetan's analogy can only deal with one question at a time, which meant that one was not really dealing with the notion of being as the universe of everything. Moreover, by dealing with such questions by precision (one at time) rather than by abstraction (dealing with the essential and excluding the irrelevant), Cajetan's analogy can only account for now this, and then that, "being." From this classic analogy of being, according to Lonergan (1990, 360; 1992, 392-93), there results a conceptual content of being. Cajetan's proportional analogy of being can give us a concept of being in any particular object, but it cannot give us a unifying notion of being. As we shall find, Lonergan will establish first, a new paradigm for understanding being and secondly, a new paradigm for analogical understanding.

Lonergan does not define a conceptual content of being for either particular being, or being, more correctly in the universal sense of all being. Instead, he (1992, 374) makes a definition of being in the "second order," which assigns the manner in which human intellect comes to determine the meaning of being.

We also note that while the terms, "concept," "idea" and "notion" are commonly used as synonyms, Lonergan (1992, 35, 39, 332, 417, 667; Doran 1990, 565) sharply distinguishes these terms. A notion is a conscious, dynamic anticipation of what one will know and affirm when one understands and judges. The paramount example of a notion is heuristic notion. A concept, however, is a formulation. It implies a content of thought. There can be two types of concept: the heuristic concept that formulates a heuristic notion, and an explanatory concept that results from insight. An idea, moreover, is "the content of an act of understanding."

Lonergan (1992, 665) sums up the notion of being by writing that:

> The pure notion of being is the detached, disinterested, unrestricted desire to know. It is prior to understanding and affirming, but it heads to them for it is the ground of intelligent inquiry and critical reflection. Moreover, this heading towards knowing is itself a notion, for it heads not unconsciously, as the seed to the plant, nor sensitively, as hunger for food, but intelligently and reasonably, as the radical *noêsis* towards every *noêma*, the basic *pensée pensante* towards every *pensée pensée*, the initiating *intentio intendens* towards every *intentio intenta*.

He continues (1992, 665):

> ... since the pure notion of being unfolds through understanding and judgement, there can be formulated a heuristic notion of being as whatever is to be grasped intelligently and affirmed reasonably.

The notion of being, according to Lonergan (1972, Lect 12, p1 [Ch. 12], 62;1992, 372, 374), is the notion of the "objective of the pure desire to know." Now, if being is "all that is known" and "all that remains to be known," being is unrestricted in its intention. On that account, being includes things that are not known, so in this life we cannot have a concept or an idea of being, we can only have a notion of being.

More importantly, because the notion of being is prior to inquiry and reflection, and because it grounds that inquiry and reflection, Lonergan observes (1992, 380-81) that "the notion of being is all-pervasive: it underpins all cognitional contents; it penetrates them all; it constitutes them as cognitional." In terms of underpinning cognitional contents, the notion of being selects data, drives us towards understanding and demands the unconditioned. The notion of being also constitutes cognitional contents as cognitional by bringing human knowing to its term in knowing being.

Of critical interest to us, and deserving more attention, is how Lonergan (1992, 380-81) holds the notion of being to penetrate all cognitional contents. In the first place the notion of being is the "supreme heuristic notion." Before each cognitional content, the notion of being is that notion of what will be known through that content. When each content emerges, what is to be known through that content becomes what is known through that content. The notion of being is thus a "universal anticipation" which will be filled in, bit-by-bit by the emergence of each cognitional content. When a content emerges it not only ends part of that anticipation, it becomes part of what is anticipated. Lonergan notes that before all answers, the notion of being is the notion of the totality of what is to be known through all answers. However, he also notes that when all answers are known, the notion of being becomes the notion of the totality known through those answers.

After our laborious exposition of what Lonergan means by the notion of being, our task of understanding of how it is analogous is considerably more manageable. Lonergan asks (1992, 385) whether the notion of being is univocal or analogous. Yet the question is puzzling, for he reminds us in the next paragraph that the distinction of the univocal and the analogous regards concepts. The notion of being, as he reminds us in his notes to *Insight* (1972, Lect 12, p3 [Ch. 12) 64), is not a concept. Nonetheless, when answering the question, Lonergan (1992, 385) does tell us that, "Concepts are said to be univocal when they have the same meaning in all applications, and they are said to be analogous when their meaning varies systematically as one moves from one field of application to another." He also answers the question of how the notion of being can be univocal or analogous. It is apparent that Lonergan may be presenting a new form of analogy that does not fit the analogical models applied to concepts, though it is certainly a model that fits in with Finnis' definition (1983, 11) of an analogous term as "a term whose meaning shifts systematically as one uses it."

This new form of analogy is exactly what Lonergan does present (1992, 385), writing that "the notion of being may be named analogous inasmuch as it penetrates all other contents; in this fashion it is said that *esse viventium est vivere*, the being of living things is being alive." This analogy is in the form of one notion penetrating other cognitional contents. Thus, the form of this notional analogy is of the same notion penetrating different cognitional contents, even though these particular contents differ.

We should not let the simplicity of this analogy detract from either its profundity, or its implications. This form of analogy effectively transcends the restricted, concept-based analogies of attribution [proportion] and proportion [proportionality]. If an analogy is taken on the basis of inquiry, as it is here, distinctions of proportion and attribution fade away. Moreover, such an analogy is open to the unrestricted and infinite. This means that this analogy is more suited to mysteries, which are infinite, and also that this analogy is open to all answers. As a final point, we note that this form of analogy, as based on the spirit of inquiry, accords better with the intellectualist focus on human knowing, rather than concepts. In an analogy based on inquiry, what is constant through different objects being analogically related, is not any concept, but the same notion within human intellect that penetrates those different contents.

3.8 Genuineness *(Insight)*

In the requirement of genuineness, we find another of Lonergan's analogies (1992, 500). He argues that the requirement for genuineness is analogous because the requirement varies in content in different cases. To illustrate this point, he gives two cases in which we may find different contents in the requirement of genuineness. There is first the genuineness found in an unspoilt character who has no need of reflection. In the second place, there is the genuineness "won back" by the repentant character who attains genuineness by reflection and purgation.

Lonergan (1992, 500) uses these distinguishing cases to make the point that genuineness involves "a starting point in the subject as he is, a term in the subject as he is to be, and a process from the starting point to the term." He argues that the requirement of genuineness is analogous, because of the varying contents and demands, in different subjects, of the development from what a subject is to what the subject should be.

We would be thwarted if we were to try to fit the requirement of genuineness into a Thomist form of analogy. It fits neither the strict form of proportion [proportionality] nor attribution [proportion]. However, we can consider the analogy of genuineness' requirement in the light of an analogy based on inquiry, in a manner similar to the notion of being. In the cases of genuineness, which Lonergan outlines, we do not have a concept of genuineness, but a notion. We thus propose that, just as the notion of being was analogous in its penetration of different cognitional content, the requirement of genuineness is analogous because it penetrates different cases, in which the requirement of genuineness varies from case to case.

3.9 Analogy in Heuristic Structure *(Insight)*

Our last example from *Insight* is Lonergan's "protracted analogy" (1997, 85-88), in which the features of classical heuristic structure are compared to an analogous feature in statistical heuristic structure. He begins by noting that "just as the classical inquirer seeks to know the 'nature of ...,' so the statistical inquirer will seek to know the 'state of ...'" He proceeds through eight other steps, until he reaches the tenth step of this analogy, in which he notes that just as classical law is in need of verification, so too the statistical state demands verification. There is a similarity between, on the one hand, the structure, and need for, reasonable affirmation, which is constituted by judgement, in classical law, and on the other hand, statistical law's need for verification.

If we wish to do so, we can fit this analogy into the Thomist model of an analogy of proportion [proportionality]. We can discern an analogy based on the isomorphism of classic and statistical inquiries' structures. However, to limit the analogy to only this model, would direct the analogy towards a conceptualist framework. In the light of our previous examples from *Insight*, such restriction of Lonergan's horizon would now be imprudent. A more accurate outlook would be to note that in each of the ten respective features of classical and statistical heuristic structures, he outlines a notion of some part of heuristic structure. He then shows how this notion is present in, or penetrates, the corresponding features of statistical and classical structures. Another way of putting this point is to say that the analogy between classical and statistical heuristic structures is based on human intellect making similar inquiries in corresponding features of the two structures.

3.10 The Fundamental Set of Analogies
(Understanding and Being)

Just after noting the metaphysician's analogy, Lonergan outlines (1990, 202-3) "A standard analogy in metaphysics," which is the analogy of form to potency that originates with Aristotle, and which represents his effort to answer the question of what, and what sort of thing, is "actuality." He warns us (*Metaphysics*, IX, 6, 1048a 25-30) that "we not only ascribe potentiality to that whose nature it is to move something else, either without qualification or in some other way, but also use the word in another sense, in the pursuit of which we have discussed these previous senses." Aristotle thus alerts us to the different uses and meanings of the same concept in his analogy. So, in expressing the meaning of "actuality," Aristotle notes (*Metaphysics*, IX, 6, 1048a 30 - 1048b 5) that actuality means "the existence of the thing." This does not however, mean existence by the same way that we may, for example, find a statue potentially within a block of wood. Actuality means something else, but while the meaning of actuality can be reached by induction, from particular cases, it cannot be universally defined. Thus, because it cannot be adequately defined, Aristotle encourages us to "be content to grasp the analogy." He proposes that actuality is to potentiality as: waking is to sleeping, so too is seeing to unopened eyes. We can gain a grasp of actuality, Aristotle writes, if we let actuality be defined by one member of the antithesis, and potentiality by the other.

Lonergan (1990, 203) also cites Aristotle's analogy (*De Anima*, II, 412b 10 - 413a 10) that illustrates the nature of the soul. The soul, writes Aristotle, "is substance in the sense which corresponds to the account of a thing." To help us grasp this point, Aristotle asks us to suppose that the eye were an animal. Sight then, would be its soul, for sight is the eye's substance that corresponds to its account. If the sight were removed, the eye would no longer be an eye. While Aristotle does not provide an essential definition of the soul, he does give us some grasp of it by relation or proportion. In particular, he draws our attention to the soul's inseparability from the living body.

The important aspect of these analogies is their structure. Aristotle's analogy of proportion [proportionality] neither sets out to grasp the essence of, nor to define, the understood object. It sets out to understand how the relation of the object to another corresponds to the relation between a second set of objects known to us. Analogy by proportion thus sets out to understand through grasping the relations of isomorphic sets of terms. In such sets, no similarity is asserted regarding the contents of the sets. What Lonegan asserts (1988, 133-34) is that "the network of relations in one set of terms is similar to the networks of relations in other sets." Aristotle (*Metaphysics*, IX, 6, 1048b 5-10) uses a helpful formula to explain the use of his analogy. One can analogically understand actuality, in relation to potentiality, in the same way as one can grasp that, "as *A* is in *B* or to *B*, *C* is in *D* or to *D*."

It is important to note that, in this text, Lonergan is not so much advancing his own idea of analogy, as he is outlining "traditional analogies." Significantly, he holds (1990, 203) that it is through his study of human knowledge that we can approach these "traditional analogies" in a way in which we can control them. So, while Aristotle focussed on the use of concepts in these analogies, Lonergan seeks to explore these analogies on the basis of human inquiry. Although Lonergan does not rule out the utility of the "traditional analogies," he does hold that the analogies become more useful if we base our analogical inquires on knowing, rather than concepts.

3.11 Four Cases of Analogy *(Method in Theology)*

Apart from his chapter on "systematics" Lonergan only makes four brief mentions of analogy in *Method in Theology*. While these examples of analogy do not reveal much of what he could mean by analogy, we should mention them because of their presence in *Method in Theology*. In the first place, Lonergan refers (1994, 3) to an analogy of science. He acknowledges those "bolder spirits" who propose that, "Science properly so called is the successful science they have analyzed. Other subjects are scientific in the measure they conform to its procedures and, in the measure they do not, they are something less than scientific." While he rejects the efficacy of this "analogy of science" for theological method, the analogy does reflect Lonergan's position in his article on the "Isomorphism of Thomist and Scientific Thought" (1988, 133-41). Where he and the "bolder spirits" would agree is that an analogy lies in two activities having the same, or similar structures or procedures, while their actual contents differ. It is thus proposed that theology could be conceived analogously with science in an analogy based on the isomorphic nature of the two inquiries.

Secondly, *Method* contains a reference to the Cassirer's contrast between mimesis and analogy. Lonergan notes (1994, 86-87) that while mimesis signifies what is imitated, analogy signifies its original. Cassirer argues that analogy involves some signification of the original, rather than an attempted mimicry. The key point on analogical expression is that, rather than having a direct material similarity with its object, as in mimesis, analogy reflects pure relations. "The context is rather communicated by a *formal* analogy between the phonetic sequence and the sequence of contents designated; ..." Cassirer (1953, I, 193) then observes how variations in tone reflect variations in the object of expression. By referring to Cassirer's analogy of expression, the analogical expression apparently works because by varying the relations of expressions one varies the meaning, and thus the object of what is expressed. If one were pushed to fit this analogy into a Thomist paradigm, one could possibly posit it as an analogy of proportion [proportionality]. However, rather than contorting the analogy into something it may not be, it is better to observe that the analogy works because of the presence of relations between the object and its phonetic representations.

Thirdly, Lonergan mentions (1994, 225-27) the more straightforward historian's analogy, in which "the present and the past are said to be analogous when they are partly similar and partly dissimilar." The historian's analogy corresponds then, to the commonsense analogy, in which one object can be analogically understood by the similar "core" that it shares with another object. In this case, of the historian's analogy, the essential point is that the analogy relies on the similarity of the objects being conceived analogously. One can only validly conceive the past on the basis of an analogy with the present to the extent that it has commonality with the present. Another key point is Lonergan's reminder that even if we conceive the past by analogy with the present, this does not mean that we presume to know the present in its entirety. As we shall find below, this is a timely reminder that when we conceive an object by analogy with another, we may have to revise our understanding of that object if our understanding of the analogate changes.

Fourthly, *Method* (1994, 333) contains a reference to an analogy of theological methods. The basic point is that methods are analogous, and not similar. In the light of Lonergan's statements, and of his points on pages three to four, he evidently means that theologians of differing allegiances have analogous methods because, though their contents differ, their procedures are structurally similar. The analogy of methods is thus another case of analogy being based on the isomorphism of human inquiries.

4. An Analogous Conception of the Divine Persons

Our foregoing investigations have covered only brief instances of analogy in Lonergan's writings. We now turn to a more detailed and substantial example. By investigating his "Analogous conception of the divine persons," (1964c, 65ff) we shall be able to explain something of the process of forming an analogous conception of a divine mystery. In the light of both our previous investigations of analogy, and our exposition of this important case of analogy, we shall be better able to determine Lonergan's meaning (1994, 336) of systematics' promotion of an "understanding of the mysteries of faith ... from analogy."

This treatment of the analogous conception of the divine persons is divided into three basic sections. In the first place, Lonergan (1964c, 77) develops a "technical formulation" of the exact problem to be faced. The primary aim of such a technical formulation is to clarify the implications of the doctrines being understood. The second aim of the technical formulation is to bring to light the apparent contradictions in the doctrine.

Lonergan secondly proposes (1964c, 77) a hypothetical solution to the problem raised and formulated in the first step. He maintains that if one is to suppose an intelligible solution, by way of analogous conception, one may gain an understanding of how the problems may be solved.

The third step is to "pass judgement" on the hypothetical, analogous solution, by which Lonergan (1964c, 77, 86) aims to determine why his solution is to be preferred above any others. Having now briefly outlined the three sections with which we are to deal, we now turn to our detailed investigation of this analogy.

4.1 Technical Formulation

If Lonergan's intention is to provide understanding through an analogous conception, we may be surprised that his first step (1964c, 79) is to make a "strict deduction from the truths of faith through metaphysical notions and principles." The deduction that divine procession is *per modum operati*, he states, is "theologically certain." How is such deduction and certainty a contribution to understanding? In the first place, deduction and its "certain conclusions" are simply part of doctrines, which we set out to understand in systematics. The first two steps of Lonergan's "deduction" establish the doctrine to be understood. The first step is to argue, through exclusion, until we are left with a procession *per modum operati*. In the second place, by positive argument, he establishes that divine procession is *per modum operati*. The turn to systematics comes more definitely though, with the third step, which uncovers the root of an apparent contradiction. In this third part we find the usefulness of this technical formulation to the general process of forming an analogous conception.

If we follow Lonergan's (1964c, 66-68, 77-81) concrete example, we find an apparent contradiction in the doctrinal affirmations (DS 75, 125, 150 1300/TCF 7, 12, 16, 322), that God is one, and that God is from God. The latter affirmation would imply some form of polytheism. Conversely, the oneness of God would imply the absence of a procession of God from God. Lonergan eliminates the apparent contradiction by identifying the divine processions as internal, not external. But such an elimination is insufficient because all eliminations are simply negative propositions. The negative elimination of apparent contradiction does not show us how divine nature differs from created nature. More importantly, this elimination does not show how the apparent contradiction is not so. One can only positively state how it is that procession and unity in God can be simultaneously affirmed, without contradiction, in the second part of Lonergan's argument.

Lonergan's first part is not a conclusion for the sake of increasing certitude. Rather, it is a conclusion intended as a technical formulation of the exact problem, which is presented by doctrines and is to be resolved by our analogous conception. We are thus led to the beginning of analogical knowing, which is in human questioning. In that light, we can better understand the importance, as Lonergan maintains (1964c, 77), of formulating technically the problem that faces us. He means that without a clear and accurate presentation of the difficulty to be solved by analogical understanding, this same understanding will be deficient, especially in terms of resolving the apparent inconsistencies within the doctrine. We conclude then, that Lonergan is encouraging the technical and specific formulation of questions, so that inquirers know exactly what they are seeking and on what level of human knowing they are seeking it.

We also note a further point on "the question." The question, or problem with a divine mystery, is not a question of the divine essence itself, because as we noted above, the divine essence is only the remote mover of human intellect. The proximate mover is divine revelation. The question is thus more concerned with how human intellect can find intelligibility in revealed truth. Our focus, in the question, is on our mode of knowing and how we can humanly conceive the truth of the divine mystery. It is important to bear in mind the point that the heuristic object of analogous conception is a humanly intelligible answer to the question of how it can be conceived that the divine processions are what they are. We note that this object is not alien to the object of scientific understanding. It is akin to investigating gravity and asking, not about the essence of gravity, but how we can understand those laws of gravity, which experimental physicists are satisfied with as being verified.

4.2 The Hypothetical Solution I: *How the Solution is Attained*

In the first place, we note Lonergan's particular solution (1964c, 81) in the case under scrutiny. He argues that "If one supposes intelligible emanation in the divinity, one concludes that there is procession *per modum operati* in the divinity." From Lonergan's outline of what this statement determines, we can assemble several key aspects of analogous understanding. First, his phrase, "if one supposes," indicates that the settlement of the previously formulated problem lies in a hypothetical principle of solution. Secondly, the hypothetical nature of this principle adds not certitude, but understanding of how the mystery may be so. Thirdly, *per modum operati* is an intelligibility that is not proportionate to the divine essence, but one that is proportionate to human intellect. The increase in understanding is thus mediate, imperfect and analogous.

Lonergan emphasises (1964c, 81) that his hypothetical solution is *hypothetical*. This means that the principle of intelligible emanation within the divinity is neither demonstrable, nor deducible, nor is it a conclusion. Intelligible emanation is simply supposed. The reason offered is that one is seeking the principle of divine procession. He thus writes that "it cannot be demonstrated that a divine procession *per modum operati* is an intelligible emanation; for from what is less determinate one can not conclude to what is more determinate." We would add here the doctrinal statement (DS 3041/TCF 137) that the mysteries of faith are beyond human demonstration. If the mysteries themselves are beyond human demonstration, then even more so are the mysteries' principles beyond demonstration.

Our previous two paragraphs indicate that the hypothetical solution to problems raised with regard to a mystery is beyond reason acting alone. On the other hand, Lonergan also emphasises (1964c, 81) that the solution to a mystery's problems is not revealed, nor is it to be found in the authoritative sources of one's faith. As he notes, the properly theological principles, which give the basis for the mysteries, are not revealed. We note that the principle of mysteries could only be communicated if the divine essence entered into and actuated human intellect. Such revelation or actuation is something that does not happen to natural human intellect in this life. Lonergan accordingly states that the principles of the mysteries are not attained by reason alone, but neither are they attained by faith alone. He importantly adds that the principles are not attained by a deduction from faith and reason. The principles of the mysteries are attained from an understanding that comes from an insight resulting from one's reason inquiring under the guidance of faith.

Lonergan makes the further point (1964c, 82) that one cannot attain the principles, provided by analogous conception, by a mere investigation of authorities. While it is possible to follow authorities and thereby conclude principles, he emphasises that no mere inspection of authorities can give one an understanding of a systematic analogy. One may face the challenge then, as to where in one's sources one finds one's hypothesis. Lonergan counters such a possible challenge (1964c, 30-31) by noting that even when one's analogical understanding of the mysteries is somehow suggested in one's sources, in its formal aspect, systematics' analogy can never be proved to be present in one's sources. This means, for example, that despite its explaining the data of the Scriptures, Thomas' psychological analogy is not found expressed in those same Scriptures. Analogical understanding simply introduces a hypothetical element. When faced with questions of intelligibility, one seeks a solution that may help suggest such intelligibility. That solution is never deduced, but discovered. In that light, Lonergan writes that, "the view that theology is simply about pure and mixed conclusions can not be admitted." The mysteries and their sources raise questions for understanding. Yet the mysteries do not offer such solutions. We note that if they did contain their solutions, they would not be mysteries and any analogical understanding would be superfluous.

Lonergan proposes (1964c, 81) that the solution to problems with mysteries comes from neither reason alone, nor from faith alone. In the light of the latter negation, he also recalls that the solution does not come from an inspection of one's sources. The solution, he emphasises, comes from an understanding of a hypothesis that comes from reason inquiring under the enlightenment of faith. Another way of putting this point is that one neither finds one's principle of solution in one's sources, nor does one logically deduce it from either reason or sources of revelation. Rather, one discovers the principle of solution as an act of intelligent insight into the mysteries. Such insight, as we discovered in chapter five, is neither deducible, nor is it at the beck and call of human intellect. Instead, insight's advent is sudden and unpredictable. It occurs as the result of inquiry, yet just when, and if, it arrives is never certain. Moreover, one's hypothesis, discovery or insight into the mysteries does not come easily. Insights into mysteries are as hard, if not more difficult, to attain than the insights of natural knowledge. If insights into mysteries were easy and attainable with certainty, systematics would be an effortless enterprise, requiring not the puzzlement and inspiration of genius, but only the routine of mediocre intellect. We also note that, as an insight, our insight into the mysteries provides us with a grasp of the intelligible possibility of what the mystery may be, not with certain knowledge of the mystery.

The facts that one's hypothetical solutions come from human reason inquiring in the light of faith, and that such solutions are not necessarily found in one's sources, helps clarify the point that there is a distinction, in the terms and relations expressed in systematics, from those used in one's sources. To express one's understanding of doctrines within a system, one has recourse to new, insightful, creative terms and relations. Lonergan (1994, 346) uses the example of Thomist Trinitarian theory, which employed terms such as "procession, relation, person." While such

terms have their technical meaning, they are not found in the sources of
the doctrines, which Thomas was expressing. The terms, we note, may
not even be implied within those sources. Lonergan also uses the example
of physics to illustrate this point. In that science, the technical terms
mass and temperature stand to the terms heavy and cold in the same way
that the terms of systematics stand to one's theological sources.

We note that Lonergan, Aquinas, and those who follow in the Thomist
tradition, are certainly not alone in using terms not found in one's sources
when explaining doctrines based upon those sources. By way of clear
example, John Macquarrie explains (1977, vii) that he uses the concepts
of Martin Heidegger to provide the basis for a contemporary theology,
which articulates the Christian faith. As another example, Bultmann
(1969, 160n13, 167n5, 262n3, 324) expressed a similar debt to Heidegger.

Lonergan argues (1994, 346-47) that the distinction between the terms
of theological systems and sources necessarily follows on from the development of understanding, as acknowledged by the First Vatican Council
(DS 3020/TCF 136). We hold that such a development of terms occurs
because systematics relies on insights, which are creative. Systematics goes
beyond the truths of doctrines to introduce hypothetical and systematised
answers to inquiries. It is because of this creative aspect that we should
expect new terms to be used in systematics. We also note that the development of new terms also relies on the use of creative insight over and
above logic and deduction. If logic were our only resource, creativity would
be stifled, and we would be confined to using only those terms found in
our sources.

We note Lonergan's acknowledgement, in *Verbum* (1997, 204, 218),
that conceptualists will not think much of a theology that considers itself
to be only a hypothesis. Rather than denying this charge, he positively
affirms that analogical understanding is simply hypothetical. He points
out that while we can demonstrate God's understanding, by reasoning
from pure perfections to pure act in God, we can in no way demonstrate
that the mode of divine understanding necessitates a divine Word. He
notes that "Psychological trinitarian theory is not a conclusion that can
be demonstrated but an hypothesis that squares with divine revelation
without excluding the possibility of alternative hypotheses." Such is the
case with Thomas Aquinas (*Summa Theologiae*, I,32,a1ad2), who quite
openly admitted his Trinitarian theology to be hypothetical. Lonergan's
response (1997, 218-19) to the conceptualists is to alert us to those shortcomings of conceptualism and the idolisation of certitude, which we have
also outlined above. We recall here our earlier chapters on the Aristote-

lian principle of science, and how, by default, theology became conceived as a deduction of certitude from known causes. We thus note that Lonergan's conception of specifically analogical understanding, as being based on postulated principles, follows his general conception of understanding in definitively breaking from the cult of certitude and deduction that characterised pre-modern science.

4.3 The Hypothetical Solution II:
The Nature of the Hypothetical Solution

Lonergan (1964c, 66-68, 81) emphasises that, by the hypothetical solution, one seeks the principle of the divine mystery. One's analogous conception thus results from one seeking what is first in, and underpinning, the divine mystery. In the analogous conception, one seeks an understanding of some intelligible principle of the mystery's being what it is. In the particular case of the divine processions, it is insufficient to state that the Son as God is from himself, but the Son as begotten is not from himself. To make such an affirmation meaningful and affirm the intelligibility of the mystery, one must find the bases on which the Son is from himself and not from himself. The question at hand is therefore not a question of theology's conclusions, but a question of principle. That is, if one can grasp something of the principle of divine procession, one can then understand how the Trinity may be so. Theological understanding's hypothetical solution thus aims for a principle by which the mysteries can be made intelligible. Without a grasp of such a principle, the mysteries remain unintelligible, discordant and incoherent to us.

Lonergan makes the point (1964c, 81-85) that the understanding, which is attained in the hypothetical solution is "mediate, imperfect, analogous, and obscure." We are familiar with his affirmation of these aspects of theological understanding, but we can now gain a better viewpoint of what they mean.

In the first place, the understanding is mediate. In our particular example, this means that we do not understand how the divine processions may be so by experiencing, then understanding, the essence of the processions themselves. Rather, our understanding comes by supposing that divine processions can be conceived by the similitude of intelligible emanation in human beings. This particular case also applies to the general process of analogous, systematic conception. Our manner of conception is mediate because we understand our object, not in itself, but in reference to a second, somehow similar, object.

Secondly, the understanding is analogous. Lonergan earlier notes (1964c, 75) that an analogous determination occurs when an unknown object's mode is determined by its similitude to a second, but known nature. Also, analogical understanding occurs when we conceive an object by grasping the form of a lesser species that nonetheless has some intelligible resemblance to the object of intellect (Lonergan 1988, 82). In our particular case, we have the divine processions, which are transcendent, infinite, and unattainable by human intellect's natural operation. These processions, however, are understood by understanding the similarity that we can find in intelligible emanations, which are finite, and attainable by human intellect.

Thirdly, Lonergan argues (1964c, 85) that the hypothetical solution is not only mediate and analogous, but also imperfect. This imperfection comes from several causes. We follow the point that a mystery is understood to the extent that its principle is understood. However, the mystery is not understood to the extent that its principle is not understood. In the case of the divine processions, Lonergan notes that even though the many elements pertaining to the procession *per modum operati* may be reduced to a single ground, or principle, that ground itself is not perfectly understood by human intellect.

First, the ground of divine procession is an infinite and rationally conscious act. However, as Lonergan notes (1964c, 85), we cannot know the infinite positively, we can only know it negatively, as regards the infinite's differences from the finite. Secondly, we conceive the divine processions according to their similitude with our own rational and moral consciousness. This consciousness, as Lonergan notes, is lived by us, rather than being perfectly known. If we add the imperfection of our knowledge of our own consciousness to the gulf between infinite divine consciousness and our finite, mortal consciousness, he rightly indicates that our consciousness is not a perfect or proportionate image of God. In the third place, our analogous conception is imperfect because it is supposed, rather than deduced or concluded from the sources of reason or revelation. Lonergan thus establishes in the particular case the general truth that, because of the imperfection of our knowledge of even humanly attainable objects, because of the gulf between the proportions of divine and mortal objects and because a hypothetical solution is supposed, our understanding of the divine mysteries will always be imperfect.

It can be proposed that the inherent imperfection of our analogy somehow reduces or weakens the reality of the mystery that we affirm. Lonergan argues though (1964c, 85), that the weakness of our analogy does not weaken or demean the divine mysteries, but the analogy's weakness reflects the eminence of divine nature over created nature. As noted in *Dei Filius* (DS 3016/TCF 132), "the divine mysteries of their very nature so exceed created intellect that, even when they have been handed over in revelation and accepted in faith, they nonetheless remain hidden by the veil of that very faith and, as it were, shrouded in darkness as long as we are exiled from the Lord in this mortal life ... ." This means that when we acknowledge an analogy's imperfection, weakness or insufficiency, we do not demean the dignity of the mystery itself. Rather, we affirm the excelling nature of the mystery over and above human and created nature.

Lonergan's point should be read in the light of both *Dei Filius* and of Thomas' reflections on whether the names predicated of God and creatures belong first to God, or creatures. Aquinas' answer (*Summa Contra Gentiles*, I,34§6) is that the names predicated of God belong primarily and more properly to God. The perfections that we ascribe to God exist first, and more excellently, in God and they only exist secondarily and in a lesser, created manner in creatures. These perfections flow from God, their cause. So, these perfections belong to, and are applied primarily, in the order of reality, to God. However, these perfections are known by us first as they exist in creatures. So, in our order of knowing, God's perfections are known first by the manner in which they are represented in creatures. Aquinas reconciles the excelling nature of God with the more humble nature of creatures, through which we understand God:

> ... because we come to a knowledge of God from other things, the reality in the names said of God and other things belongs by priority in God according to His mode of being, but the meaning of the name belongs to God by posteriority. And so He is said to be named from His effects.

4.4 Analogy's Positive Contribution to Understanding

We stress that our primary concern is with Lonergan's method, not with the contents of his analogous conception. However, a good illustration of this method is found in his point (1964c, 83-84) that if one supposes there to be divine intelligible emanation, then "there follows all that pertains to a divine procession and all that we [Lonergan] have already proved from the truths of faith under the name procession *per modum operati*." We note that Lonergan does actually conclude from intelligible emanations to divine procession *per modum operati*. But what contribution to our knowledge of the mystery does it provide? In the first place, he notes that we are not to expect that such deduction intends an increase in certitude, for the principle of intelligible emanation is not known, but supposed. Furthermore, even though the same conclusion comes from the supposed principle as comes from the truths of faith, this does not prove the verity of the principle. Another principle could possibly give the same conclusion equally well, or better. In this light, we find reinforcement for Lonergan's position (1964c, 83, 85; 1994, 336) that systematics' understanding does not set out to prove doctrines, nor does it add certitude to doctrines. That this understanding does not increase certitude is further borne out by the fact that the principles furnished in analogical understanding are not deduced from known truths, they are supposed and postulated. It is on the basis of supposition, not demonstration, that we gain understanding of the truths of faith.

If we turn our attention away from certainty, to understanding, then the postulated principle attained by analogous conception does have significance. Where we previously had no understanding of how divine procession could be *per modum operati*, our analogous conception allows us to have an intelligent grasp of a divine infinite act that is rationally and morally conscious. Lonergan acknowledges that such an understanding is imperfect, mediate and analogous, because it is an understanding of divine mystery by analogy with a humanly accessible reality. However, as he puts it (1964c, 84), this is some understanding, and it is the sort of understanding praised by Vatican Council I (DS 3016/TCF 132). We now turn to addressing the specific attainments of this understanding.

The specific achievement of analogously conceiving a divine mystery lies in understanding how it could be that the mystery is so. In other words, analogous conception allows us to grasp why it is that the mystery can be what it is. In short, analogous conception finds intelligible possibility within a mystery. We note that such intelligent understanding of the "why" and "how" of a mystery was the object sought in the first stage in which the problem was stated. The intelligibility of the mystery is the heuristic content in the statement of the problem with the mystery. By saying that one needs to know the basis of the divine processions, Lonergan means (1964c, 66, 84-86) that we are seeking the principle—the why and how, of the divine processions. In this present case, he proposes that if we suppose divine intelligible emanations, we can grasp how it is that the Son is both of himself and not of himself, how the Spirit is of himself and not of himself and how the manner of the Son's and the Spirit's not being from themselves is different to each other.

We find that Lonergan's approach parallels Aquinas' method, outlined in *Verbum* (1997, 219-20). Theological understanding results from the human desire to know *quid sit deus*. Thus, "To ask *quid sit* is to ask:

Why?" Moreover, to ask *quid sit* is to inquire into the formal cause. Nonetheless both Aquinas and Lonergan were aware that the desire to know the essence of God represents a desire for a supernatural goal that is unattainable by natural human intellect. Yet the impossibility of completely fulfilling this desire does not mean, for Aquinas, a retreat from theological understanding and a resort to simply "teaching catechism," nor does it mean as Lonergan puts it (1964c, 67), simply making verbal affirmations. Systematic theology takes up the image of God that we can find in created nature. Through the analogy of that nature, according to the mode of intelligible procession, we can grasp why it is that God can be Father, Word and Spirit. That understanding, Lonergan reminds us (1997, 219-20), is limited and imperfect because of its analogical character. While this understanding falls far short of an essential understanding of the divine essence, he notes that the analogous understanding far exceeds what could be attained by the light of natural reason. As Aquinas observes (*Summa Contra Gentiles*, I,q8§1), such an understanding is profitable, for, "to be able to see something of the loftiest realities, however thin and weak the sight may be, is ... a cause of the greatest joy."

By grasping something of the grounds, the *quid sit,* the "what, how and why," of a mystery, analogous conception reduces seemingly inconsistent elements into an intelligible unity. Under "The Act Whereby the Goal is Obtained," Lonergan writes (1964c, 12) that the attainment of such a synthetic viewpoint is a key objective of theological understanding, so that theological understanding seeks an understanding of many elements simultaneously. We note that this goal corresponds to one of the attainments of insight that we examined earlier in this book. Where there is multiplicity in the data presented to human intellect, insight reduces such multiplicity into intelligible unity. We further note that such reducing to intelligible unity achieves an intelligent grasp of the relations between the different elements at hand.

In our specific case under investigation, we find the apparently contradictory doctrinal affirmations, regarding the Son and the Spirit, reduced to an intelligible unity on the basis of an intelligible principle attained in analogous conception. With Lonergan (1964c, 84-85), we find that there had been apparent conflict between the intelligibility of the procession of the Son and the Spirit, and their consubstantiality with the Father. Lonergan acknowledges that a direct reconciliation of the conflict is impossible, because, we note, we cannot quidditatively understand God. However, the conflicts can be reconciled by the unifying insight, that the divine processions have an intelligible ground in "an act that is both infinite and dynamically conscious." Thus, from the analogous conception of intelligible emanation in the divinity, we can grasp that in God the consubstantiality is because of that act's infinity and that the divine processions are because of the dynamic consciousness in the divinity.

To explain the unifying attainment of analogous conception, we can contrast the goal of a unifying insight with the process of deducing conclusions. Lonergan makes the point (1964c, 30) that deducing conclusions from mysteries does not provide understanding. Instead, "deductions from revealed mysteries clearly and distinctly manifest problems. The more numerous and the more exact the deductions, the more numerous and the more difficult are the manifested problems." We found this exact difficulty under "the problem" above, in which deductions from the doctrines simply manifested apparent contradictions and unintelligibility in the mystery of the Trinity. Lonergan then notes (1964c, 30-31) that such problems are irreconcilable if we remain on the level of judgement, by using only deductions and conclusions. Such problems can only be reconciled by some intelligent grasp of the mysteries. Lonergan thus rejects the view that theology can be simply about conclusions, whether these conclusions be "pure" or "mixed." The resolution of the mysteries' apparent contradictions can only come by discovering an intelligible principle, which comes from the hypothetical, analogous solution that we have explored above.

We have spoken about the unifying insight that analogy provides to theological understanding. It is important to clarify something of the nature of this insight. We may ask if the insight into the transcendent object is the same as the insight into the object proportionate to human understanding, by which we understand the mystery?

We can answer this question if we take up Lonergan's distinction of analogous and univocal concepts. He proposes (1992, 385) that "Concepts are said to be univocal when they have the same meaning in all applications, and they are said to be analogous when their meaning varies systematically as one moves from one field of application to another." Before proceeding with this point, though, we re-emphasise Lonergan's insistence that meaning is ultimately found not in the concept, but the insight. Accordingly, we expect an univocal act of understanding to be a proportionate insight—one that gains a grasp of the essence of the object. Furthermore, if understandings of two objects are expressed by the same univocal concept, we expect the same insight to be grasped in both acts of understanding. For example, if I predicate, in a univocal manner, the same concept: intelligible procession, of two human beings, I am expressing a grasp of the same insight into the qualities of both persons. In other words, my univocal grasp of intelligible procession indicates that this quality is present in the same way, and in the same order, in both objects.

If, however, the concept is analogous, and its meaning varies systematically, we express not a different concept, but different insights into meanings. An analogical act of understanding thus varies in its grasp of intelligibility by way either of the objects' content, or of their proportion, or both. By way of content, the "notion of being," is always analogous, because when one predicates "being" of two, or more, objects, the content of what exists, always varies. Thus, what is "being" always varies from object to object. "Being" accordingly varies in meaning, as to the content of being in concrete cases, as we apply "being" to one object or another. By way of proportion, I may analogically predicate intelligible procession of both a human being and God. Here, I mean intelligible procession, as humanly present in a creaturely, finite proportion and immediately grasped in a humanly intelligible, manner. On the other hand, I mean "intelligible procession" in God in an infinite, transcendent proportion, and beyond immediate grasp by my natural human knowing.

If, as Lonergan states, analogous concepts systematically vary in meaning as they are applied to different objects, then we note that by univocal concepts, or predication, one expresses the same insight into two objects. That is, an insight of the same order and content is grasped in both cases. Analogical concepts or predications, however, express insights that have some similarity, but differ in order or content, or both of these. We should note here that the above understanding of analogy is impossible in conceptualism, in which the concept dictates the content of the insight.

To clarify the insight that we gain into the divine processions, we must note that when we suppose intelligible emanation in the divinity, we must allow for some differences between divine emanation and mortal, finite intelligible emanation. The relations between the Son, the Spirit, and the Father differ from the relations between the contents of our own intellectual process. Accordingly, while there are similarities leading us to a certain insight, this insight differs and must be refined according to the real differences between the transcendent object and the finite analogate. We shall take up the issue of such refining below.

In the context of an analogous conception of the divine processions, Lonergan notes (1964c, 28) that what we can know about God from the light of natural reason differs greatly from what we can know about God through the light of an analogous conception. It is important to note

Lonergan's statement that the difference between the two modes of know-ing is not only with respect to the solutions that they provide, but the difference is also with regard to the problems that they face. He notes that common to both modes of knowing is the question of the knower— *quid sit Deus?* The difference in the problems, though, lies in whether or not human knowing is operating under the light of revelation. Unaided human reason can argue from pure perfections by the ways of affirma-tion and eminence. Furthermore, whatever natural human reason attains is demonstrated. However, without revelation, there is no question and thus no problem, of such mysteries as the Trinity, the Incarnation, Di-vine Grace, the Sacraments. To understand a mystery, such as the Trinity, one first needs revelation. Without this revelation there is no problem and thus no desire to understand the mystery. However, with the added data that faith finds in revelation, one can then seek an analogous con-ception by which one can understand how that mystery can be so. Thus, while a philosopher can demonstrate that God is conscious, only a theo-logian operating under the light of faith can suppose that God is dynami-cally conscious and that there are intelligible processions in the divinity. Moreover, the theologian proposes dynamic consciousness in God, not because one demonstrates it or understands its essence, but because in this principle of dynamic consciousness, one finds the basis for the reso-lution of the difficulties of intelligibility that one finds in the Triune God (Lonergan 1964c, 28; 1997, 207-8, 213).

We can now better understand Lonergan's characterisation of system-atics (1994, 337) as "the Christian prolongation of what man can begin to know by his native powers." He argues that this approach correlates with medieval procedure, but contrasts sharply with the more modern tendency to separate systematic theology and philosophy, a separation that doubly affected theology and philosophy. First, without any notion of philosophy's association with systematic theology, some people assumed that systematic theology was no more than extra philosophy and that it lacked religious significance. From the converse school, others, such as Barth (1975, I, xiii, 6) or Calvin (*Institutes*, II, iii), presumed that phi-losophy, or natural theology, could only attain objects other than the Christian God. Philosophy was thus deemed useless, if not anti-Chris-tian. Secondly, the separation simultaneously weakened systematic theol-ogy and natural theology. As a separate discipline, systematics suffered an inability to relate to what people could know by their natural abilities. Natural theology also suffered because its more difficult philosophical concepts could not be related to their corresponding religious expressions in systematic theology.

Lonergan argues (1994, 337) that the separation of philosophy and theology results from the assumption that the truths of philosophy, and we add, of theology, have an altogether objective existence that is independent of the mind that thinks these truths. However, the modern shift in focus to the subject debunks the objectivity of truth. In *Verbum,* Lonergan insists (1997, 75-76) that truth "exists only in a mind." Even so-called "eternal truths" are only eternal because they exist within the mind of God. We would recall the point that proof, or the human establishment of truth, only takes on acceptability and precision within a specific horizon. That horizon is hardly independent of the thinking subject, it is the result of his or her intellectual, moral and religious conversion.

One can also observe that philosophy's and theology's separation or confusion results from an inadequate distinction of differentiated and undifferentiated consciousness. An undifferentiated consciousness fails to either distinguish or relate religion and philosophy because it deals with religious, moral and intellectual consciousness at once. Differentiated consciousness, alternatively, can distinguish within the subject when one is operating intellectually, morally or religiously (Lonergan 1974, 131-32). Philosophy on the one hand, and religion or theology on the other hand, are distinguished by the one being an entirely natural operation of human consciousness, while the other involves supernatural activities such as revelation. The integration and continuity, of the two, results from philosophy's, religion's and theology's being products of the one human subject, who at one time philosophises with natural reason alone, and who theologises at another time on the same object with illumination of faith. Such an integration, we emphasise, is impossible without a sufficient account of the subject's activities, such as that provided by Lonergan.

As we have indicated above, the specific integration of philosophy and systematic theology occurs on the side of the inquiring subject. The subject can, in the one instance, desire to know what one can achieve by one's natural powers. One can ask further questions that, when answered, prolong or add to what one can naturally know. The prolongation of natural knowledge thus begins heuristically. One's questions are then answered in the first instance, by the transforming illumination of faith, which is theology's principle (Lonergan 1964c, 8; 1994, 249, 251). Faith allows one to extend one's knowledge of truth by believing. Human reason thus operates under the illumination of faith, to gain a knowledge of the naturally unknowable mysteries, so that, having some revealed knowledge, reason can proceed to some understanding of these same mysteries. Lonergan's essential point (1962, 249, 250) is that systematics is neither faith alone, nor reason alone. Systematics is a human subject's operation, with faith added to all of one's natural powers. Theological understanding thus arises when human intellect appropriates revelation and seeks insights into this revelation.

4.5 Judgement on the Analogy

We now turn to the question of why any one analogy is to be preferred above another. We first need to bear in mind that, in itself, analogical understanding, as understanding, is neither true nor false. Understanding of the mysteries of faith, as Lonergan writes (1964c, 19) "pertains to the first operation of intellect, whereas truth or falsity are found formally only in the second." As noted previously, systematics' understanding neither sets out to prove doctrines, nor does it add certitude to doctrines. Because analogous understanding is not true or false in itself, we cannot pass judgement on the value of an analogy, on the grounds of certitude. How then, can we pass judgement on an analogous conception?

First, an analogy must deal with the concrete situation at hand. In the case of the divine processions, Lonergan notes (1964c, 86) that we can speak either about an abstract definition of procession, or about the concrete mode of procession. The abstract definition is inadequate to the divine processions, because this definition prescinds from concrete reality and does not account for the differences between modes. We thus note that a purely abstract definition of procession could not distinguish between the processions of the Son and the Spirit. Lonergan emphasises that an analogy should deal with the concrete mode of the divine mystery at hand. It is thus clear that an analogy should deal with the concrete questions at hand. In the case of the Trinity, an analogy should not deal with an abstract concept of processions. The analogy must deal with the concrete reality of two different divine processions. The first criterion for a good analogy is whether it resolves the concrete questions raised by the mystery.

Lonergan also makes a point that both warns us and establishes a condition for effective analogy. First, he reminds us (1964c, 85, 87) of the First Vatican Council's teaching, that the understanding of a mystery is sought "from the analogy of what is naturally known." We are thus cautioned that any analogical understanding will be mediate. So, we again emphasise that analogous conception cannot give us an understanding of the essence of a mystery. This means that analogical understanding is necessarily imperfect, an imperfection reinforced by the fact that the principles, which analogy manifests, are neither deduced nor demonstrated, but simply postulated. Despite our best efforts, and notwithstanding the number of questions an analogy may solve, analogy never penetrates to the very core of a mystery, which remains hidden, in its essence, from the minds of mortal human beings.

Lonergan adds an important clarification. He writes that (1964c, 87), "since we know the supernatural only analogously, it follows that we know the supernatural only mediately. Therefore, it remains that the analogy is to be drawn from natural realities." But, as he also notes, all mediate knowledge must have its basis in some immediate knowledge. In the case of analogous conception, this immediate knowledge is of naturally known realities. By itself, this point may seem unspectacular, even banal. It does however, present another condition for effective analogy. If one were to attempt to grasp a divine mystery by analogy with another mystery, one would simply have no understanding of either mystery. We note that human insight is directly into what is accessible to and attainable by, natural human intellect. An analogous conception of the divine mystery therefore, must be through a grasp of an object immediately attainable by human intellect. If we attempt to understand one mystery by analogy with another, we do not attain insight into the mystery, but confusion. We clarify, though, that our point here is that we could not understand a mystery by *analogy* with another mystery. This point in no way excludes an understanding of a mystery by its *interconnection* with the other mysteries.

In *De Deo Trino* (1964c, 88-90), we read three pages of Lonergan's thoughts on why an analogy for the divine processions should be restricted to only a spiritual mode of proceeding, rather than only to a spiritual nature, or even a spiritual procession. Lonergan finds that only a conscious procession, in accord with what is in act in human beings, is adequate as an analogy for the divine procession. This is because only such a natural procession has similitude to the divine processions. We thus find another condition for effective analogy, that between the immediately understood natural object and the mystery, there must be a real similitude. As Lonergan states, "an analogy has its foundation in a similitude."

The requirement for similitude comes from the form of analogous understanding. We do not understand the mystery directly, but we understand it to the extent that a notion penetrates both a mystery and a created object. Lonergan expresses the need for real similarity in *Insight* (1992, 312-13). He writes that to understand analogically, we must first understand some concrete situation, *A*. If another situation *B* is similar to *A* then it can be argued that *B* can be understood in the same manner as *A*. Such analogical understanding, Lonergan notes, relies on the assumption that "similars are similarly understood." Accordingly, one makes a transition from one understood particular case, to another similar particular case or to the general case, which one aims to understand by reference to the first particular case. He notes then, "We appeal to analogies and we generalise because we cannot help understanding similars similarly." He again makes a key warning on analogy being an understanding based on similarity. Most basically, the real similarity must be present. If the two cases are significantly dissimilar, the analogy is questionable. Further questions must be answered on how the insight into one object may be revised, modified or complemented so as to more accurately grasp the second object.

An analogy is thus valid only to the degree that there is similitude between the objects related by that analogy. This means that systematics' analogy, is valid only, as Lonergan puts it (1964c, 12) "to the extent that there exists a similitude between creator and creature." Lonergan accordingly warns us that we need to avoid generalising on insufficient grounds. His warning on generalisation holds just as true for understanding by analogy. If there is a dissimilarity between the object understood and the object through which it is understood, one's insight into the intended object needs to be complemented, changed, or even revised (Lonergan 1992, 313).

If we return to *De Deo Trino* (1964c, 88), we find that our analogies need to be systematically restricted to that which sufficiently resembles God. For example, we may seek an analogy of God in nature, which consists of vegetables, minerals, animals and human beings. Only human beings, Lonergan notes, can provide a sufficient similitude to God and then only in human beings' spiritual nature is this similitude found. The material or biological natures possessed by natural beings simply do not resemble God, and so God cannot be analogously conceived through them. We also note that when we take a created attribute, we need to abstract from its created imperfections to form an analogy adequate to conceiving the divine presence. Thus, any created object, through which we propose to understand the divine mysteries by analogy, must be subjected to the corrections of the way of affirmation, negation and eminence.

The key question now is whether creatures actually do have a similitude to God. If no such similitude exists, any attempt to understand God on the basis of our understanding of creatures would be strictly equivocal. A traditional justification of natural objects having similitude to God comes from Aquinas (*Summa Theologiae*, I,q13,a5c), who bases his position on the argument that creatures, as effects of God, do manifest something of God. By their similarity to God, as effects to cause, creatures exhibit something of God, even though they only do this imperfectly. Thomas supports his position with Saint Paul's statement (Romans 1:20) that "The invisible things of God are clearly seen being understood by the things that are made." A further argument is that purely equivocal predication between God and creatures would mean that there was no real agreement between God and creatures at all. However, Thomas argues (*De Veritate*, q2,a11) that because God's essence is the likeness of creatures, and because God knows creatures by knowing his essence, there must be some non-equivocal predication possible of God and creatures.

We note that Aquinas recognised that any analogical predication of God is possible only where there is similitude between creatures and God. Thus, analogy relies on a creature's likeness to God. We observe, though, that this likeness is a one-way relation, which makes Thomas' analogy both possible and imperfect. All creatures are effects of God, and are ordered to God. Thomas accordingly argues (*Summa Theologiae*, I,q13a7c) that creatures have a real relation to God himself, and manifest something of God's perfections. With such a likeness, by way of creatures being effects, a positive, analogical understanding is possible. However, the likeness of creatures to God involves real relation to God, not the reverse. God has no real relation to creatures. In fact, God is altogether outside of the realm of creation so that creatures are like God, but God is not like creatures. Moreover, creatures only have an imperfect likeness to God, which means that a creature, while having some likeness to God, never reaches full and perfect resemblance to God. Accordingly, we emphasise again that an analogous conception of a divine mystery can never give an immediate, direct or quidditative understanding of the mystery.

From Aquinas (*Summa Theologiae*, I,q27,a1,ad2), we can take an example of the restriction and refinement of analogy. As Lonergan later does (1997, 206-7), he argues that an analogy for the divine processions can not be found in all creatures, not even most creatures; it can only be found in rational creatures. The reason for such restriction of the analogy is simple. Whatever proceeds by non-rational, or "outward" processions is distinct from its source. However, what proceeds by intelligible procession is not necessarily distinct. So, as "the divine Word is of necessity perfectly one with the source whence He proceeds, without any diversity" it is necessary then, for any valid analogate to be likewise a procession whereby that proceeding is not distinct from its source. For example, an attempt to analogically understand the Trinitarian processions by a vegetative procession will be invalid because it cannot preserve the indistinction of essence of the three Persons.

When reading Lonergan's *De Deo Trino*, we may be surprised that the first stage of his analogous conception of the divine processions does not deal with the divine processions. In fact, his first stage (1964c, 70-74) is to spend several pages clarifying the nature of intelligible emanation. Why this is so is partly because he follows Aquinas in conceiving the divine processions by analogy with human intelligible emanations. So, by explaining the nature of intelligible emanations, Lonergan is simply dealing first with those elements that do not presuppose other elements. If we were to first suppose that intelligible emanations could be an analogy for the divine processions, we would be proceeding unintelligently, having no real grasp of what it was by which we were trying to understand the divine processions. However, the complementary side to presenting one's analogate first is the need for that object to be correctly understood. We know that analogical understanding is to grasp the mode of an unknown nature, by relation to a similar, but known, nature. It is necessary then, that if we are to adequately understand a second object by analogy, the first object by which we grasp the second must itself be correctly understood. Accordingly, if we incorrectly understand the first object, that error will be compounded when we endeavour to analogically understand the second (Lonergan 1964c, 75; 1992, 313). In both *De Deo Trino* (1964c, 68-69) and *Verbum* (1997, 10-11), Lonergan expends much effort on correcting misconceptions of human understanding, most notably the Scotists' position. He corrects such misconceptions because when human intellectuality is misunderstood, the divine processions that we analogously conceive through human intellectuality become even more misunderstood. We thus find that in the general case of analogy, if we are to understand similar objects similarly, there must be a correct understanding of the first object. Otherwise, our understanding will be quite mistaken in understanding the second object. The result of such misunderstanding is great obscurity when one attempts to understand a divine mystery by analogy with a misunderstood created reality (Lonergan 1992, 313; 1997, 192).

The need to understand accurately the created object, through which we analogically understand the divine mystery, leads us to understand how systematic understanding can develop. The analogy is derived from what we naturally know. We furthermore note that our understanding of created objects is always in a state of development. Accordingly, the more and better one understands a created object through which one analogically understands the mysteries, the more developed and refined will be our understandings of those same mysteries. Thus, because our natural understanding grows, so too does our analogical understanding of supernatural objects.

In the context of the conditions for effective analogy, we can better understand the role of the traditional, analogical *via affirmationis, negationis, et eminentiae*. Analogy first allows us to positively affirm a similarity between the created object and the divine mystery, thus allowing us to gain a similar insight into the mystery. Lonergan (1962, n45; 1988, 82, 269a), however, recalls the Fourth Lateran Council's statement (DS 806/320): "one can not know an instance of similarity between creator and creature that is so great that there does not remain to be known an even greater dissimilarity between them." So, secondly, the mystery does not have any created imperfections, so these must be removed, or negated, from our analogous insight into the mystery. Thirdly, it must also be recognised that the mystery absolutely superexceeds the proportion of any created object. This means that our insight has to be open to the transcendence of the mystery, rather than being closed and categorical of the object.

The way of affirmation, negation and eminence was a theme taken up by Aquinas (*Summa Theologiae*, I,q12,a11c, q12a12c, q13a1c, q84,a7ad3; *Summa Contra Gentiles*, I,14§2). His basic position begins from the argument that we can know God by comparing him to creatures. From natural philosophy, we can know God as the principle of creatures. As principle, we can then grasp God's remotion from his creatures, that is, how God super-exceeds all the perfections of his creatures. More importantly, we can grasp something of the creaturely imperfections that God cannot possess. Aquinas accordingly argues that we can attain some intelligent grasp of God by reasoning out what God is not. In this way, Thomas follows the path that had been favoured by Pseudo-Dionysius and other neo-Platonist influenced Christian writers, namely, the *via negativa* or *via remotionis* (Copleston, 1985, II, 348). Thomas, however, added a new dimension to the *via remotionis*. He noted that we can gain some understanding of what God is by grasping just what God is not. Thus, by removing imperfections from our concept of God, we can gain some understanding of God. As Thomas states, this is because "we know each thing more perfectly the more fully we see its differences from other things; for each thing has within itself its own being, distinct from all other things." Thomas adds another helpful clarification, that creaturely attributes are not denied of God because of any defect on God's part. We are thus lead to the third manner of grasping God. God is removed from creatures because he "super-exceeds" the perfections of all creatures. In short, Aquinas teaches that we know God's relationship to creatures insofar as is required for us to know Him as the cause of all creatures, and that creatures are different to God, inasmuch as God is not part of what He causes. Moreover, creatures are not "removed" from God by any defect on the part of God, but because he superexceeds all of His creation.

According to Aquinas, we can know God, not just by the *via negativa* and *via remotionis*, but by the affirmative way, knowing God *per excessum*. We can analogically predicate qualities of God in a "super-eminent" way, recognising that the perfections in creatures, by which we understand God, pre-exist in God in a way far exceeding the manner in which creatures manifest these perfections. So, affirming something of God means making an affirmative statement about God. While this adds a positive content to our knowledge, we follow Aquinas in cautioning that, while any such analogical knowledge we gain is positive, it is imperfect and never complete.

Lonergan (1964c, 86-87) also stresses the need for an analogy to be systematic. This means first, that to proceed implicitly and unthematically is insufficient. Similar is the approach of simply creating a new analogy for each new question. In the first case, we would hold that the unthematic and implicit approach, rather than advancing towards understanding the mystery itself, would retreat from the mystery. In the second case, Lonergan notes that rather than intelligently resolving problems with the mystery, one would simply heap up a rhetorical supply of examples, none of which would actually furnish an intelligible resolution of the problem at hand.

The more satisfactory approach, in Lonergan's view (1964c, 86-87), is to seek a systematic analogy in which one seeks an analogy that begins from elements that do not presume an understanding of other realities. Furthermore, the systematic analogy will be such that all further questions pertaining to the mystery will be resolved by virtue of that analogy. An effective analogy will not only resolve one's immediate question, but it will resolve further questions that arise as one considers a mystery. By way of example, an analogy of goodness self-diffusing does not meet the systematic requirements of an analogous conception of the divine processions. Such an analogy cannot answer questions of why there are but two processions in the divinity. Neither can such an analogy answer the question of how the two divine processions differ from one another.

In *De Deo Trino* (1964c, 83), Lonergan notes that the analogous conception leads us to conclude to the same realities as are affirmed in the doctrine of the Trinity:

> On the supposition, then, of a divine intelligible emanation, there follows all that pertains to a divine procession and all that we have already proved from the truths of faith under the name procession *per modum operati.*

If we follow Lonergan's writings immediately prior to this remark, we find that if we suppose the principle of intelligible emanation in God, we can conclude to the truths affirmed in the doctrine of the Trinity. We have already investigated the relevance of this deduction as regards understanding and knowledge. We now need to add another condition for effective analogy. In the concrete case of the divine processions, the analogy of intelligible emanation works because it explains how the Son is both from himself and not from himself, how the Spirit is both from himself and not from himself, and how the Son's and Spirit's not being from themselves actually differ. Were intelligible emanation incapable of showing how these truths are so, the analogy would essentially be useless. A general condition for analogy then, is that an analogy will be effective and useful when it can explain how it is that the truths of faith are what they are. A good analogy will thus simply manifest the intelligible grounds for the truths of faith that are concluded from doctrines.

We can now concisely deal with the question of whether an analogous conception is probable or not. We can also ask how we may determine if an analogy is either approaching, or departing from, certitude. As we have seen above, analogy simply rests upon a hypothesis and expresses merely supposed principles. How then is such a hypothetical understanding to be given any sense of probability? First, one can ask if the analogy squares with the revealed truth that it is supposed to express (Lonergan 1997, 204). If the analogy conflicts with the revealed truth, it is insufficient. But what of the positive side of approaching certitude? To this end we turn to the "consequent" truth of a hypothesis. A hypothesis, as Lonergan writes (1964c, 24), "is that conceptual and also verbal expres-

sion which enunciates a principle, which proceeds from an act of understanding, and which resolves the basic or initial problem." The initial
success or probability of a hypothetical analogy thus reflects analogy's
heuristic origin that we described above. In short, hypothetical analogy is
probable to the extent that it solves the question put to it. Moreover, the
more problems a hypothesis solves, the more probable and the more approaching certainty it will be. The more certain it becomes, he adds, the
more it excludes other possible ways of solving the same problems. We
further note Lonergan's point (1964c, 87, 92) that the more problems a
hypothesis solves the more it approaches certainty. In this light we have
another condition for effective analogy, namely, that it will solve not just
one problem, but it will resolve every other theoretical question on the
mystery at hand. In the case of the analogous conception of the divine
processions, the hypothesis of intelligible emanation works because it can
account, not only for the presence of processions of distinct, though consubstantial divine persons, but also for questions such as why two, and
only two, divine processions can be conceived.

5. CONCLUSIONS

What does Lonergan mean (1994, 336), in taking up the First Vatican
Council's affirmation (DS 3016/TCF 132) that we can attain an understanding of the mysteries from the analogy of what human reason naturally knows? Answering this question is difficult, because Lonergan made
use of a variety of analogies, without specifying a definition, or set of
meanings of analogy (Crowe 1983, 38). However, in the light of our
research, we can say confidently that Lonergan, especially in his earlier
writings, used and fostered Thomist forms of analogy. Later though, he
went beyond specifically Thomist analogies, to develop and use his own
forms of analogical understanding, with the most important case found
in the "notion of being," investigated above. The form of analogy used in
the notion of being transcended scholastic distinctions of attribution [pro-
portion] and proportion [proportionality] by introducing a new paradigm of analogy based on the knowing processes of human inquiry.
Lonergan's analogy based on notions could thus both encompass and go
beyond the Thomist forms of analogy. In the analogical paradigm, in
which an analogous notion penetrates different contents, one could possibly include Thomist forms of analogy. Yet the concept-based distinctions of attribution and proportion fade, because Lonergan's analogy, based
on inquiry, simultaneously simplifies the method of analogical understanding and frees analogy from such conceptual bounds. This latter no-

tion of analogy being "freed" is important, for in a notional, inquiry-based analogy, one is no longer tied to particular forms of relations in analogates. One is free to find the way that a notion penetrates other objects, in whatever way one may legitimately find that penetration. To take an idea from Lonergan in another context (1994, 344), in a notional analogy, one is not bound to the relation forms discovered or dictated by others, but by basing analogical understanding in the very operations of human intellect one is not dependent on others, a person is on one's own. We would thus hold that analogy, no less than insight in general, is not dependent upon external circumstances, but upon inner conditions, specifically the penetrating notion. Analogy, for Lonergan, thus occurs when the same notion penetrates two objects, one proportionate to human intellect, the other mysterious, and with that notion one can resolve problems of intelligibility associated with that mystery.

Our research has uncovered different forms of analogy. However, as we have found the basis of analogy to be in human inquiry, we should avoid the tendency to base divisions within analogical understanding upon the difference between analogical and quidditative knowledge, or between analogical and quidditative concepts. With the more free and productive foundation for analogy being in human inquiry, Crowe (1983, 38) is correct in writing that the different meanings of analogy are best determined by basing one's distinctions on the role of understanding.

First, the most strict and rigorous definition of analogy concerns a human understanding that can attain a partial understanding, but cannot attain a full, direct or proper understanding, of its object. As Crowe points out (1983, 38), while such analogical understanding is neither proper nor direct, but partial, this understanding is some understanding and thus a positive contribution to one's grasp of an object. This mode of analogy is most applicable to mysteries, of which humans cannot attain quidditative understanding. We found such analogy, strictly speaking, in Lonergan's writings on the notion of being and on the Trinity. In such strict applications of analogical understanding, one understands, not the object itself, but another object that has some similarity or relationship to the object in which we are interested. Within a Thomist paradigm of analogy, this relationship may be an attributive or proportional similarity. However, as we have importantly seen, Lonergan both simplifies and strengthens analogical understanding by holding that in analogy, one can base one's understanding on a notion that penetrates those different objects. We also note that a systematic analogy seeks a principle, by which one can resolve a series of questions about a mystery. That principle, because we are dealing with non-quidditative or partial understanding, is always hypothetical and imperfect.

The second, broader definition of analogy concerns an understanding that is indirect, but one that involves at least the possibility of all terms in the analogy being understood. Such an example is in the analogies of proportion [proportionality] between classical and heuristic structures, and Thomist and scientific thought. Crowe points out (1983, 38-39) that while there is an actual analogy of four terms in the form "(A : B : : C : D)" and one may indirectly understand some terms, one may nonetheless directly understand all four terms. Such direct and proper understanding would exclude analogy in its strict sense. Moreover, this form of analogy of proportionality is less suited to understanding the mysteries of faith, because it allows for the possibility of directly understanding such objects, which would not do justice to the humanly incomprehensible nature of the mysteries.

The third, even less restricted and less technical sense of analogy, involves common sense understanding one situation by analogy with another situation. We noted this commonsense view of analogy above. The historian's use of analogy, in which one understands the past by its partial similarity to the present, fits into this model of analogy (Lonergan 1994, 225-27). Such a broad, attributive, analogy would be less suited to understanding the mysteries, because of its tendency towards metaphor, rather than analogy.

In this light, we note the vital distinction, to which Crowe draws our attention and that we have also found in Aquinas, between systematic analogy and the mere proliferation of metaphors. In *De Deo Trino* II (1964c, 86-87), Lonergan makes a similar distinction, only he opposes systematic analogy to the rhetorical piling up of examples. To whatever we may oppose it, systematic analogy, in Lonergan's words, distinctly resolves a series of problems of intelligibility, by virtually resolving all theoretical questions on a given mystery. Aquinas' (*De Veritate*, q2a11c; *Summa Theologiae*, I,q13a6c) caution on metaphor tells us that we would gain more understanding into the symbol, rather than into the object we are really trying to understand. Crowe notes (1983, 39) that systematic analogy is more likely to be found in the first two usages of analogy and the use of metaphor is more likely in the second two. On this point he draws our attention to Lonergan's paraphrase (1992, 567, 772) of Quintillian, "almost every word we use is a metaphor." Our language, especially in its commonsense mode, is loaded with metaphors. The words we use for cognitional operations serve as good examples: "in-sight, grasping, catching on, under-standing." We need to take care, when using either these, or more complex metaphors, not to confuse them with systematic analogies.

The distinction of analogy from metaphor helps us recall that we cannot apply any analogy to a particular mystery. A systematic analogy, while not being verifiable, needs to meet certain conditions, as outlined above. Of these conditions, the most important criterion is that the analogy must bring intelligibility to a mystery by answering the questions we bring to it.

A purely logical outlook would be confused by Lonergan's different uses and meanings of analogy. What should be clear, though, after our previous investigations, is that Lonergan does not hold to a purely logical framework, though we reiterate that he does not reject logic, he simply puts it into the wider context of method. Crowe (1983, 38) draws our attention to Lonergan's comments (1990, 53-54) on Aquinas' method:

> Helpful here is his [Lonergan's] remark on Thomas Aquinas, to the effect that he is not a systematic thinker in the sense that logic requires, but [he] uses terms and explains them with the degree of precision the occasion demands, which may not be at all the degree that another occasion demands.

Lonergan further observes (1990, 53-54) that Aquinas' method was far removed from "setting down definitions, axioms, and postulates, and then deducing." Such a logical method is more akin to the approach of Scotus, who dealt with *actio* by stating that he used *actio* in fifteen senses, and then listed each of these fifteen senses. However, Aquinas deals with now this and then that instance and meaning of *actio*. Thomas' method takes a "series of questions and answers," and correlates more to a process of "presentations, inquiry, insight, conception, and sufficient conception to deal with the question at hand." We note a similarity between Lonergan's citation of Aquinas' method and our observations on Lonergan's use of analogy, and we note that Lonergan's method is also opposed to Scotus' procedure. On the one hand, Crowe observes that (1983, 38), for Lonergan, "analogy itself is an analogous term with various meanings. But nowhere ... does Lonergan offer a list of these meanings." On the other hand, Lonergan notes that Scotus "lists all fifteen" meanings of *actio*. Also relevant is his observation (1990, 54) that in Thomas' work, people simply have to determine in each case what the meanings of the

Thomist terms may be. Crowe observes (1983, 38) that this is Lonergan's pattern of thinking on the meaning of analogy. We need to understand each occurrence of the term "analogy" in its own context, without the guidance of either a defined list or of logical analysis.

Having outlined the meaning of understanding attained from analogy, we recall the point, that systematics' "imperfect, analogous, obscure, and gradually developing understanding is also synthetic." It is intrinsic to human intellect to proceed from resolving single objects, to ask how these single objects could be related to one another. So, "after individual mysteries have been considered separately, further questions arise with regard to the relation of the mysteries with one another and with the final end of man." Lonergan observes (1964c, 12) that when such questions are answered, we attain a "synthetic" understanding. That understanding is the subject of our next chapter.

NOTE

[1] From here on, and where relevant, we shall use the modern terms "attribution" and "proportion," and enclose the Thomist terms "proportion" and "proportionality" in square brackets.

Chapter 9
Understanding the Mysteries "from Interconnections"

As we have now covered understanding of the mysteries from analogy with what we naturally know, we turn to understanding attained from the mysteries' interconnections. To clarify the object of our investigation, we should recall Lonergan's citation (1994, 336) of the First Vatican Council (DS 3016/TCF 132). He notes that the mysteries can be understood, by reason acting under the guidance of faith, "both from the analogy of what it [reason] naturally knows and from the interconnection of the mysteries with one another and with man's last end." We are now investigating the next division of systematics' understanding. This chapter will ask how this understanding, from interconnections, is possible, and what form this understanding takes.

Before exploring understanding through interconnections, we should note two points. The first is on the division of systematics' understanding. We acknowledge that Church Council documents are not always philosophically precise accounts. Councils simply use the words that convey a point that has been agreed upon by their participants. Accordingly, it is not always absolutely essential to break up a discussion of systematics' understanding into distinct sections, as done in this investigation. However, we have done so, because such a division is certainly not excluded by the Council, and because dividing up our investigation adds more clarity and precision to this work. The second point is that, while we shall examine several theological texts from Lonergan, our intention is not to evaluate the content of his theology, but our intention is to determine the method that he is using. To address understanding attained from interconnections, this chapter will first explore two preliminary examples, which give us a basic idea of how we may understand an object better through its interconnections with another object. We shall then investigate Lonergan's theory behind understanding attained from interconnections. We shall thirdly examine several cases in which Lonergan attained an understanding from the interconnections of mysteries. Fourthly, before drawing our conclusions, we shall take up three examples of understanding mysteries through their interconnection with humanity's last end.

1. Preliminary Examples of
Understanding from Interconnections

To help us to grasp the workings of understanding from the interconnection of mysteries, we propose to deal first with two examples of understanding by interconnection, in which either one, or both, of the objects being intelligibly interconnected are not mysteries. Through these
two examples, we shall gain an easier entry into understanding how one
can understand an object by its interconnection with another. In doing
so, we can grasp more easily how we can attain understanding by grasping the interconnection of mysteries with each other, or with our last
end. In this section, we shall explore how we can understand by grasping
the interconnection of one non-mystery with another non-mystery, namely
the interconnection of method in theology with other scientific
endeavours. In our second case, we shall examine an example of how a
mystery of faith is understood by its interconnection to a non-mysterious
reality, namely, when grace is conceived in its relation to cognitional structure.

Our first example involves the interconnection of two non-mysterious
objects. Lonergan's reply (1971a, 224-25), to a charge from Karl Rahner,
reveals interconnections between transcendental method and theological
method. Rahner asserts that "Lonergan's theological methodology seems
to me [Rahner] to be *so generic that it really fits every science,* and hence is
not the methodology of theology as such, but only a very general methodology of science in general, illustrated with examples taken from theology" (McShane 1971, 194-95). Rahner's complaint suggests that
Lonergan's theological methodology does not bring out what is specific
to Christian theology in its own subject matter. However, we find more
significant the reverse, though unwritten, side of Rahner's charge, that
Lonergan's theological methodology has the same intentional structure
as any other scientific pursuit.

Lonergan (1971a, 224-25) does not spend much effort in defending
himself against Rahner's specific and explicit complaint. He is more concerned with bringing out what is positive in the truth behind Rahner's
statement and with explaining some connections. To get to the foundation of Lonergan's response, we should first recall his emphasis on the
theologian as the subject doing theology. He reminds us of his crucial
point, with which we are now familiar, that if one retains an Aristotelian
perspective, one would conceive theology in terms of its objects. However, if one holds a methodological viewpoint, one's emphasis would shift
from objects to the operations of the operating subject of theology. We

should also note Lonergan's reminder (1971a, 224-25) that if we expose the "basic and invariant structure of all human cognitional activity," we may realise a transcendental method which outlines the conditions of possibility for all the special methods proper to all areas of human inquiry. Moreover, we recall the statement that "Such a method will be relevant to theology, for theologians always have had minds and always have used them."

Upon the preceding foundation, we find a reminder that transcendental method is specifically relevant to theology in the two-phased and fourfold divisions of transcendental method, which yield eight functional specialties within theology. From the reverse side, of theology, this relationship means that functional specialisation within theology is based on the transcendental method, which is common to all areas of human inquiry. We may make this point in other words: The four-fold and two-phased structure of theology is *because of* the structure present in transcendental method, which is present in all intentional acts of the human mind. A key aspect of the understanding one may attain from this interconnection, is that one better understands theological method in its relationship to another object, namely transcendental method.

We should note the form of the basic interconnection in this example. The key question is how one can relate Lonergan's theological methodology to transcendental method. The answer is simple, yet important. Theological method is because of transcendental method. That is, theological method takes its intelligibility from transcendental method. As Lonergan puts the point (1971a, 225), "theologians always have had minds and always have used them." The essential point is that transcendental method, as the operation of the human mind, comes first, before theology. If one wishes to pursue theology, one must use one's mind. Theological method is because of transcendental method, because of the relationship one's specialised operations has to the general operations of one's own mind.

From Lonergan's writings on this topic (1971a, 233), we discover something of this understanding's fertility. That theology's functional specialisation is based on a common transcendental method means that "the eight functional specialties we [Lonergan] have listed would be relevant to any human studies that investigated a cultural past to guide its future." This reality leads us to two basic interconnections. First, Lonergan explicitly tells us that we can grasp a methodological interconnection between different religious confessions. If their relevant theologies are based upon transcendental method, each religion can use its own sacred traditions within a methodological theology. Lonergan claims that such an approach is useful because in a day of ecumenism and of dialogue with non-Christians, it helps to employ a method which can be adapted, by slight adjustments, to very different investigations. Secondly, there is implied in these statements an opportunity to relate, or to positively interconnect, different areas of study by the application of transcendental method to these areas. We could thus propose a way of intelligibly relating different faculties within a university by adopting an interdisciplinary methodological structure for all areas of human inquiry, which is based on transcendental method.

Our second example of attaining understanding from interconnection involves a mystery being understood in relation to a non-mysterious object. In "Thesis V" of his *De Ente Supernaturali*, Lonergan argues (1946, n157) that "Internal actual grace consists essentially in second acts of intellect and will which are vital, principal, and supernatural." By tying together grace with "intellect and will," he means to explicate an interconnection between grace and cognitional structure. In Thesis V, Lonergan both relies, and expands, upon the implications of this interconnection. This thesis thus provides a helpful example of understanding by interconnection.

The first methodological point of interest is in Lonergan's answer to the question, "what is an internal actual grace?" He replies (1946, n161), in part, that internal actual grace consists in acts of both intellect and will. That is:

> internal actual grace in the possible intellect is a certain act of understanding, for instance, the light of faith in second act, or an illumination by the Holy Spirit as the source of understanding, knowledge, wisdom, counsel; and this act of understanding is a second act produced immediately by God in us, without our being in any way efficient causes. Again, internal actual grace as received in the will is an act of willing a supernatural end ... which act is produced immediately by God in us, without our being in any way efficient causes.

Lonergan effectively makes the point that in the mystical life, the internal actual grace of God does not enter human life in an altogether unintelligible manner. He means that there is some intelligible connection between internal actual grace and another intelligible object. By explaining that internal actual grace is "a certain act of understanding, ... an illumination" and "an act of willing a supernatural end," Lonergan shows the point of connection between internal actual grace and human living. That connection is in the structure of human intentional consciousness, in which grace enters human mystical life by way of understanding and willing. We further note that the intelligible connection yields a reason for grace's so entering Christian life. Internal actual grace is manifested as an act of understanding or an act of willing because of human life's intentional constitution.

Secondly, some elements in Lonergan's proof (1946, n165ff) manifest useful examples of interconnections. In particular, we note the conception of a supernatural act that is formally free. By focussing on the human subject, he shows the interconnection of formally free supernatural acts and cognitional structure. First, he explains that supernatural act, which is a practical judgement, must proceed, somehow, from a first act of understanding. Furthermore, this first act of understanding must be supernatural, for if it is not supernatural, then a practical judgement, and its ensuing resolve, could not be supernatural. In other words, for there to be a formally free and supernatural act of will, there must essentially be a principal and supernatural act of understanding. In terms of interconnection, we find that in this section, Lonergan brings together grace and cognitional structure. The supernatural, formally free act enters into human life not just in the same structure as human intentionality, but the supernatural, formally free act actually presupposes, and both illuminates and prompts this human intentionality. There is, again, we note, an interconnection based on the reason for, "the because of," an object's existence. This "reason for" is that the manner of a supernatural, formally free act is intelligible in being because of human intentional structure.

We thirdly note Lonergan's minor premise (1946, n168), that "Second acts of intellect and will, which are vital, principal and supernatural, have all the properties of an internal actual grace." After stating this premise, Lonergan shows the fecundity of understanding attained from interconnections by deducing internal actual grace's properties from the concept of such acts.

These deduced properties include: that actual grace is distinct from infused virtue, that "an infused virtue is not sufficient for a supernatural act," an object requiring more than motion to be sufficient to be a supernatural act, that every supernatural act requires internal actual grace. Moreover, Lonergan deduces that internal actual grace: "is required for every supernatural act," "consists both in the illumination of intellect and in the inspiration of will," "gives both physical and moral powers," is divisible into ordinary and special aid, and includes deliberate as well as undeliberate acts. Some more properties deduced are that grace: can be called operative to the extent that our mind is moved but not moved and is cooperative to the extent that our mind is moved and moves (Lonergan 1946, n168-73).

Lonergan (1946, n174-79) cites eight other properties of internal actual grace. Along with the properties cited above, these deduced properties show the fertility of understanding, in particular understanding attained from interconnections. This fertility is manifested by one insight generating further insights. We should also note that Lonergan shows, not just a rhetorical connection, but a real interconnection between the mystery of internal actual grace, and human cognitional structure. We may ask what may be the use of such an exercise. The essential answer is that by determining the connection of grace and intentionality, we discover the "point of entry" of such grace into human life. We thus have a much clearer understanding of internal actual grace and its implications. That the implications and different aspects of this grace become clearer, is made evident by Lonergan's ability, once he has established the interconnection, to outline eighteen properties of internal actual grace. We also propose that by determining this interconnection, he brings together cognitional theory and mystical theology, two disciplines that otherwise may remain apparently alien to one another.

More methodologically important to us, in the more general sense, is that we have repeatedly seen that by drawing intelligible interconnections, we can understand the underlying reason for a mystery. That reason is more often than not expressed in the "because of" in a statement, which is an element easily overlooked. Our main observation, in both of our reflections on Theological Method and Internal actual grace, is that by understanding attained into interconnections, one of the most fruitful aspects of this understanding is the grasp of the reason for, or the basis or ground of, an object under consideration. As Doran notes (1995 1:181) such an understanding makes systematics an exercise of explanatory understanding of how those objects relate to one another, rather than common sense description of how those objects relate to us.

2. Lonergan's Theory Behind Understanding the Mysteries from their "Interconnections"

2.1 Attaining a single viewpoint

To help us better understand a key aim of Lonergan's method of arranging the mysteries so as to yield intelligible interconnections, we should first recall that understanding unifies manifold data into a single intelligible. As we found in chapter five, understanding yields intelligible unity from sensible multiplicity. In that light, we note Lonergan's comment (1964a, 44) that "characteristic of one who understands is the apprehension of what is many from the unity of a single viewpoint." In theology, he continues, as we attain greater understanding, then all the more can we reduce the manifold truths about God to a single truth, while at the same time, we can apprehend the many truths about God through this single truth.

The preceding point is made more clear, from a negative perspective, in Lonergan's attack on conceptualism (1997, 218-19). To the extent that one abandons the pursuit of understanding, one will fail to grasp the connections between different objects. By showing the intrinsic ineffectualness of conceptualism, he also brings out the reality for intellectualists, that understanding will unite many different data, within a single act of understanding. In the further light of Lonergan's comments in *De Constitutione Christi* we grasp that it is not only data that understanding can reduce to a single viewpoint. In what he later (1985b, 106, 181, 196-97) called the "downward mode," we find that understanding can also arrange manifold truths so that they can be intelligently apprehended in a single viewpoint.

Before investigating how such a viewpoint is attained, we should bear in mind Lonergan's point (1964a, 54) that while we are dealing with infinite mysteries, which cannot in themselves be positively conceived, we can gain some positive understanding of the infinite. This positive understanding is possible inasmuch as one can grasp the many negative conclusions of theology from a single viewpoint. We can thus grasp something of the relationships between the mysteries. Such understanding will naturally be imperfect, but it will be a real understanding. To Lonergan's point, we may add that there could be an understanding that transcends the intelligible union of negative concepts, while still not being an understanding of the infinite. That is, one could propose a partial, but nonetheless positive, understanding of the infinite. By way of example, we could point to our concept of one hundred, by which we can negatively understand infinity by noting that infinity is not one hundred. By our progressive concepts of one thousand and one million, we can gain a positive, though incomplete, understanding of infinity. A concept of one million transcends a concept of one hundred, by positively moving us towards, though never reaching, a concept of infinity.

Having introduced a key aim of attaining understanding of the mysteries by interconnections, we now turn to investigating how this uniting viewpoint may be attained.

2.2 The Manner of Attaining a Single Viewpoint

In *De Constitutione Christi* (1964a, n44), Lonergan concisely outlines the manner in which the mysteries can be interconnected with one another and how we may attain understanding from this interconnection. He puts forward the key proposition that "the many truths we know about God admit being so arranged that one truth may be grasped as being the ground of some second truth." To justify this position, he appeals first to "the link between the theses of natural theology" and secondly, to the statement of the First Vatican Council (DS 3016/TCF 132) on the "interrelationship of the mysteries." This statement is significant for two reasons. In the first place, Lonergan shows some authority for his position on arranging the mysteries so that one becomes the reason for another. In the second place, he appeals to the same text of *Dei Filius*, as the one he later cites to outline the function of systematics, in *Method in Theology* (1994, 332). Lonergan's citation of the same text, in both instances, means that we are correct to interpret this sort of "arrangement of the mysteries" in *De Constitutione Christi*, as being the same as the interconnection of the mysteries, to which he refers in *Method in Theology*.

In *De Constitutione Christi* (1964a, n44), Lonergan continues to explain the reason for such arrangement of the mysteries. On the one hand, he notes the reason for our knowing many truths, or why we have complex knowledge, about the one God who is simple. This reason is the imperfection of our knowledge. "For while God knows what is composite through a knowledge that is simple, we know what is simple through a knowledge that is composite." The other side of this reality is that we are capable of arranging such truths that we do know about God, into an order by which one truth can ground some second truth. To the extent that we can attain such arrangement, Lonergan holds that we can understand something of these truths. We would also note here, in the light of our reflections on the natural desire to know God, that the attainment of such a viewpoint is a natural desire of human intellect. To grasp all divine truths in a single viewpoint, in a manner similar to God's universal and simple knowledge, is a natural human desire. It is the natural desire for the beatific vision.

2.3 Causes of Knowing and Causes of Being

We need to clarify whether understanding, attained from the interconnections of mysteries, posits causes of being or causes of knowing. To this end, we recall Lonergan's (1964a, n47; 1985b, 79) repeated citation of Aristotle's distinction between the *causa essendi* (cause of being), and the *causa cognoscendi* (cause of knowing). Importantly, we note Lonergan's reminder that a cause of knowing is not necessarily a cause of being, but it is some truth which is a grounding truth for another, second truth. Lonergan's favourite example for this distinction is in the moon's phases and sphericity. We may say, for example, that the moon is spherical because we observe it passing through various phases. In this case, the phases are hardly the cause of the moon's sphericity. They are simply the cause of our knowing *(causa cognoscendi)* the moon's sphericity. If, on the other hand, we conclude that the moon passes through its phases because of its sphericity, then we are talking about both a cause of being, as well as a cause of knowing, as the moon's sphericity both causes its phases, and allows us to know that such phases exist.

Lonergan argues that (1964a, n47), in theology, we cannot posit causes of being in God, first, because we cannot know the essence of God and secondly, because there are no causes of being in God. When we interconnect the mysteries, in Lonergan's own words, "when our knowledge of God is constituted through many truths interrelated to each other through grounding truths," that grounding truth is not a cause of being, but a cause of our knowing the mystery. Thus, we must take heed again that what we attain in systematics, specifically systematics as the interconnection of mysteries, is not the essence of God, only an understanding of the revealed truths about God.

2.4 Interconnection and the *Ordo Doctrinae*

We have previously written on the order of teaching *(ordo doctrinae et disciplinae)*. Lonergan's reflections (1964a, n46) on understanding the mysteries by interconnection provides new light on the order of teaching. With him, we may briefly recall that the way of discovery proceeds, somewhat haphazardly, along the path from observed realities to the causes of those realities. Such, for example, is the order in chemistry whereby one proceeds from sensible data to determine the periodic table of the elements. Conversely, the way of teaching begins with causes, and proceeds to explain what is more readily observed by us. In chemistry, one may thus begin from the periodic table, to go on to explain any of the myriad of compounds that we may observe.

In theology, Lonergan explains (1964a, n46), the order of teaching occurs when reason, under the illumination of faith, attains some under-

232 Matthew C. Ogilvie: *Faith Seeking Understanding*

standing of the mysteries of faith. Here, we start, not from revealed data, but with the grounding truths, from which we proceed to the revealed realities that are better understood by our grasp of the grounding truths.

To illustrate and to defend his procedure, Lonergan appeals (1964a, n46) to the methodological authority of Aquinas, and observes that in the *Summa Theologiae* (Prologue), Aquinas' aim is to proceed along the way of teaching, to deal first with those questions whose solutions do not presuppose other solutions. In other words, Aquinas' intent is to deal with one's given topics in a systematic and orderly account. Lonergan notes that the contrast between the order of discovery and the order of teaching is best displayed within book four of Aquinas' *Summa Contra Gentiles*. Here, for example, in chapters two to nine, Aquinas argues in the manner of discovery against this, and then that, doctrinal question of fact on the Divine Generation. In chapters ten to fourteen, however, Aquinas embarks on an ordered exposition of how one may conceive the Divine Generation, with consequent arguments presupposing the truths established in previous arguments.

2.5 The Primacy of either Analogy or Interconnection

A question may be raised as to whether Lonergan intends us to pursue an understanding of the mysteries, first in their interconnections, or first by analogy. While we may be tempted towards the former position, we find that this is not Lonergan's position. We have a hint in *Verbum* (1997, 219), where Lonergan does refer to theological understanding as occurring "both from the connection between the mysteries and from the analogy of nature." This understanding, "from the interconnection ...," is within the context, and under the mantle, of analogical understanding. Both before, and after mentioning understanding by interconnection, Lonergan makes it clear that this understanding is part of analogical knowing and understanding. We shall return to this specific point at the end of this section.

What is possibly disputable in *Verbum* is indisputable in *De Constitutione Christi*. In n45, Lonergan outlines: (1) how we cannot directly understand the essence of God and (2) how we can attain an analogous, though imperfect understanding of God. He then explains that we can only analogously know individual truths about God. So, when we settle the grounding truths for these subsequent truths, the grounding truths cannot escape our analogies' imperfections. This statement clearly makes understanding by interconnection dependent on analogical understanding of individual truths. We find definitive evidence for Lonergan's giving first place to analogous understanding in his most clear statement that "our imperfect understanding of divine mysteries ... consists in the fact that we conceive divine realities analogously and then so arrange our analogous concepts that one becomes the reason for some other."

By way of example for the arranging of analogous concepts, Lonergan writes (1964a, n45) that in "the tract on the Trinity," we first analogously conceive the processions, the relations, and the persons. Only after analogously conceiving these elements of Trinitarian theology, do we proceed to "conclude from the processions to the relations and from the relations to the persons." Lonergan notes that all these elements are conceived at once in a single viewpoint, so they form an understanding, albeit an imperfect one, of the Trinity. We note, moreover, that while this example shows how mysteries can be arranged so that one becomes the reason for another, it also shows how an understanding of one's objects, even if only an analogous understanding, is necessary if one is to make any intelligent interconnections of these same objects.

If we return to our earlier point, from *Verbum*, we can resolve some of the confusion over this issue. People may be confused because understanding attained from interconnections is invariably tied up with analogical understanding. Understanding attained from interconnections, as we noted before, is part of analogical understanding. Here then, lies the solution to our problem. Analogical understanding of an individual object must come first if we are to have any understanding of a mystery. However, when we understand different mysteries through their interconnections, that understanding remains part of, and contributes more, to the analogical understanding of those mysteries. This is important to remember, if we are not to assume that we can intelligibly interconnect the essences of these mysteries. We also find Anthony Kelly's point (1989, 91), that understanding attained from interconnections "open[s] up the field of meaning in which the various analogies can do their work," gains more force if we see interconnections as part of analogical understanding. Essentially, analogy comes first. It does not retreat, but it remains and is complemented, by interconnections when we grasp them.

2.6 A Question

Before completing this section, we should note that Lonergan's reflections on interconnection, most notably those in *De Constitutione Christi* (1964a, n43), can seem to be based on an Aristotelian concept of science:

"For science is the certain knowledge of realities through (a knowledge of) their causes." Under such an Aristotelian framework, it seems natural that one's understanding should come from making logical, even deductivist, connections. In our following sections, we contend that even though he earlier held to such a view of "science," Lonergan freed himself of its constraints and eventually surpassed it altogether. We turn now to examining, in specific detail, cases in which he has understood mysteries, by grasping their interconnections with one another.

3. Examples of Interconnections

3.1 The Ontological and Psychological Constitution of Christ

In his spirited article, "Christ as Subject: A Reply," Lonergan refers (1988, 182) to an *analogia fidei*, a parallelism, which may be drawn between ontological and psychological statements about the person of Jesus Christ. This parallelism provides fertile ground for our investigation into understanding attained from the interconnections of the mysteries. Lonergan proposes interconnections between the mysteries of the ontological and psychological constitutions of Christ. By the time Lonergan wrote "Christ as Subject," these interconnections were already set out in *De Constitutione Christi* and they were to recur in *De Verbo Incarnato*. He summarises (1988, 182-83) the major interconnections, or "main parallel statements," as he calls them:

> ... as there is one person with a divine and a human nature, so there is one subject with a divine and a human consciousness. As the person, so also the subject is without division or separation. As the two natures, so also the divine and the human consciousness are without confusion or interchange. As the person, so also the subject is a divine reality. As the human nature, so also the human consciousness is assumed. As there is a great difference between 'being God' and 'being a man,' so also there is a great difference between 'being conscious of oneself as God' and 'being conscious of oneself as man.' As the former difference is surmounted hypostatically by union in the person, so the latter difference is surmounted hypostatically by union in the subject. As the two natures do not prove two persons, so the divine and the human consciousness do not prove two subjects.

Lonergan thus links, or connects, the subject (psychological constitution) of Christ, with his nature (ontological constitution). The key methodological question is whether this interconnection is strictly only a logical or rhetorical connection, or if it is something more. In *De Verbo*

Incarnato (1964d, 383-84), we find a concise statement, that the constitution of the mind of Christ depended, in reality, on his ontological constitution. In this example, we have a preliminary statement that the reason for the constitution of the consciousness of Christ was in his ontological constitution.

Lonergan deals with this point more directly in *De Constitutione Christi*. He writes (1964a, n89) that, "in the order of being Christ is ontologically constituted as man prior to his being psychologically constituted as conscious man." In the order of being, at least, the psychological constitution of Christ is interconnected to his ontological constitution in a manner of dependence. This interconnection can also be framed in the manner with which we are now familiar, namely, that the mysteries (here the ontological and psychological constitutions of Christ) are arranged so that one, (the ontological constitution) becomes the reason for the other (the psychological constitution).

Making that interconnection, between the ontological and psychological constitution of Christ, a connection that is based on the principle of the hypostatic union of Christ, allows Lonergan to make intelligible a number of aspects of Christ's consciousness. By way of three examples, we note that Lonergan (1964d, 333-35, 347) makes intelligible the manner in which we can make distinctions within Christ's knowledge. First, one should make distinctions in Christ's knowledge upon the basis of its principles, not its objects. Thus, as God, Christ exercises divine knowledge; as man, Christ exercises human knowledge. Secondly, he proposes that the mystery of Christ's knowledge is demanded by, or because of, his person. In the mystery of Christ there must be both ineffable and effable knowledge. There must be ineffable knowledge for Christ the man to know divine mystery. There must also be effable knowledge for him to reveal divine mystery in an incarnate manner. Thirdly, Lonergan notes that Christ is "one undivided subject of two unconfused consciousness," because of his hypostatic identity of being God and man. Christ's psychological constitution is thus intelligible, in terms of being "because of" his ontological constitution.

Finally, Christ's psychological kenosis illustrates, directly and concisely, the general pattern of parallel between, and interconnection of, the mysteries. Lonergan (1964a, n90) states specifically that Christ's psychological kenosis is consequent to, that is, because of or dependent upon, his ontological kenosis. So much is clear, but we may not be altogether clear on what may be the principle behind Christ's psychological constitution. Lonergan points to this principle when he writes that "since the divine and human natures neither interchange [n]or mix together in the Christ who is both God and man, similarly, from the hypostatic union, the divine and human consciousness neither interchange [n]or mix together." This arrangement of the mysteries of Christ's ontological and psychological constitution comes down to a basic interconnection. That is, the principle of the psychological constitution of Christ is his ontological constitution, which is expressed by the principle of the hypostatic union. This example reveals a basic pattern of understanding the interconnection, namely that the reason for, or the "because of," a mystery is manifested in that grasp of interconnections.

3.2. The Sinlessness of Christ

A short but revealing text is Thesis 13, of *De Verbo Incarnato*, on "Christ's Sinlessness" (1964d, 416-23). Lonergan's thesis also clearly manifests the difference between doctrines and systematics. Parts one and two of the thesis are primarily concerned with affirming the realities that (1) "Christ the man did not sin," and (2) "Christ was not able to sin." In reading these parts, we find that Lonergan's primary mode of operation is to cite relevant Catholic authorities to support his case. From "Part three, section four," however, we see a significant switch in methodology, in that he begins to explain *why* it is unthinkable that Christ could sin. That *why*, is the link, or interconnection, between the mysteries of Christ's sinlessness, and his Hypostatic Union. In the first part of Lonergan's argument, he writes (1964d, 420):

> *Argument*: If Christ the man sins, a divine person sins. But that a divine person should sin is unthinkable. Therefore it is unthinkable for Christ the man to sin. As to the *major premise*: If Christ the man sins, some person sins; and there is no person in Christ the man except a divine person. Therefore the conclusion follows.

He goes on (1964d, 421) to note that Christ's sinlessness would be the act of a person exercising his own liberty. For Christ to sin then, would be both an unthinkable denial of his eternal Filiation, and an equally unthinkable denial of the eternal Paternity.

The foregoing reflections presuppose a knowledge and understanding of the Hypostatic Union, and of Trinitarian theology. We importantly note that Lonergan's systematic must presuppose these mysteries, for this is manifestly an example of taking a mystery, be it the Hypostatic Union, or the Trinity, and arranging these mysteries with Christ's sinlessness, so that the former mysteries, in their turn, become the reasons for the latter mystery. Lonergan can thus provide an intelligible answer to the question of why it is that Christ is sinless, and at least a partial answer to how this sinlessness may be so.

3.3 Marriage and Christ's Love for the Church

In his article "Finality, Love, Marriage," Lonergan expounds some most valuable interconnections. To understand the specific interconnections, by which he makes the sacramental mystery of marriage more intelligible, we should first note his observation (1988, 20-21) that:

> a concrete plurality of rational beings have the obediential potency to receive the communication of God himself: such is the mystical body of Christ with its head in the hypostatic union, its principal unfolding in the inhabitation of the Holy Spirit by sanctifying grace, and its ultimate consummation in the beatific vision which Aquinas explained on the analogy of the union of soul and body.

This statement, which itself links many mysteries, prepares us for the interconnection that Lonergan expounds (1988, 33-34), between marriage and the relationship of Christ and the Church. That is, marriage is the sacrament, or the sign, of the union of Christ and his Church. That union is proposed as the "primary reason and cause" of Christian marriage. This interconnection is, of course, a traditionally recognised relationship. In this regard, Lonergan cites (1988, 27) the position of Pius XI's encyclical *Casti Connubii* (DS 3712/TCF 1831). The cause of marriage and conjugal love is this divine-ecclesial relationship. The love of Christ and Church, then, "is to be effective as well as affective." This means, methodologically, that Lonergan posits the mutual love of Christ and Church, as being the model, the cause and the reason, of Christian marriage. He thus follows the traditional Catholic position of arranging the mysteries so that one, the charity between Christ and Church, becomes the reason and cause of another mystery, Christian marriage. Importantly, we note that such an arrangement of the mysteries not only manifests an intelligible relationship between the mysteries, but by grasping this cause of marriage we can grasp the reason for some of the elements of marriage, namely "two lives at one till death, lived in intimacy, lived in pursuit of a common goal." These three elements, of course, are based on the previous mystery of Christ's love for the Church.

3.4 *De Deo Trino*—"The Divine Missions"

After his systematic exposition of the divine persons, "in themselves," in *De Deo Trino* II, Lonergan (1964c, 216) addresses the question of the divine missions. Importantly, he notes that the divine missions are significant not only in themselves, but also in their relationship to other mysteries, with which theology deals. Accordingly, we shall follow Lonergan's exposition of how the mystery of the divine missions is related to the mystery of the divine persons in themselves, and how the divine missions throw light on the other mysteries that are interconnected with them.

Under the question, "Is a divine person sent by the one from whom he proceeds?" Lonergan (1964c, 223) shows the intelligible interconnection of divine relations and the divine missions. In the first place, he notes that if we are to understand mission in the manner in which the New Testament speaks, one can maintain that "a divine person is sent by that person or by those persons from whom the person who is sent proceeds." This means that the divine missions are intrinsically interconnected with the divine persons. Such a position, we find later, is not new, for Lonergan writes (1964c, 224-25) that "Catholic theologians generally teach that the relation of origin of the person sent is included within the notion of mission." The significance of this position is that, when a divine person is sent by a divine person, the real relation is included in the notion of mission. Thus, because the real relation in the divinity is the same as the relation of origin, we say that a divine person is sent only by the person or persons from whom the sent one proceeds. The methodological implication of this statement is that the divine missions are caused by the divine relations of origin, which are the reasons for the divine missions. From Lonergan's connecting the mysteries, we gather something of why and how the divine missions are, and we also gain a notion of what the divine missions might be.

We later find Lonergan arguing (1964c, 226ff) to the point that the mission of the divine person is sufficiently, and solely, constituted by a divine relation of origin. Without unduly concerning ourselves with the contents of Lonergan's arguments, we can appreciate the methodological significance of his points. In the first place, by establishing that the divine relations of origin are necessary to the divine missions and in the second place, by establishing that all else but the divine relations of origin are superfluous to the constitution of the divine missions, he gives us (1964c, 231) a clear, intelligible understanding of the manner in which the divine missions are so. That is, they are caused by the divine relations of origin, with no other cause or reason.

Lonergan draws a number of parallels between the Trinity and the Incarnation, and sanctifying grace as it is received by human beings. First, there is the reality that in the Incarnation, the act of assumption of human nature exceeds the proportion of the assumed, human, nature. In a similar manner, Lonergan notes (1964c, 234) that when the Holy Spirit is bestowed on the justified, through his own proper perfection, a subsistent nature is made holy, and pleasing to God. Thus, because the uncreated gift of the Spirit, and the created holiness exceed the proportion of the subsistent nature, that sanctifying grace likewise exceeds the proportion of the human nature.

Secondly, Lonergan (1964c, 234) more directly relates the Trinitarian relations and our life of grace. He does this by noting: first, that only the Son is Incarnate and secondly, that in its bestowal, the Spirit is given on the basis of its own proper perfection, as noted above. However, as Lonergan notes, the giving of one's total love is identical with giving oneself, so that in the Spirit's bestowal, the Father and Son give their own total proceeding love, so that they are said to give their own selves and in this way come to dwell in the justified. Thirdly, once one has grasped the foregoing points, Lonergan explains that the Father, Son and Holy Spirit "understand, will, constitute, and act differently in the incarnation than they do in the bestowal of the Spirit."

This means that first, there are, from our Trinitarian theology, four real divine relations which are identical with the divine substance, which means that there exist four modes supplying the basis for an "external imitation" of the divine substance. Secondly, there are four absolutely supernatural beings which are strictly uninformed, the *esse secundarium* of the Incarnation, sanctifying grace, the habit of charity, and the light of glory. Lonergan's third, most important point (1964c, 234-35), then, is that the *esse secundarium* of the Incarnation is "a created participation in paternity." In that regard, it bears a special relationship to the divine Son. Sanctifying grace, on the other hand, bears a special relationship to the Holy Spirit, by way of its being a participation in active spiration. The habit of charity, on the other hand, possesses a special relationship to the Father, by way of participating in passive spiration. Lastly, the light of glory, by being a participation in filiation, leads us, as the children of divine adoption back to the Father. This means, significantly, and in brief terms, that the life of grace, in terms of sanctifying grace, charity and the light of glory have a Trinitarian basis and structure. Thus, the Trinity, in terms of the divine relations of origin is the reason, the cause, and the parallel model for the life of grace.

We find a particular interconnection involved in the divine processions and our justification, as Christians. In the first place, Lonergan reminds us (1964c, 238) that the divine missions are constituted from the divine processions and relations. The divine missions, he also notes, are ordered to one another through their constitution. In the second place, he notes that, from the words of Galatians, we can gather that the mission of the Son is to effect our adoption as sons, while it is this adoption that grounds the mission of the Holy Spirit. Such is, as Lonergan calls it, a "connection," and we observe that here he has intelligibly related two mysteries so that the first (our divine adoption) is the basis, cause and reason for the second, (the indwelling of the Spirit.)

On that connection, Lonergan recalls (1964c, 238-39) that the Holy Spirit is sent on the basis of special and notional divine love. That special, divine love, however, is that by which the justified are loved as ordered to the divine good. Furthermore, in the light of God's operating all in the light of his order of justice, this special divine love supposes a reason, such reason being found to be the Son himself, "who is both mediator and redeemer." Lonergan thus shows both an intelligible connection and a reason for the sending of the Holy Spirit in love.

In making another connection, Lonergan further notes that in the light of Christ's baptism, which is the exemplar of our own, we can understand how Christ's redemptive work brings about God's loving those justified in Christ. The Father loves the justified, just as he loves his own Son. It thus follows that if the Father loves us in the same way as he loves his own Son, this love means that the Father would love and give to us though the Holy Spirit. In Lonergan's words (1964c, 239):

> Once this is grasped, the order of the divine missions is in some manner understood: for the mission of the Son was that the Father might be able to love us just as he loves his own Son; and then there is the mission of the Holy Spirit in that the Father does love us as he loves his own Son. Indeed, this love that is, as it were, proper to the divine persons implies and grounds an absolutely supernatural order.

This means for us, as regards method, that Lonergan draws a parallel structure, an isomorphism, between the justification of Christians, and the Trinitarian relations. Moreover, he clearly shows us how our justification comes about, in being caused by and grounded in the Holy Trinity.

4. INTERCONNECTIONS WITH "MAN'S LAST END"

4.1 The Trinity and Human Fulfilment

To situate the place of the justified in the Trinity, Lonergan first notes (1964c, 253) that in any case of love, there is effected a quasi-identification of the beloved with the lover. That is, those affiliated in love aspire to a common good and they take part in seeking this good in a mutually ordered fashion. Accordingly, the beloved and lover do not act only as individuals, they also possess some common life. In God, Lonergan continues, God loves himself, so that in him divine love means complete identity. The divine act of willing is thus none but God himself and the Holy Spirit, who proceeds in God as God's proceeding love, is also God himself. In a similar fashion, Lonergan notes that God the Father is within the Son and the Son is within the Father. Moreover, this "being within" is just as "the known is in the knower [and] as the beloved is in the lover:" This union of identity is because "those who possess a single act of existence, a single act of understanding, a single act of knowing, and a single act of loving ... dwell within each other most perfectly."

In terms of the final destiny of human beings, Lonergan notes (1964c, 253-54) that "all else that exists in addition to God is both known and loved by God." There exist, he states, others who are present in God as the known in the knower and the beloved in the lover. Such is the case with justified persons, who are within God, not according to any consubstantiality, but according to the "quasi-identification" of love. Those who are counted among the brethren of Christ are thus present in the Divine Word by which the Father speaks himself and all else. Moreover, the justified are present in the proceeding Love by which the Father and the Son love themselves and all else. The key reality here, is that the end of human beings is not separate from the Trinity, but that our end is intimately connected with the Trinity. Those who respond to Christ, those whom Christ loves and knows, exist not just as individuals, but in union with him, being "mutually present and dwelling in him and in each other as the known is in the knower and as the beloved is in the lover."

Following on from the above, Lonergan further states (1964c, 254) that just as Christ taught not his own teaching, but the doctrine of the Father, and just as he did his Father's will, not his own will, so too he does not take members to himself without uniting them also to his Father. This means that the divine persons, the blessed in heaven and the justified who live on earth, are all "mutually present in each other as the known is present in the knower and as the beloved is present in the lover." Ultimately, this means that the final human goal is life in the Trinity, to share in the mutual indwelling of the Trinity by being united to them, in the manner described above. As Lonergan later explains (1964c, 259), in the state of justifying grace, the justified thus share in the Trinitarian life itself, being caught up into the processions themselves, in the grace of Christ, by "believing the Word we might interiorly understand and speak true words, and then through the Word and on the basis of sanctity he sent the Spirit of the Word so that linked to the Spirit by love and made living members of the Body of Christ we might shout out 'Abba! Father!'"

4.2 The Hypostatic Union and "Man's Last End"

In *De Constitutione Christi* (1964a, n73), Lonergan draws a parallel between the Hypostatic Union in Christ, and humanity's last end. This interconnection is based on the human end being in the beatific vision, in which we apprehend the divine essence itself. That is, "the very divine essence adorns the created intellect." This attainment of the beatific vision is linked, Lonergan maintains, to: (1) our elevation to this end by way of our justification, in which we receive an uncreated gift and (2) the Hypostatic Union, which not only causes our justification, but allows us to attain our end.

The interconnection is three-fold. In the three cases described above, the divine perfection is united to creatures. Moreover, in each case, the union presupposes a created and contingent term. The Hypostatic Union implies not only the Word's infinite act of existence, but the "substantial and secondary esse" received in Christ's human essence. Likewise, a human sinner's justification involves the uncreated divine gift of the Spirit, which is received, as an "accident" in the soul. So too, the beatific vision implies not only the existence of the divine essence, but that it serve as the intelligible species within an intellect (Lonergan 1964a, n73).

4.3 The Sacrament of Marriage

We have earlier noted Lonergan's connection of marriage with the love of Christ and his Church. We should now make specific the connection between marriage and humanity's last end. In the first place, in taking up Pius XI's statement on the connection of marriage with Christ's love for the Church, Lonergan follows (1988, 27-29) in noting that conjugal love's reflection of the Christ-ecclesial love is meant to lead husband and wife in daily virtue, and lead them in charity towards God and neighbour.

This means that, ultimately, marriage is a sacrament that develops a couple in charity in order to attain their ultimate end in God. In this developing charity, which reflects the divine-ecclesial love, husband and wife are called to advance together, "from the level of nature to the level of the beatific vision." Lonergan (1988, 30) thus connects marriage with our last end by being ordered towards God on the levels of appetition, reason and grace. He notes (1988, 33-34) that as a sacrament of "the union of Christ and his church," marriage is the active sacrament of realising another in Christ. And, just as marriage's reason and cause is Christ, so its final drive is towards the pinnacle of Christian perfection in which all members of the "mystical body" of Christ are known and loved, as "other selves."

5. Conclusions

This chapter's main concern has been the form taken by an understanding attained from the interconnections of the mysteries, with each other, and with humanity's ultimate end. In a crucial text, from *De Constitutione Christi* (1964a, n44), Lonergan provides an outline of such an understanding, explaining that "the many truths we know about God admit being so arranged that one truth may be grasped as being the ground of some second truth." This essentially means that, by taking one truth at a time and by dealing first with those truths which do not presuppose other truths, we can arrange the truths of faith to thus assemble an intelligible system in which each truth is related to other truths. This relating of one truth to others is achieved by way of showing how a truth is the reason, and ground of existence, for one or more other truths. Importantly, this explanation means that the interconnections are not merely rhetorical parallelisms by which we can conceive models of relationships between the mysteries. Lonergan would rather hold that real relationships exist between the mysteries and that these relationships are intelligible and accessible to human intellect, albeit in an imperfect manner.

From Lonergan's practice, which we have investigated above, and from his statement in *De Constitutione Christi,* we observe that when he proposes an attainment of insight into the mysteries through their interconnections, not only "entire" mysteries, such as the Trinity or Grace, are understood in their interconnections, but also truths within such "entire" mysteries can be intelligibly interrelated, to give our understanding depth and greater precision. Parts of the mysteries are themselves able to be intelligibly interconnected, so that we attain a deeper understanding of the entire mystery at hand. Such was the case when we found, within the mystery of the Trinity, that the mystery of the divine missions could be intelligibly interconnected with the mystery of the divine relations of origin.

We also observe how the mysteries, or truths of faith can be arranged to yield such a fertile understanding. In the first place, this manner of arrangement is not the product of a strictly logical deduction from one's doctrinal sources. Logic and deduction alone cannot relate the mysteries to one another or to humanity's last end. It is "wisdom," as Lonergan called the intellectual operations, which we may call intelligent insight and discerning judgement, that can order the questions and resultant answers of theology so that one may grasp the relevant principle/s and thus be able to resolve a series of problems in a systematic and orderly manner.

On aspects of understanding attained from the mysteries' interconnections, we note that the understanding, which we have described above, helps us towards attaining a single viewpoint of the mysteries of faith. This single viewpoint results from our being able to progressively relate more mysteries to each other. The more we understand the mysteries in their relationships, the more we can apprehend them at once. We may illustrate this single viewpoint with the issue of the moon's sphericity and phases. As we noted above, we can know the moon's sphericity by the cause of knowing, which is its phases. However, what is more important is that once we have grasped the interconnection between the moon's sphericity and phases, we can grasp both the phases and sphericity in the one viewpoint.

The foregoing reflections help clarify Lonergan's point (1994, 336, 340) that systematics promotes a unified apprehension of doctrines. By resolving problems of apparent contradiction, and by arranging the mysteries into an intelligible set of interconnected realities, systematics presents a unified understanding of the mysteries that makes the mysteries assimilable by human intellect.

Lonergan (1973, 27) shows the need for the mysteries of faith to be worked into a unified viewpoint by citing the example of Abaelard's *Sic et Non*, which shows how one could argue from scripture, tradition, and reason, for both the affirmation and denial of each of one hundred and fifty-eight propositions. Similarly, Gilbert of Porée argued that there could be "questions" in theology. Such questions existed if a proposition could be both affirmed and denied on the basis of authority or reason. The key point is that by only citing doctrines, or by only drawing logical conclusions from the doctrines, we can face a multiplicity of apparently contradictory conclusions. Something more than doctrinal citation and logical deduction is needed, if theology is to be coherent and assimilable.

Historically speaking, Lonergan (1973, 27-28; 1994, 104) holds that the medievals, especially Aquinas, solved the problem of apparent contradictions by seeking the principles behind the doctrines. The medievals, however, faced the compounding challenge of ensuring that their principles of solution were not themselves incoherent. To attempt the reconciliation of apparent contradiction in doctrine, Aquinas found that the best solution was to find one's principles of solution within an established, coherent, system of thought. In Thomas' time, as Lonergan notes, one could do no better than to take over Aristotle's system, adapt and adjust it, and conceive one's expression of Christian faith within such a system. Furthermore, Aquinas is hardly unique in such an effort. In modern times, Bultmann (1969, 160n13, 167n5, 262n3, 324) has taken from Heideggerian philosophy the basic set of terms with which to understand the message of the New Testament.

Importantly, by using a coherent system of thought, a theologian can discover principles of the mysteries and then arrange the mysteries into a coherent, assimilable whole. By way of example, we can take Aquinas' resolution of a problem (*Summa Theologiae*, III,q2,a1; *Summa Contra Gentiles* IV, 35§5). On the authority of Cyril, Gregory Nazianzen and Damascene, it seems that there is only one nature in the person of Christ. This position is clearly against the authoritative doctrine of Chalcedon. While Thomas takes as authoritative the definition of Chalcedon, he resolves the problem by taking up the definition of nature from Aristotle's system of thought. By taking this understanding of "nature," Aquinas is able to affirm, against monophysitism, the doctrine of two natures in the one person of Christ.

We can also take the example of Lonergan's Trinitarian theology (1964c, 66-68, 79-81), which we explored above. If we make a strict deduction from the Trinitarian doctrines, we can be left with the apparently conflicting conclusions that God is one, and that God is from God. To resolve this conflict and to allow us to escape the problems of polytheism or denial of divine processions, Lonergan pursued his systematic analogy of the divine persons, as investigated above. This analogous conception of the divine persons brought intelligible unity to the mysteries by providing an intelligible basis on which we could discover coherent connections between the manifold doctrinal affirmations about the Trinity.

To take another perspective on systematics' unifying understanding, we note Aquinas' point that human intellect desires to grasp all things in a single act of understanding. As we have earlier found, human intellect's drive is to understand and to understand all things. For Aquinas, this human desire remains unsatisfied until our intellects are united to the divine intellect, knowing all things through one act of understanding (Lonergan 1997, 97-98). We acknowledge, with Aquinas, that the realisation of this goal is supernatural. However, there remains the human desire to understand, as much as possible, by a unifying act of understanding. Human intellect desires to understand, and relate together, parts of knowledge that previously had been apparently disconnected. In the terms with which we are more familiar, we can recall that understanding unifies data, so that sensible multiplicity is reduced to intelligible unity. So too, understanding can take a multiplicity of doctrinal conclusions, and reduce these, by creative insight, to an intelligible unity. We find that Thomas acknowledges that in this life, human intellect cannot discover an intelligible principle by which all else can be understood. However, he does hold to a limited and fruitful understanding that is possible by the imperfect, though nonetheless useful principles that can be discovered in this life.

We emphasise Lonergan's point (1964c, 30, 36) that to provide a unified understanding of the mysteries, and so resolve the doctrines into an assimilable whole, is simply not possible by citing doctrines, or making doctrinal deductions. He argues that concentration on the dogmatic, and seeking to establish the facts, to the exclusion of the systematic, makes one prone to conclude a multiplicity of mysteries from the one divine revelation. One may, he further argues, find technical expressions for God's revelation, and one may be able to amass conciliar statements, papal definitions and testimonies from patristic and theological sources. However, if one still excludes an ordered compendium of these elements, one may be surprised to find devout people retreating into a form of biblicism, or other rejection of the multiplied, and seemingly unrelated doctrines. The "ordered compendium" of the mysteries is especially attained by systematics when it pursues an understanding of the mysteries from their interconnections. That is, one may relate the mysteries to each other, and to people's concrete lives, in the manner Lonergan has outlined (1964a, n44), by ordering the truths of faith, so that one becomes the reason for another.

The unifying of doctrines, we note, is a mental synthesis of concepts. Such a synthesis, Lonergan notes (1997, 64-65), is not the fusing of two concepts into one. That would simply result in confusion, for concepts always remain distinct. What can happen, is that the concepts may remain distinct, but the intelligibilities that they express may be merged into one. Lonergan clarifies that "where before there were two acts of understanding, expressed singly in two concepts now there is but one act of understanding." The result of such an exercise will be a single intelligible, a single though composite object of one act of understanding.

Anthony Kelly (1989, 91-92) explains the "single viewpoint," which systematics promotes, by conceiving understanding attained from interconnections as providing "a certain holographic image" of the relevant mystery. On the specific mystery of the Trinity, Kelly maintains that a "theological hologram" would provide a composite viewpoint, from which we can appreciate the mystery of the Trinity from a variety of angles. Kelly's imagery is very helpful, but he does not intend it to be taken literally, for holography involves not only a real image, but also a stereoscopic virtual image (Sears 1982, 800-2). By conceiving the understanding attained from mysteries' interconnections along literal "holographic" lines we may mistakenly believe that such understanding only involves virtual, rhetorical, or imaginary interconnections. Kelly's model of "interconnections" can reach its full strength if we conceive the understanding, attained from the interconnections of the mysteries, as involving an arrangement of the mysteries into a three-dimensional matrix, in which increasing number of mysteries can be apprehended in their relations with other mysteries. Such a model means that mysteries are not approached in a linear, deductivist manner, but that with increasing understanding, each mystery can be appreciated from a variety of perspectives.

The above conclusions apply equally to the interconnections of the mysteries with humanity's last end. Some additional points are noteworthy, though. In the first place, understanding a mystery through its interconnections with our ultimate end helps to relate that mystery more clearly to human life and living. Such understanding of interconnections allows the mysteries to become more concrete, and to have a more profound effect on spirituality. In the popular language of our day, the mysteries can become "more relevant" to "real life." We would maintain that, by being able to intelligently interconnect the mysteries with our final end, the mysteries become more meaningful and significant, and more able to be appropriated on a deep and personal level.

Our past two chapters have dealt with the manner in which we may attain an understanding of the mysteries of faith. Having grasped something of the nature of that understanding, we now turn our attention to the attainments and value of Lonergan's functional specialty, systematics.

Chapter 10
Value and Place of Systematics

We have covered both the function of systematics and the ways in which systematics can attain an understanding of the mysteries of faith, from analogy with what human reason naturally knows and from the interconnections of the mysteries. We now turn to the usefulness and place of systematics. Specifically, we shall examine the ways in which systematics provides a personal appropriation of the mysteries, which is useful for teaching, apologetics, and communicating the mysteries to a variety of cultures. We shall also examine systematics' contribution to a "scientific" understanding and to theological pluralism and systematics' balance of cultural and dogmatic concerns. This chapter will end by assessing the value of systematics in providing a framework for understanding.

1. PERSONAL APPROPRIATION

As we shall explore below, systematics is most useful for teaching, communicating, or defending the mysteries of faith. However, the foundation for such utility is in systematics providing a personal appropriation of the mysteries' intelligibility. As we have found, systematics' promotion of theological understanding helps one to attain more than rote-learned doctrinal formulae. Systematics effects a personal understanding of the doctrines' meaning, so that one appropriates the meaning and implications of the mysteries. Lacking this understanding, we can be like the sergeant-major, to whom Lonergan refers (1997, 193-94). With his manual-at-arms, our military friend can repeat all the terms, principles and reasons contained in his book. But this man does not have a genuinely intelligent grasp of the book's contents. He lacks the understanding that systematics brings, which allows one to grasp personally the meaning of the principles behind the book and ultimately allows one freedom from the book. For want of understanding, our sergeant-major would find teaching difficult. To questions about the book's contents, he could only answer by repeating the book's content. Against such shortcomings, Lonergan insists (1994, 351) that "one must understand what one has to communicate." Only when one has understood a mystery for oneself, can one pass on a grasp of a mystery to one's different audiences. Aristotle (*Metaphysics*, I, 2, 982a 10-15) similarly insisted that teachers were more wise and better able to teach by having an understanding of the matter one was addressing.

As specifically regards theology, systematics promotes personal appropriation of both the contents, and the very method, of theology. First, as concerns theology's results, systematics promotes a personal understanding of the mysteries, by taking the mysteries and formulating a conception of the mysteries, which is intelligible within a personal religious, social and cultural horizon. We can clarify this personal appropriation by recalling that systematics' insight is no different from insight in general by relying upon one's inner conditions, not upon outer situations. Insight depends upon our own personal grasp of intelligibility, our personal solution to a question, whether this be intelligibility in data, or intelligibility of a truth. By challenging us, prompting us, and encouraging us to pursue such insight, systematics ensures that our understanding of the mysteries is personal, and independent of the concepts of others.

Systematics also contributes to personal appropriation, specifically in its finding intelligibility in the connection of the mysteries with humanity's last end. As we noted in chapter nine, by understanding a mystery through its interconnections with our last end one can more manifestly relate a mystery to human life and living. This means that systematics promotes an understanding of the mysteries which, rather than remaining remote and detached from human life, become more concretely a part of human life. This brings about a personal grasp of a mystery's meaning in a person's life and goes no small way towards nourishing one's personal spirituality.

In the broader realm of theological method, we should recall that Lonergan's lifework was directed towards helping others towards personal self-appropriation. In *Insight*, he encouraged us to follow the book, not as a prescription of what one should do, but as a guide to aid the reader in grasping for oneself the dynamic, conscious activities that constitute human knowing. Similarly, he proposed *Method in Theology* (1994, xii) as a work that helps one discover within oneself the intentional operations that go into doing theology. Importantly, Lonergan's theological method (1994, 344), and systematics in particular, provide a self appropriation that leads one to genuine independence. By basing his method upon the very structures immanent within human knowing, and by his commitment to the intellectualist tradition, he can offer a theology that, in content and method, allows one a greater freedom than simply being able to take the concepts or method of another and use these for oneself. Rather, this method allows one freedom to reformulate concepts, to devise one's own expressions of religious realities and to find for oneself the operations present in doing theology. In short, one has freedom from others' concepts and expressions of method, "One is on one's own."

2. AN UNDERSTANDING FOR TEACHING

On systematics' usefulness for teaching, we recall Aquinas' distinction (*Quaestiones Quodlibetales*, IV,q9a3 [18]) between removing student's doubts, and teaching them so that they grasp an understanding of the faith. For removing doubts, appeals to authorities are sufficient. However, to generate some grasp of the grounds, of the truth of the mysteries, some understanding of how the mystery is so must be communicated. In Aquinas' work, we find support for our contention that, to communicate a grasp of the mysteries of faith to students, one must go beyond doctrines and pass on the limited but helpful understanding gained in systematics. Effective teaching is only possible when the mysteries of faith are understood, and worked into a whole that is attainable and intelligible to the minds of the students.

Systematics provides understanding useful to teaching in several ways. First, by allowing a grasp of a mystery's nature, systematics allows one the imperfect, but nonetheless profitable understanding that gives personal insight into what that mystery may be. When that insight is attained, one may recast one's inherited definitions and concepts into new concepts that better meet the needs of one's time and culture. Secondly, the unifying understanding, which systematics provides, allows one a firmer grasp of one's faith and gives one a greater versatility of expression in one's reflections upon that faith. Thirdly, systematics presents a methodical, assimilable viewpoint of the mysteries, which one is able to follow in an ordered and systematic fashion. In particular, systematics' understanding into the interconnections of the mysteries allows teachers to present such a systematic presentation of the mysteries. This systematic, or orderly presentation, is the order of teaching, to which Lonergan often refers, and contrasts with the order of discovery.

To illustrate this contrast of the order of teaching, which we find in systematics, with the order of discovery, found more readily in doctrines, we turn to Aquinas' work, which Lonergan follows in maintaining that communicating an understanding of the mysteries requires an order of teaching different to the order of discovering the doctrinal facts of a mystery. The discovery of facts follows an irregular path. Issues are resolved as they arise, some secondary issues are likely to be concluded first, and teachers are likely to settle issues as they arise in argument. This order can result in different aspects of a mystery being settled, without these aspects being intelligibly related. Such an approach, Aquinas complained (*Summa Theologiae*, Prologue), results in frequent repetition and brings weariness and confusion to the reader. In sharp contrast with the order of discovery, one, in the order of teaching, defers deliberation over issues that assume the results of other issues. To generate understanding, a teacher starts with questions whose resolution presupposes no other solutions. This was the approach Thomas employed in his *Summa Theologiae* (Lonergan 1994, 345-46). It is an approach greatly aided by systematics' unifying understanding of the mysteries.

Lonergan (1988, 122) uses Trinitarian theory to illustrate concretely the difference between the order of discovering facts and the order of teaching, or communicating understanding. First, in proving, or removing doubt about the Trinity, Lonergan cites the conventional wisdom that considers it best to begin with the dogmatic affirmation of three consubstantial persons. One then argues that, because the persons are consubstantial, their real distinctions cannot be based on distinct absolute perfections, so they must be based on relations. One then argues that, in order to ground distinctions, the relations must be relations of origin. Next, one argues that relations of origin presume processions. Lastly, one proposes that the only processions, in God, are analogous to those in human consciousness. With Lonergan, we find that this approach exemplifies the order of discovery, in which one argues by setting and solving difficulties. The only understanding of the nature of the processions in God occurs when one moves from the strict proof of the processions, to the existence of an analogy of the processions.

However, if one aims not so much to prove the Trinity, as to teach some understanding of what the Trinity is, one does better to follow the order of Aquinas' *Summa Theologiae* (I,q27,Intro), which directs one's attention towards forming a unifying understanding that can be expressed in humanly attainable concepts. For teaching, Aquinas argues that one should pursue the aims, which we find in Lonergan's later functional specialty, systematics. We find in Aquinas, an endorsement of a unifying, ordered understanding, which uses analogous conceptions of the divine mysteries. Lonergan argues that (1988, 122), in this ordered understanding, one begins with the question that requires no prior answers, that being the notion of God. One may then clarify the way in which we may conceive processions in God, by asking if there are processions in God. One could not yet inquire about the Son's procession from the Father, as this would presuppose resolution of the notion of person. Having clarified the way that we may conceive processions, we can then clarify the divine subsistent relations. Lastly, having clarified the mutually opposed subsistent relations, we may foster some grasp of how it may be that the divine persons are distinct, yet consubstantial. This order of teaching *(ordo doctrinae)*, leads a student to grasp not only the conclusions of Trinitarian theory, but also the principles and grounds of the Trinity.

We can now understand better how systematics makes an invaluable contribution to teaching. We should ask, though, why the orders of discovery and teaching differ. The difference cannot, Lonergan notes (1988, 122), be based on any order or priority within God, for nothing in the Trinity is prior or posterior. The order of discovery follows the order with which human intellect can gain an understanding of the mysteries. Lonergan notes first (1997, 215), the order of our concepts *"in fieri,"* which is illustrated by our latter exposition of how one would gain an understanding of the Trinity. Secondly, there is the order of our concepts, *"in facto esse,"* illustrated by the "proof" of the Trinity. The difference in orders, he explains, is not due to any property of God Himself, but is due to the systematic order of our concepts. Lonergan's account for the difference in the orders of discovery and teaching thus relies upon his focus on the inquiring subject, and upon his analysis of the human subject's intentionality.

3. An Apologetic

Systematics also has apologetic usefulness. However, we would be misled to presume that systematics could assist an apologetic by way of proving the mysteries of faith. This book has already shown that systematics is concerned neither with proof, nor with fortifying the certitude of doctrines. One would be disappointed with systematics as an agent for proof, because its analogies and proposed interconnections are hypothetical, necessarily imperfect, and never more than probable. If, however, we accept systematics as manifesting intelligible possibility, we have a more realistic apologetic. If systematics provides an understanding of how the mysteries may be so, the apologetic value of that understanding is that, by establishing intelligible possibility, we discover possible being. We can take Lonergan's point (1997, 57) that, "Intelligibility is the ground of possibility, and possibility is the possibility of being; equally unintelligibility is the ground of impossibility, and impossibility means impossibility of being." By showing the intelligibility of the mysteries, systematics simultaneously shows the possibility of the mysteries' existence. The advantage of this understanding, and the grasp of possible being, is in the resolution of the contentions of adversaries, who argue against the mysteries by pointing to the mysteries' supposed unintelligibility.

To be outwardly apologetic, to show to non-Christians how Christian mysteries are intelligible and thus possible, Lonergan observes (1973, 23-24) that systematics has its historical antecedents in the work of the second and third century apologists, who explained what Christians truly believed to an audience whose horizons were outside Christianity. The apologists could not possibly have fulfilled their purpose by citing authorities and doctrinal sources that were not accepted by the pagans. Lonergan argues that the apologists had to "enter into the mind of the pagans, to discern what they would accept as legitimate assumptions, and to proceed from that basis to a clarification of Christian doctrine." Effectively then, the apologists did not undertake a proof of doctrine. Their activity was towards intelligibility, by creating a new conception of Christian faith that would be readily understood by pagan hearers.

Lonergan also (1971c, 139; 1974, 45) cites the example of Thomas Aquinas, who had to present Christian faith within a new, developing and challenging environment. Specifically, Lonergan finds that, in the *Summa Contra Gentiles*, Aquinas did not simply restate Christian faith by rearranging its doctrines, neither did he use older, established categories. Thomas' achievement was to present a new conception of Christian faith within the cultural horizon of the Greek and Arabic thought, which was simultaneously challenging Christian doctrine and becoming part of the cultural context of Aquinas' audience. He developed a new understanding of Christian faith, which made the faith intelligible within the horizon of the new thought that was penetrating his own concrete, and developing culture. In the context of showing how he would manifest Catholic truth and set aside contrary positions, we note Thomas' comment (*Summa Contra Gentiles*, I,2§2-4), that because the Moslems and the pagans accept none of the Christian sources, he resorted to "the natural reason," to which all are forced to give assent. His method was to take the Moslem and pagan systems of thought, and present Catholic faith with conceptions that were intelligible within these systems. We note that by developing new conceptions of Christian truth, which were intelligible within non-Christian horizons, Aquinas and the apologists used creative insights to assemble these new expressions. No amount of strictly logical deduction could help Christian theology go beyond its old boundaries and reach such new modes of expression.

Lonergan's own work on the hypostatic union shows both the need for, and provision of, an ongoing, apologetic understanding. Within a Catholic horizon, the dogma remains constant. However, while one age found it sufficient to adore the mystery, and another found it reasonable to account for the union with metaphysical descriptions of nature and person, our age has brought new questions and challenges. Lonergan notes (1985b, 91-94) that modern psychology and critical philosophy, as well as hermeneutics and critical history demand "something both different and more exacting." We need today, he continues, to be able to conceive how it could be that a divine person could live a fully human life. In "Christology Today," we see how, by using the insights of modern scholarship, especially modern philosophy, he presents an expression of how one divine person could simultaneously be the subject of a divine consciousness and a human consciousness.

Lonergan's main point (1985b, 74) is that, while the faith itself remains the same, each age brings about new contexts in which older conceptions of the faith do not meet the questions of the day. To make the faith intelligible and thus promote the possible being of the mysteries to ongoing contexts, new expressions of the mysteries are required, that meet the exigences of these different times. Such work, we have found, is possible by the operation of systematics, in its ongoing, developing work of presenting expressions of the mysteries' intelligible possibility.

4. An Understanding for Ongoing Cultures

Our investigations have shown Lonergan's (1973, 22; 1994, xi) serious concern for theology's relationship with culture and his conception of theology as mediating a religion's value and function to a culture. If we accept this view of theology and accept that cultures are ongoing, developing and manifold, and if we acknowledge that a religion's meaning does not occur in a vacuum but only takes on intelligibility within a concrete cultural context, then theologians face the challenge of making a religion intelligible to people in the manifold cultural contexts within which a religion is found. This challenge is compounded by the ongoing, developing nature of cultures. One culture develops into another, a plurality of cultures can interact and spawn new cultures. The key question is how one can intelligibly present a religion's meaning and function to a culture that possesses its own common sense, cultural values science, scholarship and philosophy.

Yet one may ask if Barth (1975, I,I,72) is not right by stating that when it is accepted that Church proclamation should be positively related to culture, the result can be that "A proclamation that accepts responsibilities along these … lines spells treachery to the Church and to Christ Himself." We would respond with Lonergan and Macquarrie (1977, vii, 13, 14), that to be intelligible, a theology must use the language of a culture

within which theology finds itself. Tillich (1968, III,4) also acknowledges the danger of the Christian message being lost in cultural adaptations. He maintains, however, that risk is no reason for evading the serious task of making Christianity intelligible to all people. The question
here is not whether one defects from one's Christian message in whole or
part, when presenting it to specific cultures. Rather, the question regards
how one can present one's religion, be faithful to its authentic message,
yet make this religion able to be intelligently appropriated by concrete
cultures. The issue at hand is whether one wishes to bring one's gospel to
all peoples, (Matthew 28:19) or whether one believes that all nations
should bring themselves to one's own culture, so that they may receive
that gospel.

In parallel to the apologetic and teaching functions of theology, no
amount of repeating doctrines can make the mysteries intelligible within
different audiences' concrete cultural life and history. This is a point stated
clearly by Rahner's (1978, 289) observation that "the official teaching of
the church must also be interpreted and brought into contact with contemporary ways of thinking, and this cannot be done by merely repeating
this official teaching." Systematics, however, specifically aims to meet this
need by conceiving the mysteries in terms intelligible within their concrete, cultural contexts. Lonergan (1973, 58) thus sees systematics concerned with the concrete effect of God's grace on humanity and our world,
in addition to the "supernatural" aspects of theology. Systematics promotes an understanding of the mysteries in terms of its audience's acquired culture. It does this by using not only religious categories, but also
categories from more human fields of study, most notably philosophy.
On this point, we note that systematics, as Lonergan (1994, 336) envisages the specialty, seeks an understanding of the mysteries that incorpo-
rates analogy with what human reason naturally knows. If one seeks such
an understanding so in line with what we naturally know, it must necessarily be on the level of a specific culture and time. Attaining such an
understanding can accordingly allow one to present this understanding
to the ongoing culture within which one finds oneself.

By way of example, we recall Lonergan's citation (1973, 23) of Fuller's
The Foundations of New Testament Christology (1979, 243ff), which shows
both the need for, and exercise of, an understanding formed for different,
ongoing cultures. The New Testament's varying expressions of the Gospel show an awareness, on the part of its authors, that failing to present
the Gospel in culture-appropriate forms, would have lead to misappre-
hension and misunderstanding of the Gospel. We also recall Lonergan's

references (1973, 25-26; 1985b, 74; 1994, 344, 347) to the presentation of God to different levels of human consciousness, which find different presentations of God intelligible. We note that by building upon and revising earlier conceptions of God, Clement and Origen promoted, not a denial of the doctrine of God or the realities affirmed by Scripture, but a new understanding of God in line with the philosophic and cultural contexts of their times. These early developments show that, while the faith itself remains constant, it needs to devise new conceptions of its doctrines to meet the demands of different times.

We should not presume that our time is immune from ongoing cultural developments. Our own culture, and the world's contemporary cultures, bring a range of new and pressing problems for theology. Lonergan argues that, in today's world, people may have familiarity with Church doctrines. However, from within new, developing cultural contexts, these same people rightly ask what these doctrines could possibly mean to them. As we found, under "An Apologetic," today's philosophical contexts have generated new questions about the meaning of Chalcedon's doctrine in the modern world. To work towards answering such questions is systematics' task. It serves ongoing cultures by forming understandings that are intelligible within those ongoing cultures. This service is two-fold. First, systematics takes questions of intelligibility from the culture within which it finds itself. Secondly, systematics cannot seek to answer those questions by citing doctrines formulated in possibly alien or remote cultures. Rather, it expresses the mysteries both by analogy with what a given culture naturally knows, and intelligibly relates those mysteries, with each other and to the ultimate end to which a people of a concrete culture aspire.

In the light of the above, we understand Lonergan's point (1994, 352), that development can occur when one's religious message is preached to different cultures, or varying differentiations of consciousness. Systematics is thus an ongoing and developing enterprise, in its concern with discovering and adapting new conceptions of the mysteries to different peoples. In this endeavour, we recall that an essential part of systematics' function is to attain an understanding of the mysteries, by analogy with what human intellect naturally knows. If what human intellect naturally knows develops and varies across cultures and differentiations of consciousness, systematics, in its various contexts, will likewise develop in its conceptions of the mysteries. As Macquarrie states (1977, 14), "recognition of the cultural factor is equivalent to acknowledging that there is no final theology." As culture develops, theology likewise has to develop to become intelligible within its culture.

5. Systematics and Communications

The issue of systematics and ongoing cultures raises the closely related issue of systematics and the following functional specialty, communications. We can take two perspectives on this issue. First, as Lonergan argues (1994, 132, 351, 355), systematics cannot be the end-point or completion of theology. Without communications, the remaining seven functional specialties, including systematics, simply "fail to mature." Systematics, for all its worth, requires an outward-oriented expression of its results. Theology requires a specialty which can manifest its results to those who have not necessarily participated in the first seven functional specialties. Unless it is to become an introverted discipline with no relevance to people's concrete lives, theology needs that functional specialty which effects "its external relations." Systematics, in particular, can overcome problems of apparent irrelevance if it is the basis for communications. Communications is specifically concerned with bearing the results of theology to people outside of the main theological process, but who nonetheless have an interest in theology's results. The range of such people naturally includes people of other cultures, other differentiations of consciousness, or other disciplines. Communications is thus about presenting theology's results to different people who possess a myriad of common meanings.

Communications complements and completes the work of systematics by leading others to share in the meanings one has discovered. Lonergan argues (1994, 362) that to do this presupposes three factors on the communicator's part. First, the communicator must have knowledge of the meaning one intends to share. To this end, the first seven functional specialties are at one's service. Then, meaning is constitutive of living, so one must live out the meaning one intends to communicate. Thirdly, because meaning is effective, one must practise that meaning, because "actions speak louder than words." These factors imply communications' dependence on the previous functional specialties. Most notably, communications depends upon systematics, for one finds it difficult to intelligently communicate what one does not understand. However, even systematics needs complementing by communications, so that its meaning can be conveyed to all peoples.

We propose that systematics occurs within the systematician's own cultural and social horizons. Questions are raised within a culture, and a good systematician answers those questions in a manner intelligible to that culture. A classicist would presume the systematician's work to be intelligible within the contexts of all other peoples, who should aspire to the successful systematician's dominant culture. However, the empirically-minded systematician wishes to communicate one's message to others, just as Christianity, in the spirit of Matthew 28:19, intends its message for "all nations." Those who bear that message with an empirical notion of culture need to broaden their own horizons to embrace also a reliable, familiar, and sympathetic understanding of the culture to which they are addressing that message. Lonergan insists (1994, 362) that such a broadening of one's horizons should not be superficial, but that communicators use the cultural resources and language of a people creatively, and sincerely. We say "sincerely," because if one uses the resources of a culture in a patronising or merely utilitarian way, a communicator will interfere with a culture. Lonergan's vision, however, is for communications to take advantage of, and embrace, a culture so that one's message is not disruptive, but simply a "line of development within the culture."

One may ask what essential difference there may be between systematics and communications. After all, is not systematics concerned with presenting new understandings of the mysteries within new cultures? What then, is the added dimension of communications? The answer to this question lies in a personal appropriation of the empirical notion of culture. An empirically-minded systematician will realise that, despite one's ability to deal with questions raised by one's culture and one's corresponding ability to devise new conceptions of the mysteries appropriate to that culture, even the best systematician belongs to a specific culture and one's systematic conceptions will be made in the terms of that culture. Communications occurs when one takes the results of one's theological investigations and translates these into the cultural horizon of other people. Such an answer, however, requires a certain humility on the systematician's part. Despite our awareness of cultural diversity, we may sometimes be tempted to believe ourselves transcultural, and beyond cultural boundaries. Such belief, we argue, is only a new form of classicism and a trap for modern thinkers who sometimes presume the fine flower of civilisation to be that in which we now find themselves. Rather than presuming that those who wish to share in systematics' results should aspire to our civilisation, communications puts the onus onto theologians to take their message, and express it in forms intelligible to other hearers.

We can make two further points on why systematics should be complemented by communications. First, systematics usually occurs within a narrow range of media. Questions are raised in books and monographs, occasionally issues are raised in learned discussions in mass media. Those questions are answered by systematicians in similar media. But the majority of religious believers do not tune into serious debates in mass media. Even fewer read the learned journals of theology. People in our own culture generally read the popular press, are entertained or sometimes "infotained," by television. Alternatively, people may listen to the stories of their village elders or dance in illustration of tribal myth. Systematics, in its normal practice, does not feel at home in such media, but it should not feel ashamed of this. It is more the role of communications to take the message of systematics, mould it, reshape it, and formulate it, so that it is both intelligible and attractive to those who do not read the monographs. In communications, systematics' results are translated into effective homilies, transposed into the common sense language of the popular press, or even arranged into a human movement that brings new life to a culture.

We secondly note that communications plays a vital role for a properly empirical theology. One cannot deduce all questions that could be raised in relation to the mysteries of faith. An empirical theology will find questions raised in the concrete, everyday lives of people encountering a religion. Systematics partly depends on communications to provide further questions for reflection. When communicators find that their hearers have questions that remain unanswered, systematicians will need to seek better analogies, and newly discovered interconnections that can edify and encourage religious life.

This section has outlined communications' complement to systematics. We now turn to the other perspective on this issue, namely communications' dependence upon systematics. While we have noted systematics' provision of a personal appropriation of the mysteries, which is yet to be transposed into other cultural terms, communications still relies first upon that very personal appropriation provided by systematics. As we noted in our section on systematics and teaching, for one to effectively communicate, one must first intelligently grasp what one is communicating. It is personal insight into a mystery that provides the basis from which one can communicate that mystery to various audiences (Lonergan 1994, 351). To attempt communication of a mystery that one does not personally understand would likely be communicating, not what one understands, but merely a doctrinal formulation or dogmatic statement. While such formulations, or definitions can be helpful, one who seeks to communicate with clarity relies not upon formulations, but upon personally acquired insight, in which true clarity resides. We also note that communications' reliance upon systematics demands ongoing development in systematics. Without the development of new conceptions of the mysteries, communications will stagnate, for it would be left attempting to present one's message to the modern world, with conceptions of the mysteries more suited to a bygone time.

To use a helpful illustration, one who attempts communications without systematics can be no better than a courier who delivers a message that he does not understand. One's delivery may be efficient, and one may deliver the precise contents of a country's intentions. But that courier can be of no help if the recipients ask, "What does this message mean?" To communicate with the understanding provided by systematics is to be more like the ambassador, who understands with clarity the meanings provided by her country, and who also understands the culture of her host nation. It is the ambassador, not the courier, who can translate the message of her country into the language of her hosts, defend that message, answer questions about it, and ultimately make that message part of her hosts' lives. So it is also with systematics and communications. Without systematics, we remain inarticulate carriers of our religious message. With systematics, though, we have a message that is personally appropriated, and we are thus able to bear that message far more intelligently to our hearers.

To end this section, we note that, because communications' function is to make systematics' results accessible to others, communications requires a base that goes beyond culture, and enables it to cross cultural barriers. That transcultural base, in Lonergan's work, is his transcendental method, which outlines the intentionality common to all people. Despite objections to the contrary, Lonergan's basing theological method on a transcendental method provides a foundation from which inter-cultural communication is possible. He argues that all people gain cognitive meaning from experience, understanding and judgement, and that all people share in responsible decision and being in love. It is on the basis of these common aspects of human mental life, that he would argue that cross-cultural communication is not only possible, but able to be actively encouraged.

6. A Scientific Understanding

Especially in his earlier works, Lonergan often refers to theology's "scientific" understanding. From our investigations of systematics, we can throw light on how this functional specialty attains a "scientific" understanding. First, we note Lonergan's citation (1964c, 8) of Aquinas' *Quodlibetal* questions (IV, q9a3 [18]). As we have noted before, Aquinas stated that a disputation may be directed either to removing doubt, or to instruction and generating understanding. If one's aim is removing uncertainty about a matter, Aquinas argues that one best argues by appeal to the authorities recognised by one's audience. However, Aquinas also notes that,

> there is the magisterial type of disputation in the schools, whose goal is not the removal of error but the instruction of the listeners in such a way that they may be led to an understanding of the truth the master intends to bring out. In this case, recourse should be had to reasons that investigate the root of the truth and which make one understand how what is said is true. Otherwise, if the master determines the question by appeal to bare authorities, the listener will indeed be made certain that the matter is so; but he will acquire no scientific knowledge or understanding and will go away empty.

Lonergan (1994, 330-31) makes the same essential point as Aquinas, by criticising "Denziger theology," or Christian positivism, which simply appeals to church authority and propagates its doctrines. While such an exercise may make a reader certain of what is so, on the authority of the church, the reader attains no inner understanding of the doctrines.

Aquinas promoted a "scientific" knowledge that grasps both the root of a truth, and the reasons for how that affirmed truth is so. This notion of "scientific" knowledge corresponds to Aristotle's vision of science as being concerned principally with understanding. While we cannot reject a scientific concern with certitude, Lonergan points out (1964c, 7-9, 40-41) that if one seeks certitude to the exclusion of understanding, one can only gain a "crude and undigested knowledge of realities." Such a knowledge, he adds, lacks scientific knowledge in the term's authentic sense. Moreover, one seeking only certitude may gain conceptual certainty of a reality, but one will have no synthetic apprehension of all the elements of the matter. By way of illustration, we note that any dolt may be certain, on the authority of Einstein and other eminent scientists, of the relationship "$e=mc^2$." However, only one with a scientific understanding can use this knowledge for any practical purpose. One needs an understanding of the principles and nature of this relationship to grasp that, in a nuclear reaction, the energy released will be equal to the mass change, multiplied by the constant of the speed of light, squared. We add that if one has

262   Matthew C. Ogilvie: *Faith Seeking Understanding*

grasped neither the formula's meaning, nor the essence of the relation-ship between mass change and energy release, one is powerless to defend the formula against anyone who is unprepared to accept the authority of Einstein on this matter.

We should note that, in providing "scientific" understanding, Lonergan's vision of systematics reflects a shift from proof to conversion. Proof may aim for certitude, but that certitude abstracts from concrete living and thinking. Lonergan (1994, 338) argues that, within a concrete, methodi-cal framework, conversion, not proof, is basic. Such conversion, "trans-forms the concrete individual to make him capable of grasping not merely conclusions but principles as well." In this regard, we recall Aquinas' point (*Summa Theologiae*, II-II,q8,a1c), that understanding is a knowledge pen-etrating to the inward nature of a thing. He states that "Understanding implies an intimate knowledge, for *intelligere*, [to understand] is the same as *intus legere* [to read inwardly]." Thomas contrasts understanding, which penetrates to the very essence of a thing, with sensitive knowledge, which is only concerned with external qualities. With regard to the nature of an object, Aristotle (Metaphysics, I, 3, 983a 24-25) also notes that we only truly know a thing when we think we recognise its cause. We thus con-clude that a knowledge of an object, no matter how "certain," will re-main incomplete if no understanding of cause, or principle, is present.

It is worth noting that Aquinas, Aristotle and Lonergan (1964c, 7), in his earlier writings, held to a notion of science as "certain knowledge of realities through a knowledge of their causes." Despite this problem, this notion of science nonetheless sought after intelligibilities, through a reality's cause. When Aristotle, Aquinas, or Lonergan in his early days, write of a "scientific" understanding, this understanding has some positive correla-tion with the aims of modern science. Our earlier investigations showed that modern science is not so much concerned with authorities and de-ductions, as it is concerned with discovering intelligibilities within ob-jects. So too, Lonergan's model of systematics is concerned with discover-ing intelligibilities within its object, the divine mysteries. He argues (1962, 253-54; 1997, 218-19) that if, like the medieval Aristotelians, one aban-dons scientific concern for intelligibility in favour of "certitudes," one will be powerless to deal with challenges or problems presented by those who do not accept one's authorities. However, if one pursues intelligibil-ity within the mysteries, one not only reflects a key concern of modern science, one is also equipped to deal with the manifold challenges pre-sented by culture, science and ongoing contexts.

7. Cultural Intelligibility Balanced with Doctrinal Continuity

As a functional speciality within theology, systematics brings transcultural intelligibility to the mysteries. However, systematics also avoids a problem of doctrinal instability. When theologians attempt to make the mysteries intelligible across different cultures, they often risk doing injustice to their doctrinal tradition. Lonergan's vision of systematics, however, balances cultural intelligibility with doctrinal continuity. His commitment to making the mysteries intelligible across many cultures is evident throughout his *Method in Theology*. We also note that Lonergan (1994, 332) remained a "Roman Catholic with quite conservative views on religious and church doctrines," though we would clarify that he did not mean himself to be a reactionary conservative. Rather, Lonergan was a conservative in the sense of maintaining the doctrinal continuity of his tradition. His account of systematics is a helpful model for those who wish to treat culture with the modern, empirical outlook it deserves, while simultaneously remaining faithful to their religious heritage.

How does Lonergan achieve this balance? We should note that, first, doctrinal continuity occurs because: human intentionality remains the same, there is the transcultural gift of God's love, there remains past genuine achievement, but most importantly, there is the permanence of dogma. We also note that development in systematics occurs when systematics is done either for, or within, different cultures or varying differentiations of consciousness. Under such conditions, one may ask whether developments and cultural transpositions of understanding the mysteries do not represent a betrayal of one's church doctrines. More conservative people may find Lonergan's systematics to be an unjustified adjustment, or an abandonment, of one's religious heritage. Such an attack on theological understanding is not new, however, and we find such an attack being made on the followers of Thomas Aquinas, by Archbishop John Peckham (Lonergan 1964c, 49), namely that the Thomists relied upon new 'philosophic dogmas' that put 'idols' and "the vanity of conflicting questions" into the house of God. Peckham's essential problem was with the novelty of the understanding presented by Aquinas and his followers. We can pacify Peckham and other conservatives who fear systematics as contra-doctrinal, by noting, with Lonergan, that because doctrines is concerned with the affirmation and verification of the mysteries, and systematics is concerned with understanding those mysteries, that two distinct activities are performed in doctrines and systematics. New understandings do not mean rejection of older judgements about the mysteries. Theological understanding complements affirmations of the mysteries. Moreover, systematics is properly concerned with understanding. It thus in no way aims to establish proof, or disproof for that matter, of the mysteries, systematics simply intends to determine how the mysteries are so, not that they are so.

Systematics then, in no way compromises doctrinal continuity. Not even the most conservative Catholic could successfully argue that asking how a mystery could be, and seeking an answer to this question, could necessarily involve a lack of faith in that mystery. A simple example may be helpful here: Unless one wishes to embrace an unpleasant alternative, no conservative Catholic could maintain that, upon being told that she would mysteriously conceive the son of God, Mary fell from God's grace and sinned by asking how this would be (Luke 1:26-34). Mary simply exercised her natural human desire to understand, the same desire shared by all people. Lonergan's approach to systematics takes a similar form. In the faith thematised in foundations, one affirms the mysteries in doctrines. In systematics one accepts those doctrines in faith, asks how they could be so, and proposes hypothetical, analogous answers to those questions. Doctrinal continuity is maintained by systematics' reliance upon doctrines and because of the doctrines' permanence. Cultural intelligibility is maintained because, while the doctrine may remain the same, the questions about those same doctrines and the answers given to those questions, vary from culture to culture and between varying differentiations of consciousness.

8. Systematics and Pluralism

Lonergan's repudiation of classicism and his commitment to an empirical notion of culture are reflected in his generally positive attitude towards pluralism in theology. Interestingly, *Method in Theology*'s chapter on systematics contains no explicit reference to pluralism. Nonetheless, there is an implication of pluralism within systematics, in Lonergan's (1994, 344-45, 352-53) description of developments occurring when a religion encounters new cultures and varying differentiations of consciousness. This section will outline several ways in which Lonergan's theological method can account for theological pluralism. We shall then propose several ways in which systematics can contribute to effective and positive theological pluralism.

Lonergan (1985b, 243; 1994, 150-51, 326-27) finds three broad sources of pluralism, including: pluralities of common sense, varying differentiations of consciousness, and the presence or absence of conversion. In the first case, pluralism occurs when theology is transposed from one culture to another. Such pluralism occurs when an empirical notion of culture is acknowledged, and one affirms the need to take one's theological message to a variety of cultures, each having its own languages, resources, and common sense. This pluralism, according to Lonergan (1971b, 2; 1985b, 243; 1994, 276, 326), is more concerned with communications, rather than generating doctrinal pluralism. Simply put, the goal of communicating one's gospel to different people "calls for at least as many preachers as there are differing places and times, and it requires each of them to get to know the people to whom he or she is sent, their ways of thought, their manners, their style of speech." In this way, communications, as we outlined above, is pluralist to the extent that a communicator wishes one's message to reach a plurality of people.

Lonergan argues (1994, 150, 276, 326) that a second source of theological pluralism is found in the effort to take a religious message to people of varying differentiations of consciousness. He cites several differentiations of consciousness, which are worth outlining, to help us appreciate the pluralism necessary in communicating one's message to such differentiated consciousness. First, undifferentiated consciousness remains within the world of common sense. Common sense consciousness, according to Lonergan, operates in a world of assimilation and proverb, with a more concrete mindset that focuses on the present situation, without using scientific definition or systematised inquiry. Common sense consciousness thus considers objects primarily as they relate to oneself. Scientifically differentiated consciousness on the other hand, is concerned with precisely defined terms, systematic relationships between objects, logical and methodological procedures. Scientific consciousness is thus less concerned with objects as they relate to oneself, and more concerned with objects as they relate with one another. To illustrate the contrast between scientifically differentiated consciousness and common sense consciousness, Lonergan cites (1985b, 239-43; 1994, 258, 274-75) Eddington's two tables. On the one hand, one operating with common sense will describe a table that is "brown, solid, heavy." The scientist, though, will describe a table made up of colourless, mostly empty space, with the occasional "wavicle" making up the mass of the table. Lonergan also outlines a religious differentiation of consciousness, in which ascetism works towards its attainment in mysticism. Such consciousness, he argues, operates beyond the world mediated by meaning, by being caught up in self-surrender to the gift of God's love. A fourth, scholarly differentiation of consciousness, exists in which one adds, to one's own cultural common sense, a penetrating understanding of the common sense present in another culture. Lonergan also points to another, philosophic, differentiation of consciousness in which one operates from the starting point of the data of consciousness. We have not outlined all of the possible differentiations of consciousness, nor have we examined the way in which various differentiations of consciousness can coincide. The essential point remains though, that we have illustrated several differentiations of consciousness, and these imply the need for pluralism in our communications.

A classicist cannot appreciate varying differentiations of consciousness. If however, we appreciate that different people operate within various worlds of meaning operative within varying differentiations of consciousness, there results both the imperative and an explanation for a pluralism in the expression of a religion. Expressing the Trinity, for example, by way of a scientifically differentiated consciousness that can appreciate concepts such as person, substance and procession, is useful within that context, but entirely unsuitable to an audience whose common sense consciousness demands a more concrete image, which is more immediately relatable to everyday life. The presence of varying differentiations of consciousness will thus require a pluralism of expressions, unless a religion wishes to eliminate from its fold those who do not share a common differentiation of consciousness. We should note, though, Lonergan's argument (1994, 276, 329) that such pluralism of expression again involves a pluralism primarily in communications, rather than in doctrines, for what is plural is normally not the religious reality itself but the manner of expressing that reality to different people.

We should note that the forms of pluralism, to which Lonergan refers, cannot be accounted for by a classicist system of thought. For the classicist, legitimate pluralism is impossible because one assumes immutability, permanence and self-evidence. The self-evidence presumed by classicism is most important, because it assumes one legitimate cultural outlook, one form of differentiated consciousness. If one does not find the classicist's arguments self-evident because of some cultural difference, the classicist is likely to assume this as due to some deficiency in the other culture. The pluralist, on the other hand, acknowledges the existence of manifold cultural traditions, and within those traditions, one foresees the possible occurrence of varying differentiations of consciousness. The classicist would approach such cultures and differentiations of consciousness by demanding that people abandon their cultural and intellectual heritage in favour of the one true culture. On the other hand, one may take an empirical approach to culture, discover that cultures are ongoing, contingent, developing, and manifold. As Lonergan writes (1974, 184; 1994, 302-63), if one adds respect to a knowledge of such cultural variations, there results pluralism. The classicist may object that a pluralist outlook gives no grounds for unity in faith. Lonergan's response would be that the genuine ground of unity is found, not in uniform formulations, but in the common response of being in love with God. By accepting God's love, he would argue that we are united in religious conversion, which also leads to moral and intellectual conversion.

Conversion, where it exists positively, can be expressed in a number of ways, so that legitimate pluralism is always possible. However, in mentioning conversion, we turn to the third source of pluralism, which Lonergan identifies (1971b, 38; 1985b, 247-48; 1994, 276, 326, 330). Where there is a lack of conversion, a certain "perilous" pluralism results. Such improper pluralism comes from failure to respond to the gift of God's love, when one fails to seek the truly good or worthwhile, or when one falls victim to the manifold errors concerning human knowing. Such pluralism is not the result of taking a message to different people. It results from human unauthenticity's arriving at a different message from its failure to respond to the transcendental precepts: be attentive, be intelligent, be reasonable, be responsible and be in love.

Lonergan's distinction, of a third, unsafe form of pluralism, from two other forms of pluralism based on concerns with communications, helps us to understand his point (1985b, 96n4) that pluralism is more applicable to catechesis and communications:

> In catechetics, and more generally in communications ... the rule is pluralism, for one has to express the Christian message in the language and style appropriate to a class of people in a given culture. Still such pluralism does not imply that there are many, diverse Christian messages; and it is the task of the theologian to ascertain just what is the one message that the many communicators present to the many different audiences.

This text is illuminating, as it shows the form of pluralism Lonergan has in mind when he refers positively to pluralism. For him, pluralism lies in the manner of communicating the Christian message. Despite the cultural adaptations one makes in expressing one's message, that message remains the same in essence. Hence, Lonergan's pluralism is a theological pluralism, rather than a religious pluralism, for within his method, he can allow for many theologies, but these all remain theologies of the one religion. While there may be a plurality of communications' contents, these all remain communications of the same intelligible object yielded by one and the same religious revelation. It would thus appear that, while Lonergan encourages the presentation of many conceptions and expressions of his religion's message, that message remains ultimately based on a singular religion, so the message remains likewise singular, and not plural. We could contrast such theological pluralism, which ultimately relies on an assumed revelation from God, with the pluralism investigated by religious studies, which, as a secular discipline, is more concerned with the human search for the divine. As religious studies examines any and all confessions, and any number of revelations, it is clear that religious studies will uncover a pluralism of religions, with a corresponding pluralism of messages, and an even greater pluralism in the communication of those messages.

Essentially, a plurality of religions is possible within religious studies because it treats any and all religions. Theological pluralism, on the other hand, occurs within the personal conversion of the theologian who is dedicated in mind, heart and soul, to one's religion. To admit plurality of messages would be to abandon that commitment to faith and life. For one who accepts a specific set of data from revelation and is committed to the God who revealed it, pluralism can only legitimately occur in the expression of the religion's mysteries. This is the form of pluralism we find in Lonergan's work.

The foregoing investigations have outlined pluralism insofar as Lonergan envisages it, primarily for communications. We should now propose some ways in which the function of systematics can foster positive, authentic theological pluralism. First, systematics fosters pluralism by its origin in questions of intelligibility. Systematics, like all human intentional activities, begins from human wonder, the drive to know. Systematics specifically begins from questions of how the mysteries could be so, that is, how we can conceive the mysteries in relation to naturally knowable objects and in relation to each other. Pluralism in systematics can result from the different questions that intelligence places before the mysteries. Because not all theologians ask the same questions about God, we can assume that different questions will be raised and a plurality of different, though not actually opposed, answers may be given. Rahner (Rahner and Thüsing 1980, 4) puts the point well, noting that one can approach Christology from a number of viewpoints. One can begin with questions of philanthropy, thanatology, or eschatology. Rahner argues that all such questions can find their answer in the Church's confession of Christ. Those answers, we also note, are likely to be specialised, in line with their corresponding questions. We may thus find a pluralism of systematic Christologies. Jesus may be found intelligible in one work as saviour from sin, in another work as liberator of the oppressed, in yet another work as the Incarnate Word, consubstantial with the Father. Such pluralism simply reflects the questions that theologians put to the same mystery. This pluralism, however, does not mean that one theology, which develops in response to a particular question, necessarily contradicts another theology that developed in response to another question.

Systematics' concern to understand the mysteries from the analogy of what human reason naturally knows can also encourage pluralism. We would note that what people naturally know varies across cultures and across differentiations of consciousness. Thus, common sense analogies, which are drawn to find intelligibility within the mysteries, will vary from the analogies used to explain the mysteries within a more scientific context. Again, such pluralism does not imply that one analogy will exclude the validity of another. Neither Saint Patrick's common sense analogy of the Trinity, based on a shamrock, nor the more technical psychological analogy, need be exclusive if we appreciate that each analogy meets the intellectual needs and requirements of particular cultures with their specific differentiations of consciousness.

We should also note that systematics is a creative enterprise. As we have found in our study of systematics' understanding from analogy and by interconnections, systematics' understanding is a hypothetical theory put forward by creative insight into the mysteries. The very creative nature of insight means that different original thinkers will discover a plurality of analogies and manifold interconnections by which the mysteries can be understood. Unless one wishes to pursue a deductivist model of theology, such as that envisioned by classicist thinking, one would have to agree with Aquinas that "scientific" theology, which we call systematic theology, is only a hypothetical theory put forward to explain a mystery. The hypothetical nature of our understanding means that we can never exclude a plurality of other conceptions of the divine mysteries.

We finally note that pluralism in systematics allows us to distinguish systematics' pluralism from a less acceptable doctrinal pluralism. Doctrinal pluralism may be more problematic to many theologians, because this form of pluralism may imply doctrines that are ultimately right or wrong, or mutually contradictory. On the other hand, pluralism in systematics is more concerned with varieties of conception of the same doctrines. This point should be borne in mind when new theological theories emerge, lest heated arguments and accusations of heresy arise over what are ultimately issues of conception, not doctrine or belief.

9. Relevance to non-Catholic Religions

We should now say something about the relevance of Lonergan's systematics to the theologies of non-Catholic religions. We first note that, while he envisages (1994, xii, 332-33) his theological method as relevant to non-Catholic theologians, he neither offers specific ways in which his method can be so adopted, nor specifies detailed criteria for such an adaptation. However, from his statements, and our investigations, we can make some comments on how his theological method, specifically systematics, is suitable for other religions.

First, rather than finding common ground in the contents of doctrines or beliefs, Lonergan argues (1994, 109, 278) that what underpins, what is more primary, and more common to human religions, is the love of God. He proposes that the most important and basic common feature of many world religions is being in unrestricted love with transcendent reality. It is in that state of being-in-love in which Lonergan finds the most fruitful starting point for interreligious dialogue. This point concurs with the point that the foundations, which governs one's other work in theology, are based upon one's religious conversion, or love of God. If one can learn much from one's theology from adverting to one's personal conversion, there is much that one can learn and share with others, by adverting to their personal or communal conversions to transcendent reality.

We noted that, while he finds some basis for inter-religious dialogue, Lonergan does not specify particular ways in which his method may be useful to theologians of other confessions. His affirmations (1994, 150, 278, 332-33) in this regard are only general and as regards the possibility of theologians starting from different confessional starting points, he states that "the method is designed to take care of the matter." This point is made specifically in relation to the areas relevant to theological research. If one grants that the theological method may be able to handle such matters, one must nonetheless ask what forms of religion may find useful or not Lonergan's method generally, and systematics specifically.

We argue that all religions should find relevant the first four functional specialties. All religions have data that must be researched and such data must be interpreted. No religion is exempt from history and historical development, nor is any religion immune to dialectical differences, either internal or external. Less universal, however, would be the next four functional specialties. Foundations would be relevant, inasmuch as any religion's adherents are converted within that religion's horizons, and have their conscious, intentional operations affected by that conversion. Less universally applicable however, are doctrines, and even less so systematics. Specifically with systematics, a key presupposition of the specialty is that the God, whose mysteries one seeks to understand, transcends human intellect and is mysterious. Systematics is neither a complete understanding of divine mysteries, nor is it a proof of divine mysteries. As we have found, systematics involves a partial understanding by analogy and by interconnection, because God and divine mysteries so transcend human intellect that, "even when given in revelation and received by faith, they remain covered over by the very veil of faith itself" (DS 3016/TCF 132) Moreover, systematics is necessarily analogical because God, and the divine mysteries, are beyond the normal experience of natural human intellect. Systematics will have most relevance to religions in which God is believed to be transcendent, and above attainment by unaided, natural human intellect.

Following on from the necessity of God's transcendence to Lonergan's notion of systematics, we note the presupposition that God is revealed to human beings. While systematics prolongs and complements the natural knowledge that we may have of God, systematics operates upon revealed truths. Systematics would thus be useless to an agnostic philosophy that, while acknowledging the possibility of God, maintains that this God has not been made sufficiently manifest to human beings for that divine being to be known.

Systematics relies on positive affirmations regarding God and revelation. We should also note that systematics would also only be relevant where a religion manifests a positive attitude towards the human spirit. Systematics relies upon the actively inquiring, searching spirit of humanity that desires to understand what is set before its intellect. Systematics would thus be relevant to only those faiths that affirmed that the human spirit is legitimate in its search for understanding of God. An extreme Calvinist, however, would find systematics a waste, assuming that human intellect was corrupt, fallen and naturally inimical to God (Calvin, *Institutes*, II, iii). Lonergan's systematics is relevant only inasmuch as one affirms that natural human intellect is not entirely antagonistic to God, and that a sincere, searching mind, may in fact have positive insight into the revealed truths of God.

Similarly, we note that systematics is concerned with understanding divine mysteries by analogy with what human beings naturally know. In this way, systematics implies a positive engagement with the world of natural human achievement. What humanity naturally knows today is modern science, modern philosophy and modern scholarship. A religion that affirms the goodness and validity of such secular achievements is likely to feel more comfortable with Lonergan's notion of systematics. One who feels that the workings of humanity are counter to God and intrinsically hostile to divine revelation, will not readily desire to understand God in the language, terms, and thought forms of supposedly hostile secular achievement.

10. How have I Understood?

Any teacher will share this writer's experience of students who claim to understand, but do not. Gilbert Ryle (1990, 163) provides a useful set of criteria by which we can evaluate the presence or absence of understanding:

> For example, after listening to an argument, you aver that you understood it perfectly; but you may be deceiving yourself, or trying to deceive me. If we then part company for a day or two, I am no longer in a position to test whether or not you did understand it perfectly. But still I know what tests would have settled the point. If you had put the arguments into your own words, or translated it into French; if you had invented appropriate concrete generalizations and abstractions in the argument; if you had stood up to cross-questioning; if you had correctly drawn further consequences from different stages of the argument and indicated points where the theory was inconsistent with other theories; if you had inferred correctly from the nature of the argument to the qualities of intellect and character of its author and predicted accurately the subsequent development of his theory, then I should have required no further evidence that you understood it perfectly. And exactly the same sorts of tests would satisfy me that I had understood it perfectly.

We find Ryle's tests useful, not only for assessing understanding, but also for evaluating a method's effectiveness in promoting understanding. If we concede that systematics' theological understanding is never perfect, we nonetheless find useful criteria for systematics' understanding in Ryle's tests.

First, to the analogical aspect of systematics' understanding, we can apply Ryle's specific criteria that: (1) one can put an argument into one's own words, (2) one can translate this argument into another language, and (3) one can devise concrete illustrations of the more general and abstract parts of the argument. Systematics' understanding by analogy works towards putting a doctrine into one's "own words," because that analogy is with the object of human reason's natural knowledge. On the other hand, a criterion for systematics' practical effectiveness is whether a systematician can express the mysteries in the language proper to one's naturally known objects. Moreover, an effective systematician would be able to recast and reformulate doctrinal definitions, so as to express these doctrines with concepts more readily appropriated by a theologian and his or her audience.

An analogical conception of the mysteries also helps to express those mysteries in various "languages." While Ryle's criterion is linguistic, we would hold that systematics also works towards translating the intelligibility of mysteries into different cultural contexts. Systematics provides genuine understanding when it provides the basis for communications, in which one can express a mystery's intelligibility in ways comprehensible to people of different languages and cultures.

Ryle also argues that true understanding devises concrete illustrations for generalisations and abstractions. Systematics meets this criterion, in promoting a more concrete expression of the mysteries by using analogies with the concrete realities that people naturally know. Systematics will accordingly be effective in providing understanding when it conceives the mysteries in the concrete terms known by natural human intellect.

If we turn to systematics' understanding attained from the mysteries' interconnections, which involves the arrangement of the mysteries so that one is shown as the reason for another, systematics both meets and goes beyond Ryle's test of determining if one can draw further consequences from different stages of an argument. By formulating a matrix of interrelated mysteries, systematics can show not only those mysteries that consequently follow on from a particular mystery, but one can also show how that particular mystery is consequent to other mysteries. Systematics thus provides effective understanding when one can show those mysteries that follow on from a particular mystery, and also show the mystery or mysteries which are the reason for the mystery under consideration.

Understanding by interconnections can show how mysteries are related to each other, and humanity's last end. However, there is also scope for systematics to provide intelligibility by showing ways in which the mysteries are not connected. By showing how the mysteries are inconsistent with other realities, systematics can meet Ryle's criterion of being able to indicate points where a theory is inconsistent with others. Similarly Ryle argues that one who truly understands will predict subsequent developments in a theory. In this way, systematics will provide understanding when it can point to possible directions that future conceptions of the mysteries will take. Most notably, one who understands by interconnections will have some success in predicting subsequent developments in showing how more mysteries are related, by each being the reason for others.

Systematics' understanding, both by analogy and interconnections, also meets Ryle's criterion of standing up to cross-questioning. We should not expect though, that systematics would seek to withstand a cross-examination that sought proof of the mysteries. However, by showing the possible being and intelligibility of the mysteries, systematics can withstand cross-examination regarding intelligible possibility. Systematics can thus withstand the cross examinations of those who hold that the mysteries could not be so, because of their supposed unintelligibility. Systematics will be effective when it reflects Aquinas' objective (*Summa Contra Gentiles*, I,9§2-3), to resolve the doubts of adversaries, by setting forward probable arguments, that also console those who believe in the mysteries, by showing how those mysteries can be so.

We end this section by noting that systematics' understanding can be effectively tested by the broad criteria: "Does this understanding at least partially explain a mystery?" and "Does this understanding unify our knowledge of the mysteries?" As we have found repeatedly in this book, Lonergan's vision of systematics more than meets these criteria. We can evaluate the effectiveness of systematics, and the systematician's work, by the extent to which: (1) it can give new expression to the mysteries within different cultural contexts, (2) it can illustrate the mysteries in terms proper to natural human knowing, (3) it can resolve doubts of the mysteries' possible being, (4) it can show to what other mysteries a particular mystery is consequently or subsequently related, (5) it can show how a mystery is inconsistent with other objects of knowledge, (6) it can comment on the intelligibility or possible being of a mystery, (7) it can predict further developments in its understanding and (8) it effectively explains the mystery and provides a unified knowledge of that mystery and other mysteries.

II. CONCLUSIONS

Systematics' most essential attainment is its personal appropriation of the mysteries, which gives one a personal grasp of the meaning and implications of the mysteries. This personal grasp of intelligibility applies to both the methods and the content of systematic theology, so that by personal appropriation one attains authentic independence. This personal appropriation is especially valuable for teaching, apologetics, forming conceptions for ongoing cultures and for forming what has been called a "scientific" understanding.

Systematics' value to teaching is illustrated well by Thomas' contrast of settling doubts and generating understanding. We may remove doubts by appeals to authorities, but Aquinas argues (*Quaestiones Quodlibetales*, IV, q9a3 [18]) that if we do not promote a scientific understanding, our students will go away empty. Thomas did not mean that scientific understanding provided certainty. He meant a "scientific" personal appropriation of the principle, reasons for, or causes, of a mystery. This understanding of principles is most useful for teaching. With a functional specialty that promotes one's intelligent grasp of mystery, one is better able to reformulate definitions into new concepts appropriate to the intellectual horizons of one's students.

By basing its presentation on the principles of a mystery, rather than the haphazard way in which it was discovered, systematics can help teachers present the mysteries in the *ordo doctrinae,* which makes the mysteries more readily appropriated by students. The value of the order of teaching helps us avoid the problems associated with trying to teach without either due order or a grasp of the principle involved, which leads to intellectual "weariness and confusion" in students (*Summa Theologiae*, Prologue, I,q27).

Systematics' understanding is useful for apologetics, not by proving the mysteries of faith, but by explaining how the mysteries can be so and manifesting the intelligible possibility of those mysteries. Systematics is especially useful in manifesting that intelligible possibility in the concepts or thought forms of new and ongoing cultures (Lonergan 1973, 23-24). As a functional specialty, systematics is not content to preach to the modern world, with the conceptions more proper to ancient cultures. It can form understandings of the mysteries that are intelligible within new and ongoing cultures. As we noted, this does not mean an abandonment of one's doctrinal tradition, but a new expression of the mysteries that enables people to appropriate those mysteries for themselves, in terms proper to their own cultures.

By distinguishing certitude, which is more proper to doctrines, from understanding, which is more proper to systematics, we can understand how systematics can help one balance concern with maintaining fidelity to one's religious tradition with sensitivity to the needs of ongoing cultures. In systematics, one can account for a growth and development in understanding, while at the same time holding to a constancy in one's dogmas. One can also maintain a healthy plurality of systematic understandings, without compromising the integrity of one's faith.

Systematics is valuable to, and presupposed by, communications. Without the personal insight provided by systematics, communications would be the passing on of intelligibilities that were not one's own. Effective communication, in which one can address the concrete concerns of a specific culture, is possible only when systematics provides a personal appropriation, with which one can reformulate one's message, develop new conceptions and be able to translate one's message into the language of another culture. On the other hand, systematics needs complementing by communications, for only with the external relations fostered by communications, can systematics specifically and theology generally, take on wider relevance by the results of theology being presented to a myriad of people. We also found that communications is valuable to systematics, when communications is a two-way process, in which questions are addressed, in addition to answers being given. When such questions are addressed, systematics faces the need to develop new conceptions that are more appropriate to the concrete questions faced by communicators.

Against the classicist presumption of uniformity, systematics provides a framework in which effective pluralism can be promoted. We discovered the wider forms of pluralism, resulting from differing common sense, differentiations of consciousness and differing conversions, which can affect theology generally. Systematics, however, can contribute to theological pluralism, by addressing different questions, by developing many different and complementary analogies and by being creative in its discovery of new relations and intelligibilities in the mysteries.

Systematics is useful, in varying degrees, to non-Catholic religions. While we argued that the first four functional specialties were applicable to all religions, we found that systematics is useful only to those faiths that: affirm a transcendent God who has revealed certain mysteries, and which also affirm the positive function of the human intellect in genuinely seeking understanding of God. Those religions that do not uphold a transcendent God, or mysterious truths, or those religions that reject the positive role of human reason in seeking God, will find systematics less relevant.

Lastly, we asked of the value of systematics in actually providing understanding. Against Ryle's criteria, we found that systematics' analogical understanding can put a mystery into one's own words, or the words of a specific culture, and such analogies can provide concrete illustrations of the mysteries. Systematics' interconnections can help one understand the consequences of a mystery, and show upon what a mystery is based. Moreover, systematics can show up inconsistencies by showing to what a mystery may not be connected. Both analogy and interconnection also help support the mysteries against cross-questioning. This is not, we emphasise, by way of proving the mysteries, but by showing their intelligible possibility.

Having now covered the place and value of systematics, we now turn to making a review of Lonergan's presentation of systematics.

Chapter 11
Evaluations

With specific focus on systematics, this chapter will evaluate the manner in which Lonergan has met certain aims he set for his method in theology. To this end we shall: (1) evaluate how systematics meets the norms of modernity, and how systematics contributes to an understanding that is probable and imperfect, (2) examine systematics' coherence with human subjectivity, (3) respond to a challenge that Lonergan has not overcome classicism, and (4) evaluate systematics in relation to theological development. Finally, we shall (5) make some observations on the significance of Lonergan's recognition of understanding by analogy.

1. Systematics and the Norms of Modernity

In line with his statement (1973, 32) that "Along with changes in the notion of science and the notion of philosophy, it [specialisation] has been my motive in devoting years to working out a *Method in Theology*," this book has found many points of contact between Lonergan's theological method and the modern practice of science, philosophy and scholarship. In particular, this method overcomes the shortcomings of classicist approaches to theology. This section will outline the ways in which this method, particularly systematics, meets the standards of modern science, philosophy and scholarship.

Systematics, like the other functional specialties, presents an approach to theology that embodies the modern turn to specialisation. Moreover, the way in which the different specialisations are presented as functional specialties allows one to conduct specialised operations, while at the same time making a substantial contribution to the wider, ongoing, theological process.

Systematics is also part of a theological method that reflects the modern turn to empirical methodology. By basing his theological method upon an analysis of human intentionality, Lonergan gives this method a clearly empirical basis. It is important to emphasise that, like Newman (1985, 109), his intentionality analysis, and subsequently his theological method, are based upon an empirical viewpoint of human intellect as it really operates, rather than upon deduced concepts of mind or knowing. We further note that Lonergan (1992, 11ff; 1994, xii, 7) does not simply define a set of intentional and theological operations. He invites us to establish our own empirical observations of our intentionality, by using *Insight* and *Method in Theology* not as sets of prescriptions, but as guidebooks to our own operations that we can empirically discover for, and within, ourselves.

Earlier, we have found that modern scientists, characterised by Galileo, turned from the Aristotelian preoccupation with certainties and deductions, to a concern for intelligibility in observed events. We are familiar with systematics' concern for discovering intelligibility, rather than certainty. However, we should note that neither modern science, nor Lonergan's theological method, are unconcerned with attaining certainty. While science is concerned with intelligibilities, it in no way avoids certainty and approaches it whenever possible. Likewise, in the functional specialty, doctrines, Lonergan's theological method allows one to attain certainty within the horizon thematised in foundations. Systematics is nonetheless concerned primarily with intelligibility, which is discovered by intelligent insight. The important element in systematics' insight is that this insight is not reached by way of deduction from supposedly self evident principles, as was supposed by classicist thinking. Rather, systematics' analogies and interconnections result from creative insight and hypothesis. Systematics thus overcomes the classicist burden of presuming science, philosophy and theology to be concerned with necessity. Instead of necessity, systematics is concerned with hypothetical intelligibilities and attaining an understanding that is ongoing, but never more than probable.

Systematics relies upon creative insight. This point recalls modern history's constructive function, in which a historian relies on one's creative powers to build upon the information available from one's authoritative sources. By creative, or constructive insight, one can even rediscover what has been forgotten in history. Modern history's constructive aspect assumes freedom from a strictly deductive approach. Likewise, systematics is concerned with taking truths, which are attainable from one's authoritative sources, and "filling in the gaps" by a hypothetical, probable understanding of how one may relate those truths to each other and how one may understand those truths by analogy with the objects of one's natural world.

Modern science is characterised by its ongoing and ever-increasing nature. Against the static worldview of classicism, systematics shares with modern science a commitment to ongoing discoveries and development. We have repeatedly seen how systematics allows for ongoing development. Lonergan argues (1994, 352-53) that development in systematics can occur because one seeks understanding within different cultural contexts, because understanding occurs within varying differentiations of consciousness, or because dialectic can highlight error and bring its correction to light. We also noted, in our study of analogical understanding, that our understanding of mysteries can develop in parallel to our developing understanding of the objects by which we analogically understand those mysteries.

Our study of the turn to modern science also showed that it cast off the Aristotelian dependence upon metaphysics. While classicist science viewed itself as a prolongation of philosophy, and dependent upon the concepts of philosophy, Lonergan observes (1985b, 135-36) that with Newton modern science asserted its right to use its own proper conceptual framework. Likewise, Lonergan conceives systematics as a theological activity that relies upon its own set of terms that are founded upon an analysis of human intentionality. The basic terms of systematics are thus not metaphysical, but psychological. With such freedom from metaphysical concepts, Lonergan argues that systematics allowed people to find the operations of this theology within their own intentional consciousness. In turn, this allows systematics to become, like science, more concrete in its operations and applications. We should note that, for Lonergan (1994, 343), freedom from metaphysical concepts does not mean that we utterly reject metaphysics, but that making psychological terms basic yields a critical metaphysics. Metaphysics thus becomes more concrete, because one will be able to identify each metaphysical term with its corresponding element in intentional consciousness.

Modern science also turned from deduction from principles to empirical verification. We earlier found, especially in Galileo's experiments and in the quantum physicists' methodology, that modern science is concerned with observing events, forming hypotheses, and testing these hypotheses by empirical verification. We may conceive science's process of empirical verification as a testing of scientific hypotheses by the standard of whether such hypotheses explain observed phenomena, or not. We find a significant parallel here with the specific function of systematics. We note Lonergan's point (1964c, 24) that an analogical understanding of the mysteries can be evaluated in the light of whether it solves the questions put to it and whether the analogies square with the revealed truths within which they seek intelligibility. While modern science deals with observable natural phenomena and systematics deals with revealed truths, both disciplines support the probability of their hypotheses by referring those hypotheses back to the phenomena or truths they aim to explain. Another perspective on this parallel between modern science and systematics, is that the probability of both rely upon their success in resolving problems of intelligibility.

A most important aspect of systematics' meeting of the norms of modernity is its focus on the human subject. Lonergan's theological method generally, and systematics specifically, parallel modern science's and modern philosophy's focus on the intentional operations of the human subject. However, we note that while we have found Lonergan's theological method generally, and his functional specialty systematics specifically, to have overcome the constraints of classicism, and risen to the challenges of modernity, others have accused him of not overcoming classicism. We shall deal with this accusation later in this chapter.

Having outlined the manner in which systematics meets the standards of modernity, we can clarify Lonergan's response (1994, 351) to the accusation that systematic theology is elitist and difficult. Interestingly, he makes no effort to show how systematics is not difficult or elitist. Rather, he notes that theology, specifically systematics, must deal with difficult issues. Systematics is difficult, but so too are other fields of study, such as mathematics, science, and philosophy. His essential point is that if our theology does not match the difficult standards set by other disciplines, the practitioners of those other disciplines will be able to dominate theology. Because modern science is difficult, and often complex, a theology that meets science's modern standards will have its comparably difficult and complex aspects.

Systematics is also notable for its understanding that is imperfect, and probable, two aspects that correlate with the practice of modern science. We now turn to explaining these aspects of systematics.

In accord with the theological understanding envisaged by the First Vatican Council (DS 3016/TCF 132), systematics can present only an *imperfect understanding*. First, systematics' understanding is imperfect because of its necessarily analogous nature. We have dealt with this analogous understanding and its inherent imperfection in chapter eight above. It suffices now to recall the main point at hand, namely, that God's essence is not directly knowable by natural human intellect. Lacking a supernatural act, such as the beatific vision, finite human intellect can only grasp the infinite divine quiddity by an indirect, analogous, and therefore imperfect act of understanding. That analogous understanding, we further recall, is hypothetical and thus never complete or unconditioned. We note moreover, that the imperfection of our analogous understanding of the mysteries extends to our understanding of the mysteries from their interconnections. That understanding from interconnections relies upon our prior analogous understanding, and takes on analogous understanding's inherent imperfection.

Lonergan (1997, 215-17) draws support for the imperfection of systematics' understanding from Aquinas' writings (*Summa Theologiae*, I,q1,a2c, a7c, a7ad1m). Following Thomas, he notes that one may operate in this life under the guidance of divine revelation, working towards some grasp of God's essence. The fullness of that understanding, however, will always remain beyond the reach of natural human intellect. Moreover, even in his masterful Trinitarian study, Aquinas never intended his psychological analogy to supplant the divine essence as the sole sufficient principle of explanation. Thomas' psychological analogy could only provide an imperfect understanding, in a way similar to a side-door through which we only gain a partial look.

Aquinas took up human intellect's inherent imperfection in understanding the divine mysteries in his *Summa Contra Gentiles* (IV,1,§4). In particular, he emphasised our intellects' disproportion to the divine essence. From a more positive perspective, through His revelation, God remains in harmony with our intellect by bringing us, little by little, towards the perfect, through stages of development in our apprehension of revelation. But while this understanding is towards perfection, it cannot itself reach a complete understanding of God, because the human intellect, in its present state of being connected with the sensible, "cannot be elevated entirely to gaze upon things which exceed every proportion of sense."

From our investigations of systematics, we discover the necessary imperfection of the understanding, which we attain into the mysteries. Our understanding of the divine mysteries is analogical, in the downward mode of human intentionality, and thus bound to the created objects' lack of proportion to the divine essence. Despite the profitability of our understanding, it never in this life completely reaches the divine essence itself.

In a manner similar to its inherent imperfection, systematics' understanding never attains complete certainty. At best systematics' understanding can only achieve *probability*. In this way, systematics parallels modern science in its pursuit of probable theories, rather than deduced certainties. Moreover, Lonergan's advocacy of an understanding that makes no pretensions to attaining certainty reflects Aquinas' view of theology. Thomas (*Summa Contra Gentiles* I,9§3) proposed that Book Four of his *Summa Contra Gentiles*, which employed a method with which Lonergan (1994, 336) would closely identify systematics, would make use of "probable arguments."

The shift from classicist to modern, empirical thinking can illustrate a key reason for systematics' merely probable understanding. Systematics occurs within a determinate culture and a specific time. Moreover, systematics' understanding originates with specific questions and each ongoing, developing culture has its own set of new and developing questions that lead to correspondingly new answers. Thus, just as culture is ongoing, developing, but never complete, so too the questions that cultures raise regarding the mysteries may be manifold, ongoing and developing. Notwithstanding the fact that human intellect will always raise more questions about the mysteries than it can answer, human cultures will never raise all the questions pertinent to the mysteries. A culture may reach a new level of understanding, but no culture will ever reach ultimate understanding of the mysteries. We mean that one age may ask certain questions that lead to germinal answers. A later age, building on past achievements, may have more developed and more differentiated questions, which lead to ever-increasing acts of understanding. On this point, Lonergan notes (1964c, 25-26) the specific example of developing Trinitarian theory. While Augustine and Aquinas addressed the same Trinitarian doctrine, Augustine expounded the doctrine with a psychological analogy. Thomas, alternatively, developed this analogy to include both psychology and metaphysics. Aquinas' understanding, we further note, was formed within a culture holding to a static worldview. In our own day, Lonergan has continued the development in understanding by asking and answering questions about the Trinity, not only in psychological and metaphysical terms, but also within the modern world's horizon of modern philosophy and science. Importantly, this achievement cannot be terminal, because we can expect future scholars to always meet and answer questions proper to the cultural and scholarly development of their own times.

We also affirm that systematics' understanding can only ever be probable, due to the difference in proportion between the divine essence and human intellect. As no human understanding is proportionate to the divine essence, we conclude that despite whatever understanding we may have, that understanding will be incomplete. In this light, we recall the Fourth Lateran Council's affirmation (DS 806/TCF 320) that no similarity can be observed between a finite object, and the infinite God, without there being an even greater dissimilarity. As systematics' analogical understanding conceives the divine mysteries according to their similarity with created objects, we can only conclude that no question about the nature of a divine mystery can be analogically answered, without there being further questions being raised. Accordingly, when we attempt to understand God, Lonergan notes (1988, 82) that "the further one pushes the issue, the clearer it becomes that there is much we do not know." This position echoes the First Vatican Council's declaration (DS 3016/TCF 132) that, despite our acceptance and positive understanding of revealed truths, our understanding of such truths will never reach complete understanding, and will remain only probable.

Systematics' probable character is also manifest in the difference between doctrines and systematics. Doctrines, or dogmatics, as Lonergan writes (1964c, 28-29), are determined by revealed truth or naturally known truth. The assent to doctrines is an act of judgement, which provides certainty. Conversely, systematics' understanding is not a conclusion from revelation or reason. Systematics' conception is a hypothesis neither found in one's doctrinal sources, nor reasonably demonstrable. Systematics' understanding is probable because it is only a hypothesis put forward to explain a mystery. Lonergan cites (1997, 204) the example of Thomas' Trinitarian theory, which could be demonstrated neither from reason or revelation. It is simply a hypothesis that squares with what revelation declares. Importantly, as Aquinas indicates (*Summa Theologiae*, I,q32,a1 ad2m), the hypothetical, probable, nature of such understanding means that other possible hypotheses cannot be excluded.

We note that, even though systematics' understanding is merely probable, we should not fall into an uncritical relativism regarding different hypothetical theories put forward by systematics. As we have seen in chapter eight, systematics' understanding can be more probable, or less probable, depending on how many questions it can answer. The more problems a hypothesis solves, the more probable that hypothesis will be. Moreover, systematics' resolution of problems illustrates the value of an understanding that is only imperfect and probable. While the arguments systematics puts forward may not be complete or demonstrative, systematics' understanding does give us some intellectual relief in our study of the mysteries of faith. That our understanding is probable, rather than improbable, means that our understanding solves problems of intelligibility, and approaches, though never reaches, an ultimate understanding of God. Aquinas makes a similar point, when he states (*Summa Contra Gentiles*, I,8§1) that "to be able to see something of the loftiest realities, however thin and weak the sight may be, is, as our previous remarks indicate, a cause of the greatest joy."

The imperfect and probable nature of systematics manifests significant parallels with modern science. Like modern science, systematics is an ongoing, never fully completed enterprise. While both disciplines approach the fullness of truth, neither makes any pretensions to having ever reached perfection. They accept readily their ongoing, developing nature in which their understanding is positive, but never perfect, probable, but never absolutely certain.

2. COHERENCE WITH HUMAN SUBJECTIVITY

In its different aspects, systematics would be less possible, or even futile, if it was incompatible with the natural operations of human intellect. Systematics has the clear strength of being coherent with human intellect. This coherence comes from Lonergan's emphasis on meeting the problems of theology by attending to the very nature of human intentional consciousness, and by basing his theological method generally, and his conception of systematics specifically, upon the operations of human intentionality.

Lonergan's open account of human intentional consciousness puts him in a more positive stance towards human intellect than writers such as Barth or Calvin. Calvin held (*Institutes* II,iii*)* that fallen human nature was corrupt of mind and will. Likewise, Barth (1975, I,I, 6, 19, 28-30, 89, 90, 196, 199, 209, 238, 246) held that human reason was Godless, inimical to belief, undisposed towards God's Word and lacking in active capacity for the Word of God. To hold that human intellect is so depraved that it cannot apprehend God, without contradicting its own natural operations, is a negative, pessimistic and almost misanthropic viewpoint that would argue for discontinuity of human intellect and divine grace and faith. We find relevant here Macquarrie's statement (1977, 50):

> The Calvinist believes that he himself, as one of the elect, has been rescued from this sea of error and that his mind has been enlightened by the Holy Spirit. However much he may insist that this is God's doing and not his own, his claim is nevertheless one of the most arrogant that has ever been made. It is this kind of thing that has rightly earned for theology the contempt of serious men.

While Macquarrie's charge of arrogance may be strong, we would find that a Calvinist or Barthian would ultimately assert some form of intellectual superiority over the rest of "unenlightened" humanity. Lonergan's account of human knowing, on the other hand, asserts no special privilege or ability on the part of Christian theologians. His account is per-

haps more humble, but it has the advantage of allowing a person to operate with coherence between, and equal intellectual integrity in, secular
and religious fields of study.

Lonergan's account of natural human intellect, which can actively, positively cooperate with the grace of God, is a viewpoint more affirming of
the human person, and our natural capacities. His position allows us to
view ourselves as creatures whose intellectual activities, in doing theology, are continuous with our intellectual operations in the "natural realm."

Lonergan shares a generally affirmative attitude towards human intellect, with scholars like Rahner and Macquarrie. Macquarrie argues (1977,
v, 25) that Christian theology should be coherent with the other results
of human intellect's operation and that any Christian theology must have
"philosophically defensible foundations." Behind Macquarrie's statements
is a positive outlook on humanity that sees any acceptable theology as
being coherent with human intellect. Rahner (1978, xi, 1-2) makes similar points more specifically. He finds vital the theologian's tasks, to situate
Christian faith within the contemporary intellectual horizon and to reflect upon the question of how one can be a Christian with "intellectual
honesty." Rahner essentially shares Lonergan's view that theology should
be coherent with, affirming of, and edifying to, the human spirit. This
approach ultimately is more acceptable, more inviting and more open to
dialogue than the confrontational approach represented by Barth and
Calvin. We should note, though, Rahner's point (1978, 289) that a religion cannot be brought into positive contact with the concrete minds of
people simply by repeating that religion's official teachings. Such teachings may be valuable as doctrinal definitions, but they are not always
formulated in a manner coherent with the intellects of those to whom
the doctrines are addressed. Fulfilling that need is very much the role of
systematics.

Lonergan's theological method is coherent with human intellect because it is based on an analysis of human beings and their concrete intellectual operations. Lonergan (1974, 3) bases this theological method upon
an intentionality analysis that "begin[s] from people as they are." As we
have earlier noted, this approach parallels that of Newman (1985, 109),
who emphasised an investigation of human knowing, as it existed, and
not as it was supposed to have been. Moreover, Lonergan's investigation
of human intellect resulted in his identification of different intentional
activities, which are governed by the transcendental precepts: be attentive, be intelligent, be reasonable, be responsible and be in love. Most
importantly, these transcendental precepts are applicable to all areas of

human intellectual activity. So, when the transcendental precepts are thematised in Lonergan's theological method, we find a method coherent in its operations with the operations applicable to a human subject's other interests. While Rahner (1971a, 194-96) may have had problems with a method so broad in its application, the strength of Lonergan's method is that it allows and encourages human intellect to operate in theology in the same way it does in any other human pursuit. By being based upon the universal operations of the human mind, this method is coherent, first, with a human mind and secondly, with a human being's other intellectual activities.

To take systematics most specifically, we find this functional specialty's coherence with human intellect manifested by its operational genesis in concrete questions. In *Method in Theology* (1994, 336), Lonergan states that systematics is concerned with attaining an understanding of how the mysteries can possibly be what they are. Our investigation of systematics' understanding by analogy showed that this understanding was prompted by concrete questions regarding the intelligibility of doctrines. So too, understanding attained from interconnections arose from questions concerning the relationships of different mysteries. The essential point is that such questions, and their resultant answers, are coherent with human intellect, because the questions are concrete questions raised by real human beings who greet the mysteries with questions of how the mysteries could be so.

We also note that systematics attains an understanding that is probable, ongoing, and creatively insightful. These aspects of systematics are coherent with human intellect because these are aspects of human intellect as it concretely exists. On the other hand, a classicist model of theological understanding would seek an understanding that was certain, logically deduced, and static. Such an understanding would be inconsistent with concrete human intellect.

We should also note that in being coherent with, and based upon, human intentionality, systematics' basic terms are not metaphysical, but psychological (Lonergan 1994, 343). We first note that having psychological terms as basic means that people can find the operations of such a theology within themselves and be aware of their operation. With a psychological base, theology can thus become more concrete in its operations.

Lonergan also argues (1994, 343) that having such a psychological base leads to a critical metaphysics. He means that if metaphysical terms are derived from an intentionality analysis, for each and every metaphysical term, there will be a corresponding element of intentional consciousness, which will help clarify valid terms, while simultaneously eradicating empty or misleading terms. Such a critical metaphysics has two positive functions. First, critical metaphysics provides a heuristic structure, as a definite horizon within which one can raise questions. Secondly, as a point of illumination of analogous understanding, a critical metaphysics can settle differences between literal and metaphorical meanings and between notional and real distinctions.

Another attainment of systematics in terms of its foundation in, and coherence with, intentional consciousness, is that it can both escape authoritarian constraints upon, and admit development in, one's method. If one's method is based on intentional consciousness, it can and should develop parallel to the development of intentional consciousness. Moreover, if method is based on intentional consciousness, it is up to each person to discover that intentional consciousness within oneself and to work out one's method accordingly. In that way, one becomes independent from others' selections of method (Lonergan 1994, 343-44).

3. Has Lonergan Overcome Classicism?

William Shea (1976, 275) proposes a supposedly "straightforward and devastating" criticism of Lonergan: that despite his awareness of "the shift from classical [*sic*] to contemporary culture, ... the classical [*sic*] remains determinative of his own positions in philosophy, theology and even method." One's first impression is that Shea fails to distinguish "classicism" as a worldview from "the classical" as the genuine achievements of former time. If one is to equate classicist philosophy with classical achievement, Lonergan may be guilty as charged, for he envisages (1994, 352) theology as an ongoing process, in which today's theology builds upon past achievements.

The notion that Lonergan remains beholden to classicism is both unfortunate and mistaken, though it seems to be widespread, for Shea (1976, 275) cites scholars who raise charges that "run the gamut from his [Lonergan's] failure to meet adequately points raised by contemporary studies in language, myth and symbol to his unreserved devotion to the Catholic doctrinal tradition." These scholars include Charles Davis, Leslie Dewart, Langdon Gilkey, James Mackey, Schubert Ogden and W. Richardson. One could ask if such scholars could have made such statements after taking account of Lonergan's work in *Insight*. After reading Lonergan's chapter on "Doctrines" (1994, 295-33), one cannot accept that Lonergan expresses "unreserved devotion to the Catholic doctrinal tradition." At best, this accusation implies naive acceptance of Catholic doctrines on Lonergan's part, at worst it implies fundamentalism. Neither option squares with Lonergan's writings, or, for that matter, the manifold recollections of those who knew him personally.

If classicism is the belief that there is only one, normative culture, and that all must subscribe to the ideals of that culture, one is hard-pressed to find Lonergan so instructing us to enforce our theology, either in its content or its methodology, upon all peoples in the same manner. On the contrary, we repeatedly find him encouraging us to find theological method within our own intentional consciousness and to reformulate and express our religion in ways appropriate to varying cultures and people (Lonergan 1994, xi-xii, 7, 11, 18-19, 326-30, 332-33, 344, 352-53).

Hugo Meynell argues (1978, 407-8) that those who believe that Lonergan failed to outgrow classicism generally fail to differentiate classicism and the practice of systematics. Systematics is simply an attempt to understand the mysteries of faith. Where authors, who presume Lonergan to be classicist, could stumble, is in his proposal that systematics deals with the mysteries, or truths of faith. If one takes such a statement in isolation, one could mistakenly think that he is proposing some sort of understanding of immutable truths established within a classicist framework. However, systematics is part of an ongoing, critical theological process that includes doctrines, which is concerned with the truths of faith, not in any uncritical or classicist manner, but in a way taking account of the manifold issues affecting doctrines, including doctrinal development. We further note that systematics is concerned with promoting an understanding, of doctrines, to a wide variety of peoples and cultures, so systematics can hardly fit the basic monocultural criterion of classicism. Meynell sums up the situation well (1978, 407), writing that:

> ... 'classicism' is the insistence that there is but one culture, and is very apt to issue in insistence on uniformity of expression; whereas a non-classicist 'systematics' can discern and therefore accept a unity of belief in a wide variety of forms of expression.

Meynell also observes that many commentators on Lonergan cite chapter Nineteen of *Insight*, which deals with general transcendent knowledge, including the existence of God, as an example of Lonergan's own classicist leanings. We concur with Meynell that this chapter, no less than Lonergan's other work, does not fall into the classicist error, which is the belief that there is only one culture and that theological arguments should only be presented within the horizon of this culture.

These observations should reassure us that contrary to being classicist, Lonergan has definitely broken away from the classicist horizon.

4. Development in Systematics

We have already investigated some sources for development in systematics. We now turn to several other ways in which we can conceive such development. Lonergan (1994, 352-52) puts forward development stemming from dialectic. Such dialectical development is possible within systematics because its understanding is imperfect, hypothetical, never certain, but only probable. Our chapter on understanding by analogy showed that one can pass judgement on one's understanding according to its effectiveness in solving problems of intelligibility. When an understanding of the mysteries no longer solves such problems, or when it creates more problems than it solves, it becomes necessary to develop and revise that understanding. Such dialectical development in systematics is evident in the conception of "Limbo," which for many years intelligibly explained the fate of unbaptised infants. Despite this conception's possible efficacy in former times, developments in culture and philosophy have rendered "Limbo" an ineffective and sometimes destructive explanation. While no new explanation has yet won widespread acceptance, we find in "Limbo" an example of the need to revise and develop the explanations furnished by systematics.

Lonergan argues (1994, 353) that revision may occur for cultural in addition to theological reasons. This is simply because theology does not occur in isolation, but it occurs within a given cultural context and works to mediate a religion to that cultural context. Systematics thus has to revise its earlier explanations in the light of new developments in culture, which include the revisions of a culture's science, philosophy and scholarship. In that way, Doran notes (1995, 2:332), systematics will never be terminal, but shall develop always, as culture develops. The issue of ordaining women to priestly ministry serves as a good example. Aquinas' explanation (*Summa Theologiae*, Suppl,q39,a1c,a3ad4m), that women are unable to receive holy orders due to their "state of subjection," is entirely unacceptable in today's culture. While the doctrine is still open to theological debate, even one who staunchly supports the official Catholic position on women's ordination would have to agree that the systematic explanation for that doctrine has required radical revision. In a less controversial situation, Lonergan's article "Christology Today" (1985b, 74-

79) shows how systematic theology needs to, and can, be developed and revised to meet new cultural challenges. The article manifests an appreciation for the substantial challenge presented by modern scholarship to Christological and Trinitarian theology, most notably in modern understandings of person, identity, human consciousness and subjectivity. In Lonergan's work, we see that to answer such concerns with the language of Chalcedon is manifestly insufficient. However, to defend the doctrine of Chalcedon, he makes a valuable contribution by developing new conceptions of person, identity, consciousness and subjectivity, that go some way to meeting the challenges of modern scholarship.

We can advance two further reasons for systematics' need for, and contribution to, development and revision. In the first place, there is the nature of our understanding itself. Human understanding, especially understanding of mysteries, is never a terminal, complete understanding. Such understanding only belongs to God. Finnis makes a similar point (1980, 399-400), reminding us that "our pursuit of understanding is laborious, developmental, and never nearly completed; we need images, figures, symbols, to help us understand even the most abstract terms and relations; and our learning and discovery are always harassed by oversight, muddle and lapse of memory." Newman (1974, 90, 148-51) makes the point clearer by noting that, when we are presented with a great idea, even the most inspired teachers cannot communicate a full understanding of that idea without taking great time and effort to do so. The full elucidation of a great idea, he reminds us, takes much time, and much thought. Moreover, the more an idea is a "living" reality, the more complex will it be in its various aspects. If we acknowledge the mysteries of faith as being "great" and if we acknowledge God, and the divine mysteries to be living realities, our understanding of those mysteries must be in a process of ongoing development and revision.

The nature of the mysteries also implies that our human understanding of them will be in constant development. If our understanding of those infinite mysteries is finite, there must always be room for development by way of augmenting and correcting our understanding. Newman (1974, 151) expresses this point well:

> ... as a mystery implies in part what is incomprehensible, so does it in part imply what is not so; it implies a partial manifestation, or a representation by economy. Because then it is in a measure understood, it can so far be developed, though each result in the process will partake of the dimness and confusion of the original impression.

Systematics is a humble functional specialty. It recognises that it has limits, and that it remains in a process of development and revision. While we may now be in a higher stage of development than previous times, it is important for those doing systematics to bear in mind that their work is part of an ongoing process, and that future generations will build upon and correct our current work. In an advanced world, they may laugh at us or even find us offensive.

We note that systematics promotes a positive reformulation and development of understanding the mysteries because of its emphasis on creative insight. The analogies and interconnections that systematics uncovers are not logically deduced, but discovered by creative insight. Systematics, being within the intellectualist tradition, has an advantage over conceptualism, which is more prone to deduction and thus either inertia or destruction. When conceptualism has logically deduced all its conclusions from its self-evident principles, it finds it difficult to change without breaking down and rejecting its former findings. Intellectualist-based systematics however, fosters creativity, the freshness of new insights and discoveries of the hitherto unknown. We do not mean that Lonergan rejects logic, for logic can be later used to evaluate the coherence of systematics' insights. We mean that systematics uses creativity, in addition to logic, in an ongoing, ever-developing, methodical enterprise.

We end this section by noting that there is development in understanding and there is development in doctrines. The two forms of developments are different, and Lonergan (1985a, 15) was aware of this fact at the beginning of his theological career. Doctrinal or dogmatic development concerns the determination of the truths of faith. Systematics' development, or the development of theological understanding concerns developments in the understanding of those doctrines. Failure to recognise this distinction can have serious effects for theology, as we found in the case of Peckham's complaints against the scholastics.

5. Analogy and Official Catholic Teaching

We have examined Lonergan's achievement in expounding the implications of *Dei Filius'* affirmation (DS 3016/TCF 132), that we can understand the mysteries of faith by analogy with what human intellect can naturally know. He uses the First Vatican Council to outline systematics' function, in which analogical understanding plays an essential role. However, understanding the mysteries by analogy has an even longer and more venerable tradition within the Catholic faith. Most notable in this regard is Thomas Aquinas, who encouraged and promoted such analogical understanding. It is thus interesting that, while Catholic tradition has a long history of employing understanding by analogy and while the First Vatican Council is most explicit and direct in its affirmation of theological understanding by analogy, subsequent official documents of the Catholic Church should often neglect this aspect of theological understanding. Moreover, we find it surprising that the same text from *Dei Filius*, as cited by Lonergan, should be cited by official Catholic documents without mention of understanding by analogy. In this regard we can take texts from the Second Vatican Council, *Veritatis Splendor* and the *Catechism of the Catholic Church*.

First, in *Optatam totius*, the decree on the Training of Priests (n16), the Second Vatican Council states that in the course of priestly theological studies, "lastly, in order to throw as full a light as possible on the mysteries of salvation, the students [for the priesthood] should learn to examine more deeply, with the help of speculation and with St. Thomas as teacher, all aspects of these mysteries, and to perceive their interconnection." While this text does not specifically cite *Dei Filius*, it is disappointing that a key text from the Second Vatican Council should mention understanding attained from the mysteries' interconnections, without making any reference to understanding the mysteries by analogy.

Even more interesting is the *Catechism of the Catholic Church*. The *Catechism* notes (n41) that "All creatures bear a certain resemblance to God," and that "we can name God by taking his creatures' perfections as our starting point, ..." However, the *Catechism* twice refers to *Dei Filius,* specifically on the understanding of the mysteries. These citations refer: (1) to "The mutual connections between dogmas, and their coherence, [which] can be found in the whole of the Revelation of the mystery of Christ" (n90) and (2) to the virginal conception of Christ, an event the meaning of which "is accessible only to faith, which understands in it the 'connection of these mysteries with one another'..." (n498). We should emphasise that both of these texts have footnotes that indicate citations from Vatican Council I's *Dei Filius* Chapter IV, (DS3016). Despite these citations, the *Catechism* refers to only the understanding of mysteries attained from interconnections, without any mention of understanding attained from analogy.

The citation of only one aspect of theological understanding also occurs in Pope John-Paul II's *Veritatis Splendor* (n110), which has a footnote to "*Dei Filius*, Chap. 4: DS, 3016." However, the Pope's text encourages moral theologians to "develop a deeper understanding of the reasons underlying its [the Magisterium's] teachings and to expound the validity and obligatory nature of the precepts it proposes, demonstrating their connection with one another and their relation with man's ultimate end." Again, we find a direct and explicit citation of the same text as that used by Lonergan to explain systematics' function. Nonetheless, while Lonergan explains systematics' function in terms of analogy and inter-connection, we find another official Catholic document referring only to understanding attained from interconnections.

We can greet these truncated citations of *Dei Filius* with surprise. To explain why, however, may take another volume and this section of our book can only present some preliminary speculations. In the first place one could suggest that the documents, to which we referred above, were composed by officials who had been brought up and educated within a classicist-minded environment. Such a mindset is more comfortable with a logical and deductivist system of thought. We recall, in this regard, Kleutgen's view of theological development as limited to discerning the logical bonds between the Church's revealed truths (McCool 1977, 10). We would suggest that because classicist thinkers are more comfortable with logical connections, they would feel a greater affinity to the affirma-tion that we can understand the mysteries by their interconnections. While we would certainly not wish to make a sweeping claim of classicism against the Second Vatican Council and church officials, we suggest the possibil-ity that remnants of classicist thinking within the Catholic Church made it more appealing to focus on interconnections as a way of understand-ing. We should note, though, that the understanding through intercon-nections, which Lonergan proposes as merely probable and creative, would still be far removed from the classicist notion of deducing connections in a logical, supposedly certain system of thought.

On the negative side, one may suggest that classicists, or those affected by such thinking, will feel uncomfortable with analogical understanding, which is: hypothetical and creative, rather than simply logical; probable, rather than certain; and manifest of intelligible possibility, rather than adding extra proof. Such an approach is anathema to a classicist and at least unsettling to a classicist-influenced person. We can thus propose the possibility that a lingering desire for certainty, deduction and proof within theological speculation, has meant that official Vatican documents have mentioned the aspect of interconnections within theological understand-ing, to the apparent exclusion of understanding from analogies.

Our discovery here leaves much room for further fruitful research. Nonetheless, regardless of the reasons behind the neglect of analogy, we can positively affirm the achievement of Lonergan in drawing our attention to an overlooked aspect of systematic theology. It would be to contemporary theology's benefit to look back to a Council, which is often maligned on account of its unpopular statements on Papal infallibility, and take heed with Lonergan of one of its more positive achievements in presenting a balanced view of theological understanding. It is to his credit to have taken a fuller view of *Dei Filius'* teaching, and to have applied it in a contemporary context.

6. Conclusions

This chapter has found systematics to be coherent with the standards of modern science, philosophy and scholarship, and with human intellect. In meeting the standards of modernity, we have found that systematics embraces a developing understanding, which is imperfect and never more than probable. By being coherent with human subjectivity, systematics accounts for that subjectivity as it exists in different cultures, so that systematics does overcome problems associated with classicism. Lastly, we found that Lonergan has positively renewed the tradition of theological understanding by analogy, which has been unfortunately neglected in some quarters.

Lonergan's presentation of systematics thus effectively bridges the gaps which have existed between faith, reason and culture. While this is a difficult and perhaps risky exercise, it is one that is nonetheless necessary, as Tillich reminds us (1968, III,4). In systematics, Lonergan takes up the First Vatican Council's affirmation (DS 3008-43/TCF118-39) of both faith and reason, which avoids the extremes of fideism and rationalism. Lonergan, however, adds a further concern for culture, which overcomes the classicist hurdle and he adds an account for modern standards, which produces a theology and a theological understanding specifically, which affirms faith, reason and culture, and meets the difficult standards of modernity.

Lest we fall into a new classicism, we should avoid the expectation that Lonergan's achievement is perfect and definitive. However, we should acknowledge his great achievement in presenting a functional specialty, in which systematics' coherence with faith, reason, culture and modern standards allows the theologian to operate with intellectual honesty. Lonergan presents a model of systematics that allows faith to be animated by the questions and answers of reason and also allows belief to become a substantial part of modern societies, by way of systematics' coherence with the cultures and scholarly standards of those societies.

We have rejected the view that Lonergan is classicist. He has overcome classicism by presenting a method for theological understanding which is both modern and faithful to one's religious tradition. The readiness of some to accuse Lonergan of classicism is perhaps caused by the difficulty of such a task. However, such accusations may pay him an indirect compliment by testifying to the level of his achievement in fulfilling his goal.

Lastly, we note that Lonergan has made a valuable contribution to theology in recovering the teaching of *Dei Filius* on theological understanding. By emphasising the understanding of the mysteries by analogy, he has done well to highlight an element of understanding, which has too often been neglected.

It now remains for us to make some concluding evaluations regarding the value and achievement of Lonergan's presentation of systematics. To this conclusion, we now turn.

Chapter 12
Conclusion

This book has investigated the function of systematics as a functional specialty within Lonergan's *Method in Theology*. We have given these investigations depth by placing systematics within the contexts of Lonergan's theological method and of the motivations behind, and foundations of, systematics. We have augmented this investigation by further exploring the meaning of systematics' understanding attained from analogy and interconnections and by examining the usefulness and place of systematics. To conclude this work, we shall make three brief reflections. First, we shall place systematics within the context of Lonergan's "new beginning" for theology. Secondly, we shall review the exact function of systematics. Thirdly, we shall summarise systematics' usefulness and grounding concerns.

1. SYSTEMATICS AND LONERGAN'S NEW BEGINNING

Lonergan proposed a new beginning for theological method that would account for, and meet, the standards of modern science, philosophy and scholarship. If we first consider his theological method in a wider context, we first emphasise that his theological method did not nullify all previous theological achievements. However, faced with the perception of theology as a second-rate, decadent and ineffectual discipline, which did not meet modern standards, he held that theology required fundamental changes. The modern shift from a classicist to an empirical notion of culture reinforced his conviction that only a new beginning could raise Catholic theology to the standards demanded of a modern discipline. This search for a new beginning reflects the ambitions of Newman and Aquinas. Newman argued (1974, 69) that Christianity needed to uphold its genuine traditions, while simultaneously making genuine and constructive use of the available sources and methods of modern scholarship. Aquinas likewise reformed the presentation of his tradition to make it intelligible and persuasive within the new context of Greek and Arabic thought that influenced his culture. Lonergan similarly aimed to uphold his religious tradition, while also renewing his tradition's theology so that it could constructively use the best achievements of modernity. This aim clearly and positively responded to Leo XIII's call to renew and augment the old with the new. Lonergan, however, was more successful than others, including Leo, the modernists and the rationalists. One failed to positively and constructively engage the methods of modernity, preferring to take only the more acceptable of modern results. The others failed in bridging the gap between the Church's traditional teaching, and their new doctrines. Lonergan's strength was to present a method by which one can discern clearly "his respectful attention to, learning from, and critical reorientation of both tradition and modernity" (Doran 1995 2:301).

Systematics is clearly grounded in Lonergan's *novum organon* for theology, which yielded a theological method based upon the operations of human intellect. The success of that new beginning has been evident in the ability of that method to identify and promote functional specialties within theology, which bring theology closer to the standards and methods expected of modern scholarship, and which also make theology more manageable to theologians who must now operate with the specialised methods appropriate to their occupation.

Systematics is part of Lonergan's "new beginning," but as the promotion of understanding the mysteries of faith, systematics is not an entirely new exercise. It is similar to speculative theology, with which theologians have long been familiar. Systematics also conforms to the First Vatican Council's descriptions of theological understanding and it corresponds to the intent of Aquinas' theology, especially in the *ordo doctrinae* found in the two Summae. Lonergan's presentation is new, however, in conceiving systematics as a specialty within a theological method that is divided into distinct functions within the process from data to results.

No less than any other part of Lonergan's theological method, systematics needed to positively account for and balance the demands of religious tradition, modern standards, an empirical notion of culture and the operations of human intellect in reason and faith. First, systematics is not a set of empty speculations, but the promotion of intelligibility within the truths of faith. Its impetus, and reference point, is in the Church doctrines that systematics tries to understand. This means that systematics remains clearly within the theologian's religious horizon.

Secondly, systematics meets modern standards, most manifestly by being a specialised theological function. Like modern science, systematics is ongoing and ever-increasing. In its hypothetical solution to problems, systematics also reflects modern history's creative, constructive, function. Systematics is also based upon the empirically discovered operations of human intellect. This empirical emphasis on the subject means that systematics is not a prescribed set of deduced procedures, but a functional speciality that can be discovered in the concrete operations of the theologising subject. The evaluation of systematics' probability, with regard to the number of problems it solves, also reflects modern science's turn to empirically verified possibility. Systematics also manifests the establishment of an autonomous methodology, proper to its operations, which yield the conditions of possibility for discovering intelligibility within revealed truths.

Systematics also clearly reflects an empirical notion of culture. Instead of employing a classicist approach to understanding, systematics embraces cultures as manifold, ongoing and developing. Lonergan's method promotes the development and reform of systematics to meet the variations of consciousness and common sense in manifold cultures. This commitment to an empirical notion of culture is vital under the horizon that conceives theology as mediating between a culture and a religion. If culture is conceived along classicist lines, theology will be seen as a permanent and universal attainment. When culture is conceived empirically, theology, including systematics, faces the substantial challenge of adapting itself to the manifold needs of different cultures.

Systematics is also coherent with human intellect, by being based upon the human mind's concrete operations. Being founded upon the operations of active intellect, systematics not only has a transcultural base, it is also continuous with the cognitional operations used in all fields of human endeavour. Moreover, because it is intended as an aid in discovering one's intentional and theological operations, systematics facilitates the self-discovery of the inquiring subject.

Systematics can successfully account for, and balance, faith, reason, an empirical notion of culture and modern standards, because of Lonergan's theological method's foundation in an analysis of human intentionality, which yielded his transcendental method and identified the transcendental precepts: be attentive, be intelligent, be reasonable, be responsible and be in love. Importantly, because this method is transcendental, not categorical, it begins with human inquiry operating with the pure "question" or desire to know. This transcendental method, upon which systematics and the other functional specialties are based, allows human intellect to pursue questions relevant to any and all cultures, and any and all objects of human endeavour. The method's transcendental nature also promotes ongoing development and revision. Moreover, the focus on the intentional subject, in Lonergan's method, allows for the integration of natural and "supernatural" operations, in reason and faith. Particularly in systematics, transcendental method's heuristic foundation, and focus on the subject, enable one to account for the operations of the human subject, who uses both faith and reason to find intelligibility within the divine mysteries by using one's faith to guide one's reason.

2. The Function of Systematics

Systematics essentially seeks intelligibility within the mysteries of faith, specifically an intelligibility appropriate to the culture out of which particular questions arise. In pursuing understanding, systematics' primary concern is neither with belief, nor faith, nor the doctrinal affirmations of mysteries, but the question of how it could be that the mysteries are so. Systematics takes over from doctrines, in which the mysteries are affirmed and posits questions of intelligibility concerning these mysteries. Systematics, rather than adding to certitude or faith, manifests intelligible possibility, by showing how one can conceive something of the nature of mysteries and how those mysteries may be related to each other and to humanity's end.

Systematics' understanding is both analogical, and from the interconnections of the mysteries. Understanding the mysteries by analogy means that human inquiry can yield a notion that penetrates both a naturally known object and a mystery. While analogy can take the form of proportion and attribution, we have found Lonergan's exercise of analogical understanding to transcend such conceptual limits. Analogy yields only a partial understanding, but this understanding is useful in manifesting a hypothetical and intelligible principle of the mystery. By analogy with naturally known objects, systematics can manifest to human intellect how a mystery can possibly be.

From the interconnections of the mysteries with each other and with humanity's end, systematics manifests the intelligibility of mysteries in their relationships. This understanding shows how the mysteries are the reasons for other mysteries and how these mysteries are, in turn, grounded by other mysteries. Similar to the way in which we grasped that a circle's roundness is because of the equality of its radii, systematics, by proposing an intelligible matrix of the mysteries, can propose the manner in which the mysteries are because of each other and how our end is also because of these mysteries.

Systematics' understanding fulfils, at least partially, the human desire for insight into revealed truths. It intends resolution of apparent incoherence between human intelligence and these truths, which in their doctrinal presentation can seem incoherent with each other, unintelligible and impossible to be. Following the general pattern of insight, systematics releases the tension of human inquiry, which can remain unresolved insofar as doctrines propose mysteries which are apparently unintelligible. Systematics is also creative and not necessarily deductive, because doctrines and revelation do not provide information on how the mysteries may be conceived, in themselves or in relation to each other. By interconnecting the mysteries within humanity's "perceptual field" and by proposing hypothetical analogies that can explain the mysteries, the insightful systematician can manifest, in a humanly attainable manner, the intelligible possibility and intelligible unity of the mysteries. We have seen, very importantly, that systematics' understanding is fertile. An effective analogy, or creative interconnection of the mysteries will resolve not only the initial problem at hand, but also help resolve a series of problems. In this light systematics nourishes the *ordo doctrinae* by providing a principle, or set of principles, under which the mysteries can be intelligibly ordered to be more effectively assimilated by students or hearers, without suffering the intellectual weariness associated with the order of discovery.

3. Usefulness of and Need for Systematics

To illustrate the need for systematics, we can recall Aquinas' reflection (*De Veritate*, q18a8ad4m) on Aristotle (*De Anima*, III, 7 431a 14-29):

> According to the Philosopher, the intellective soul is related to the phantasm as to its objects. Consequently, our understanding needs conversion to phantasms not only in acquiring knowledge but also in using knowledge once it is acquired.

From our work on understanding, we are aware that intellect needs an image with which to form an insight. However, we note Aquinas' point that intellect also needs a sensible image with which to use knowledge once it is attained. We propose that Aquinas means that to make use of knowledge for teaching, communications, apologetics, or any other reason, one needs a humanly attainable object with which one can work, and which one's hearers can appropriate for themselves. In this light, we can posit the need for systematics. Once one has attained doctrines or knowledge of the facts of faith, one needs conversion to a humanly attainable intelligibility of the realities affirmed by these doctrines. Without such conversion, doctrines remain unusable. Systematics serves a vital purpose in fostering conversion to, and a personal appropriation of, the intelligibility of the mysteries. Without the personal appropriation and understanding that systematics brings, the mysteries remain unintelligible and unable to be used for teaching, communications or any of the other purposes we have outlined. With this understanding, however, one has the power to intelligently articulate the mysteries in one's teaching, defence of tradition, or communication with diverse cultures, and to place those mysteries within one's intellectual culture.

The key to systematics' necessity and usefulness is its promotion of personal appropriation of the mysteries. Systematics' understanding makes the mysteries more understandable, rather than being utterly remote from human minds. Even if we cannot attain a full understanding of those mysteries, we can attain a partial understanding, which resolves at least some of the intellectual discomfort we may have in the face of such objects. However, we should recall that, despite the academic value of systematics, its usefulness is not restricted to the halls of learning. Lonergan's concern was also pastoral, and systematics takes on pastoral significance by forming the basis of communications, by which academics and non-academics can personally profit from the results of theology.

Aristotle (*Metaphysics*, I, 2, 982a 10-20) provides an insight into why systematics should be necessary for theology, by stating that the basic qualification for teaching others is understanding, which is the basis of wisdom. Not only for teaching, but for the manifold functions of communications to different cultures and differentiated consciousness, apologetics and contributing to positive pluralism, systematics is the basic requirement for the theologian. Without this understanding, one is left with only conceptual doctrinal definitions. By the personal, intelligent appropriation of the mysteries, systematics allows one to reformulate, recast and redefine doctrines so that one may intelligibly present the mysteries: to students, to a plurality of cultures and in different forms of communications. Moreover, by appropriating the principle of a mystery, one may place it in the order of teaching, rather than the order of discovery, so that hearers may more readily appropriate the meaning and significance of that mystery. Most importantly, systematics is necessary in manifesting the intelligible possibility of a mystery, for without an understanding of how the mystery may be so, one's teaching, apologetics and communications may be left empty.

Systematics is also valuable in aiding a theologian's self-appropriation. Like Lonergan's theological method in general, systematics does not rely upon conceptual prescriptions of how a theologian should theoretically operate. Lonergan's account of systematics presents a guide to intentional operations that the theologian can discover within oneself. We note that he does not intend his method to guarantee results. He (1994, 5-6) rejects the notion that,

> method is ... a set of rules that, even when followed blindly by anyone, none the less yield satisfactory results. I should grant that method, so conceived, is possible when the same result is produced over and over, as in the assembly line or 'The New Method Laundry.' But it will not do, if progressive and cumulative results are expected.

In the first place, Lonergan's method relies upon insight, which is neither strictly logical nor invariably deduced, but creative and unpredictable. Moreover, instead of providing a prescription or formula for almost predetermined results, systematics, and Lonergan's general theological method, bring order and light to theologian's operations by helping one identify one's intentional operations and by helping the theologian to direct and focus one's operations more properly to the task at hand. By having a knowledge of what one is doing, when one is doing theology, one's efforts can thus be spent more constructively on the matter at hand.

Systematics is an urgent need for modern Catholicism. Like other faiths, Catholicism faces the challenge of balancing the demands of faith, reason and culture. We have seen how systematics achieves this balance and helps one remain faithful to one's tradition, while simultaneously presenting one's tradition intelligibly within new cultural and scholarly contexts. Systematics is also needed because of the gulf that often exists between Catholic doctrines and the communication of those doctrines. To many, doctrinal documents of the Catholic Church are unintelligible and unable to be appropriated into their concrete living. A key problem with Catholic doctrines is that debate over them has focussed too much on the doctrinal issues concerning the verity or otherwise of the proposed facts of Christian life. We propose that systematics is needed to present the reasons how and why the realities affirmed by doctrines are what they are. Moreover, modern Catholicism needs appreciations of how those doctrines may be made intelligible within the manifold contexts in which they find themselves. Regrettably, Catholics too often find that their faith is communicated to them by way of affirming which doctrines are right or wrong, without sufficient insight into their meaning and significance. This writer has been disappointed, for example, to find that the *Catechism of the Catholic Church* has been distributed to many Catholic school teachers as a primary resource for school-age religious education. This approach first violates Pope John-Paul II's intent, stated in the *Catechism*, (p6), that it should "encourage and assist in the writing of new local catechisms, which take into account various situations and cultures." Secondly, merely "teaching catechism" may make hearers certain of doctrinal verity, but, as Aquinas reminds us (*Quaestiones Quodlibetales*, IV,q9a3 [a18]), it will send away students empty, with no understanding of what those doctrines may mean.

Systematics fills the gap between doctrines and communications by presenting an intelligible, humanly attainable, conception of the mysteries. It does this by formulating analogies, with which systematicians can present models of how the mysteries may be so. Such analogies bring clarity to the mysteries by helping human intellect form a notion that penetrates both the mysteries and objects proper to human knowledge. Moreover, systematics provides a framework under which the mysteries are intelligible in their relationship to each other and to our human end. Such an understanding, we argue, is not an option for contemporary Catholicism, it is essential, lest Catholicism's teaching degenerate into the passing on of doctrinal formulas, which ever-fewer people understand.

4. Conclusion

What would Lonergan have thought of our work? We trust that we have come to a fuller and better understanding of the functional specialty, systematics, and its place within his theological method. But he would be disappointed to see us stop at this point. While we may have achieved much, our real work is to use our personal appropriation of our own intentional operations in theological understanding and to use this self-knowledge in focussing and guiding our energies in doing theology. Lonergan would be happier if we did not see this book as a terminal point. He would be far happier to see it as an exercise in self-appropriation, which formed the basis of fruitful work in developing new systematic understandings for our contemporary world.

That self-appropriation, rather than a set of prescribed categories or a fixed "new method laundry" is more vital because, fifteen years after Lonergan's death, we find ourselves in a new social and ecclesial situation. Most of us no longer work under classicist assumptions, nor is our church, in the main, a conservative one facing down the prospect of nihilism overtaking society. As Lonergan prophesied in 1965, (1988, 245), classical culture would be jettisoned, but not without being replaced by new movements. Today, we have a more liberal, historically-minded church and theological academy that exist within a world for which nihilism is no longer a threat but reality (Doran 1990 4-5). Increasingly, the dominant intellectual force of our time is post-modernism, to which we agree with Doran (1990, 5-6) there are only three serious alternatives. First, there is "deconstructive normlessness," which we find an increasingly dominant force, but one that has served to reinforce despair in the abilities and potential of knowing subjects. When we discussed judgement in chapter five, we noted Fingarette's (1963), and Janov's (1981) observations that the inability to exercise judgement is a symptom of neurosis. "Neurosis" would seem a fitting metaphor for the postmodern movement that despairs so much of the knowing human subject, that critically founded understanding is traded for the extremes of lazy tolerance and deconstruction. In such an intellectual environment, it is possible to produce meaningless nonsense and have it published, as displayed eminently in the Sokal *Social Text* hoax, as described by Michael Ruse (1999, 1-12).

If some despair in the human subject's abilities, there are some who take the second, less academically popular option of "an educated and sincere but misguided return to classicism and dogmatism" (Doran 1990, 5-6). Such an approach reminds us of Lonergan's warning (1988, 245) that there would be "formed a solid right that is determined to live in a world that no longer exists." One finds such attitudes in the various reactionary Catholic conservative movements that vary in their actual beliefs and professed loyalties, but are united in their belief that what they call "modernism" is wrong and that the solution to Catholicism's woes is a return to a previous golden era, even if that era is more golden in memory than historical reality. If in the post-modern left we find despair in the human subject, we find in the conservative right an arrogant self-confidence in their ability to exercise "right judgement" without a corresponding concern for understanding or moral sensitivity. The overriding metaphor for the right would seem to be psychopathology. So often we see in its various movements the myth of pure intellect, with right reason emphasised to the exclusion, or detached ignorance, of human values, which in Lonergan's words (1994, 122), would be "something less than the life of a psychopath."

Against the unfruitful options of the left's neurotic flight from reality and judgement, and of the right's psychopathic flight from understanding and value, there lies the third option, which Doran (1990, 6) identifies as finding for ourselves the discovery of the norms of human genuineness. It is the option of Lonergan's "perhaps not numerous center," (1988, 245) which is willing to put the hard effort into reconciling the old and the new by diligently working out the transitions required to maintain fidelity to both tradition and modernity. This book has found that for Lonergan, the basis for those transitions and reconciliation is in the self-appropriation of the human subject. From that foundation, the discovery that theologians have minds and use them, and can use them well, one can go beyond dead-ends and advance the cause of theology. It is that cause for which we are confident that Lonergan's model systematics will be of great service.

We can now end our investigation by recalling Aquinas's question, with which we opened this investigation: "What is God?" The true value of systematics would lie in partially answering that question. It cannot be answered by despair in the subject's abilities, and it cannot be answered by dogmatic formulations more suited to a bygone era. Rather, an answer to "What is God?" whether the question is raised in an remote and speculative context or one that is proximate and more concrete, would be founded upon the theologian's self-understanding of what it is to understand, how one can raise effective questions, and how one may go about answering those questions. That is the program of systematics, and it is a program to which we hope to diligently apply the self-appropriation we have attained though our investigation.

Bibliography

Anselm. 1974. *Anselm of Cantebury,* Volume One. Edited and translated by Jasper Hopkins and Herbert Richardson. London: SCM.

Aquinas, Thomas. 1942. *Quaestiones Disputatae et Quaestiones Duodecim Quodlibetales,* Volumen V, *Quaestiones Quodlibetales.* (Editio VII) Turin: Marietti.

_____. 1952-1954. *Truth [De Veritate],* Translated by Robert W. Mulligan (Volume 1), James V. McGlynn (Volume 2) and Robert W. Schmidt (Volume 3). Chicago: Henry Regnery.

_____. 1957. *Commentary on Aristotle's De Anima.* In *Aristotle's De Anima, In the Version of William of Moerbeke, and the Commentary of St. Thomas Aquinas.* Translated by Kenelm Foster *et al.* London: Routledge and Kegan Paul.

_____. 1961. *Commentary on the Metaphysics of Aristotle,* Volumes I and II. Translated by John P. Rowan. Chicago: Henry Regnery, 1961.

_____.1963. *Commentary on Aristotle's Physics.* Translated by Richard J. Blackwell, Richard J. Spath and W. Edmund Thirlkel, introduction by Vernon J. Bourke. London: Routledge and Kegan Paul.

_____. 1975. *Summa Contra Gentiles.* Translated with an Introduction and Notes, by Anton C. Pegis (Book One), James F. Anderson (Book Two), Vernon J. Bourke (Book Three) and Charles J. O'Neill (Book Four). Notre Dame: University of Notre Dame Press.

_____. 1981. *Summa Theologica,* Translated by the Fathers of the English Dominican Province. London: Sheed and Ward.

Aristotle. 1991. *The Complete Works of Aristotle.* Ed. by Jonathan Barnes. The Revised Oxford Translation. Bollingen Series LXXI•2. Princeton: Princeton University Press.

Armstrong, Karen. 1994. *A History of God, From Abraham to the Present: the 4000-year Quest for God.* London: Mandarin.

Athanasius. 1978a. *De Decretis (Defence of the Nicene Council).* Translation by Newman, with revisions. In Philip Schaff and Henry Wace, eds. *A Select Library of Nicene and Post-Nicene Fathers of the Christian Church.* Second Series. Volume IV, St. Athanasius: Select Works and Letters. Grand Rapids: Eerdmans.

_____. 1978b *De Synodis (On the Councils of Arminum and Seleucia).* Translation of Newman, rev. by Archibald Robertson. In Philip Schaff and Henry Wace, eds. *A Select Library of Nicene and Post-Nicene Fathers of the Christian Church.* Second Series. Volume IV, St. Athanasius: Select Works and Letters. Grand Rapids: Eerdmans, 1978.

Bacon, Francis. 1973. *The Advancement of Learning.* Ed. by G. W. Kitchin, introduction by Arthur Johnston. London: J. M. Dent and Sons.

Barth, Karl. 1975. *Church Dogmatics,* Volume I: "The Doctrine of the Word of God," Part One. Edited by G. Bromley, and T. Torrance. 2d ed. Edinburgh: T & T Clark.

Becker, Carl L. 1958. *Detachment and the Writing of History: Essays and Letters of Carl L. Becker.* Ed. by Phil L. Snyder. Ithaca: Cornell University Press.

Bettenson, Henry, ed. and translator. 1987. *The Early Christian Fathers: A Selection from the Writings of the Fathers from St. Clement of Rome to St. Athanasius.* Oxford: Oxford University Press.

Boly, Craig S. 1991. *The Road to Lonergan's "Method in Theology": The Ordering of Theological Ideas.* Lanham: University Press of America.

Brown, Raymond E., Joseph A. Fitzmyer, Roland E. Murphy, eds. 1989. *The New Jerome Biblical Commentary.* London: Geoffrey Chapman.

Bultmann, Rudolf. 1969. *Faith and Understanding*, Volume I. Edited with an introduction by Robert W. Funk, translated by Louise Pettibone Smith. London: SCM.

Butterfield, H. 1958. *The Origins of Modern Science 1300-1800*, (new ed). London: G. Bell and Sons.

Calvin, J. 1960. *Calvin: Institutes of the Christian Religion*, Volume I. Edited by John T. McNeill, translated and indexed by Ford Lewis Battles. Library of Christian Classics, Volume XX, Philadelphia: Westminster Press.

Carrithers, Michael, 1986. The Buddha. In *Founders of Faith*. Oxford: Oxford University Press.

Cassirer, Ernst. 1953. *The Philosophy of Symbolic Forms*, Volume One: Language. Translated by Ralph Manheim. New Haven: Yale University Press.

Chesterton, G. K. [nd]. *The Secret of Father Brown*. London: Cassell and Company.

Collingwood, R. G. 1989. *The Idea of History*. Reprint of 1961 ed. Oxford: Oxford University Press.

Collins, James. 1956. *A History of Modern European Philosophy*. Milwaukee: Bruce.

Copleston, Frederick. 1985. *A History of Philosophy*, New York: Doubleday Image Books.

Corcoran, Patrick, ed. 1975. *Looking at Lonergan's Method*. Dublin: Talbot Press.

Crowe, Frederick. E. 1980. *The Lonergan Enterprise.* Cambridge, Massachusetts: Cowley.

_____. 1983 Lonergan's Early Use of Analogy: A Research Note—with Reflections. *Method: Journal of Lonergan Studies*, 1: 31-46.

_____. 1989. *Appropriating the Lonergan Idea*. Edited by Michael Vertin. Washington: Catholic University of America Press.

_____. 1992. *Lonergan*. (Outstanding Christian Thinkers Series, edited by Brian Davies). Collegeville: Liturgical Press.

Daly, Thomas V. 1982. The Peaceful Intellectualist Liberation from Logic. *Catholic Theological Review*, 4:26-32.

_____. 1991. Learning from Lonergan at Eleven," *Method: Journal of Lonergan Studies*, 9: 44-62.

_____. 1996. Letter from Hawthorn, Melbourne; to the author on 19 January.

Danaher, William J. 1988. *Insight in Chemistry*. Lanham: University Press of America.

_____, ed. 1993. *Australian Lonergan Workshop*. Lanham: University Press of America.

Darwin, Charles. 1962. *The Origin of Species: By Means of Natural Selection Or the Preservation of Favoured Races in the Struggle for Life*. Sixth edition of 1872. New Foreword by George G. Simpson. New York: Collier.

_____. 1993. *The Autobiography of Charles Darwin, 1809-1882: with original omissions restored.* Ed. with appendix and notes by his grand-daughter, Nora Barlow. New York: Norton .

Deferrari, Roy J. 1986. *A Latin-English Dictionary of St. Thomas Aquinas*. Boston: St. Paul Editions.

Dessain, Charles S. 1970. Cardinal Newman and Bernard J.F. Lonergan S.J. Lecture given at Lonergan Congress, Florida. In Florida Congress Papers, 1970, Volume One.

Doran, Robert M. 1990. *Theology and the Dialectics of History*. Toronto: University of Toronto Press.

_____. 1995. *Intentionality and Psyche*. Vol. 1 of *Theological Foundations*. Milwaukee: Marquette University Press.

_____. 1995. Theology and Culture. Vol. 2 of *Theological Foundations*. Milwaukee: Marquette University Press.

Drake, S. 1978. *Galileo Studies*. Ann Arbor: University of Michigan Press. Cited in William Danaher. 1988. *Insight in Chemistry*. Lanham: University Press of America

Ferré, Frederick. 1967. Analogy in Theology. In Paul Edwards, ed. *The Encyclopedia of Philosophy*, Volume One. New York: Macmillan Company and The Free Press.

Fingarette, H. 1963. *The Self in Transformation: Psychoanalysis, Philosophy, and the Life of the Spirit*, New York: Basic Books.

Finnis, John. 1980. *Natural Law and Natural Rights*. Clarendon Law Series, edited by H. L. A. Hart, Oxford: Clarendon Press.

_____. 1983. *Fundamentals of Ethics*, Washington, D.C.: Georgetown University Press.

Fuller, Reginald H. 1979. *The Foundations of New Testament Christology*. Glasgow: Collins.

Geiselmann, Josef Rupert. 1966. *The Meaning of Tradition*. Volume 15 *Quaestiones Disputatae* series. London: Burns and Oates.

Heelan, Patrick A. 1965. *Quantum Mechanics and Objectivity: A Study of the Physical Philosophy of Werner Heisenberg*. The Hague: Martinus Nijhoff.

Heidegger, Martin. 1951. *Kant Und Das Problem Der Metaphysik*, 2d. ed. Frankfurt: Vittorio Klostermann.

_____. 1962. *Kant and the Problem of Metaphysics*. Translated by James S. Churchill. Bloomington: Indiana University Press.

Heisenberg, Werner. 1962. *Physics and Philosophy: The Revolution in Modern Science*. Harper Torchbook edition. New York: Harper and Row.

Hoenen, Petrus. 1933. De origine primorum principiorum scientiae. *Gregorianum*, 14:153-184.

_____. 1938. De philosophia scholastica cognitionis geometricae. *Gregorianum*, 19, 498-514.

_____. 1939. De problemate necessitatis geometricae. *Gregorianum*, 20:19-54, 321-50.

Hutchinson, Eliot D. 1942a. The Period of Elaboration in Creative Endeavour. *Psychiatry*, 5: 165-76.

_____. 1942b. The Phenomenon of Insight in Relation to Education. *Psychiatry*, 5: 499-507.

_____. 1943. The Phenomenon of Insight in Relation to Religion," *Psychiatry*, 6: 347-357.

_____. 1949a. The Nature of Insight. In Patrick Mullahy, ed. *A Study of Interpersonal Relations*. New York: Hermitage Press.

_____. 1949b. The Period of Frustration in Creative Endeavor. In Patrick Mullahy, ed. *A Study of Interpersonal Relations*.

_____. 1949c. Varieties of Insight in Humans. In Patrick Mullahy, ed. *A Study of Interpersonal Relations*.

Irenaeus. 1981. *Against the Heresies*. Translated by Alexander Roberts and W. H. Rambaut. In Alexander Roberts *et al* (editors), *The Ante-Nicene Fathers: Translations of the Writings of the Fathers down to A.D. 325*. Volume I: The Apostolic Fathers—Justin Martyr—Irenaeus. Grand Rapids: Eerdmans Publishing.

Janov, Arthur. 1981. *The Primal Scream*, (with a new foreword by the author). New York: Perigee.

John-Paul II. 1993. *Veritatis Splendor*, (Encyclical Letter Regarding Certain Fundamental Questions of the Church's Moral Teaching). Australian Edition. Homebush, Sydney: St Pauls.

Kant, Immanuel. 1990. *Critique of Pure Reason*. Translated by Norman Kemp Smith. London: Macmillan.

Kelly, Anthony. 1989. *The Trinity of Love: A Theology of the Christian God*. Volume Four, New Theology Series, General ed., Peter C. Phan. Wilmington: Michael Glazier.

Lamb, Matthew, ed. 1981. *Creativity and Method: Essays in Honor of Bernard Lonergan*. Milwaukee: Marquette University Press.

Langlois, Jean. 1964. The Notion of Being According to Lonergan. In Frederick E.
Crowe, ed., *Spirit as Inquiry: Studies in Honor of Bernard Lonergan, S.J.*, (Special issue
of *Continuum*), Chicago: Saint Xavier College.

Leo XIII. 1879. *Aeterni Patris* (On the Restoration of Christian Philosophy). In Thomas
Aquinas. 1981. *Summa Theologica*. Translated by the Fathers of the English Dominican Province. Rev. ed. London: Sheed and Ward.

Loisy, Alfred. 1950. *The Origins of the New Testament*. Translated by L. P. Jacks. London:
George Allen and Unwin.

Lonergan, Bernard J. F. 1959. *De Intellectu et Methodo*. *Reportatio*, mimeographed
edition. Rome: St. Francis Xavier College. [ET by Michael G. Shields. Toronto:
Lonergan Research Institute of Regis College, 1990.]

_____. 1962. The Method of Theology. Institute given at Regis College, Toronto,
July 9-20, 1962. Typescript by Nicholas Graham, Toronto: Lonergan Research
Institute, Regis College, 1984.

_____. 1964a. *De Constitutione Christi: ontologica et psychologica, Supplementum*.
Editio quarta. Rome: Gregorian University Press. [ET by John F. Brezovec.
Worthington, Ohio: Pontifical College Josephinum, nd.]

_____. 1964b. *De Deo Trino: Pars Dogmatica*. Editio altera et recognita. Rome:
Gregorian University Press.

_____. 1964c. *De Deo Trino: II Pars systematica, seu Divinarum personarum conceptio
analogia*. Editio tertia et recognita. Rome: Gregorian University Press. [ET by John F.
Brezovec. Worthington, Ohio: Pontifical College Josephinum, nd.]

_____. 1964d. *De Verbo Incarnato*. Editio Tertia. Rome: Gregorian University Press.
[ET by Charles Hefling. Boston College, 1990]

_____. 1971a. Bernard Lonergan Responds. In *Foundations of Theology*, ed. By Philip
McShane. Dublin: Gill and Macmillan.

_____. 1971b. *Doctrinal Pluralism*. (The 1971 Pere Marquette Theology Lecture.)
Milwaukee: Marquette University Press.

_____. 1971c. *Grace and Freedom: Operative Grace in the Thought of St. Thomas
Aquinas*. Ed. by J. P. Burns, introduction by Frederick E. Crowe. New York: Herder
and Herder.

_____. 1972. *Lonergan Notes Insight*. Copy held at Lonergan Centre, Sydney.

_____. 1973. *Philosophy of God, and Theology: The Relationship between Philosophy of
God and the functional Specialty, Systematics*. (St. Michaels' Lectures, Gonzaga University, Spokane, 1972.) London: Darton, Longman and Todd.

_____. 1974. *A Second Collection: Papers by Bernard J. F. Lonergan, S.J.* Edited by
William F.J. Ryan and Bernard J. Tyrrell. London: Darton, Longman and Todd.

_____. 1976. *The Way to Nicea: The Dialectical Development of Trinitarian Theology*.
Trans. by Conn O'Donovan from the first part of *De Deo Trino*. London: Darton,
Longman and Todd.

_____. 1984. Questionnaire on Philosophy: Responses by Bernard J. F. Lonergan,
S.J. *Method: Journal of Lonergan Studies*, 2:1-35.

_____. 1985a The *Gratia Operans* Dissertation: Preface and Introduction. Ed. by
Frederick E. Crowe, *Method: Journal of Lonergan Studies*, 3/2:9-46.

_____. 1985b. *A Third Collection: Papers by Bernard J.F. Lonergan, S.J.* Ed. by
Frederick E. Crowe. New York: Paulist Press.

_____. 1988. *Collection*. Ed. by Frederick E. Crowe and Robert M. Doran. 2d ed.,
revised and augmented. Toronto: University of Toronto Press.

_____. 1990. *Understanding and Being: The Halifax Lectures on Insight*. Ed. by
Elizabeth A. Morelli and Mark D. Morelli. 2d ed., rev. and augmented. Toronto:
University of Toronto Press.

_____.1992. *Insight: A Study of Human Understanding*. Ed. by Frederick E. Crowe and Robert M. Doran. 5ᵗʰ ed., rev. and augmented. Toronto: University of Toronto Press.

_____. 1994. *Method in Theology*. 2ⁿᵈ ed. Reprint. Toronto: University of Toronto Press. Original 2d ed., London: Darton Longman and Todd, 1973.

_____. 1997. *Verbum: Word and Idea in Aquinas*. Ed. by Frederick E. Crowe and Robert M. Doran. Toronto: University of Toronto Press.

McCool, Gerald A. 1977. *Catholic Theology in the Nineteenth Century: The Quest for a Unitary Method*. New York: Seabury.

Macquarrie, John. 1977. *Principles of Christian Theology*. Rev. ed. London: SCM.

Mascall, E. L. 1966. *Existence and Analogy: A Sequel to "He Who Is."* London: Libra.

Meynell, Hugo. 1976. In Defence of Method. *The Month*, 9: 48-53, 60.

_____. 1978. On Objections to Lonergan's "Method." *Heythrop Journal*, 19: 405-410.

_____. 1989. Bernard Lonergan. In David F. Ford, *The Modern Theologians: An Introduction to Christian Theology in the Twentieth Century*, Volume I. Oxford: Basil Blackwell.

_____. 1991. On Being an Aristotelian. *Heythrop Journal*, 32: 233-248.

Mullahy, Patrick, ed. 1949. *A Study of Interpersonal Relations: New Contributions to Psychiatry*. New York: Hermitage Press.

National Conference of Catholic Bishops (U.S.A.). 1993. *The Challenge of Peace: God's Promise and Our Response*. Washington: United States Catholic Conference.

Neuner, J. and Dupuis, J., eds. 1983. *The Christian Faith: In the Doctrinal Documents of the Catholic Church*. Rev. ed. London: Collins, 1983.

Newman, John Henry. 1973. *The Letters and Diaries of John Henry Newman*, Volume XXV. Edited with notes and introduction by Charles Stephen Dessain and Thomas Gornall. Oxford: Clarendon.

_____. 1974. *An Essay on The Development of Christian Doctrine*, (the edition of 1845.) Ed. with an introduction by J. M. Cameron. Harmondsworth: Penguin.

_____. 1985. *An Essay in Aid of A Grammar of Assent*. Ed. by I. T. Ker. Oxford: Clarendon.

Newton, Sir Isaac. 1962. *Sir Isaac Newton's Mathematical Principles of Natural Philosophy and His System of the World. Philosophiae Naturalis Principia Mathematica*, translated into English by Andrew Motte, 1729. Rev. translation, with appendices by Florian Cajori. Berkeley: University of California Press.

O'Collins, Gerald. 1975. *Has Dogma a Future?* London: Darton, Longman and Todd.

O'Neill, Graeme. 1989. Voyage of Exploration. *The University of Melbourne Gazette*, Spring: 2-4.

Ogilvie, Matthew C. 1992. The Human Ineffable or Beatific Knowledge of Jesus Christ while He lived on this Earth, as expounded by Bernard Lonergan in his Twelfth Thesis on the Incarnate Word. (*De Verbo Incarnato*, Third Edition, Rome, Gregorian University Press, 1964). Master's thesis. Sydney College of Divinity.

_____. 1997. The Importance of Experience: An Opportunity for Clarification. *Compass: A Review of Topical theology*, 31:37-41.

Origen. 1936. *Origen on First Principles*. Koetschau's text of the *De Principiis* translated into English, with an introduction and notes by G. W. Butterworth.) London: SPCK.

Ott, Ludiwg. 1974. *Fundamentals of Catholic Dogma*. Translated by Patrick Lynch, edited in English by James Bastible. Rockford, Illinois: Tan.

Pascal, Blaise. 1966. *Pensées*. Translated with an Introduction by A. J. Krailsheimer. Harmondsworth: Penguin.

Pitt, Valerie H, ed. 1975. *The Penguin Dictionary of Physics*. Harmondsworth: Penguin.

Plato. 1989. *The Collected Dialogues of Plato: Including the Letters.* Ed. by Edith Hamilton and Huntington Cairns. Bollingen Series LXXI, Princeton: Princeton University Press.

Platt, Washington and R. A. Baker. 1931. The Relation of Scientific "Hunch" to Research. *Journal of Chemical Education*, 8:1969-2002.

Rahner, Karl. 1961. *Theological Investigations I: God, Christ, Mary and Grace.* Translated by Cornelius Ernst. Baltimore: Helicon.

_____. 1971a. Some Critical Thoughts on "Functional Specialties in Theology."In Philip McShane, ed. *Foundations of Theology: Papers from the International Lonergan Conference 1970.* Dublin: Gill and Macmillan.

_____. 1971b. *Theological Investigations VII: Further Theology of the Spiritual Life.* Translated by David Bourke. London: Darton, Longman and Todd.

_____. 1978. *Foundations of Christian Faith: An Introduction to the Idea of Christianity.* Translated by William V. Dych. London: Darton Longman and Todd.

_____. 1990. *Faith in a Wintry Season: Conversations and Interviews with Karl Rahner in the Last Years of His Life.* Ed. by Paul Imhof and Hubert Bialowons, translation edited by Harvey D. Egan. New York: Crossroad.

_____. 1994. *The Content of Faith: The Best of Karl Rahner's Theological Writings.* Ed. by Karl Lehmann and Albert Raffelt, translation ed. by Harvey Egan. New York: Crossroad.

Rahner, Karl and Wilhelm Thüsing. 1980. *A New Christology.* Translated by David Smith and Verdant Green. London: Burns and Oates.

Rees, Jessica. 1983. *Sing a Song of Silence: A Deaf Girl's Odyssey.* (npl): The Kensal Press.

Richardson, Alan. 1964. *History, Sacred and Profane.* London: SCM

Riley, Philip Boo. 1980. The Development of Doctrine: A Study in Bernard Lonergan's Method in Theology. Ph.D. diss., McMaster University.

Ross, W. D. (Sir David). 1949. *Aristotle's Prior and Posterior Analytics.* Rev. text with introduction and commentary. Oxford: Clarendon Press.

_____. 1960. *Aristotle.* 5th rev. edition. London: Methuen.

Ruse, Michael. 1999. *Mystery of Mysteries: Is Evolution a Social Construction?.* Cambridge (Mass): Harvard University Press.

Ryle, Gilbert. 1990. *The Concept of Mind.* Harmondsworth: Penguin, 1990.

Sacred Congregation for the Doctrine of the Faith. 1982. *Inter Insigniores*, (Declaration on the Admission of Women to the Ministerial Priesthood, 15 October, 1976). Text in Austin Flannery, general ed. *Vatican Council II*: Volume II, More Postconciliar Documents. Dublin: Domincan Publications.

Sala, Giovanni B. 1994. *Lonergan and Kant: Five Essays on Human Knowledge.* Translated by Joseph Spoerl, ed. by Robert M. Doran. Toronto: University of Toronto Press.

Sears, Francis W. *et al.* 1982. *University Physics.* 6th ed. Reading, Massachusetts: Addison-Wesley, 1982.

Sharpe, Eric J. 1988. *Understanding Religion.* London: Duckworth.

Shea, William M. 1976. The Stance and Task of the Foundational Theologian: Critical or Dogmatic? *Heythrop Journal*, 17: 273-292.

Sykes, Stephen W. 1983. Absolute Dependence. In Alan Richardson and John Bowden, eds. *A New Dictionary of Christian Theology*, London: SCM.

Tallon, Andrew. 1997. *Head and Heart: Affection, Cognition and Volition as Triune Consciousness.* New York: Fordham University Press.

Tillich, Paul. 1968. *Systematic Theology*, (Combined Volume). Digswell Place, Great Britain: James Nisbet.

Tracy, David. 1970. *The Achievement of Bernard Lonergan.* New York: Herder and Herder.

_____. 1975. *Blessed Rage for Order: The New Pluralism in Theology.* New York: Seabury.

Vatican, Second Council. [Vatican Council II]. 1984a. *Dei Verbum,* (Dogmatic Constitution on Divine Revelation, 18 November 1965.) Text in Austin Flannery, general ed. *Vatican Council II: The Conciliar and Post Conciliar Documents.* New Rev. Ed. New York: Costello.

_____. 1984b. *Optatam totius* (Decree on the Training of Priests, 28 October, 1965.) Text in Austin Flannery, general ed. *Vatican Council II: The Conciliar and Post Conciliar Documents.*

Vertin, Michael. 1983. Dialectically-Opposed Phenomenologies of Knowing: A Pedagogical Elaboration of Basic Ideal-Types. In *Lonergan Workshop IV.* Ed. by Fred Lawrence. Chico, California: Scholars Press.

Walgrave, Jan Hendrik. 1972. *Unfolding Revelation: The Nature of Doctrinal Development.* London: Hutchinson.

Catechism of the Catholic Church. 1994. Official Edition for Australia and New Zealand. Homebush, Sydney: St Pauls.

Index*

*Authors' names in the Bibliography are not indexed.